Taxpayer Rights and Revenue Powers

Taxpayer Rights and Revenue Powers

by

Peter Howarth

ATTI, Formerly one of HM Inspectors of Taxes
Howarth Consulting

and

Robert Maas

FCA, FTII, FIIT, TEP
Blackstone Franks LLP

LexisNexis™ UK

Members of the LexisNexis Group worldwide

United Kingdom	LexisNexis UK, a Division of Reed Elsevier (UK) Ltd, Halsbury House, 35 Chancery Lane, LONDON, WC2A 1EL, and 4 Hill Street, EDINBURGH EH2 3JZ
Argentina	LexisNexis Argentina, BUENOS AIRES
Australia	LexisNexis Butterworths, CHATSWOOD, New South Wales
Austria	LexisNexis Verlag ARD Orac GmbH & Co KG, VIENNA
Canada	LexisNexis Butterworths, MARKHAM, Ontario
Chile	LexisNexis Chile Ltda, SANTIAGO DE CHILE
Czech Republic	Nakladatelství Orac sro, PRAGUE
France	Editions du Juris-Classeur SA, PARIS
Germany	LexisNexis Deutschland GmbH, FRANKFURT and MUNSTER
Hong Kong	LexisNexis Butterworths, HONG KONG
Hungary	HVG-Orac, BUDAPEST
India	LexisNexis Butterworths, NEW DELHI
Ireland	LexisNexis, DUBLIN
Italy	Giuffrè Editore, MILAN
Malaysia	Malayan Law Journal Sdn Bhd, KUALA LUMPUR
New Zealand	LexisNexis Butterworths, WELLINGTON
Poland	Wydawnictwo Prawnicze LexisNexis, WARSAW
Singapore	LexisNexis Butterworths, SINGAPORE
South Africa	LexisNexis Butterworths, DURBAN
Switzerland	Stämpfli Verlag AG, BERNE
USA	LexisNexis, DAYTON, Ohio

First published in 2004

Published by LexisNexis UK

A CIP Catalogue record for this book is available from the British Library.
ISBN 0754519457

Typeset by Columns Design Ltd, Reading, England
Printed and bound in Great Britain by Antony Rowe Ltd, Chippenham, Wilts

Visit LexisNexis UK at www.lexisnexis.co.uk

Preface

The introduction of self-assessment simplified some of the procedures of dealing with assessments. However, many people (including myself) did not immediately appreciate that it created a fundamental shift in the entire administration of the tax system. When self-assessment was introduced the Revenue deliberately sought to create a balance between the powers conferred on the Revenue and the rights given to taxpayers. Many people within the Revenue still do not seem to me to appreciate the effect of this brave attempt to move from the Revenue driving the tax system, towards the Revenue and the taxpayer becoming partners in the administration of the system.

Prior to self-assessment tax advisers could manage with an understanding of the Taxes Act 1988 and could get by without too much knowledge of the Taxes Management Act 1970. In the self-assessment era the Taxes Management Act has acquired as much importance as the tax legislation itself.

Since the introduction of self-assessment I have been tempted to write a book on the Taxes Management Act. When Peter Howarth suggested to me that we should write it together I leapt at the opportunity. I hope that readers will feel that this was an effort worth making. However, I discovered years ago that the downside of writing is that it is important to get everything 100 per cent right. I would welcome readers pointing out to me those areas where they feel we have got it wrong, or where they feel that the explanation is inadequate, so that mistakes can be corrected in later editions of the book.

The preface is an author's opportunity to acknowledge the help that they have had from others in writing the book. I would particularly like to thank Jill Holland and Pauline Monu for typing my share of the manuscript. I would also like to thank Robert Lillycrop for putting me right in relation to the current procedures of the General Commissioners. Peter would like to thank Sabrina Kuhn at LexisNexis for her patience whilst we tried to get it right. Also Gena Shackleton, Jane Cartmel and his wife Bernadette for their continuous encouragement, and the partners at Haslam Tunstall for their understanding.

Robert Maas and Peter Howarth
June 2004

Contents

Table of Statutes

Table of Statutory Instruments

Table of European Legislation

Table of Cases

A

B

C

D

E

F

G

H

I

T

V

W

X

Chapter 1

Introduction

1.1 When income tax self-assessment was introduced, a conscious effort was made to try to include new rights for taxpayers to counterbalance the new powers being given to the Inland Revenue. That was ten years ago! In the interim the government have on a number of occasions strengthened the Revenue's powers, but little or no consideration has been given to maintaining the balance that the draftsman originally conceived.

1.2 Nevertheless, things are not wholly one-sided. The taxpayer does have rights, albeit many practitioners seem either to overlook these or are reluctant to assert them.

1.3 It is difficult to see how a practitioner can nowadays protect a client's interests without a clear understanding of the extent of taxpayer rights and the limitations of the Revenue's powers. These limitations and powers are mainly contained in the Taxes Management Act, although for companies the likelihood of eventual separation of corporation tax from income tax has long been mooted and the draftsman took the opportunity of corporation tax self-assessment to introduce corporation tax management provisions, separate from the income tax ones. These largely follow the income tax provisions, but differ in significant areas – and of course there are some corporation tax areas, such as group relief, which have no income tax equivalent.

1.4 In this book we have tried to review the income tax provisions and to avoid repeating too much when we move on to corporation tax, highlighting instead the areas of difference. A phenomenon of tax law (and we suspect law generally) is that when a new tax is introduced or provisions applicable to one tax are extended to another, the draftsman tries to keep the same administrative framework but reflect in the new legislation lessons that have come to light and interim changes in Revenue procedures. The result is that there are more differences than most of us would want. We suspect that most would prefer a single set of administrative rules that apply across the taxes and that are updated regularly. Sadly that is not what we have. Accordingly it is important to appreciate where differences lie.

1.5 In this book we have sought to deal only with rights and powers in relation to income tax, capital gains tax and corporation tax. The rights and powers in relation to the other taxes administered by the Revenue (inheritance tax, stamp duty, stamp duty revenue tax, stamp duty land tax and petroleum revenue tax) largely follow those for income tax, but are not identical. The administrative provisions in relation to national insurance contributions similarly, although increasingly moving towards the income tax rules, are still separate. We have also not considered the administrative provisions of other non-tax legislation administered by the Revenue, such as student loans, the national minimum wage and tax credits.

1.6 A knowledge of taxpayer's rights does not of course require one to enforce them. At the end of the day the agreement of tax liabilities is not a game to be played wholly within the rules. Rather it is a confrontation between a Revenue official, whose aim is to collect as much tax as he legitimately can, and the taxpayer and his advisers, who wish to protect as much of the taxpayer's wealth as is lawfully permissible. In such a confrontation the rules are an aid, to be invoked where they will assist a party, but to be ignored where their enforcement would serve little or no purpose.

1.7 What is important is that the taxpayer or his adviser knows the rules. There is nothing wrong in deciding not to stand on the client's rights, or in volunteering information which you do not think the Revenue are entitled to, or even recommending the payment of tax that you do not believe to be due. However, you ought to do these things consciously and deliberately, and be clear in your own mind why you are doing them.

1.8 In most cases it will be to save costs. Pyrrhic victories may be intellectually satisfying but the client cannot be expected to be appreciative of a professional fee note that exceeds the tax at stake in a dispute – unless he was warned of the position and has made a conscious decision, as some do, to fight something on principle, without too much regard to the costs.

1.9 Saving time is also saving costs. However, before volunteering information which you do not believe the Revenue are entitled to in order to save time, you need to consider whether it will indeed have that effect. Most practitioners have experience of Revenue enquiries where, when answers are provided to the initial questions, the Revenue raise fresh issues and the case drags on, often creating a suspicion that the Revenue are reluctant to close the case without collecting some tax. Whilst the Revenue officially deny that this happens and contend that needlessly prolonging an enquiry does reflect badly on an inspector, experience suggests that the Revenue's controls are not always as good as they would like people to believe.

1.10 When self-assessment was introduced, the Revenue made a policy decision not to disclose the reason for opening an enquiry. Whilst the reasoning behind this may be understandable, when combined with the concept of finality under which the Revenue are in effect allowed only one bite a year at the enquiry cherry, the result often seems to be that the inspector does not adopt a focused approach to an enquiry, but raises myriad issues many of which may appear insignificant in terms of tax at risk. In such circumstances volunteering information to an inspector who enjoys fishing red herrings is more likely to increase the costs of an enquiry than to reduce them.

1.11 Enquiries into tax returns are a good example of how useful a knowledge of rights and powers can be. An enquiry starts when an enquiry notice is served on the taxpayer and a letter requiring information is sent to his accountant (although, particularly in the case of an aspect enquiry, it is increasingly being copied to the client). This often contains a time limit, normally 30 days, for providing the information. This letter is not part of the statutory enquiry procedure. The inspector has invented the time limit. Nothing serious will happen if it is not met. The inspector will either send a reminder or issue a formal information letter. That is not to say that the time limit should be ignored. If you cannot comply it is courteous to let the inspector know in advance. Clients can get scared when they receive a section 19A notice, so it is sensible to warn the client that it might come but not to worry unduly. However, it is important to know that it is not a statutory deadline. Neither you nor the client should worry if it is not met. You should not allow yourself to be pressurised by the Revenue into giving an ill-considered reply, or into supplying documents that you have not had time to review simply because you believe that you need to meet that target date.

1.12 The Revenue often say that they 'need' or 'require' a meeting with the client. Meetings can be a helpful way to speed up the resolution of an enquiry. But the Revenue does not 'need' a meeting; if it did parliament would have given it power to require one. The Revenue have no power to interview anyone (except in relation to national insurance and possibly tax credits). Even the Special Compliance Office (SCO), the Revenue's serious investigation arm, have no power to require a taxpayer to attend a meeting – although, except where a criminal prosecution seems likely, it would be counterproductive to refuse to attend a meeting with SCO.

1.13 Again, that is not to say that it is unwise to attend meetings. However, taking the client to a meeting is doing a favour for the Revenue. If you are doing someone a favour, commonsense suggests that you should do it on your terms, not theirs. It also suggests that you should have a policy towards meetings. Is there any point in taking the client to a meeting at an early stage in an enquiry when the inspector may be on a fishing expedition, trying to reel in as much information as possible? Is there any point in taking him to a meeting which is likely to cover accounting or bookkeeping queries when you wrote up the books? Is it fair to keep him sitting around for half of the meeting while you discuss issues with the inspector? It is likely to be far more productive for you to resolve with the inspector in advance of any meeting all of the issues within your own knowledge. Many people take the view that an early meeting between the accountant and the inspector is very useful, as it can clarify issues and help the inspector to understand what information is likely to be available, but that a meeting with the client present ought to be a sort of last resort, when the only outstanding issues are things that only the client is likely to know the answers to.

1.14 How many client meetings do you have without an agenda? Why should you have a meeting with the Revenue without a detailed agenda? We would stress the word 'detailed'. What do you want out of a meeting and what do you think the inspector wants out of it? Do you really want the client (and perhaps you) to be caught by surprise by the Revenue raising an issue on which the client has not had an adequate opportunity to refresh his memory? If you were given a detailed agenda you could legitimately tell the inspector that you are not going to allow the client to answer questions outside the scope of the agenda.

1.15 What about books and records? Under section 19A you can be required to produce them to the inspector. However, it is up to you where you produce them. The inspector has no power to insist on coming to the client's business premises. He has no power to require you to parcel up the books and send them to him. What do you think is the most appropriate place to produce the records? In many cases it is likely to be at your office. Unless they are very voluminous it is unlikely to be at the client's premises. If you send the records to the inspector for how long is he entitled to keep them? The answer is that, as he is not entitled to require them to be sent to him, he can keep them only for as long as you allow him to. Again that is not to suggest that you should be awkward and put a time limit on how long he can keep them. The last way to achieve a speedy and satisfactory agreement with anybody is to be aggressive. However, if it is inconvenient to the client not to be able to refer to the records why not ask for them back after a reasonable period? Worse, if the inspector raises detailed questions on the records do you really want your client to attempt to answer them without your asking for the records back first, so that he can understand the query?

1.16 The Revenue sometimes issue threats about 'lack of co-operation' if you decline to attend meetings or ask for the return of the records. 'Co-operation' comes from the Latin, 'co' means with or together, and 'opera' means work. In other words it means 'working together' not 'doing as you are told' by the inspector. Standing on your client's rights is not a lack of co-operation. Not providing within a reasonable period information that the inspector wants may be – but undoubtedly only if the information is relevant to his enquiry, ie you should co-operate in resolving the enquiry but there is no need to co-operate in helping him to mount a 'fishing expedition' into your client's overall financial affairs. If you decline a meeting and ask the inspector to put his queries in writing, you are co-operating if you respond reasonably promptly. It also of course needs to be realised that there is no requirement on anyone to co-operate with the Revenue. The significance of co-operation is in relation to penalties. Most tax related penalties are 'up to' a specified amount. In assessing what penalty to charge, the Revenue take account of the degree of co-operation. However such penalties can normally only arise if there has been negligence (or fraud). If the enquiry produces little or no extra tax, co-operation or the lack thereof is irrelevant in monetary terms. It is, of course, very relevant in speeding up the enquiry; but a quick settlement is not necessarily an appropriate one.

Chapter 2

Administration of the Tax System

The Inland Revenue

2.1 Income tax and corporation tax are administered by the Inland Revenue. The Revenue, in theory at least, are not part of the government but an independent body set up to collect and manage taxes. The Revenue are managed by a body of Commissioners. This is an unfortunate name, as the members of the completely separate bodies set up to hear tax appeals are also called Commissioners. The Commissioners responsible for the tax system are usually called the Commissioners of Inland Revenue. They are collectively referred to as the Board or the Board of Inland Revenue. The Commissioners are appointed by the Queen (undoubtedly on the recommendation of the government) and hold office during her pleasure, ie they can be removed only by the Queen [IRRA 1890 s 1]. They are required to have their chief office in London and also to keep other offices in such other places as they deem necessary. Such offices must be kept open on the prescribed days and during the prescribed hours [IRRA 1890 s 3]. As it is the Commissioners themselves who have the power to prescribe the hours this is a fairly pointless direction [IRRA 1890 s 39]. Revenue offices are open during normal office hours five days a week, except on bank holidays, but some also open at other times (such as on 31 January if it occurs at a weekend) where it is felt appropriate.

2.2 The Commissioners of Inland Revenue have "all necessary powers" for carrying into execution every act of Parliament relating to inland revenue, ie the revenue of the UK collected or imposed as stamp duty or taxes and placed under the management of the Commissioners [IRRA 1890 ss 1(2), 39].

2.3 The Commissioners are required to appoint such staff as they consider appropriate [IRRA 1890 s 4]. They must appoint Inspectors and Collectors of Taxes, who must act under the direction of the Board [TMA 1970 s 1(2)]. They can appoint a person as an Inspector or Collector generally or for a specific purpose and are deemed to have appointed a person for a specific purpose if he is authorised for that purpose under the Board's administrative practice [TMA 1970 s 1(2)–(2B)].

2.4 Any function conferred on the Commissioners can be exercised by any officer of the Commissioners acting under their authority (unless a statute specifically specifies otherwise). However, statutory instruments must be made by the Board itself [IRRA 1890 s 4A].

2.5 Where something is to be done by Revenue staff the older legislation refers to an inspector, but more recent Acts refer to an officer or an officer of the Board. The reason for this change is to give greater flexibility in the use of staff to the Revenue, so that staff below inspector level can be used to do some work previously done by Inspectors of Taxes. The three terms, inspector, officer and officer of the Board, are used interchangeably in this book. In general we have tried to use 'inspector' if the legislation refers to an inspector and 'officer' if it specifically refers to an officer.

2.6 It is specifically provided that any legal proceedings or administrative act relating to any tax which is begun by one Inspector or Collector can be continued by another (and any Inspector or Collector can act for any division or other area) [TMA 1970 s 1(3)]. The legislation does not appear to confer any similar authority on other officers of the Board.

2.7 This may be pertinent in relation to self-assessment. A tax return is required to be delivered to the officer who gave the notice to make the return [TMA 1970 s 8(1)]. Notice of rejection of a Revenue correction to a return must be given to the officer by whom the notice of correction was given [TMA 1970 s 9ZB(5)]. Perhaps more importantly, it appears that only the officer who opens an enquiry can make a jeopardy amendment [TMA 1970 s 9C(1), (2)]. Similarly, it appears that it is only the officer who opens an enquiry who can issue a section 19A notice (although any officer can open an enquiry not merely the one by whom the return was issued) [TMA 1970 s 19A(1), (2)]. It is probably only that officer who can issue a closure notice [TMA 1970 s 28A(1)]. Even if the officer concerned is an Inspector it may be questionable whether TMA 1970 s 1(3) permits a different Inspector to issue a section 19A or section 28A notice. These do not appear to be administrative acts as they require the officer to exercise a discretion. Even if they are, the normal principle is that, in cases of conflict, a specific statutory provision overrides a general one and a later provision overrides an earlier one. On both these grounds the specific wording of ss 19A and 28A may well override s 1(3). This probable requirement for a specific officer to be involved in actions consequent on an earlier action is emphasised by FA 1998 Sch 18 para 95(5) which specifically sets this out in relation to corporation tax self-assessment.

The tribunals

2.8 Tax law is extensive, varied and complex. This being so it is inevitable that there will be frequent disagreement between the Revenue and taxpayers, on how the law is to be applied to certain facts or even about what the true facts are. To resolve such disputes a reasonably straightforward appeal system has developed. In many cases the taxpayer has a choice. He can take his dispute before a local tribunal, the General Commissioners, or to a special tribunal, the Special Commissioners. Some matters have, by law, to be heard only by the Special Commissioners (such as appeals relating to offshore matters, insurance companies, tax assessments made by the Board of

Inland Revenue as opposed to local officers, see **7.16**), or just the General Commissioners (notably appeals in personal allowance disputes under TMA 1970 s 42). There are some exceptions, for example, disputes over land values will be heard by the Lands Tribunal [TMA 1970 s 46D].

2.9 A detailed review of the rights and procedures relating to various appeals can be found in **Chapter 7**. This chapter takes a look at the administrative provisions to be found in the Taxes Management Act relating to the appointment and serving of tax officials and the appeal commissioners.

The General Commissioners

2.10 The first tribunal is one established to deal with appeals and certain other powers given by the Taxes Acts. For this 'Commissioners for the general purposes of the income tax' are appointed. They are referred to as the General Commissioners. The Lord Chancellor has power by regulation to change their name [F(No2)A 1992 s 75]. This power was inserted because at the time there was a suggestion that the public might confuse the Appeal Commissioners with the Commissioners of Inland Revenue and thus lack confidence in their independence, but subsequent Lord Chancellors seem to have dismissed this concern. The General Commissioners are organised into divisions as defined by the Lord Chancellor and governed by the Council for Tribunals (Tribunals and Inquiries Act 1992). These divisions are for administrative purposes only and a hearing by the 'wrong division' would not invalidate a decision.

2.11 A General Commissioner is very much a layman, usually selected by a local advisory committee. They are persons of integrity, character and understanding who have knowledge of the local community. They need not have any knowledge of tax law, their task being to decide what the correct facts are in any case presented to them. All General Commissioners must retire by their 75th birthday [TMA 1970 s 2(7)].

2.12 There are some administrative differences between the countries making up the United Kingdom because in England, Wales and Northern Ireland a General Commissioner is appointed, and dismissed, by the Lord Chancellor [TMA 1970 s 2(2)], whereas in Scotland it is the Secretary of State who assumes this responsibility [TMA 1970 s 2(3)]. Also in Scotland, a sheriff is an ex-officio General Commissioner for his district [TMA 1970 s 2(4)].

2.13 Proceedings before the General Commissioners are still valid even if there has been a defect in their appointment, or if one of them has continued beyond his 75th birthday [TMA 1970 s 2(8)]. It is really 'hopeless' to try and have a second chance at an appeal by arguing some defect in administrative procedure, such as the wrong division heard the appeal. In *Sinsbury v Burgess ((1968) 47 ATC 397)* the High Court dismissed an appeal brought by the taxpayer on the grounds that the wrong division of General

Commissioners had determined assessments; the judge actually describing the appeal as 'hopeless'.

2.14 Serving as a General Commissioner is not a financially rewarding occupation because they are not remunerated. They may, however, be paid such out of pocket travelling and subsistence allowances as the Lord Chancellor (in Scotland, the Secretary of State) may determine [TMA 1970 s 2(5)].

2.15 Each division of General Commissioners must appoint a clerk who is paid for his services. They may themselves dismiss their clerk, but he may also be dismissed by the Lord Chancellor (in Scotland, the Secretary of State). A clerk must retire at the age of 70 unless the General Commissioners think it is in the public interest that he continue, but in any event he cannot continue beyond the age of seventy five [TMA 1970 s 3]. The clerk is usually legally qualified, but on occasions an ex-tax inspector may be appointed. His role is to guide the Commissioners in the appeal procedures and to arrange meetings. Although he is usually present at meetings his absence would not invalidate a decision (see *Venn v Franks (1958) 38 TC 175*). Where, due to a reorganisation of divisions of Commissioners under TMA 1970 s 2(6), a clerk loses his office or suffers a reduction in his emoluments he is entitled to compensation for loss of office (The Clerks to General Commissioners (Compensation) Regulations 1973, SI 1973/900, made under FA 1972 s 130).

2.16 General Commissioners, and their clerks, are protected from liability for any costs arising out of any act or omission in the execution of their duties unless:

(*a*) the proceedings relate to their being tried for a criminal offence; or

(*b*) it is proved they acted in bad faith.

It follows that a person must have acted reasonably and in good faith to attract this statutory protection [TMA 1970 s 3A(2)].

2.17 However, all is not lost for the hapless taxpayer who finds himself barred from seeking redress as a court may, instead, order the Lord Chancellor (in Scotland, the Secretary of State) to pay such costs [TMA 1970 s 2A(3)]. It does, however, seem odd that the Lord Chancellor is empowered to make the regulations specifying the circumstances under which a Court may order him to pay costs and how any such amount is to be decided [TMA 1970 s 2A(4)]. He does not, however, have a completely free hand, as any such regulations must be approved by Parliament.

2.18 The extent of the meaning of 'acted in bad faith' is not yet subject to case law, probably because the argument arises, thankfully, in only rare instances, and also because the rule is quite new; it was introduced only from 1 April 2001 by the Access to Justice Act 1999 and as yet only applies to

England, Wales and Northern Ireland. Some assistance may be obtained by looking at cases the courts have sent back to the Commissioners, such as *R and D McKerron Ltd v IRC [1979] STC 815* in which the court ruled that the Commissioners had been unreasonable when they determined an appeal when the appellant's solicitor had left the room for a very short period, and ordered a re-hearing. Presumably in such circumstances the wasted costs of the first hearing could be claimed.

The Special Commissioners

2.19 TMA 1970 s 4 deals with the appointment of 'Commissioners for the special purposes of the Income Tax Acts', who are referred to in the legislation as the Special Commissioners. One of the Special Commissioners is designated as the 'Presiding Special Commissioner'.

2.20 Unlike the General Commissioners, who need no qualifications, a Special Commissioner must have at least 10 years standing in the legal profession [TMA 1970 s 4(2)]. This means qualification under Courts and Legal Services Act 1990 s 71, so a Special Commissioner will always be a barrister or solicitor. Deputy Special Commissioners may be appointed to facilitate the performance or functions of a Special Commissioner and they must also be suitably qualified [TMA 1970 s 4A].

2.21 Like the General Commissioners, Special Commissioners are governed by the Council of Tribunals (Tribunals and Inquiries Act 1992) and are appointed, and dismissed, by the Lord Chancellor. They must retire at the age of 70, subject to a public interest extension to the age of 75 [TMA 1970 s 4(3A); Judicial Pensions and Retirement Act 1993 s 26]. Unlike the General Commissioners they are salaried.

2.22 The function of the Special Commissioners is to execute the duties and powers assigned to them in the legislation [TMA 1970 s 4(5)].

Conflict of interest

2.23 No Commissioner, whether General or Special, may act in any matter in which he has a personal interest unless the parties to the proceedings expressly consent [TMA 1970 s 5]. In this regard the personal interest has to be 'direct and certain'. This can mean a very small financial interest in the outcome of an appeal (see *R v Holyhead General Comrs, ex p Roberts (1982) 56 TC 127*).

Official declarations

2.24 All tax officials and Commissioners must make a declaration, as laid down by TMA 1970 Sch 1 on taking up office. The wording differs slightly depending on the status of the official but they all relate to the confidentiality of information received in the execution of their duties [TMA 1970 s 6]. A common theme of each declaration is that there will be complete secrecy on all matters relating to official duties, unless disclosure is required to carry out those duties or for the purpose of a prosecution for a tax offence or any other case required by law.

Presumptions in proceedings

2.25 In legal proceedings there is a presumption that anything purported to be done by a Revenue officer shall be assumed to be valid unless the opposite is proved [IRRA 1890 s 24]. Under this there is an assumption that any notice is presumed valid unless it can be shown not to be. This was confirmed in *B and S Displays Ltd v Special Comrs [1978] STC 331* and more recently in *R v IRC, ex p Taylor [1988] STC 832*. So attempting to see Revenue reports to prove that there was a valid reason for a formal order is another hopeless task as anything the Revenue does is assumed by law to be correct and in order unless the appellant can prove the opposite. An appellant would have clear practical difficulties with this.

2.26 Usually only a legally qualified person can present proceedings in Court but for tax purposes proceedings in the magistrate's court (sheriff's court in Scotland) may be taken by anyone employed by the Revenue even if they are not legally qualified, provided that the proceedings relate to a taxation matter. Proceedings in the County Court can, however, only be taken by a legally qualified person [IRRA 1890 s 27].

Rewards

2.27 In many tax investigations there is speculation that the Inspector of Taxes has an informant. Anyone who is tempted to become a Revenue informant may be interested to know that the Board of Inland Revenue can give rewards to those giving them information about an offence, or to anyone who helps them to recover a fine or penalty.

2.28 Before deciding that this could be a full time occupation, perhaps consisting of a life of sitting in public bars eavesdropping on conversations, it would be best to carefully note that rewards are at the sole discretion of the Board of Inland Revenue and they cannot be obliged to make one, nor be forced into agreeing an amount. This was confirmed in the early case of *Riach v Lord Advocate ((1932) 18 TC 18)*. Mr Riach argued that the Revenue had agreed to pay him £30,000, this being 10 per cent of the sums recovered because of his information. They only paid him an ex gratia sum of £250, so he sued for the rest. The court dismissed his claim on the grounds that the Revenue could not enter into any agreement to pay awards because their power to pay them was only discretionary. In any event amounts in excess of £50 must have Treasury consent. This was recently reaffirmed in the case of

R (on the application of Churchouse) v IRC [2003] EWHC 681 (Admin), [2003] STC 629) [IRRA 1890 s 32].

Mitigation powers

2.29 The Board of Inland Revenue may mitigate any penalty or fine imposed under any relevant taxes act (but excluding inheritance tax legislation per IHTA 1984 s 260) or stay or compound any proceedings for recovery of any fine or penalty. This power can also be exercised after judgement has been obtained. (IRRA 1890 s 35].

Chapter 3

Returns of Income and Gains

Income tax and capital gains tax

Notification of chargeability

3.1 The tax collection system begins with a requirement to notify the Revenue if a person is liable to pay income tax or capital gains tax. The current legislation defining those liable to do so is at TMA 1970 s 7(as amended by FA 1994) and is effective from 1995/96. For all practical purposes this is now far enough back in history not to cause to much worry about the previous provisions. However, for the curious, or those in deep trouble, the rules were not significantly different from the current ones.

3.2 This requirement will mainly affect individuals and trustees, but companies can also be liable to income tax, in which case they too are caught by these provisions. The requirement is that anyone liable to pay income tax or capital gains tax, who has not received a tax return for completion must notify the Revenue by the 5 October following the end of the tax year for which there is a liability [TMA 1970 s 7(1)].

Example

Peter has a salary paid under PAYE and so does not receive an annual self-assessment tax return from the Revenue. In the tax year 2003/04 he starts to receive income from a part time business. He must notify the Revenue by 5 October 2004.

3.3 Unless liable at the higher rates of tax there is, however, no requirement to notify in the following circumstances:

(*a*) all liability is satisfied via the PAYE system [TMA 1970 s 7(4)];

(*b*) all income has tax deducted at source and there is no liability to higher rate taxes [TMA 1970 s 7(6)];

(*c*) the only income is from company dividends and there is no liability to higher rate taxes [TMA 1970 s 7(6)];

(*d*) there is no tax liability for the year; this seems obvious in view of the fact that the section is aimed at those liable to pay tax, but it is nevertheless specifically spelled out at TMA 1970 s 7(7).

3.4 To enforce compliance with these provisions there are penalties for those who default. These can amount to a maximum of the actual tax liability for the year concerned. However, those who have missed the 5 October deadline have an escape if they realise before the following 31 January, because there is no penalty if the tax is paid by then.

EXAMPLE

An individual has a tax liability of, say, £1,000 for 2003/04 and has not received a tax return form for completion. He must therefore advise the Revenue by 5 October 2004. After this date he is in default and has a liability to a maximum penalty of £1,000 (his outstanding tax). He can, however, avoid this if he pays the tax by 31 January 2005 [TMA 1970 s 7(8)]. The liability relevant to the calculation of a penalty is the net amount after all reliefs and the deduction of tax at source [TMA 1970 s 8(1AA)].

3.5 The Revenue say that the most common failures under TMA 1970 s 7 are:

(*a*) by those commencing a business;

(*b*) the creation of a trust;

(*c*) capital gains by those within the PAYE system and so not accustomed to receiving a tax return; and

(*d*) capital gains made by certain types of trust in which the beneficiaries become liable to the tax.

3.6 The Revenue do have the power to extend these statutory deadlines [TMA 1970 s 118(2)] but say that they will never do so for failure to notify offences under TMA 1970 s 7. This seems reasonable. In most cases it is realised that a deadline cannot be met for one reason or another when it becomes imminent. In such circumstances it is sensible to ask the Revenue for more time and they may, or may not, agree. It would be odd to want to notify liability but need more time to do so. Applying for such an extension in itself would be notification. The route for those who think they may have a good reason for late notification lies in the mitigation of penalties and an argument that there should be no penalty at all in the individual circumstances of their case by virtue of the second part of TMA 1970 s 118(2) (see **14.87**).

3.7 There is no laid down form of notification so a verbal one will suffice. However, if the Revenue fail to act on it, it may be difficult to convince them that the notification was given. It must, therefore, make sense to notify the Revenue in writing and review the position well before

5 October to ensure that the notice has been processed. If the deadline is close it is suggested that recorded delivery is used. It is not necessary to wait to quantify the income before giving notice. The purpose of the notification is to give the Revenue an opportunity to issue a tax return in good time for it to be completed by the 31 January due date. It is not necessary to spell out either the source or the amount of the income. It is, however, advisable to do so if this is readily available. If the amount is small the Revenue may decide that it is not worthwhile to issue a return or may deal with the adjustment through the taxpayer's PAYE notice of coding.

3.8 A failure to notify offence can indicate a lax attitude to tax compliance in general and so might prompt the Inspector to call for the books, records and other information and mount an investigation. Some Inspectors feel that those who have not taken their responsibilities to notify a liability to tax seriously may well also approach the keeping of accurate and up to date records in a cavalier fashion. The result could be an uncomfortable, and potentially expensive, period of Revenue scrutiny. Tax Inspectors tend to like these cases because the failure to notify offence is easy to demonstrate, so there is no pressure to justify the investigation by demonstrating incorrect records. It follows that more than the usual degree of care ought to be taken when preparing accounts and tax returns in failure to notify cases.

Income tax returns

3.9 A person can be required to complete a return of his income and gains for a tax year. This requires him to give such information in the specified format, and provide accounts, statements and documents with the return, as may be reasonably required [TMA 1970 s 8(1)]. At present the Revenue do not normally demand that accounts or other documents be submitted with a return by individuals, partnerships or trustees; in fact they positively discourage it. The exception is for sub-contractors in the construction industry who must submit their forms SC60 with their tax return. If an employee of a non-UK resident employer who works in the UK for a continuous period of 30 days or more is asked to make a tax return and the duties he carries out in the UK are performed for the benefit of a UK resident (or a non-resident trading in the UK) he can be required to include particulars of any earnings paid to him, whether or not he is taxable on them in the UK [FA 1974 s 24]. A return must also include a self-assessment, ie a calculation of the tax payable. A self-assessment is not required if the return is submitted by 30 September after the end of the tax year (or, if later, within two months of the notice to submit a return) [TMA 1970 s 9].

3.10 The fact that the Revenue discourage the submission of accounts ought not to create a deterrent from submitting them. It is clear from TMA 1970 s 29(6)(a) (see **6.8**) that the legislation envisages a taxpayer volunteering additional information with his return. The Revenue accept that where this is done they cannot refuse to accept the information. There are two main reasons why a taxpayer might wish to submit accounts and other additional information. The first is that this may fend off an enquiry. If there is something in a return that looks odd or gives the Revenue cause for concern the only way they can normally satisfy their curiosity is by opening an enquiry. However, if the taxpayer has anticipated any questions and provided answers in advance, the Revenue might well be satisfied with those answers. The second is that the Revenue cannot raise a discovery assessment where the information that gives rise to the discovery was sent with the tax return. Accordingly the more information the Revenue are sent the greater the protection against discovery the client obtains. In practice accounts are likely to contain additional information to that required by the Standard Accounts Information page of the tax return. At a minimum, the expenses are likely to have been analysed under different heads in the accounts.

3.11 In a return, there is no need to disclose interest or deposits with the National Savings Bank, other than investment deposits, if it does not exceed £70 [ICTA 1988 s 325].

3.12 A tax return may require details of any assets acquired, and the person from whom they were acquired, although the following assets are excluded from this requirement:

(*a*) any within TCGA 1992 s 51(1) (rights to gambling winnings);

(*b*) any within TCGA 1992 s 121 (non-marketable government securities);

(*c*) any within TCGA 1992 ss 263, 268, or 269 (passenger vehicles, decorations for valour, foreign currency for personal use);

(*d*) chattels with a value of less than £6,000;

(*e*) trading stock,

[TMA 1970 s 12].

The current return form does not require such information.

3.13 If the chargeable gains accruing to an individual in a tax year do not exceed the exempt amount for that year (ie, the CGT annual allowance) and the aggregate amount or value of the consideration for all chargeable disposals of assets made by him in the year does not exceed four times that exempt amount, a statement to that effect satisfies the requirements of a notice under s 8 to the extent that it requires information for the purposes of establishing the amount in which he is chargeable to capital gains tax for that year [TCGA 1992 s 3A(1)]. For this purpose, if there is no deduction for losses the chargeable gains means the gains after taper relief, but if losses fall to be deducted it is the amount before both losses and taper relief [TCGA 1992 s 3A(2)]. This also applies to personal representatives in relation to the year of death and the two following years [TCGA 1992 s 3A(4)].

3.14 The format of a return must be that required by the Revenue, ie their form must be used [TMA 1970 s 113(1)]. Using a photocopy is not welcomed by the Revenue but is acceptable, provided it includes the notes as well as the numerical entries. This is because the Revenue wish to ensure that everything they want to be before a taxpayer when he completes and signs a form actually is. It is, however, pointed out that photocopying forms is a breach of copyright but, when done on an individual basis, the Revenue will take no action. However, if done on a large scale for commercial gain they will seek to enforce their copyright (see Statement of Practice SP5/87).

3.15 The use of computer generated forms is permitted provided the software is approved by the Revenue. The approved software is listed on the Revenue website in the section on internet filing.

3.16 A tax return form may be served on a person by delivery to his last known private address, place of business or employment. This may be done by physically leaving it there or sending it by post [TMA 1970 s 115].

3.17 Once a person is required to complete a return there are deadlines for the delivery of it to the Revenue. This time limit is the 31 January following the end of the tax year (eg for the year 2003/04 the return must be delivered by 31 January 2005), with the proviso that a period of three months must be allowed for completion of returns issued for completion after 31 October [TMA 1970 s 8(1A)].

3.18 The Revenue has, helpfully, given illustrative examples of the working of this rule. They say:

(*a*) If a return notice is given on one day in a month it is due on or before one day earlier in the third following month (eg a return notice dated 13 February 2005 has a filing date of 12 May 2005).

(*b*) If a return notice is given on the first day of a month it is due on or before the last day of the second following month (eg a return notice dated 1 February 2005 has a filing date of 30 April 2005).

(*c*) If there is no 'corresponding date' in the third following month it is due on or before the last day of that month (eg a return notice dated 30 November 2004 has a filing date of 28 February 2005).

[Per contents of Revenue letter of 15 March 1997 reported in *Simon's Direct Tax Service* E1.806.]

3.19 There is an alternative, earlier filing date for those who do not wish to calculate their own tax liability or for employees who would like any tax underpaid to be collected via the following year's PAYE system. These have to be with the Revenue by 30 September, or within two months if it is a late issued return [TMA 1970 s 9(2)].

3.20 A partner in any trade, profession or business must include his share of partnership income on his own personal tax return, even though there may also be a return of the same information by the partnership. The amount he returns must be the same as that reported on the partnership return [TMA 1970 s 8(1B)]. It appears that he must do this even if he believes those amounts to be incorrect. Clearly, in such circumstances he ought also to give the correct figures and explain how the difference arises.

3.21 A person making the return must include a declaration that it is correct and complete to the best of his knowledge [TMA 1970 s 8(2)]. This means that the return must be signed by the taxpayer in person. The Revenue will accept the signature of someone under an enduring power of attorney if the taxpayer is unable to sign because of physical or mental incapacity (Statement of Practice A13).

3.22 If the tax return filing date is close but there is difficulty obtaining the final and correct figures for entry then the Revenue will accept a return containing provisional figures. It was once the case that these would only be accepted if there was a good reason and an explanation for the use of a provisional figure was submitted with the return, together with a date by which the final figure would be advised. This changed with effect from 23 October 2001. Provisional or estimated figures are now acceptable even if no explanation and no final date for provision of the correct figure is given. The Revenue take the view that a taxpayer must still make his best efforts to make a full and complete return by the statutory filing date otherwise the use of provisions and estimates is not justified. Thus, using them may lead to an enquiry into the return.

3.23 The case of *Dunk v Havant General Comrs [1976] STC 460n* is the lead case for the Revenue's views, particularly the words of Goulding J:

> 'what the taxpayer has to declare is "that the return is to the best of his knowledge correct and complete". If … a taxpayer finds circumstances that make the best of his knowledge more than usually unreliable, it is open to him to put against a figure for a particular item of income such words as "Estimated", "See accompanying memorandum", or something of that kind, and explain the circumstances. If he has done his best – and, of course, he is under a duty to use all proper sources of knowledge – he will not, in my view, be guilty of making a false statement providing, as I say, he puts in a genuine estimate and, if necessary, explains that it is not very reliable'.

3.24 This was confirmed by the Court of Appeal in the case of *Alexander v Wallington General Comrs [1993] STC 588* in which Lloyd LJ, referring to the words of Goulding J, said:

> 'I hope that the taxpayer will pay good heed to those words, because they represent a correct statement of the English law and practice on this subject'.

3.25 Figures of income in the return should be rounded down and deductions and credits rounded up. The tax figures may also be rounded

3.26 Returns that are obviously incomplete are sent back to the taxpayer for correction. When this happens the Revenue will usually allow a further 14 days for rectification, unless the return was in any event late or it was an 'unsatisfactory return', ie it did not meet the requirements of s 8, eg it is not in prescribed form, not signed, supplementary pages were not included, etc. The Revenue have power to amend a return (or amendment) themselves within nine months of the delivery of the return or amendment to correct obvious errors by giving notice of such an amendment to the taxpayer. A taxpayer may, however, reverse such a correction within 30 days of its issue [TMA 1970 s 9ZB].

3.27 Any claims for reliefs must be included on the tax return [TMA 1970 s 42].

3.28 Electronic lodgement (see **14.51**) is permitted by approved persons using approved software and hardware. However, a hard copy must be signed prior to transmission. Electronic lodgement has not been successful and the Revenue are phasing it out and replacing it with Internet submission, either by taxpayers themselves or their agents.

3.29 Taxpayers have had very little success when trying to argue that they have actually made returns by pointing out that the Revenue can go and obtain the information elsewhere. It was common practice in the pre self-assessment days for agents to enter 'per PAYE' and 'per P11D' on returns instead of taking the trouble to research the figures. It is clear that such a practice was, and still is, incorrect, as was made quite clear in the case of *Cox v Poole General Comrs and IRC [1990] STC 122n.*

3.30 If a person who has been required to submit a return does not do so, the Revenue are entitled to determine the tax due by estimating it. Any such determination can only be replaced by a completed return. There is also a range of penalties for late submission of a tax return.

3.31 After a return has been submitted it can be amended by the taxpayer, by notice to the Revenue, at any time in the 12 months after the filing date [TMA 1970 s 9ZA]. There were some changes to this right from 1 May 2001. Prior to this date no amendment could be made if the Revenue had commenced an enquiry. This no longer applies. An amendment can now be made even if an enquiry is underway; it will not, however, be effective until the enquiry is closed and does not limit the scope of the enquiry [TMA 1970 s 9B]. The Revenue's view is that the amendment provisions do not prevent them from seeking penalties if the original figures were incorrect due to fraud or negligence (see Revenue Interpretation RI 195).

3.32 The Revenue can also amend a tax return to correct obvious errors or omissions, such as errors of principle or arithmetical mistakes, within nine months of receiving the tax return (or within nine months of the taxpayer amending the return under TMA 1970 s 9ZA). Such a correction must be made by notice in writing to the taxpayer. The taxpayer is entitled to reject the amendment within 30 days of receiving the notice. The Revenue also have power to amend a tax return, by notice to the taxpayer, whilst an enquiry is in progress, if the officer forms the opinion that the amount stated in the self-assessment is insufficient and that, unless the assessment is immediately amended, there is likely to be a loss of tax to the Crown [TMA 1970 s 9C]. If the enquiry relates only to an amendment to the return, the assessment can only cover additional tax attributable to that amendment [TMA 1970 s 9C(3)]. Such an amendment is known as a jeopardy amendment. A jeopardy amendment cannot be appealed against until after the enquiry is completed. This means that the tax is immediately payable subject to the right to apply to the Commissioners to postpone all or part of it.

3.33 Such amendments are comparatively rare, although the Revenue tell their staff, 'Where a taxpayer will not agree to make a payment on account and you are of the opinion that tax is at risk you should consider making a jeopardy amendment' (Enquiry Manual, para 1951). They go on to point out that 'the legislation is silent about the circumstances in which a jeopardy amendment might be appropriate'. They suggest that the officer should consider making a jeopardy amendment where he discovers or suspects that the taxpayer intends to dispose of assets, to become non-resident, to apply for bankruptcy (or, in the case of a company, go into liquidation), or the taxpayer may be about to go to prison. They also say that the officer should consider making such an amendment 'where the taxpayer refuses to co-operate but only if you have already established with some degree of certainty that the self-assessment is deficient' (para 1953).

3.34 An entertaining case on the subject of tax returns is *Moschi v General Comrs for Kensington [1980] STC 1*. It probably covers most points involving the failure to complete a tax return. It is a case that deals with the pre self-assessment era, but is still relevant. Mr Moschi, having been served with tax returns for a number of years, initially did not complete them at all and suffered a penalty for this failure. To avoid further penalties he then completed the forms but inserted no figures; instead he wrote 'to be ascertained'. He was told that this was not acceptable so he then re-submitted the forms, but this time against the entry for 'trades and professions' he inserted a reference to a letter advising that his income could be found by reference to the accounts of five named companies. The General Commissioners found him in default and awarded further penalties. Mr Moschi then appealed to the High Court but the Court said that the fact that the Revenue has information through other channels does not satisfy the requirements of a person to deliver a full and complete return.

Enquiries

3.35 Having notified the Revenue of a liability to pay tax and then completed a tax return the matter does not necessarily end. The Revenue may 'enquire' into the return, any amendment to that return or any claim or election related to the return. They must give written notice of the intention to make such enquiries. The powers to do this in respect of individuals, partnerships and trustees can be found at TMA 1970 ss 9A (re income tax and capital gains) and 12AC (partnerships). In plain language this means that the Revenue have the legal authority to investigate a tax return.

3.36 The enquiry notice is given by a letter sent to the taxpayer telling him that an enquiry into the tax return is being made. Enclosed with the letter should be the relevant Code of Practice 11 (COP 11) relating to self-assessment enquiries. If an agent is acting the Revenue will, at the same time, advise him of the enquiry notice and send him a copy.

3.37 A strict time limit is imposed on the Revenue within which they can start an enquiry. In most circumstances this time limit expires 12 months from the 'filing date', so it is important to understand what is meant by 'the filing date'.

3.38 For all taxpayers, except companies, the filing date is the 31 January following the end of the tax year concerned. Thus, for the tax year 2003/04 the normal filing date is 31 January 2005.

3.39 A later filing date applies if the Revenue issue the tax return after 31 October following the end of the tax year (eg after 31 October 2004 in respect of a return required for the year 2003/04). In such a case, the filing date is three months from the day on which the notice to make a return is given (eg where the Revenue send a return relating to the tax year 2003/04 for completion on 1 December 2004, the filing date would have been 29 February 2005).

3.40 If the Revenue issue a return late it is normally because the taxpayer has failed to notify liability within the statutory time limit.

3.41 The Revenue can commence an enquiry into a return only within certain defined periods. For individuals, partners and trustees these are:

(*a*) 12 months from the filing date, if the return was delivered (or amended) on or before the filing date.

(*b*) The quarter day next following the first anniversary of the day the return was delivered, if the return was delivered (or amended) after the filing date. The quarter days are 31 January, 30 April, 31 July and 31 October.

[TMA 1970 s 9(2).]

3.42 Some examples, as follow, may help in the understanding of this.

(*a*) A return for 2003/04 has a normal filing date of 31 January 2005. If it is delivered to the Revenue on or before 31 January 2005 the 'enquiry window' will expire on 30 January 2006, ie 12 months from the filing date.

(*b*) The Revenue issue the return for the year 2003/04 on 1 December 2004, so it has a filing date of 28 February 2005 (the return is issued after 1 October so the filing date is three months from issue of the return). The 'enquiry window' will expire on 28 February 2006, ie 12 months from the filing date.

(*c*) A return for the year 2003/04, issued by the Revenue before 1 October 2004, is delivered to the Revenue on 1 March 2005. Its normal filing date was 31 January 2005. The enquiry window' expires on 30 April 2006, ie the quarter date following the first anniversary (1 March 2006) of the delivery of the return.

In normal circumstances an enquiry into the return cannot be made outside these time limits.

3.43 In the first year of the self-assessment system there was an outcry when the Revenue issued notices on the last day of January so that taxpayers could only have received them after 31 January. The Revenue withdrew such notices after agreeing that the correct interpretation of the legislation required the taxpayer to receive the enquiry notice by the 30 January not for the Revenue merely to have issued it before then.

3.44 This interpretation was further emphasised by the Special Commissioners in the case of *Wing Hung Lai v Bale [1999] STC (SCD) 238*. In this case an enquiry notice had been issued on 27 January 1999. The Special Commissioner accepted that the accountant had received his copy on Monday, 1 February 1999 and that the taxpayer had received his notice on Tuesday, 2 February 1999. The Special Commissioner decided that the notice was invalid. This was because the service of a s 9A notice is governed by the Interpretation Act 1978 s 7, which states that 'service is deemed … to have been effected at the time which the letter would be delivered in the ordinary course of post'. It had therefore to be decided what 'the ordinary course of post' was in this case. The Special Commissioner looked at two helpful notices.

3.45 The first was a practice direction from the Queen's Bench Division on 8 March 1985 in which it was said:

> 'to avoid uncertainty as to the date of service it will be taken (subject to proof to the contrary) that delivery in the ordinary course of post was effected:
> (a) in the case of first class mail, on the second working day after posting
> (b) in the case of second class mail, on the fourth working day after posting
> "Working days" are Monday to Friday, excluding any bank holiday'.

3.46 The second was a Code of Practice by the Post Office that promised delivery of second class post within three working days of posting and also defined working days as Monday to Friday. Therefore, the notice could not have been delivered within the 'ordinary course of post' because three working days took it to Monday, 1 February 1999, and four working days to Tuesday, 2 February 1999.

3.47 The Revenue are permitted only one bite of the cherry. A return that has been the subject of one notice of enquiry cannot be the subject of another – although an amendment to the return can be enquired into separately if the enquiry window on the return itself has closed but that for the amendment (normally 12 months after the end of the quarter in which the amendment was made) is still open [TMA 1970 s 9A(3), (5)].

Determination of appropriate case

3.48 There are some circumstances where there is more than one method of calculating a liability because the source of income falls within the provisions of more than one Schedule. When this happens the law permits the Inspector to determine which should be used. There is no right of appeal against this decision. The Inspector can only use such power in relation to computing profits under Sch D Cases I or II or amounts within Sch D Cases III, IV or V [TMA 1970 ss 9D, 12AE].

Trusts

3.49 The Revenue can require trustees to submit an income tax return, to contain such information as may reasonably be required and to deliver with it such accounts, statements and documents relating to information contained in the return as may reasonably be required [TMA 1970 s 8A(1)]. They can serve a notice on any one trustee or on all of them [TMA 1970 s 8A(1)]. In practice they send a tax return to only one trustee. The time limit for submitting the return is the same as that for individuals [TMA 1970 s 8A(1A)]. The return must include a declaration that it is correct and complete to the best of the trustee's knowledge and belief [TMA 1970 s 8A(2)]. The notice to make the return can require different information, accounts and statements for different periods or in relation to different descriptions of income and different descriptions of settlement [TMA 1970 s 8A(3), (4)]. Subject to this, the rules in relation to individual tax returns also apply to returns of trustees. The limit on the need to supply information on capital gains considered at **3.13** also applies to trustees but by reference to the reduced exempt amount that the trust attracts [TCGA 1992 Sch 1 para 1(5A)]. As indicated at **14.7**, a trustee who authorises the receipt of income arising from trust property by a beneficiary (or an agent of the beneficiary) is not required to take an action for the purpose of the assessment of the beneficiary to tax if the beneficiary (or agent) actually receives the income and the trustees make a return of the name and address of that person and the amount of income concerned under TMA 1970 s 13 (see **4.2**) [TMA 1970 s 76(1)]. In other words if the trustees mandate income direct to the beneficiary it is for the beneficiary not the trustees to declare it on a tax return.

Partnerships

3.50 Where a trade, profession or business is carried on by two or more persons in partnership the Revenue can require the submission of a partnership return [TMA 1970 s 12AA]. This has a different purpose to an individual's tax return. A partnership is a transparent entity for tax purposes (technically it is not an entity at all) and as such is not a taxpayer. The individual partners are liable for the tax on their individual shares of the partnership income. The partnership return is therefore an information return – although the enquiry provisions enable the Revenue to enquire into the partnership return it is obviously more convenient to everyone to have one enquiry, where the information ought to be readily available, rather than having separate enquiries into the return of each partner, where the Revenue would want to investigate the calculation of the partnership profits.

3.51 An officer of the Board can by notice require 'such person as is identified in accordance with rules given with the notice (or a successor of his)' to make and deliver a partnership return and to deliver with it such accounts, statements and documents relating to information contained in it as may reasonably be required [TMA 1970 s 12AA(2)]. Alternatively (or even additionally), they can require any or all of the parties to make the return [TMA 1970 s 12AA(3)]. In practice, partners can choose to nominate one particular partner to receive and complete the partnership return (Income Tax Self-Assessment Manual, para 503). If they do not do so the Revenue will choose, but in practice, as long as one partner signs the return, they do not normally seem concerned as to whether it is the partner to whom the return was addressed or a different one. If the partners are all individuals, the time limits for the submission of personal returns applies. If the partnership is a mixture of individuals and companies, the time limit is the latest of the individual (see **3.17**) or company (see **3.62**) limits [TMA 1970 s 12AA(4), (5)].

3.52 A partnership return must include:

(*a*) a declaration of the name, residence and tax reference of each of the partners (who were partners at any time during the period for which the return is required);

(*b*) the dates of changes, if there have been partnership changes during the return period;

(*c*) a declaration by the person making the return that it is correct and complete to the best of his knowledge or belief;

(*d*) the like particulars with respect to any disposal of partnership property as if the partnership were taxable on chargeable gains; and

(*e*) a partnership statement,

[TMA 1970 ss 12AA(6), (7), 12AB].

3.53 The partnership statement must show, for the period in respect of which the return is made and each period of account ending within that period:

(*a*) the amount of income or loss from each source which has accrued to or been suffered by the partnership for the period;

(*b*) the consideration received in respect of each disposal of partnership property during the period;

(*c*) each amount of income tax that has been deducted from (or treated as paid on) such income;

(*d*) the amount of each tax credit that has accrued to the partnership for the period;

(*e*) the amount of each charge on income of the partnership; and

(*f*) the amount of any such income, loss, consideration, tax credit or charge that is to be attributed to each partner (by reference to his profit share),

[TMA 1970 s 12AB].

3.54 The rules on amending, correcting and enquiring into a partnership return broadly follows those for individual returns [TMA 1970 ss 12AB–12AD]. A partnership return can be amended only by the partner who made the return or his successor, and notices given by the Revenue have to be given to that partner. It appears that, strictly, a person cannot have a successor unless he 'is no longer available' [TMA 1970 s 12AA(11)]. In practice the Revenue do not normally enforce this. Where a successor is possible he will be the person for the time being nominated for the purposes of s 12AA by a majority of the partners. In the absence of such a nomination the Revenue can nominate any of the partners [TMA 1970 s 12AA(11)]. Where a partnership return is amended (or corrected by the Revenue) the Revenue must amend each of the individual partner's returns and tell each partner that they have done so [TMA 1970 ss 12ABA(3), 12ABB(6)].

Corporation tax

3.55 The corporation tax provisions on returns broadly follow those for income tax, although there are some differences. A company has 12 months after the end of its accounting period to give a notice of chargeability if it has not been given a notice requiring it to make a tax return. The penalty for failure to comply with this requirement is up to 100 per cent of the tax payable for the accounting period that remains unpaid at the end of the 12-month period. For this purpose the tax unpaid takes no account of any relief that may be due following repayment of a loan account under TA 1988 s 419 [FA 1998 Sch 18 para 2]. Any such penalty can be mitigated by the Revenue using their powers under TMA 1970 s 102 (see **12.60**).

3.56 A company is not issued with a tax return. Instead it can, by notice, be required to deliver a return containing such information, accounts, statements and reports as are relevant to its tax liability or otherwise relevant to the application of the Corporation Taxes Acts to the company. Different information, accounts, statements and reports can be required from different types of company. The return must incorporate a declaration that it is correct and complete to the best of the signatory's knowledge [FA 1998 Sch 18 para 3]. The return must be in the form prescribed by the Board of Inland Revenue [TMA 1970 s 113(1)]. A return form can be downloaded from the Revenue's website or obtained from the Revenue's order line. The reason that the Revenue do not automatically issue corporation tax return forms is that most companies use computer generated forms. The return must include a self-assessment and a calculation of the tax payable [FA 1998 Sch 18 paras 7, 8]. The return is not regarded as made unless the accounts and other information required to comply with the notice are included [FA 1998 Sch 18 para 4].

3.57 The notice to complete a tax return must specify the period to which it relates. It could be that the notice requires a return to a date that is not an accounting period, possibly because the accounting date was changed without the Revenue having been told. In such circumstances the return must be for the accounting period that ends during the period specified in the notice. If there is more than one such accounting period a separate return is required for each of them. If no accounting period ends in the specified period but one began during it, the return is required for the part of the period specified in the notice prior to that accounting period commencing. If the company was outside the charge to corporation tax for the entire specified period the return must cover the whole of it. If a notice is received but none of the above applies, no return need be made [FA 1998 Sch 18 para 5]. It is difficult to envisage a situation in which a company is not either within the charge to corporation tax for part of the period specified in the return or outside the charge to corporation tax for the whole of that period! Accordingly, it is unclear in what circumstances no return is required. If the company had no taxable income or gains it appears that a nil return needs to be made.

3.58 In general, as with income tax, all claims and elections must be made in a return, as far as possible. However, for corporation tax there are some claims that can only be made in a return (or an amendment to a return), namely those for group relief, capital allowances, research and development tax credits, land remediation tax credit and life assurance company tax credit [FA 1998 Sch 18 para 10]. The time limit for amending a return is extended to allow such claims to be made (see **Chapter 6**). A claim for repayment of income by virtue of TA 1988 s 6(2) (exclusion from income tax of companies within the scope of corporation tax) or by virtue of an exemption under the Corporation Taxes Acts (such as the exemption for charities), or for payment of a tax credit (if this is still possible), or for corporate venturing scheme investment relief, cannot even be made in advance of submitting a return [FA 1998 Sch 18 para 9].

3.59 Where a UK company is required to prepare accounts under the Companies Act 1985 for a period consisting of or including the whole of the period for which a return is required, the power to require the delivery of accounts as part of the return is limited to such accounts as are required to be prepared under that Act [FA 1998 Sch 18 para 11]. In *Slater Ltd v Beacontree General Comrs [2002] STC 246*, Lightman J held, in relation to a precept, that 'the Commissioners were entitled to require a profit and loss account in one of the four statutory formats appropriate to a small company. They were not entitled to more'.

3.60 A corporation tax return for a company which carries on a trade, profession or business in partnership must include any amount which is stated to be its share of any income, loss, consideration, tax, credit or charge in a partnership statement (under TMA 1970 s 12AB) for the period for which the return is made (or a period which includes any part of it) [FA 1998 Sch 18 para 12]. Obviously, if the company thinks that such figures are wrong it ought also to include the correct figures.

3.61 As with income tax, a return can also require details of chargeable assets, subject to the exclusions at **3.12** (other than under TCGA 1992 ss 51(1), 268 and 269, which are not relevant to companies). The exclusion for assets acquired as trading stock does not apply if the assets are held for the purpose of the long-term business of an insurance company. The exclusion for tangible moveable property does not apply to property within TCGA 1992 s 262(6) (terminal markets and currency) [FA 1998 Sch 18 para 13].

3.62 A completed company tax return must be with the Revenue by the 'filing date'. This is the last day of whichever of the following is the latest:

(*a*) 12 months from the end of the period for which the return has to be made;

(*b*) if the period of account (ie the period for which accounts are prepared) in which the last day of the accounting period for which the return is required is no longer than 18 months, 12 months from the end of that period;

(*c*) if that period of account exceeds 18 months, 30 months from the start of it; or

(*d*) 3 months from the date when the return was issued for completion,

[FA 1998 Sch 18 para 14].

3.63 A return can be amended by notice to the Revenue within 12 months of the filing date or, if the return was made for the wrong period, what would have been the filing date had the period for which the return was actually made been an accounting period. A notice of amendment has to contain such information, and be in such form, as the Revenue may reasonably require. [FA 1998 Sch 18 para 15]. They have not laid down any requirements. A company can amend its return during the course of an enquiry. If it does so, the amendment does not restrict the scope of the enquiry but can, if the Revenue wish, be taken into account in the enquiry [FA 1998 Sch 18 para 31(1), (2)]. In so far as the amendment offsets the amount of tax payable (including by another company) it does not take effect until after it is completed, except for the purpose of any claim under TMA 1970 s 59DA (see **8.48**) [FA 1998 Sch 18 para 31(3)].

3.64 As with income tax (see **3.32**) the Revenue can itself amend a return to correct any obvious errors or omissions within nine months from the date the return (or amendment to it) was delivered to them. Unlike with income tax, if a company disagrees with the Revenue adjustment it must re-amend the return to negate the Revenue's change. If the time period for amendment has expired, the company has three months from the date of the Revenue's amendment to reject it by notice in writing [FA 1998 Sch 18 para 16]. The rules on jeopardy amendments considered at **3.32** also apply to companies [FA 1998 Sch 18 para 30].

3.65 The enquiry procedure is similar to that which applies for income tax. The Revenue must issue a notice of enquiry [FA 1998 Sch 18 paras 24, 25]. For corporation tax this can cover not only the tax due for the year, but the Revenue can also enquire into any amount that affects, or could affect, the tax payable by the company for another accounting period or the tax liability of another company for any accounting period [FA 1998 Sch 18 para 25(1)(b)]. This extension is necessary because the carry back of losses by a company is given effect to in the return for the later year and a group relief surrender will affect the tax payable by the claimant company.

3.66 If the Revenue think that a return may have been made for the wrong period (or has become one for the wrong period as a result of a direction under TMA 1970 s 12(5A) – the power for the Revenue to direct the accounting period where a company carries on several trades) the enquiry power includes power to enquire into the period for which the return should have been made. A return is made for the wrong period if either:

(*a*) it was made for a period which is not in fact an accounting period of the company; or

(*b*) it was made on the basis that there was no accounting period ending with the specified period, but there was in fact such a period.

In such a case the period within which an enquiry can be opened is calculated by reference to the accounting period adopted in the return, not the correct one [FA 1998 Sch 18 para 26].

3.67 The time limits for amending a return (and for the Revenue to enquire into it) are extended for insurance companies and certain friendly societies which are subject to statutory rules that permit a provision to be made on a provisional basis or a periodic investigation into the company's finances [FA 1998 Sch 18 paras 85–87].

3.68 Where an amount included in a corporation tax return which is required to be included in the return (such as a group relief claim) affects the tax payable for a different accounting period or the tax payable by another company, that amount is treated as conclusively determined for corporation tax purposes in relation to that other period or company once it can no longer be altered [FA 1998 Sch 18 para 88(1), (2)]. An amount can no longer be altered for this purpose if the period within which it can be amended by the company and the period within which an appeal against a Revenue amendment can be made has closed and any appeal has been finally determined. Where any provision allows a return to be amended late, or the Revenue amend it under FA 1998 Sch 18 para 83(3) where a capital allowance claim is reduced, the above rules obviously apply by reference to that provision [para 88(3)–(5)].

European Economic Interest Groupings

3.69 A European Economic Interest Grouping (EEIG) registered in Great Britain or Northern Ireland (or which has an establishment here) can be required to make a return by an Inspector within the time limit specified in the notice, containing such information as may be required by it and to deliver with it such accounts and statements as the notice may specify. If the EEIG is registered elsewhere the Revenue can serve the notice to make a return on any UK resident member of the EEIG or, if there is no such member, on any member of the EEIG. They can serve separate notices on as many members as they think fit. A return by an EEIG must include a determination to the effect that it is to the best of the maker's knowledge correct and complete. A notice to make a return can require different information for different descriptions of income or gains, or in relation to different descriptions of member or different descriptions of grouping. If the contract for the formation of the EEIG provides that the grouping shall be bound only by two or more managers acting jointly, the return must be signed by both (or all) of them [TMA 1970 s 12A].

Records

3.70 Any individual, partnership or trustee who may be required to make a tax return under TMA 1970 ss 8, 8A or 12AA must keep all such records as may be required to enable him too make a correct and complete return [TMA 1970 s 12B(1)(a)]. So must a company [FA 1998 Sch 18 para 21].

3.71 Such records must be preserved until, what the statute calls, 'the end of the relevant day', which is:

(*a*) for those carrying on a trade, profession or business, the fifth anniversary of the 31 January next following the year of assessment or, if it is a company liable to income tax, then six years from the end of the period for which the return was required; or (*b*) in any other case, the first anniversary of the 31 January next following the year of assessment,

[TMA 1970 s 12B(1)(b), (2)].

The records to back up a corporation tax return need to be preserved for six years from the end of the return period [FA 1998 Sch 18 para 21(2)].

3.72 These rules could allow a taxpayer to destroy records while a legitimate enquiry is able to be opened or is under way. They are therefore modified in such circumstances to require the records to be preserved:

(*a*) if there is an enquiry (including one already open), until the date that enquiry is completed; or

(*b*) if no enquiry is under way but the Revenue still have power to start one, the day on which they cease to be entitled to enquire into the return (see **3.37**),

[TMA 1970 s 12B(1)(b); FA 1998 Sch 18 para 21(3)].

3.73 There is nothing to stop the Revenue demanding a return be completed for any year, no matter how long ago. In such a case the law demands that if any relevant records still exist for the year or period concerned that they are preserved until the 'relevant day' determined as in **3.71** above as if the return had been demanded 'in date' [TMA 1970 s 12B(2A); FA 1998 Sch 18 para 21(4)].

3.74 The legislation does not dictate what records should be kept, except for those persons carrying on a trade, profession or business. They are told that the records must include records of all amounts received and expended in the course of the trade, etc, and 'the matters' in respect of which the receipts and expenditure take place. If the trade involves dealing in goods, a record of all sales and purchases of such goods made in the course of the trade must also be kept [TMA 1970 s 12B(3)(a); FA 1998 Sch 18 para 21(5)]. TMA 1970 s 12B(3)(b) and FA 1988 Sch 18 para 21(6) requires all supporting documents relating to such receipts and expenditure and sales and purchases be preserved in the same way as the records. 'Supporting documents' includes accounts, books, deeds, contracts, vouchers and receipts [TMA 1970 s 12B(6)(b); FA 1998 Sch 18 para 21(6)]. Those engaged in property letting are treated as trading for record keeping purposes [TMA 1970 s 12B(6)(a)].

3.75 The duty to preserve records can be discharged by preserving the information they contain. If this is done then such copy documents are admissible in evidence. There are, however, certain types of document that must be kept in original format, namely:

(*a*) dividend vouchers;

(*b*) vouchers in relation to payments made under deduction of tax;

(*c*) forms SC60 for sub-contractors; and

(*d*) records of foreign tax deductions (or deemed tax creditable under tax sparing arrangements).

These are of course records that evidence the payment of tax (or something treated as tax) rather than of transactions or income [TMA 1970 s 12B(4), (4A); FA 1998 Sch 18 para 22].

3.76 The Revenue consider that this will specifically permit the use of optical imaging systems, provided that what is retained on disc represents a complete and unaltered image of the underlying paper document (Tax Bulletin 21, Feb 1996). It is understood that this includes a requirement to copy the back of an invoice if information, such as terms and conditions, is shown thereon. The Tax Bulletin article says that records relating to a taxpayer's obligations as an employer, such as PAYE records, must still be retained in paper form and contractors in the construction industry must continue to keep the originals of subcontractor documents and vouchers.

3.77 As might be expected, there is a penalty for those who fail to comply with these record keeping and preservation requirements. The maximum penalty is £3,000. A penalty cannot be imposed for a failure to keep those documents at (*a*) and (*b*) in **3.63** above if the Revenue are satisfied that the taxpayer can prove any facts that they reasonably require to be proved by reference to other documentary evidence [TMA 1970 s 12B(5), (5A); FA 1998 Sch 18 para 23]. There is no penalty for a failure to keep records which might have been required only for the purposes of claims, elections or notices which are not included in the return [TMA 1970 s 12B(5A)]. However, the Revenue are likely to reject the claim in the absence of such records.

3.78 The Revenue have said that penalties will only be sought in the more serious cases, such as where records have deliberately been destroyed to obstruct an enquiry or there has been a history of serious record-keeping failures (Tax Bulletin – Special Edition 1997). Apart from such cases, it is unlikely that the maximum penalty would be sought even where they feel that penalties are appropriate.

3.79 TMA 1970 s 12 does not give the Revenue power to dictate what records a business must keep. What is requisite for the purpose of enabling the taxpayer to make and deliver a correct and complete return is, at the end of the day, a question of fact. If the Revenue cannot show that the return is incorrect or incomplete there may well be an inference that the records maintained in fact satisfy the requirements. The Revenue say in SA/BK 3 (Self-assessment: a guide to keeping records for the self-employed):

> 'The precise records you need to keep to meet these requirements will depend on the type and size of your business. It is up to you to ensure that the statement of business income and expenditure in your return is adequate. Whatever form of records you maintain they must be adequate to enable you to do this.'

They go on to say:

> 'Some examples of the actual records recommended for particular types of business are given later in this document. They cannot of course cover every type of business, or different circumstances within the same type of business. So your business is unlikely to fit squarely within any of the examples given.'

The Revenue's recommendations are helpful indicia of what may be appropriate. However, most accountants would expect the appropriate record for a business to depend on its size and method of operation, so in many cases the Revenue recommendations are probably excessive in some respects.

3.80 In relation to corporation tax returns the Revenue have confirmed that records which satisfy the requirement of Companies Act 1985 s 221 to keep and preserve accounting records will also have satisfied the requirement to keep and preserve records for tax purposes (apart from transfer pricing records) (Tax Bulletin 37, Oct 1998).

3.81 Particular difficulties arise with estimates, with some Inspectors seeking to reject estimates out of hand on the basis that the record keeping requirements have not been met. If records are not available of expenditure that is known to have been incurred it is hard to see how a return can be correct without the inclusion of an estimate of such expenditure. The Inspector's obligation under TMA 1970 s 19A regarding an enquiry is not to satisfy himself that the return is correct and complete, but to satisfy himself that it is not incorrect or incomplete. It seems likely that the use of this double negative is to emphasise that there is a difference between something being correct and its not being incorrect, ie there may be scope for differences of opinion either of which would be correct or may be scope for the inclusion or omission of minor amounts which, while affecting its accuracy, do not make the return incorrect.

3.82 In any event the Revenue have said that 'in practice we will continue our long-standing approach of treating a reasonable and reliable estimate as a sufficiently accurate figure' (Tax Bulletin – Special Edition 1997). Whilst they go on to say, 'this does not relieve taxpayers of their obligations to keep proper records', this probably does no more than emphasise that a taxpayer cannot ignore the record keeping requirements and use estimates where it would be reasonable to obtain and keep accurate figures. They also say that 'an estimate which, while not a precise figure, is sufficiently reliable to enable the taxpayer to make an accurate return does not have to be identified as an estimate, in the return, although where there are doubts as to the reliability of an estimate they would expect both its use and those doubts to be brought to their attention.

3.83 The Revenue have also given guidance in Tax Bulletin 37 (Oct 1998) on the records that they feel are necessary under the transfer pricing legislation. They

> 'do not want taxpayers to suffer disappropriate compliance costs, nor to be required to prepare and retain documentation which is out of keeping with the nature, size and complexity of their business, or with the transaction (or series of transactions) in question. At the same time, taxpayers will be required to self assess accurately, and may be called on by the Inland Revenue to justify their transfer prices and the quantum of income, profits or losses incurred for tax purposes.'

They do, however, think that taxpayers need to prepare and retain such documentation as is reasonable given the complexity or otherwise of the relevant transactions and which identifies commercial or financial relations falling within the scope of the legislation; the nature, terms (including prices) of relevant transactions; the methods by which the nature and terms were arrived at (including any study of comparables and any functional analysis undertaken); the reason it is believed that that method has resulted in arm's length terms; and the terms of relevant commercial arrangements (eg contracts, loan agreements) with both third parties and affiliated customers, including any budgets, forecasts or other papers relied on in arriving at arm's length terms, etc.

Chapter 4

Other Returns

4.1 The Revenue can require third parties to make returns in specified situations to enable them to cross-check the information provided by taxpayers.

Persons in receipt of income belonging to others (TMA 1970 s 13)

4.2 Any person who is in receipt of any money or value that belongs to someone else who is chargeable to income tax on it can be required by an Inspector of Taxes to make a return giving the following details:

(*a*) a statement of all such money, value or gains;

(*b*) the name and address of the person to whom it belongs; and

(*c*) a declaration whether the person is a UK resident, or of 'full age' or an incapacitated person,

[TMA 1970 s 13(1)].

4.3 If the recipient receives the money or value jointly with another person or persons, the return must also give the name and address of that other person or persons [TMA 1970 s 13(2)].

4.4 An Inspector cannot demand information under this section if it relates to a tax year that ended more than three years before the Inspector's notice [TMA 1970 s 13(3)].

4.5 In *Lord Advocates v Gibb (5 TC 194)* the Revenue issued a notice to a firm of underwriting agents under the predecessor of section 13 asking for a list of all of their clients and the amount of profits they had received belonging to each. The Court of Session held that the firm had to make the return as the wording was broad enough to apply to cases of mercantile agency. In *Attorney-General v The National Provincial Bank Ltd (14 TC 111)* the Revenue asked the bank for a return of all cases where they received untaxed interest on War Loan and National War Bonds where the bank either acted as a trustee, held the stock as security for a customer's overdraft or loan (with the dividends being credited to the customer's account), held the stock as security given by a guarantor, or held the stock as nominee. It was held that they had to make the return in all of these circumstances where the bank held the stock as security, because it was the registered proprietor so it received the interest, albeit that it obtained the interest for the person who was entitled to it.

4.6 In *Fawcett v Special Comrs and Lancaster Farmers Auction Mart Co Ltd (69 TC 279)* the Court of Appeal (reversing the decisions both of the Special Commissioners and the High Court) held that a firm of livestock auctioneers had to make a return of sales made by it on behalf of farmers. The company contended that the section applied only where the beneficial owner was chargeable to tax on the specific receipt and that it could not apply if the receipt was simply an element in arriving at trading profits. The company also argued that, as the section applied only to receipts in respect of which its clients were chargeable to income tax and it could not know whether or not a person was selling an item in such a capacity it was impossible to comply with the notice. Whilst the Court of Appeal thought this, superficially at least, a powerful argument, it pointed out that the company can only be required to provide information which is in its possession and in cases where it had reason to believe that the vendor was not selling in a capacity of a trader it would have a reasonable excuse for having excluded the sale from its return – although it would be obliged to supplement the return if further information were to subsequently come into its possession which showed that it was mistaken. The restriction to information in the person's possession is of course a common-sense one but it is not a requirement of the legislation.

4.7 Anybody supplying the necessary information in another satisfactory format would not normally be required by an Inspector to repeat that information under the authority of s 13. The Revenue has said that it will be discriminating in the issue of notices to solicitors.

Lodgers and inmates (TMA 1970 s 14)

4.8 The Revenue can require any person it believes is letting out rooms to deliver a return in writing, stating:

(*a*) the name of every lodger or inmate resident in his dwelling house; and

(*b*) if that person has an ordinary place of residence elsewhere, the address of that place.

The notice must specify a time within which the return must be made but there is no statutory minimum period that must be allowed. The return needs to be specifically stated to be to the best of the person's knowledge. The reference to 'his dwelling house' probably prevents a notice being served on a landlord who has his own property but lets out rooms in another property.

PAYE returns (TMA 1970 s 15)

4.9 Employers must, when required to do so, provide the Revenue with such of the following information as they may require relating to each of those who are, or have been, his employees:

(*a*) name and address [TMA 1970 s 15(4)];

(*b*) particulars of relevant payments made to him [TMA 1970 s 15(5)];

(*c*) particulars of relevant payments the employer has arranged (or guaranteed or facilitated) for some other person to make, and the name and business address of the person making the payments [TMA 1970 s 15(5)(b), (13)];

(*d*) if the relevant payments have not been made by, nor arranged by, the employer but he is aware that they have been paid, the name and business address of the payer [TMA 1970 s 15(5)(c)].

Relevant payments are all payments made to the employee in respect of his employment, including expenses, payments made on his behalf and not repaid and payments to him for services rendered in connection with a trade or business, whether or not in the course of his employment [TMA 1970 s 15(6)].

4.10 Where an expense figure is an apportionment of an expense covering a number of employees or covering both the employment and some other matter, the return must contain a statement that an apportionment has been made [TMA 1970 s 15(7)(a)]. It might be sensible to also include the apportionment calculation, as the Revenue has power to ask for this [TMA 1970 s 15(7)(b)].

4.11 The notice requiring the return must specify whether a return is required for all of a person's employees or only for named individuals or a specified class of employee [TMA 1970 s 15(3)(a)]. The return is of course the forms P35 and P11D. The s 15 notice in relation to salaries is included on the employer's annual return form P35 and covers all employees. That in relation to expenses is also included on the P35 and limits the requirement to make a return to directors and employees earning £8,500 or more per annum.

4.12 Where the employer is a body of persons, such as a company or unincorporated association, both the body and the secretary or other officer performing the duties of secretary are treated as the employer, and are thus obliged to make the return. In the case of a company, but not, apparently, any other body of persons, both can be penalised for a failure to comply with TMA 1970 s 15 [TMA 1970 s 15(12)].

4.13 The notice can also require the return for an employee to state whether any benefits have been provided to him (or to any other person) by reason of his employment which could give rise to tax under TA 1988 ss 141–165 and to give particulars of such benefits [TMA 1970 s 15(8)]. These sections have of course been superceded by ITEPA 2003 ss 73–226, but the need to amend s 15(8) to reflect this appears to have been overlooked. In the case of benefits, the employer can also be required to give particulars of the amounts which may be chargeable to tax by virtue of the above provisions, ie to calculate the taxable benefit [TMA 1970 s 15(9)]. Since the introduction of self-assessment the P11D has required the employer to do this in respect of most benefits, so that the employee can then simply transpose the taxable amount onto his own tax return.

4.14 When providing details of payments and benefits the gross amount must be shown before any deductions that may be permitted by the legislation, eg expenses claims [TMA 1970 s 15(11)].

4.15 Anyone who has been concerned in making payments or providing benefits to another person's employees can also be required to provide full details including the names and addresses of the employees if these are known to him [TMA 1970 s 15(10)].

4.16 The Revenue cannot demand a return for a year of assessment that ended more than five years after 31 January next following that year [TMA 1970 s 15(2) and (10)].

4.17 Where an individual works under a contract caught by TA 1988 s 134 (now ITEPA 2003 s 44) (workers supplied by an agency) s 15 applies as if the agency were the employer of the worker [TA 1988 s 16A]. ITEPA 2003 s 44 itself of course treats the services of the worker as duties of an employment with the agency and all remuneration receivable in consequence of the agency contract as earnings from that employment, so the reason for this separate deeming is not readily apparent. It is probably to ensure that the obligation to submit P11Ds covers such workers. Section 134(6) (now ITEPA 2003 s 45) provides that, where an individual with a view to personally providing services to another person (the client) enters into arrangements with a third party (the agency) and the effect of those arrangements is to bring section 134 into play, any remuneration receivable under such arrangements, eg direct from the client, is treated for income tax purposes as earnings of the deemed employment with the agency. In such a case it is the client (or other person who pays remuneration) who is treated as the employer for s 15 purposes in relation to payments by him [TMA 1970 s 16A(1)(b)].

4.18 If a person who is employed by a non-UK employer performs duties of an office or employment in the UK for a continuous period of 30 days or more and those duties are performed for the benefit of a person resident in, or carrying on a trade, profession or vocation in, the UK, s 15 applies as if the person for whose benefit the duties are performed were the employer, but only so as to require him to make a return of the name and place of residence of the person concerned [FA 1974 s 24].

Fees and commissions (TMA 1970 s 16)

4.19 A person who carries on a trade or business can be required by an Inspector to make a return of payments, of a kind specified in the notice requiring the return, made during the period specified in the notice, being:

(*a*) payments made to someone who is not an employee for services rendered in the course of the trade or business (or if the notice so specifies a specific part of the trade or business);

(*b*) payments for services rendered in connection with the formation, acquisition, development or disposal of the trade or business by non employees; or

(*c*) payments made in respect of any copyright, public lending right or right in a registered design or design right,

[TMA 1970 s 16(1)].

4.20 A body of persons (which includes a government department, local authority or other public body, but would not include a sole trader or, probably, a partnership) which does not carry on a trade or business but carries on some other type of activity can similarly be required to provide details of:

(*a*) payments made in the course of the activity to anyone who is not an employee for services rendered; or

(*b*) payments made in respect of any copyright, public lending right or right in a registered design or design right,

[TMA 1970 s 16(2)].

4.21 In both cases the information must give:

(*a*) the name of the recipient;

(*b*) the amount of the payment; and

(*c*) if the notice so requires:

  (i) the reason for the payment;
  (ii) the period over which the services were rendered;
  (iii) the business name of the recipient;
  (iv) the business or home address of the recipient; and
  (v) any other particulars required by the notice,

[TMA 1970 s 16(4)].

4.22 If the trade, business or other activity is carried on by an unincorporated body of persons (which would probably include a partnership) the notice must be served on the secretary, or person who performs the duties of secretary, of the body [TMA 1970 s 16(3)]. 'Payments for services' for the purpose of s 16 includes commissions of any kind and payments of expenses incurred in connection with the rendering of services [TMA 1970 s 16(7)(a)]. Reference to the making of payments includes the giving of any valuable consideration [TMA 1970 s 16(7)(b)].

4.23 A return cannot be required to include:

(*a*) any payment from which income tax is deductible;

(*b*) anything where the total payments to one person do not exceed £15;

(*c*) any information that relates to tax years that ended more than three years before the information was requested; or

(*d*) payments falling within s 16A (see **4.17**),

[TMA 1970 ss 16(4), 16A(1)].

Interest paid or credited by banks, etc, without deduction of income tax (TMA 1970 s 17)

4.24 Any person who in the ordinary course of their trade or business receives or retains money and pays interest on it (whether gross or under deduction of tax) must, when so required by an Inspector, make a return of all interest paid or credited and the tax deducted therefrom in the tax year specified, together with the name and address of the person receiving such interest [TMA 1970 s 17(1)]. Although the section is expressed to apply in particular to banks (and, by the Income Tax (Building Societies) (Dividends and Interest) Regulations 1990, SI 1990/2231, to building societies) it is not limited to such organisations. It will cover any business that borrows funds to onlend to others or that receives deposits on which it pays interest. However, as the money must be received in the ordinary course of the trade it will not apply to a business that borrows money for the purpose of its trade if it is not such a financial type of business.

4.25 There is no requirement to return any information either:

(*a*) relating to monies not received or retained in the UK; or

(*b*) where the beneficial recipient of the interest is a non-resident company which has requested by notice in writing that the interest is not included in a section 17 return and the payer holds a declaration to that effect.

[TMA 1970 s 17(4)(4A)]. It should particularly be noted that there is no exclusion for interest paid to a non-resident individual, trust, partnership or other unincorporated body.

4.26 Separate notices can be served in relation to different parts of a business. This especially applies to banks, which may be served with notices at different branches on the branch manager. Where this happens any notice subsequently served on the head office is deemed to exclude transactions carried out at the branch [TMA 1970 s 17(2)].

4.27 The Inspector cannot demand information that relates to tax years that ended more than three years before the date on which the information is requested [TMA 1970 s 17(1)].

4.28 The Revenue have power by regulation to prescribe further particulars that can be required by the notice, and the form which such a notice must take, or to exclude things from the need to give a notice [TMA 1970 s 17(5)(6)]. They have done so by the Income Tax (Interest Payments) (Information Powers) Regulations 1992, SI 1992/15. This excludes from s 17:

(*a*) payments in respect of a certificate of deposit;

(*b*) payments in respect of investments held by a non-UK branch;

(*c*) where the interest is paid gross by virtue of a declaration made after 5 April 2001 under TA 1988 s 481(5)(k)(i) (which takes out of the obligation to deduct tax certain cases where the person beneficially entitled to the interest is not ordinarily resident in the UK), the notice need not include the name and address of the person to whom the interest was paid if that is not the person beneficially entitled to the interest;

(*d*) interest on TESSAs; and

(*e*) payments in relation to Personal Equity Plans,

[reg 3(1)].

4.29 The further information that can be required by a s 17 notice in cases where the person beneficially entitled to the interest has made a declaration under the Income Tax (Deposit Takers) (Interest Payments) Regulations 1990, SI 1990/2232, reg 5, that he is unlikely to be liable to pay income tax for the year is:

(*a*) the account number;

(*b*) the address of the branch where the account is held;

(*c*) if the account is a joint account notification of that fact and, if known, the number of such joint holders and their dates of birth and National Insurance numbers;

(*d*) date of birth of the account holder;

(*e*) the National Insurance number of the account holder;

(*f*) the currency in which the interest was paid, if it was other than sterling and the account in which the interest is recorded is a foreign currency account;

(*g*) whether the interest payment was the first one in respect of that account;

(*h*) a declaration that the certificate of no tax liability is still thought to be valid; and

(*i*) the name and address of the person (or persons) by or on whose behalf a certificate has been given (of non-liability to tax) in respect of the payment,

[regs 4, 5(3)].

4.30 The further information that can be required in other cases is:

(*a*) the account number;

(*b*) the address of the branch where the account is held, if that is necessary for identifying the account;

(*c*) in the case of a joint account, the fact that it is a joint account and, if known, the number of joint holders;

(*d*) where a declaration is made under TA 1988 s 481(5)(k)(i) (see **4.28**) notification of that fact and the name and principal residential address of the individual or individuals beneficially entitled to the payment (or in the case of a Scottish partnership, of each of the partners);

(*e*) if known, the date of birth and National Insurance numbers of the person or persons beneficially entitled to the interest;

(*f*) where the first interest payment on the account was made during the year, notification of that fact; and

(*g*) if the interest is recorded in a foreign currency notification of that fact and of the currency concerned,

[reg 6(2)].

4.31 The Regulations also entitle the Revenue to require the bank or other financial trader to furnish them with such information (including copies of relevant books and documents) as they may reasonably require to check the section 17 return [reg 8]. They must allow at least 14 days for the provision of such information. It can also be required to make such information available for inspection by the Revenue at such time as they may reasonably require [reg 10].

4.32 In *Eke v Knight [1977] STC 198*, where the Revenue sought a penalty for failure to comply with a Commissioners' precept for the production of her bank deposit account, the taxpayer somewhat optimistically contended that the precept should not have been made as the Revenue could have obtained the information about her deposit interest under s 17. The Court of Appeal not surprisingly felt this 'a quite untenable view'. They are quite distinct powers. Furthermore, s 17 is only available to the Revenue if they know of the existence and identity of the person liable to pay interest to the taxpayer.

4.33 The Revenue can also require the recipient of the interest to give them the name and address of the beneficial owner if the recipient has not received it beneficially [TMA 1970 s 18(1)]. The notice cannot require information in relation to a tax year ending more than three years prior to the date of the notice [TMA 1970 s 18(3A)]. The Revenue have similar regulation making powers to those in s 17 [TMA 1970 s 18(3B), (3C)]. Parts of the Interest Payment Information Powers Regulations 1992 referred to above apply to s 18 in accordance with these powers.

Payments of interest other than by banks, etc (TMA 1970 s 18)

4.34 Although s 17 applies to banking type businesses, a similar requirement to provide information is placed upon any person who pays interest. The section is headed 'Interest paid without deduction of income tax', but this is misleading for those who may be thumbing through the act as the requirements were extended in 1990 to also cover payments under deduction of tax.

4.35 Any other person by or through whom interest (or a building society dividend, a payment on redemption of a relevant discounted security or a foreign dividend) is paid can be required to give the Revenue the name and address of the person to whom the interest was paid on whose behalf it was received, as well as the amounts involved [TMA 1970 s 18].

4.36 The Regulations exclude from s 18 the same items as are listed at **4.23** above and also any payment to which a s 17 notice can apply (or could do but for the above exclusions) [reg 3(4)]. They require the provision of the information at (*a*)–(*h*) of **4.29** above [regs 4, 5(3)(b), 6(2)] and at (*a*)–(*g*) in **4.30**. They can also require:

(*a*) identification of the security or investment in respect of which the payment is made;

(*b*) if the payment is in a foreign currency and is recorded in that currency, notification of that fact and of the currency concerned;

(*c*) if the payment was made to or for two or more persons, identification of that fact and, if known, the number of such persons; and

(*d*) if the payment was made gross by virtue of a declaration under TA 1988 s 468O(1)(a) (interest distribution by authorised unit trust-residence condition of unit holder or interest distribution by open-ended investment company-residence condition of owner of share) the name and principal residential address of the beneficial owner or owners and the fact that the appropriate declaration was made,

[reg 4(1), 6(3)].

4.37 The Regulations also enable the Revenue to require the audit information described at **4.31** above [regs 9, 10].

Payments out of public funds (TMA 1970 s 18A)

4.38 Any person making payments out of public funds may be required by an Inspector to supply the name and address of anyone to whom they have paid a grant or subsidy and the amount of the payment. Those receiving grants or subsidies on behalf of another can be required to give similar details of the person on whose behalf they have received such payment [TMA 1970 s 18A(1)]. A payment is out of public funds if it is provided directly or indirectly by the Crown, by any Government, public or local authority, whether in the UK or elsewhere, or by an EC institution [TMA 1970 s 18A(6)].

4.39 Any person who issues licences or approvals or who maintains a register of such items can also be required by an Inspector to provide him with the name and address of the holder of a licence or approval and particulars of the licence or of the entry in the register [TMA 1970 s 18A(2)].

4.40 An Inspector can use this power only if, in his reasonable opinion, it is or may be relevant to a tax liability or to the amount of such a liability [TMA 1970 s 18A(4)].

4.41 Information cannot be required for a tax year ended more than three years before the date on which the information is requested [TMA 1970 s 18A(5)].

Special returns

4.42 In addition to the general return requirements under the Taxes Management Act a number of provisions contain their own requirements for a return to be made. The main ones are as follows.

Company demergers, etc

4.43 Where a company makes an exempt distribution within TA 1988 s 213 it must make a return to the Revenue within 30 days of the distribution, giving particulars of it and the circumstances and the reasons why it considers it to be exempt [TA 1988 s 216(1)]. If within five years after the making of an exempt distribution a person makes a chargeable payment which consists of a transfer of money's worth (which triggers a tax charge under TA 1988 s 214) he must make a return to the Revenue within 30 days after the payment giving particulars of the transaction, the name and address of each recipient of the payment and the amount or value of what is transferred to each [TA 1988 s 216(2)]. If a transfer is made within the five-year period which is considered not to give rise to a chargeable payment because it was made for bona fide commercial reasons and does not form part of a scheme or arrangement such as is mentioned in TA 1988 s 214(2) (and for which advance tax clearance was not obtained), a return similarly needs to be made within 30 days, giving the same information and in addition the circumstances by reason of which the payment or transfer is not a chargeable payment [TA 1988 s 216(3)(4)].

Purchase of own shares

4.44 If a company treats a payment made by it as one within TA 1988 s 219 (purchase by unquoted company of own shares to be treated as a capital payment instead of a distribution) it must make a return to the Revenue giving particulars of the payment and of the circumstances by reason of which it considers s 219 to apply [TA 1988 s 226(1)]. If the transaction is for the purpose of benefiting the trade of the company or a 75 per cent subsidiary, any person connected with the company (within TA 1988 s 228) who knows of any scheme or arrangement affecting the payment which is designed (or likely) to result in the vendor or an associate of his having interests in a company, such that had he owned them immediately after the purchase section 219 could not have applied, must give notice to the Inspector containing particulars of the scheme or arrangement within 60 days of first knowing of both the payment and the scheme or arrangement [TA 1988 s 226(2)].

Non-qualifying distributions

4.45 If a company makes a distribution which is not a qualifying distribution it must make a return to the Revenue within 14 days of the end of the accounting period in which the distribution is made (or within 14 days of the payment if it is not made in an accounting period) giving particulars of the transaction which gave rise to the distribution and the names and addresses of the recipients and the amount received by each [TA 1988 s 234(5), (6)]. The CT61 contains a space for making such a return. If it is not, in the circumstances, apparent whether a transaction creates a distribution the company must still make a return giving details of the transaction (but not of the recipients) and must supply to the Inspector such further information that he requests as he may reasonably require [TA 1988 s 234(7)]. This does not apply to an amount applied by the trustees in acquiring dividend shares under an Approved Share Incentive Plan on behalf of a participant [ITEPA 2003 s 493(3)].

Stock dividends

4.46 A company must make returns of all share capital to which TA 1988 s 349 (stock dividends) applies. A return must be made for each complete calendar quarter falling within the accounting period (plus the part of a quarter falling partly within it), or for the whole accounting period if it does not include a quarter day, in which it pays a stock dividend. The return must be made within 30 days of the end of the period to which it relates. It must show the date on which the shares were issued (and, if different, the date on which the company first became liable to issue them), particulars of the terms on which the shares were issued and the appropriate amount in cash (as defined in TA 1988 s 251(2)) [TA 1988 s 250(1)–(5)]. The Inspector can then require the company to furnish him with such further information as he may reasonably require for the purposes of TA 1988 ss 230 and 249–251. He must allow at least 30 days for such information to be supplied [TA 1988 s 250(7)].

EIS relief

4.47 If an event occurs by reason of which EIS relief given to an individual falls to be withdrawn under TA 1988 ss 291, 299, 299A or 300 (or would fall to be withdrawn but for s 300A) the individual must notify the Inspector within 60 days of his coming to know of the event. He must obviously give particulars of the event [TA 1988 s 310(1)]. Where relief falls to be withdrawn under TA 1988 ss 289(1)(ba),(c) or (d), 293, 300, 302 or 303 (or would fall to be withdrawn but for s 300A) the company, and any person connected with the company, who has knowledge of the matter must notify the Inspector within 60 days of the event (or of coming to know of it) giving particulars of the event [TA 1988 s 310(2)]. If in either case the event falls within s 300 and the person making the return knows the replacement value received (or expected to be received) the notice must include particulars of the receipt of the replacement value [TA 1988 s 310(2A)]. If after having issued a certificate under TA 1988 s 306(2) in respect of eligible shares it appears to the company or to any person connected with the company who has knowledge of the matter, that s 294 may apply so as to deny EIS relief, the company and the connected person must both give notice to the Inspector setting out particulars of the case [TA 1988 s 310(3)].

Loan interest relief

4.48 A person who claims relief for loan interest under TA 1988 s 353 must, unless the interest is paid to a building society or a local authority, furnish the Inspector with a statement in writing by the person to whom the interest is paid showing the date the debt was incurred, the amount of the debt when incurred, the interest paid in the tax year and the name and address of the debtor [TA 1988 s 366(1)]. The Revenue ask not to be sent such a statement under self-assessment, but a taxpayer who complies with such a request will be in breach of his statutory obligation (although, it appears, not liable to a penalty).

Overseas entertainers and sportsmen

4.49 The Income Tax (Entertainers and Sportsmen) Regulations 1987, SI 1987/530, require a person who makes a connected payment or connected transfer (ie in respect of UK performances by an overseas entertainer) to make a return to the Revenue for the period to 30 June, 30 September, 31 December and 5 April within 14 days of the end of that period [reg 9(1)–(3); TA 1988 s 555(7)].

Sub-contractors in the construction industry

4.50 If there is a change of control of a close company which is limited by shares and holds (or has applied for) a tax exemption certificate under TA 1988 s 561 by reason of an issue or transfer of shares in the company to a person who was not a shareholder immediately prior to the issue or transfer, the company must notify the Inspector of the name and address of the new shareholder within 20 days of the issue or of receiving information as to the transfer [Income Tax (Sub-contractors in the Construction Industry) Regulations 1993, SI 1993/743, reg 42. TA 1988 s 589].

Training courses for employees

4.51 If an event occurs by reason of which there is a failure by an employee to comply with any provisions of TA 1988 s 589(3) or (4), the employer of the employee must notify the Revenue within 60 days of becoming aware of that event, giving particulars of the event [TA 1988 s 588(6)].

Pension scheme surpluses

4.52 The Pension Scheme Surpluses (Administration) Regulations 1987, SI 1987/352, reg 3 requires the scheme administrator to make a return to the Revenue within 14 days of making a surplus payment to the employer. The return must show details of the surplus, include the date it was made and, if it is in the form of a transfer of an asset, its market value, the full name and tax reference of the scheme, the name, address and tax reference of the employer and the amount of tax deducted [TA 1988 s 602].

Occupational pension scheme

4.53 The Retirement Benefits Scheme (Information Powers) Regulations 1995, SI 1995/3103, require the administrator of a pension scheme to send a valuation report to the Revenue within one year after the effective date of the valuation for a small self-administered scheme and two years for an insurance scheme or a large self-administered scheme [reg 4]. A small self-administered scheme must also send details of a large number of specified transactions to the Revenue within 90 days after the date of the transactions [reg 5]. The relevant forms for notifying such events can be downloaded from the Revenue's website. They are:

PS 7012	Acquisition and Disposals of Land
PS 7013	Loans to Employer or Associated Employer
PS 7014	Acquisition or Disposal of Shares in Employer or Associated Employer
PS 7015	Borrowings
PS 7016	Purchase, sale or lease of miscellaneous assets from or to Employer or Associated Employers

The administrator must also send the Revenue, within 180 days after the end of the scheme year, specified information in relation to any of the following changes that took place in the year: the admission of a new employer as a participator to the scheme, changes of address of existing participating employers, the date an employer ceases to carry on a trade or business and any change in the association of one participating employer with another [reg 6]. The administrator also has to send within the same time limits details of special contributions by employers and the admission of a controlling director to membership of the scheme (or an existing member becoming a controlling director) [regs 7 and 8]. A proposal to pay benefits to a controlling director on early retirement due to ill health must be notified to the Revenue at least 28 days before they are paid (or 14 days if the benefit is connected wholly to a lump sum) [reg 9]. The administrator also has to notify the Revenue within 30 days of the end of the tax year of events to which TA 1988 ss 598, 599, 599A or 601 apply [reg 10]. Where a pension payable under a pension scheme is secured by an annuity the insurance company must notify certain transactions within 180 days after the end of its chargeable period in which the event occurs [reg 11; TA 1988 s 605].

Personal pension scheme

4.54 Under the Personal Pension Schemes (Relief at Source) Regulations 1998, SI 1998/1013, if the Revenue withdraw approval of a scheme under which net contributions have been paid, the scheme administrator must provide the following information to the Revenue within 30 days of the approval: the full name, address, NI number and tax reference of each individual who has paid net contributions after the date specified in the notice, the amount of tax relief given on the contributions, the relief actually due and the difference between the two [reg 14(2), (3)]. If an individual who has paid net contributions fails to comply with regs 5–7 (which require him to provide information to the scheme administrator) the administrator must also provide the above information to the Revenue within 30 days [reg 14(4), (5); TA 1988 s 639]. Under the Personal Pension Schemes (Information Powers) Regulations 2000, SI 2000/ 2316, the scheme administrator of a self-invested personal pension scheme must supply information to the Revenue within 90 days after the date of a transaction that consists of the acquisition or disposal of land, the borrowing of money or the purchase, sale or lease of any asset other than land [reg 4]. He must also notify them within 30 days after the end of the tax year in which the event occurs of any payment within TA 1988 s 648B(1) (return of contributions after pension date) [reg 5] [TA 1988 s 651A].

Stock Exchange transactions

4.55 The Revenue can require a member of the Stock Exchange (other than a market maker) to make a return giving, in relation to any transactions effected by him in the course of his business during the period specified in the notice, such particulars as they may specify [TA 1988 s 728(2)]. They can also require a similar return from any person other than a member of the Stock Exchange who acts as agent or broker in the UK in transactions in securities [TA 1988 s 728(3)]. They cannot ask, under either of these powers, for particulars of any transaction effected more than three years prior to the notice requiring the return [TA 1988 s 728(4)].

Movements of capital between residents of member states

4.56 The Movements of Capital (Required Information) Regulations 1990, SI 1990/1671, require a UK company which enters into a transaction that would have been unlawful under TA 1988 s 765(1) (migration of companies) but for Article 1 of the EC directive of 24.6.1988 No 88/361/EEC, to provide the Revenue with the following information within six months of carrying out the transaction:

(*a*) the name of the UK company, the nature of its trade or business, and the tax office and reference to which its accounts are submitted;

(*b*) the name of the non-resident company, its place of incorporation, the EU country in which it claims to be resident (if the transaction involved the issue of shares or debentures), the grounds on which that claim is made and the facts that support it, the nature of its trade or business and the extent to which, and means by which, the UK company had control of the overseas one both before and after the transaction; and

(*c*) a full description of the transaction, including the date it took place, the name of any person to whom shares or debentures were issued or transferred, if that person is a company, its place of incorporation, the EU country in which that person claims residence (and the grounds for such a claim and the facts that support it), any connection between that person and the UK company, full details of the shares or debentures issued or transferred, the consideration given and the reason for any underpayment and the reason for the transaction and an estimate of its effect on the UK tax liability of the UK company and other members of its 51 per cent group,

[reg 3]. The Revenue have power to ask for further information, which has to be supplied within 60 days of the date of the notice requesting it [reg 4; TA 1988 s 765A].

Relief on investment in a VCT

4.57 If an event occurs by reason of which the income tax relief under TA 1988 Sch 15B falls to be withdrawn or reduced, the individual to whom the relief was given must make a return to the Inspector within 60 days of his becoming aware of the event, giving particulars of the event [TA 1988 Sch 15B para 5].

Settlements with foreign element

4.58 If a person adds (or otherwise transfers) property to a settlement that was created before 17 March 1998, otherwise than under a transaction at arm's length or in pursuance of a liability incurred before that date, and the transferor knows, or has reason to believe, that the settlement is not UK resident or ordinarily resident, the transferor must make a return to the Revenue within 12 months of the transfer, identifying the settlement and specifying the property transferred, the date of transfer and the consideration, if any, for the transfer [TA 1992 Sch 5A para 2]. If a person who is domiciled and either resident or ordinarily resident in the UK, creates a non-UK settlement (or a UK one which is treated as non-UK under a double tax agreement) he must make a return to the Revenue within three months of the creation of the settlement, giving the date of the settlement, the name and address of the settlor and the names and addresses of the trustees at the time the return is made [TA 1992 Sch 5A para 3]. If at the time such a settlement was created, the settlor was not both domiciled and resident or ordinarily resident in the UK but subsequently becomes UK domiciled and resident or ordinarily resident, he must make a return giving the above information within 12 months of his change of status [TCGA 1992 Sch 5A para 4]. If a settlement is exported, ie becomes non-UK resident (or deemed non-resident under a double tax agreement) the trustees immediately before the export, must make a return to the Revenue within 12 months of that event, giving the date of creation of the settlement, the name and address of the settlor (or of all the settlors if there were more than one) and the names and addresses of the trustees immediately prior to the export [TCGA 1992 Sch 5A para 4]. Once one person has delivered a return under any of these provisions the liability of others to do so ceases [TCGA 1992 Sch 5A para 5].

EIS reinvestment relief

4.59 If a chargeable event in relation to EIS shares, held by an individual within TCGA 1992 Sch 5B para 3, occurs, that individual must notify the Revenue within 60 days of his coming to know of the event, giving particulars of the circumstances giving rise to the chargeable event [TCGA 1992 Sch 5B para 16(1)]. If the chargeable event is the shares ceasing to be eligible shares, because the company ceases to be a qualifying company or ceases to exist wholly or mainly for the purpose of carrying on a qualifying trade or the investor or some other person receives value from the company, the company and every person connected with the company who has knowledge of the transaction must similarly notify the Revenue within 60 days of the event [TCGA 1992 Sch 5B para 16(2)]. An event must also be notified if it would have been a chargeable event but for Sch 5B para 13B or

1A(5) [TCGA 1992 Sch 5B para 16(2A), (3)]. Where para 13B (receipt of replacement value) applies the person making the return must include particulars of the receipt (or expected receipt) of the replacement value if the person has knowledge of that value [TCGA 1992 Sch 5B para 16(3A)]. Where a company has issued a certificate under TA 1988 s 306(2), those shares are eligible for EIS relief and at least 80 per cent of the money raised by the issue is not used by the company within the 12 months permitted period both the company and any person connected with the company must notify the Revenue within 60 days of the expiry of the 12-month period (or in the case of a connected person, of becoming aware of the position) [TCGA 1992 Sch 5B para 16(4)].

Lloyds underwriters

4.60 The Revenue can require a syndicate's managing agent to deliver a return of the syndicate's profit or loss for a tax year, together with accounts and such other information which the notice may require, by 1 September in the tax year concerned or, if later, three months from the date of the notice [FA 1993 Sch 19 para 2]. There are heavy penalties for non-compliance.

VCTs

4.61 A VCT (or former VCT) must deliver a return within 12 months of the end of each accounting period (or of the day it ceased to be approved as a VCT), giving specified details of the investments held by the company [reg 22, Venture Capital Trust Regulations 1995, SI 1995/1979; FA 1995 s 73].

Corporate venturing scheme

4.62 If after an investing company has obtained relief, an event occurs by virtue of which it ceases to be a qualifying company in relation to those shares, or the relief falls to be withdrawn or reduced by virtue FA 2000 Sch 15 para 47 or 59, the investing company must notify the Revenue within 60 days of the relevant event (or if it is the receipt of value by a connected person, of coming to know of the event). If the event is a receipt of value and the company has knowledge of any replacement value received, the return must include that information. If the event occurs before the issue of the shares, the 60-day period runs from that date of issue of the shares [FA 2000 Sch 15 para 64]. If the issuing company has provided the Revenue with a certificate of compliance and an event subsequently occurs by reason of which the relief falls to be withdrawn or reduced, the company and any person connected with it who has knowledge of the event must notify the Revenue within 60 days of the event (or of coming to know of the event) [FA 2000 Sch 15 para 65].

Plant or machinery

4.63 Where plant or machinery has qualified for a first year allowance or a normal writing down allowance and it is subsequently used within 10 years from being brought into use for overseas leasing which is not protected leasing, notice of that fact must be given to the Revenue. The notice must specify the non-resident to whom the plant is leased and the items concerned [CAA 2001 s 119]. If plant is leased to two or more persons jointly, one of which is a non-UK resident who does not use the plant exclusively in a UK branch, and the leasing is not protected leasing, the lessor must give notice to the Revenue, specifying the names and addresses of the lessees, the part of the expenditure which is properly attributable to each of them and which of them is UK resident [CAA 2001 s 120(1), (2)]. If an event arises that triggers a charge under CAA 2001 s 117 (recovery of allowances in case of joint leasing) a notice must also be given to the Revenue, specifying any of the joint lessees who is not UK resident and the items concerned [CAA 2001 s 120(3), (4)]. In all of these cases the notice must be given within three months of the end of the chargeable period in which the asset is first used for such leasing (or if later within 30 days of coming to know of that fact) [CAA 2001 ss 119(3), 120(5)].

Community investment tax relief

4.64 If after an investor has obtained relief, an event occurs by virtue of which the relief falls to be withdrawn or reduced the investor must notify the Revenue of the event by 31 January after the end of the tax year in which the event occurred (or 12 months after the end of the accounting period in which it occurred in the case of a company). If the event is the receipt of value by a person connected with the investor and the investor is not aware of the event within that period, the time limit is extended to 60 days after he becomes aware of it [FA 2002 Sch 16 para 42].

Employee securities and options

4.65 Each person who is a responsible person in relation to a reportable event must give written particulars of the event to the Revenue by 7 July in the tax year following that in which it occurs [ITEPA 2003 s 421J]. The reportable events are:

(*a*) an acquisition of shares or securities or an option over shares or securities, pursuant to a right or opportunity available by reason of the employment;

(*b*) a chargeable event in relation to restricted shares or securities;

(*c*) a chargeable event in relation to convertible shares or securities;

(*d*) an event which gives rise to a taxable amount under ITEPA 2003 s 446L (artificial enhancement of value);

(*e*) the discharge of a notional loan where shares were acquired at an undervalue within ITEPA 2003 s 446U;

(*f*) a disposal of shares or securities for more than market value;

(*g*) the receipt of a benefit in relation to shares or securities which is taxable under ITEPA 2003 s 447;

(*h*) the assignment or release of an employee share option; and

(*i*) the receipt of a benefit taxable under ITEPA 2003 s 447(6) in connection with a share option,

[ITEPA 2003 s 421K]. The responsible persons are the employer, a host employer (within ITEPA 2003 s 689), the person from whom the shares or securities were acquired and (except where the securities are excluded securities) the person by whom the securities were issued [ITEPA 2003 s 421L(3)]. Excluded securities are securities issued by a national or regional government or local authority (or a joint body of such entities) and shares or securities which are listed or dealt in on a recognised stock exchange and issued by a person who is not connected with the employer [ITEPA 2003 s 421L(6)].

Enterprise management incentives

4.66 A share option can qualify as an EMI option only if notice of it is given to the Revenue by the employer company within 92 days of its grant. The notice must contain (or be supported by) such information as the Revenue may require for the purpose of determining that the EMI conditions are met. It must also contain a declaration by a director or the secretary of the employer, that in his opinion the requirements are met and the information provided is to the best of his knowledge correct and complete, and a declaration by the employee that he meets the working time commitment in relation to the option [ITEPA 2003 Sch 5 para 44]. A company whose shares are subject to a qualifying EMI option at any time during the tax year must also deliver a return to the Revenue by 7 July after the end of the tax year containing such information as the Revenue may require [ITEPA 2003 Sch 5 para 52].

Chapter 5

Information Powers

The power to call for documents (TMA 1970 s 19A and FA 1998 Sch 18 para 27)

5.1 Quite reasonably the Revenue have the right to enquire into a tax return, but this power would be very weak if they were unable to access the documents and other information that they believe are needed to enable them to check the accuracy of a return.

5.2 Accordingly, where notice of an enquiry has been given under TMA 1970 s 9A(1) or 12AC(1) (see **3.35**) the Revenue have power for the purpose of the enquiry by notice in writing to require the taxpayer, within such time as may be specified in the notice (which must be at least 30 days):

(*a*) to produce to the Revenue such documents as are in the taxpayer's possession or power and as the officer may reasonably require for the purpose of determining whether and, if so, the extent to which the return is incorrect or incomplete; and

(*b*) to furnish the Revenue with such accounts or particulars as the officer may reasonably require for that purpose,

[TMA 1970 s 19A(1), (2)].

5.3 Where the enquiry is limited to enquiring into an amendment to the return the officer can obviously only seek documents or information to determine whether the amendment is incorrect [TMA 1970 s 19A(2)(a)(ii)].

5.4 There are a number of important points to note in relation to this power.

(*a*) It operates only where notice of an enquiry has been given. This obviously means a valid notice, as an invalid one is not a notice under TMA 1970 s 9A(1). The taxpayer has no right of appeal against a s 9A notice and it is expensive to have to seek judicial review if the taxpayer wishes to challenge its validity. There is, however, a right of appeal against a s 19A notice. It is perfectly proper for the taxpayer to challenge the validity of the s 9A notice on that appeal, as, if that notice is invalid, the s 19A notice will automatically also be an invalid one. In

Wing Hung Lai v Bale [1999] STC (SCD) 238 the Inspector issued the s 9A notice on 27 January 1999 and posted it to the taxpayer by second class post. It was held to be invalid as in the ordinary course of postage, it could not be deemed to have been received (and was not received) until 2 February, which fell outside the enquiry window.

(*b*) The taxpayer is entitled to at least 30 days to provide the information. In *Self-Assessed v Inspector of Taxes [1999] STC (SCD) 253* the Special Commissioner accepted that the s 19A notice was invalid. It required the information to be supplied within 30 days of the issue of the notice and the taxpayer successfully argued that if he was entitled to 30 days to comply with the notice that period must start from the date he received the notice.

(*c*) The Revenue can seek information only 'for the purpose of the enquiry'. They cannot use s 19A to mount a fishing expedition into the taxpayer's overall affairs or to obtain information that relates to an enquiry into someone else's return or to the taxpayer's return for a different year. Prima facie anything in relation to a particular year is unlikely to be relevant in checking the correctness of a return for a different year.

(*d*) The Revenue can only ask for documents in the taxpayer's possession or power. This would not normally include his accountant's working papers, which belong to the accountant. Nor can it include documents in relation to the taxpayer's spouse or other relatives.

(*e*) The test is whether 'the officer may reasonably require' the item. This is different from whether the officer reasonably believes that he needs the document or information or whether he is acting reasonably. It is an objective test and a question of fact. At the end of the day it is for the Commissioners to decide whether anyone enquiring into the return would reasonably require the item. Reasonableness is considered further below.

(*f*) It is interesting to note that the officer is not checking that the return is correct and complete; he is checking that it is not incorrect or incomplete. Why should the draftsman have used a double negative? He normally chooses his words with care. This suggests that 'not incomplete' may be a less stringent test than complete. For example, suppose that the return includes estimates. It is impossible to say that an estimate is correct, but much easier to say that it is not incorrect.

5.5 So what is reasonable? Well it seems reasonable that the document should be relevant to the purpose for which it is required, ie to determine if the return is incorrect and, if so, by how much. So it must clearly relate to the entries on the return. Some things are obvious – a statement of interest received or the financial records of a business are clearly relevant to the figures on the return. However, that may not mean that it is reasonably required. For example, the main clearing banks show on a person's bank statement in April the total interest paid during the year and the tax deducted therefrom. As that one bank statement is all that the Revenue need to check the entry on the return it may well be that the other statements which show the individual interest figures contributing to that total are not reasonably required. If there are several ways that the Revenue can check a figure, can the information that would be necessary if they adopt the most circuitous of those routes be reasonably required or does only the information to support the most appropriate route meet that test? For example, one of the authors came across a case where the Revenue sought to justify a request for private bank statements on the grounds that dividends must have been banked and they needed to see such statements to verify the dividends. The taxpayer sent the Revenue the dividend counterfoils and said that he did not believe that the bank statements were appropriate evidence to verify the dividends. They would not show the name of the company, or whether the dividends actually belonged to the taxpayer, or if a dividend related to the year in which it was banked, or the tax credit or in most cases the amount, as dividends are not necessarily banked separately. The dividend counterfoils by contrast contain all of the information that is needed to verify the correctness of the dividend. The Revenue backed off.

5.6 Other things are less obvious. The private bank statements of a businessman, for example, normally have no direct relevance to the figures reported in his business accounts. Inspectors are told by the Revenue's Enquiry Manual to be prepared to justify requests they make for documents and information if their purpose is not obvious. Private bank statements are a highly contentious issue. If they contain business receipts then they may be relevant. However, even that is probably a question of degree. If, for example, the business does not operate a separate business account, but all business receipts are banked in the private account, the private bank statements are obviously relevant. On the other hand, if business receipts are banked in a business account but one or two are accidentally paid into the private account it is hard to see that this of itself makes the private account relevant. Even if it does, is sight of the whole of the private account bank statements reasonably required or only those pages which contain the business receipts? If the private statements were examined when preparing accounts or the tax return and information taken from them they might be relevant but otherwise they are probably not and their production ought to be resisted. The Revenue appears to agree with this because it tells its officers that the legislation does not specifically give access to private bank accounts.

5.7 Sometimes an item cannot be demonstrated to be reasonably required at a particular point in the enquiry but may become so later. Private bank statements are a good example of this. If a business has a separate business account and reasonably good records it is questionable if private bank statements can be reasonably required. On the other hand if the records are poor and the officer forms a view that they are unreliable and he needs to arrive at the profits by some other means, such as by preparing capital statements, it may be hard to resist a contention that they are reasonably required at that stage. This is why the Enquiry Manual tells Revenue staff that they should not normally seek private bank statements in their opening letters. It is not until the business books and records have been examined that a decision as to whether or not the private bank account is relevant can possibly be made.

5.8 The Revenue frequently demand items that seem to be irrelevant. Any request for non-financial records must be of doubtful validity. The Revenue consider that appointment diaries, for example, are relevant because they might help to determine the extent to which the return is incomplete. Such requests should be considered carefully. Unless the diary has been used to record financial information it is likely to be no more than a memorandum of expected future events, many of which may never have occurred, eg cancelled appointments. It is hard to imagine what help such a memorandum is likely to be.

5.9 Demands to examine an accountant's working papers are becoming increasingly common. The Revenue accept that accountancy working papers cannot be required under s 19A because they are not in the power or possession of the taxpayer. They do, however, believe that a request for 'particulars' may be made to explain the link between an entry in the records and a figure on a return. Though it needs to be remembered that a taxpayer can only be required to produce particulars within his knowledge. It is doubtful whether he can be required to ask his accountant for information to supply to the Revenue. Having said that, where the information that the Revenue require is linking documents it is generally sensible to volunteer them irrespective of the legal position. If the Revenue are provided, for example, with a trial balance so they can see the relationship between the business records and the accounts this will not only avoid prolonging the enquiry needlessly but will also obviate the risk of the officer making invalid assumptions in an attempt to guess the missing information and asking a lot of unnecessary further questions.

5.10 The best policy is probably to be aware of the Revenue's rights and powers but at the same time to consider what is in the client's best interest in the individual circumstances. Volunteering information to which you believe the officer is not entitled can speed up the enquiry. However, it can also lengthen it, as the more information you give the more issues there may be for the officer to explore or the more red herrings he may fish for. If you decide to volunteer information it is often sensible to first ask the officer why he considers it relevant, as this may indicate what sort of areas are worrying him and you may be able to produce an alternative source of information that you feel more appropriate and that ought to satisfy his concern. It is sensible when volunteering information to make clear that you do not think that his request satisfies the requirements of s 19A but are nevertheless happy to provide it. Remember also that it may sometimes be sensible to volunteer information that the Revenue have not asked for if this will explain something that appears to be worrying the officer.

5.11 In practice the Revenue always issue a precursor letter before issuing a s 19A notice. This gives the opportunity to challenge whether or not information requested falls within s 19A without the pressures of the time limit of a formal notice. Although officers tend to put a 30-day deadline in a precursor letter this is not a statutory deadline. It is no more than an expression of wishes by the officer. Nevertheless, if it cannot be met it is sensible to tell the Revenue and agree an amended target date. Some officers regard failure to meet their self-imposed target as automatic justification for issuing a formal s 19A notice.

5.12 Although the Revenue can demand original documents, copies are sufficient to comply with a s 19A order, provided they are facsimiles. The Revenue does have the power to inspect the originals, however, and can itself take copies of any documents produced [TMA 1970 s 19A(3), (4)]. The power is to require the taxpayer to produce the original for inspection. The taxpayer does not have to give the document to the Revenue. Provided that he acts reasonably it is up to him where he produces the document, eg he is entitled to decide to do it at his or his accountant's office. If he does so he must of course provide the Revenue with the facility to take copies.

5.13 There is no requirement for a taxpayer to produce any documents or particulars that may be relevant to:

(*a*) any pending appeal by him; or

(*b*) any pending referral to the Special Commissioners under TMA 1970 s 28ZA (referrals of questions during an enquiry – see **7.64**) to which he is a party,

[TMA 1970 s 19A(5)].

5.14 There are a number of things that the Revenue reminds its officers they are not permitted to do under s 19A. They cannot:

(*a*) insist that taxpayers attend meetings;

(*b*) require that documents are delivered to the Revenue's office – they need only be produced;

(*c*) obtain access to premises;

(*d*) obtain documents brought into existence for an appeal hearing;

(*e*) obtain documents relating to a year not under enquiry;

(*f*) obtain information about someone else's return;

(*g*) get information from third parties; and

(*h*) ask for general information.

5.15 There is a right of appeal against a notice under s 19A. Such appeals must be made within 30 days of the date on which the formal notice is given (see **5.2**). The normal rules that apply to appeals against an assessment to tax also apply for these appeals. The appeal notice must give the grounds for the appeal [TMA 1970 s 19A(6)–(8)].

5.16 Typical grounds for an appeal could be:

(*a*) that all, or some, of the information required is not reasonably required; or

(*b*) that documents required are not within the taxpayer's power or possession.

5.17 It is to be hoped that any appeal can be settled by agreement with the Revenue but if this proves impossible the Appeal Commissioners will consider the appeal at a hearing. If they confirm any part of the notice it must then be complied with within 30 days of the date of their decision. The Appeal Commissioners determination is final and conclusive [TMA 1970 s 19(9)–(11)]. This last point should be particularly noted. There is no right of appeal to the High Court. At first sight this might appear odd but it is in fact logical. The general rule is that the Commissioners are the sole arbiters of fact. An appeal to the High Court in other areas lies only on a matter of law. What is or is not reasonably required is a pure question of fact to be determined on the basis of the circumstances in each individual case. What may have been decided in a particular case ought to have no precedental value, because the fact that the facts of a particular case indicate that a particular document is reasonably required does not mean that the same document will be reasonably required in another case where the surrounding facts are different.

5.18 It should be noted that lodging an appeal brings the Revenue's power to require information to a halt. When the appeal is decided, even if the taxpayer loses, a completely new 30-day period commences. Accordingly, appealing, even unsuccessfully, has a side effect of significantly extending the time allowed for complying with the notice. In practice the Revenue seem reluctant to pursue appeals before the Commissioners and seem to manage without the information.

5.19 It should also be noted that the Revenue can issue as many s 19A notices as they wish in the course of an enquiry. This is reasonable, as something that is not reasonably required at the start of an enquiry may become reasonably required at a later stage. The effect of this power is that while a decision of the Commissioners in favour of the Revenue is final and the taxpayer must produce the information, a decision in favour of the taxpayer is, in practical terms, not final, as the Revenue can simply issue a fresh s 19A notice for the same information. It may be worth pointing out to the Commissioners this anomaly, as justice might suggest that if the Commissioners are unsure they ought to come down in favour of the taxpayer, as that will still leave the Revenue with the ability to try for a second bite at the cherry.

5.20 There have been a number of Special Commissoners' decisions on s 19A. These need to be approached with caution in the light of the above comments. In *Mother v Inspector of Taxes [1999] STC (SCD) 279* the notice required the production of cheque book stubs and paying-in books relating to the taxpayer's property management business. These were held to be reasonably required even though they contained information relating to other taxpayers, although the Commissioner commented that the taxpayer was entitled to provide 'as little information concerning other taxpayers as is compatible with the requirement to produce documents relating to the taxpayer's business'. The notice also required the production of dividend counterfoils which the taxpayer had mislaid. The Commissioner felt it incumbent on her to seek to obtain replacement copies at her own expense. In *Accountant v Inspector of Taxes [2000] STC (SCD) 522* it was held reasonable to expect the accountant to produce documents relating to his personal and undesignated client's bank and building society accounts even though these contained confidential client information. It was also felt reasonable to require him to prepare a balance sheet under the heading of furnishing particulars. It is difficult to see the justification for this. The legislation does not require the particulars to be furnished in any particular form. In *Guyer v Walton [2001] STC (SCD) 75* the Commissioners held that a solicitor's clients ledger client cash book and supporting records were reasonably required and that 'the rule of legal professional privilege is excluded because it is not expressly preserved by section 19A'. This is of doubtful validity. It conflicts with the later House of Lords decision in *R (on the application of Morgan Grenfell & Co Ltd) v Special Comr (2000) 74 TC 511* – see **5.53**). It is intriguing that, in the above cases, the taxpayer chose to appeal to the Special rather than the General Commissioners in relation to a question of pure fact, which one would have thought might be better considered by practical-minded businessmen untrammelled by the lawyer's approach to issues.

5.21 The above powers to call for documents and information also apply to documents and information which an Inspector may reasonably require for the purpose of making a determination under TMA 1970 s 9D(1)(c) or 12AE(1)(c) (see **3.48**) [TMA 1970 s 19A(2A)]. In the case of an enquiry into a partnership return, the Revenue can also require the production of documents or the furnishing of information from any partner who was a predecessor or successor of the partner who made the return [TMA 1970 s 19A(12)].

5.22 There are penalties for failure to comply with a s 19A notice [TMA 1970 s 97AA (see **12.50**)].

5.23 The rules relating to production of information by a company are virtually the same as those under s 19A [FA 1998 Sch 18 paras 27 and 28]. The significant difference is that with a company the Revenue have power to determine the form in which information is provided [FA 1998 Sch 18 para 27(1)(b)]. They often seek to use this power to require information to be produced in the form of a computer disk so that they can interrogate the information using a computer program. If they are instead provided with a complete print out of the information it is arguable that, as they have all of the information, a disk containing that same information cannot be reasonably required in addition. It is certainly worth taking such an argument before the Commissioners.

5.24 Where the Revenue can choose to tax amounts under either Sch D Case I or Cases III or V, or to tax an insurance company under either Case I or the I minus E basis, they can by notice require the company to produce to them such documents in the company's power or possession and to provide them with such information in such form as they may reasonably require for the purpose of making that choice. The information powers in FA 1998 Sch 18 paras 27 and 28 apply for this purpose [FA 1998 Sch 18 para 84].

The s 20 information powers

5.25 TMA 1970 s 19A and FA 1998 Sch 18 provide powers to support the self-assessment enquiry system. However, the Revenue have had a more general enquiry power since 1976. This is now contained in TMA 1970 s 20. Sections 19A and 20 are not mutually exclusive. The Revenue can, if they wish, use s 20 in the course of an enquiry into a tax return. Indeed, Inspectors have been known to threaten s 20 in response to an appeal against a s 19A notice. There is a parliamentary statement that indicates that this ought not to happen and it is worth quoting this to the Revenue if they adopt such a tactic. However, the statement specifically does not preclude the use of s 20 in place of s 19A. It reads:

> 'The powers in TMA 1970 ss 19A, 20 are not mutually exclusive. However, the Inland Revenue would not normally issue a notice under s 20 in order to obtain information that they had failed to obtain under s 19A. Very rarely, it might become clear, after the taxpayer had appealed against a s 19A notice, that s 20 was in fact the more appropriate section to use. A notice under s 20 cannot be issued by an Inspector unless the taxpayer has failed to take an opportunity to provide the information voluntarily, and may be issued only with the consent of an independent Appeal Commissioner.' [Hansard, Vol 329, col 426, 19 April 1999.]

5.26 Section 20 contains three distinct powers.

(*a*) An Inspector can, by notice in writing, require a person:

  (i) to deliver to him such documents as are in the person's possession or power and (in the Inspector's reasonable opinion) contain, or may contain, information relevant to any tax liability to which that person may be subject or the amount of any such liability; and
  (ii) to furnish to him such particulars as the Inspector may reasonably require as being relevant to, or to the amount of, any such liability, [TMA 1970 s 20(1)].

(*b*) The Board can, by notice in writing, similarly require a person to deliver such documents and information to a named officer of the Board [TMA 1970 s 20(2)].

(*c*) An Inspector, can by notice in writing, require a third party to deliver to him (or, if that person so elects, to make available for inspection by a named officer of the Board) such documents as are in his possession or power and as (in the Inspector's reasonable opinion) contain, or may contain, information relevant to a tax liability of the person into whose tax affairs the Inspector is enquiring (or the amount of such a liability) [TMA 1970 s 20(3)].

5.27 One major difference is that this provision enables the Inspector to obtain documents in the possession or power of the third party. Such a person cannot be required to furnish particulars. So an Inspector can demand to see, for example, invoices relating to transactions with someone but cannot ask for a list of transactions to be provided, unless such a list already exists.

5.28 It will be seen that there are a number of differences between the two powers. Under s 19A the taxpayer has to make documents available to the Inspector, ie he can decide where the Inspector looks at them and he retains possession of them, whereas under s 20(1) he is required to deliver the documents to the Inspector, ie he must hand them over to the Inspector or send them to his office. The test under s 19A is an objective one, ie is the document reasonably required for the purpose of the enquiry, whereas under s 20(1) it is a subjective one, ie does the Inspector reasonably believe that he needs the document? A s 19A notice can only be served on the taxpayer whereas a s 20(3) notice can be served on a third party – although as with s 19A and unlike with s 20(1) the third party is not required to deliver the document to the Inspector, he merely needs to make it available for inspection by the Revenue (at a place of his choosing).

5.29 Original documents do not have to be produced, copies can be substituted provided they are facsimiles. However, if the Inspector so requires he is entitled to inspect the originals [TMA 1970 s 20B(4)].

5.30 Documents do not include personal records as defined in Police and Criminal Evidence Act 1984 s 12 or journalistic material as defined in s 13 of that Act. Particulars do not include any material contained in such documents [TMA 1970 s 20(8C)].

5.31 Persons who have died and companies that have ceased to exist may be treated as taxpayers for the purposes of s 20 [TMA 1970 s 20(6)].

5.32 Although in many ways s 20 is wider than s 19A in other ways the taxpayer is given more protection under s 20 than under s 19A. Not all Inspectors can issue s 20 notices. To be entitled to do so an Inspector must be authorised by the Board to do so [TMA 1970 s 20(7)]. This is not a strong protection as it is understood that the officer in charge of an office, and normally his deputy, are so authorised as a matter of course. Nevertheless, it may be worth checking that the Inspector is an authorised person if it is wished to challenge a s 20 notice.

5.33 Before he can issue a notice under s 20 the Inspector must first informally request the information he wants and must give the person a reasonable opportunity to deliver it (or, in the case of a third party request, make it available) [TMA 1970 s 20B(1)]. If this does not produce the information he wants then he must obtain the consent of an Appeal Commissioner before a formal notice can be issued [TMA 1970 s 20(7)(a)].

5.34 The Appeal Commissioner must be satisfied that in all the circumstances the Inspector is justified in proceeding to issue the notice before he can give his consent [TMA 1970 s 20(7)(b)]. The taxpayer has no right of attendance at the consent hearing before a Commissioner.

5.35 In *Morgan Grenfell & Co Ltd ((2000) 74 TC 511)* the taxpayer contended that it should have been given an opportunity to make representations to the Commissioner at the time when he considered whether or not to consent under s20(7) to the issue of the notice. The Court of Appeal held that not only did the taxpayer not have a right to demand an oral hearing but also that the Commissioner had no jurisdiction to allow one. They found it difficult to see cogent reasons demanding an inter partes hearing, as opposed to a reasonable opportunity to make representations, and felt that 'in sensitive cases, such as those involving informers, it would be impossible for the Commissioners to give acceptable reason for not exercising his discretion without giving the game away' if there were a right to an oral hearing.

5.36 Although Lord Lowry gave the leading judgement, in an earlier case, *R v IRC, ex p TC Coombs & Co [1991] STC 97*, Lord Mackay of Clashfern specifically commented that in his view it followed from the terms of FA 1998 ss 20(7) and 20B(1):

> 'that one of the circumstances into which the Commissioners must enquire when an application [for consent to issue a notice] is made to him, is whether such a reasonable opportunity [to deliver or make available the documents in question] has been given and any correspondence that passes in that connection between the Inspector and the person to whom he wishes to give notice should be placed before the Commissioner. The obligation on the Commissioner to consider all the circumstances implies a duty on the officer of the Inland Revenue who appears before the Commissioner to lay before the Commissioner all the information he has about the relevant circumstances including any which might be unfavourable to the giving of the notice … In enacting those provisions Parliament obviously placed great weight on the position of the independent Commissioners and the need for the Commissioner's consent. It is important that this be given full effect.'

This view was echoed by Lord Jauncey of Tullichettle who added that the Revenue 'must only hide behind a cloak of confidence when this is absolutely necessary and not as a matter of course'. In that case the company had not complied fully with the notice. When the company's solicitor asked what was missing they received what Lord Jauncey described as 'the singularly unhelpful reply' that 'it is for your clients to decide to what extent they have complied with their obligations … and with respect the Revenue are entitled to receive their response under a notice the scope of which is not so far as I am aware challenged on the grounds of construction'. Lord Jauncey felt it 'very difficult to justify this unhelpful attitude and expressed the hope that the Revenue would bear his observations in mind in future cases'. Lord Lowry himself expressed the view that 'the Revenue are absolutely bound to make full disclosure to the Commissioners of all facts within their knowledge which could properly influence the Commissioner against giving his consent to a s 20(3) notice'.

5.37 *R v MacDonald, ex p Hutchinson & Co Ltd [1998] STC 680* is a rare case where the court questioned a s 20 notice. The Inspector had not put before the Commissioner a letter from the company saying that 'it believed that the production of the information required would be very time consuming and costly'. Nor had the company been told the issues that the Inspector felt were in contention. The judge thought it was entitled 'to a statement in short form dealing with the main issues which were in contention'. He expressed concern about the fact that the Commissioner appeared to have readily acceded to a request to dispense with giving reasons as raising a question mark as to the objectivity of the proceedings. He commented that 'the "cloak of confidence" provided by subs (8G) is available in a proper case, but it should only be sought if "absolutely necessary" … [e]ven where there are grounds for invoking that power, its effect will not normally be to remove the obligation altogether, but simply to limit the scope of the information which needs to be disclosed'.

5.38 Where a s 20(1) notice is issued a period of at least 30 days must be allowed in which to comply with it but this time limit does not apply to orders under s 20(2) (see **5.41**) [TMA 1970 s 20(8D)]. When the notice is issued the Inspector must also give the taxpayer a written summary of his reasons for having applied for consent unless doing so would (or might) identify an informant, or the Commissioner who gave the consent gives a direction that such a summary need not be given [TMA 1970 s 20(8E)]. Such a direction can be given only if the Commissioner is satisfied that the Inspector has reasonable grounds for believing that disclosure of the information would prejudice the assessment or collection of tax [TMA 1970 s 20(8H)].

5.39 If what the Inspector is demanding seems unreasonable it is important to set out any objections, with reasons, in writing and ask the Inspector to lay this before the Appeal Commissioner when he is seeking consent. He is obliged to present the full facts and so your letter must be placed before the Commissioners (see the case of *R v MacDonald, ex p Hutchinson & Co Ltd [1998] STC 680* at **5.37**).

5.40 A Commissioner who has consented to the issue of a s 20 notice cannot take part in, or even be present at, any later appeal hearing by the taxpayer concerned if the Commissioner has reason to believe that any of the required information may be adduced in evidence [TMA 1970 s 20(7AB), (7AC)].

5.41 Section 20(2) is very similar to s 20(1). In fact the only difference in wording is that 'the Board' may require the production of documents or particulars instead of 'an Inspector'. 'The Board' is of course the Board of Inland Revenue. This power is usually only used by Special Compliance Offices and even then very infrequently. The Board does not have to seek the information informally before making such an order, is not required to obtain the consent of an Appeal Commissioner to the making of an order and does not need to allow any period of time to comply with the order. In fact the only restriction is that 'the Board' can only make an order if it has reasonable grounds for believing that the taxpayer may have failed (or may fail) to comply with any provision of the Taxes Acts and that any such failure is likely to lead to serious prejudice to the proper assessment or collection of tax. Unfortunately there is no definition of serious [TMA 1970 ss 20(7), (7A), (8D) and 20B(1)].

5.42 A s 20(2) order is often mistaken for a search warrant. This is because the Inspector will turn up unannounced and hand over the notice. This will demand the production of information immediately. Typically he will then ask that he, and his team, be allowed entry to collect this. Such an order does not give a right of access to property.

5.43 The only remedy to a taxpayer who is aggrieved by a s 20(2) notice is to apply for a judicial review of the Board's decision.

5.44 The Revenue advises its officers to be sensitive about using s 20(3) because of the unreasonable burden that may be placed upon the third party or because of the sensitivity of revealing that an investigation is under way. When a s 20(3) notice is issued, the Inspector also has to give the taxpayer a copy of the notice unless a Commissioner (which does not appear to need to be the one who gave consent to the issue of the notice) directs otherwise. Such a direction can be given only if the Commissioner is satisfied that the Inspector has reasonable grounds for suspecting the taxpayer of fraud [TMA 1970 s 20B(1A), (1B)]. The Inspector must also give the taxpayer a written summary of his reasons for applying for consent to issue the notice unless either a Commissioner has made a direction under s 20B(1B) or he directs that reasons need not be given, either to protect the identity of an informer or because he is satisfied that disclosure of the reasons might prejudice the assessment or collection of tax (see **5.22**) [TMA 1970 s 20(8E)–(8H)].

5.45 The administration of s 20(3) is very similar to that for s 20(1). The consent of an Appeal Commissioner is needed, an informal request needs to be made initially, and time to comply must be given.

5.46 Most of the cases under s 20 relate to s 20(3) notices. The House of Lords was first asked to consider the provision in *R v IRC, ex p TC Coombs & Co [1991] STC 97*. In that case, a firm of stockbrokers sought to challenge the validity of the notice on the grounds that the Commissioner had not given adequate consideration to the position. Lord Lowry, who gave the main judgement, pointed out that the case for the validity of a notice is supported by a strong presumption of regularity as the Commissioner must be presumed to have satisfied himself that the Inspector reasonably held the opinion required by s 20. He alluded to the difficulty of displacing the inference if the Revenue does not explain its reasons, as happened in that case, although he accepted that, if their failure to give satisfactory evidence to the courts 'can be credibly explained, even if not entirely justified', the courts should not draw an adverse inference from such silence. In that case, the Revenue had given an informant on undertaking not to reveal either his identity or the information that he had provided. In response to the company's claim that because the Revenue refused to explain to the courts why they had sought a s 20(3) notice such a notice could never be questioned, Lord Lowry retorted:

> 'This prospect does not fill me with alarm when I reflect that Parliament has subjected an intrusive and potentially oppressive (but presumably necessary) power to what I suggest to be the effective supervision of section 20(7). Nor should the difficulty of achieving a remedy cause surprise when one considers the following points.
> (*a*) The applicant has to prove a negative.
> (*b*) What he has to prove is not a fact within his knowledge but the absence of a reasonable opinion on the part of someone else, namely, the Inspector.
> (*c*) The Inspector's opinion has to have been reasonable but need not have been correct.
> (*d*) The resolution of the question will usually depend in large measure on evidence which is not put before the Court.
> (*e*) By reason of the principle of confidentiality ... the general rule for taking account of a party's silence does not fully apply and, for the same reason, the Court cannot assess the extent to which in each case it does not apply.
> (*f*) Proceedings in which affidavit evidence is the general rule are not well suited to resolving factual questions.'

5.47 In *R v IRC, ex p Ulster Bank Ltd ((1997)69 TC 211)* the bank claimed that the notice was unduly onerous. The notice asked for statements and back up vouchers in respect of 'all sundry parties suspense accounts'. In the Court of Appeal Morritt LJ first dismissed the bank's contention that a notice had to be limited to documents which are known to the Revenue to be in the possession or power of the person to whom a notice is given. He went on to say that whilst a mere witness cannot be required to search through his records to see which if any of them may be material to a case, that is because he will not ordinarily know what the issues are, and that 'different considerations apply where the witness can be told specifically what documents he is to look for and produce'. Simon Brown LJ concluded:

> 'I see no objection to the use of the section 20 powers for "what is essentially a discovery exercise, whereby the applicant is seeking

> production of documents with a view to ascertaining whether they may be useful" … provided only and always that it is a specific discovery exercise and that in the Inspector's reasonable opinion the documents "may contain information relevant to any tax liability" (s 20(3))'.

However, too much relevance ought not to be placed on this as the High Court judge in *R v IRC, ex p Banque Internationale à Luxembourge SA [2000] STC 708* felt it 'clear that the view of Simon Brown LJ that a notice can only be valid if it is a specific discovery exercise, was a minority view inconsistent with that of the majority'. In that and other cases the courts have constantly rejected challenges based on the breadth of the notice.

5.48 In *R v IRC, ex p Archon Shipping Corp [1998] STC 1151* the judge pointed out that:

> 'There is no avenue of appeal. The decision of the Commissioner is final. He is the taxpayer's safeguard … Often the purpose of seeking documents would be lost if the Inspector had to disclose to the taxpayer the justification for the order he seeks … That is why the circumstances are put before an impartial third party. In such circumstances it seems to me that courts should be astute to avoid giving by the avenue of judicial review, what is, in reality, a second look at the Commissioner's decision … It will only be in exceptional circumstances and for clearly identifiable reasons that the High Court will interfere to set aside a notice.'

5.49 In *R V IRC, ex p Banqe Internationale à Luxembourg SA [2000] STC 708* the judge commented:

> 'Mere proof on this application that the burden is substantial is not … a matter which advances BIL's case. BIL had the opportunity to make representations to this effect to the Inspector and Commissioner before the notices were served: it did not do so. BIL could have made representations requesting notices in less burdensome form before or after the date of the notices: it did not do so. The question of the burdensome character of the notice was a matter for the Inspector and Commissioner when the notice was issued and when and if a request was made for a notice in different form.'

In general, the courts do not seems sympathetic to the burden that notices can place on third parties. In *Clinch v IRC [1973] STC 155*, which concerned the Revenue's enquiry powers under TA 1988 s 745 (see **5.128**), it was pointed out to Ackner J that the notice would require Mr Clinch to go through some 600–650 files and 6,500 index cards and it would take five months of full time work to comply with the notice. The judge thought that Mr Clinch had overestimated the time involved, but even if he was right, felt that it was Mr Clinch's own fault for not having assumed that a notice would be likely to be served on him at some stage as his office was the tax avoidance office of his Bank. He accordingly should have kept his records in such a form as to be able to readily provide the information the Revenue would be likely to require!

5.50 The taxpayer involved must normally be named in the s 20(3) notice [TMA 1970 s 20(8)]. Sometimes the Inspector may not be aware of the identity of the taxpayer to which the information he is seeking relates. In such a case s 20(8A)) allows him to ask a Special Commissioner to consent to the issue of a s 20(3) notice without naming the taxpayer. The Commissioner can make such an order only if he is satisfied that:

(*a*) the notice relates to a taxpayer whose identity is not known to the Inspector or to a class of taxpayers whose individual identities are not known;

(*b*) there are reasonable grounds for believing that the taxpayer (or any of the class of taxpayers) may have failed to comply with any provision of the Taxes Acts;

(*c*) that such failure is likely to have led (or to lead) to serious prejudice to the proper assessment or collection of tax; and

(*d*) the information which is likely to be contained in the documents in question is not readily available from another source,

[TMA 1970 s 20(8A)].

5.51 In keeping with the other provisions of s 20 the consent of a Commissioner is needed to the issue of a s 20(8A) notice, an informal request has to be made first, and time to comply must be given. Anyone served with a s 20(8A) notice can object to it by notice in writing to the Inspector within 30 days of its issue on the grounds that it would be onerous for him to comply with it. If a compromise cannot be agreed with the Inspector, the objection must be referred to the Special Commissioners for a decision. They have power to vary or cancel the notice [TMA 1970 s 20(8B)].

5.52 A notice served on the taxpayer cannot oblige him to deliver documents or furnish information relating to the conduct of a pending tax appeal by him, and one served on a third party cannot require the production of documents relating to a pending appeal by the taxpayer [TMA 1970 s 20B(2)].

5.53 A s 20(3) notice does not oblige the third party to produce a document that wholly originates more than six years before the date of the notice unless the notice itself is expressed to exclude the restriction. A notice given by the Inspector can contain such an exclusion only if the Commissioner approved the exclusion at the time he gave the consent, and one issued by the Board can do so only if they first obtain the consent of a General or Special Commissioner. In both cases the Commissioner can approve an exclusion only if he is satisfied that there are reasonable grounds for believing that tax has been (or may have been) lost owing to the fraud of the taxpayer [TMA 1970 s 20B(5), (6)].

5.54 If the taxpayer has died, a s 20(3) notice cannot be issued after six years have elapsed since the death [TMA 1970 s 20B(7)].

5.55 Barristers, advocates or solicitors cannot be served with a notice by an Inspector but can be issued with one (under any of the three subsections) by the Board of Inland Revenue [TMA 1970 s 20B(3)]. Such people cannot be required to produce anything which is subject to 'professional privilege' [TMA 1970 s 20B(8)].

5.56 The exemption for legal professional privilege was considered in *R (on the application of Morgan Grenfell & Co Ltd) v Special Comr ((2000) 74 TC 511).* The Revenue issued a s 20(1) notice on Morgan Grenfell demanding various documents in relation to advice it had received from tax counsel and its solicitors in respect of a tax scheme it had sold to Tesco. They contended that the protection given by s 20B(8) applied only to a notice served on the legal adviser and could not protect Morgan Grenfell itself from being required to disclose the advice. The Court of Appeal agreed. Fortunately the House of Lords did not. Lord Hoffman pointed out that 'LPP is a fundamental human right long established in the common law. It is a necessary corollary of the right of any person to obtain skilled advice about the law'. He also said that:

> 'the Courts will ordinarily construe general words in a statute, although literally capable of having some startling or unreasonable consequence, such as overriding fundamental human rights, as not having been intended to do so. An intention to override such rights must be expressly stated or appear by necessary implication'.

He could not understand why Parliament should 'want to preserve LPP for documents in the hands of the lawyer but not for documents (which may well be copies or originals of the same documents) in the hands of the taxpayer' and felt that there was nothing 'to create a necessary implication that LPP was intended to be excluded'. He dismissed a Revenue claim that it is important to have access to the taxpayer's legal advice in those cases in which liability may turn upon the purpose with which a person entered into a transaction as not a sufficient reason for overriding LPP and commented that 'the court must infer the purpose from the facts'. Lord Hobhouse of Woodborough thought that the question to be asked was whether, in the absence of any express words that abrogate the taxpayer's common law right to rely on LPP, there is a necessary implication (re one which necessarily follows from the express provisions of the statute construed in their context) to that effect and concluded that there was not.

5.57 A notice under s 20(3) (or s 20(8A) – see **5.50**) does not oblige an auditor to deliver or make available documents which are his property and were created by him (or on his behalf) for, or in connection with, his functions as auditor [TMA 1970 s 20B(9)(a)]. This protection is weak. It only applies to papers that were created in connection with the performance of his functions as auditor under any enactment. In other words, the auditor must have been appointed because of a statutory requirement. Partnerships, sole traders and very small companies normally have no statutory auditor requirement and thus have no protection, but the Revenue voluntarily extends the protection if an audit to statutory standards has been performed [Statement of Practice 5/90].

5.58 This protection is not general. It applies only to papers created for audit purposes. If accounts are being prepared at the same time as the audit, the papers in respect of accounts preparation may not be protected, although it is arguable that the account work was for the purpose of the audit as this could not be performed without first preparing the accounts.

5.59 A similar protection is provided for 'relevant communications' between a tax adviser and his client that are the property of the tax advisor and relate to tax advice about his client's tax affairs. The communications protected are those between a tax adviser and his client, or any other tax adviser to that client, the purpose of which was the giving or obtaining of tax advice [s 20B(9)(b), (10)].

5.60 The protections for both audit papers and tax communications do not apply to a document which contains information explaining any information, return, accounts or other documents which the person to whom the notice is issued has, as tax accountant, assisted any client of his in preparing for, or delivering to, the Revenue [TMA 1970 s 20B(11)]. A person acts as tax accountant when he assists a client in the preparation or delivery of any information, return, accounts or other document which he knows will be, or is likely to be, used for any tax purposes [TMA 1970 s 20D(2)].

5.61 The protection is also disapplied where the notice is served under s 20(8A) (see **5.50**) and the document contains information giving the identity or address of any taxpayer to whom the notice relates or any person who has acted on behalf of such a taxpayer [TMA 1970 s 20B(12)]. In other words, if the accountant or tax advisor has the ability to identify an unknown taxpayer he has to provide that information.

5.62 There is also an exception to the exceptions. The document remains protected if the unprotected information, ie that in paras **5.38** and **5.39**, is contained in some other document which has been either sent to the Revenue or inspected by an officer of the Revenue [TMA 1970 s 20B(13)].

5.63 Where the protection is disapplied it is not lost completely. All that the Revenue are entitled to see is such parts of the document as contain the information referred to in paras **5.38** and **5.39**. The Revenue have given guidance in SP 5/90 as to how this can be done in practice. After pointing out that 'the Revenue is entitled to have access to the information showing how the entry was arrived at, although information showing why the entry was arrived at in that way remains protected', it states:

> 'Where an auditor or tax advisor wishes to claim protection for part of a paper, a copy, which must be photographic or otherwise by way of facsimile, of the part which is not protected may be supplied to the

Revenue. But the original must also be made available for inspection by the Revenue on request, when the protected parts may be kept covered up if the auditor or tax advisor wishes.'

5.64 The Statement of Practice also emphasises that accountants' working papers will not be called for on a routine basis. The Revenue will continue their general policy of seeking access on a voluntary basis and will use their formal powers only where they consider it absolutely necessary. Requests will be limited as far as possible to information containing specific entries (SP 5/90 paras 10 and 11).

5.65 It should be appreciated that the protection for such link papers and tax advice correspondence applies only for s 20. It does not apply where a notice is issued to the taxpayer under s 19A. If the Revenue seek access to the audit working papers under s 19A they should normally be told that these belong to the accountant and are not within the taxpayer's power to obtain. However, the Revenue may challenge this. They define link papers as 'those papers which show how the figures in the return are derived from the figures in the prime records, are held by the agent but are available to the taxpayer'. It is undoubtedly a question of fact whether and to what extent papers belonging to the accountant are available to the taxpayer.

5.66 As a general rule, where the relationship between an accountant and his client is that of principal and principal, documents prepared, acquired or brought into being solely for his own purpose by the member as principal belong to the member. It follows from this that, if the client's instructions were to prepare accounts, the accounts belong to the client and the trial balance belongs to the accountant. If the instructions were to write up the accounting records and prepare accounts then both the trial balance and the accounts would belong to the client.

5.67 Is the position changed by Companies Act 1985, s 237? This requires the auditor to form an opinion 'whether proper accounting records have been kept by the company' and 'whether the company's individual accounts are in agreement with the accounting records' and to state in his report if these requirements are not met. It is difficult to see how a requirement for the company to keep proper accounting records can somehow shift to the company the ownership of property belonging to a third party even if it makes good a failure by the company to carry out its statutory obligations.

5.68 As indicated at **5.9**, in practice careful thought should in any event be given before refusing to supply the Revenue with link papers. It is normally likely to be in the client's interest to volunteer these whatever the legal position might be.

5.69 If warned of a pending s 20(3) order it is important to make written representations to the Inspector arguing why he should not proceed and ask that he put those representations before the Appeal Commissioner. He is bound to do this following case of *R v MacDonald, ex p Hutchinson & Co Ltd [1998] STC 680*. The time to influence an order is before it happens; there is little chance of changing it after the event.

5.70 There are, in theory at least, two possible routes by which to challenge a s 20 notice: in penalty proceedings or by way of judicial review when the notice is issued. Although the latter is a far more expensive procedure it has the advantage that if the notice is upheld, as in practice is usually the case, there is a further opportunity to comply with it without incurring a penalty. An unsuccessful challenge in penalty proceedings will result in the imposition of a penalty, although in *Monarch Assurance Co Ltd v Special Comrs and IRC [1986] STC 311*, where this was done, the Special Commissioners accepted that the company had acted in good faith and imposed a nominal penalty of 50p only.

5.71 The Courts have indicated that they do not approve of speculative orders. This was the point in *R v O'Kane and Clarke, ex p Northern Bank Ltd [1996] STC 1249*. In this case a s 20(3) notice on the bank demanded too much information relating to a named individual. The notice did not specify documents but asked for every piece of information held by the bank. The Court held that this was 'unfair and oppressive'. As a counter balance, however, have regard to *R v IRC, ex p Ulster Bank Ltd ((1997) 69 TC 211)*, see **5.47**. In this case the Court of Appeal approved the Revenue's precursor request for information required under s 20(8A) covering a period from 12 October 1979 to 12 April 1991 relating to unknown taxpayers and unspecified accounts. The bank had estimated that it would take five years, for one man working full time, to comply with the request, at a cost of £346,000! The Court of Appeal was, however, unimpressed.

5.72 Section 98 imposes a penalty for failure to comply with a notice. What if the notice asks for too much or for something that cannot lawfully be required? In *Dyson v A-G [1912] 1 Ch 158* Farwell LJ said:

> 'The duty imposed by the Act … is to make such a return as is required by the Commissioners … The duty and the penalty for disobedience are both one and indivisible and are co-extensive and if the Commissioners frame their requisition with so little care as to exceed their powers the whole demand and not merely the ultra vires portion becomes unenforceable.'

In contrast, in *Royal Bank of Canada v IRC ((1972) 47 TC 565)* Megary J decided:

> 'But where, as here, the requirements are contained in a notice divided into numbered paragraphs dealing with different matters, and the attack is made on one or more of such paragraphs, I do not see why the invalidity of those paragraphs, if established, should infect the other paragraphs, or why the notice should not be good as to the good paragraphs and bad as to the bad.'

Information for other tax authorities

5.73 The Revenue can seek information under s 20(1)–(8) and (8C)–(9) not only for UK tax purposes but also where it is relevant to a liability to tax on income or capital gains in another EU country where this is requested by the overseas country under the EU Mutual Assistance Directive (77/799/EEC) [FA 1990 s 125(1), (2)]

5.74 A s 20 notice can also be used not only to obtain information in relation to UK tax but also in relation to a tax liability in an overseas country with which the UK has a double tax agreement providing for exchanges of information [FA 2000 s 146].

Offences by tax accountants (TMA 1970 s 20A)

5.75 Tax accountants who commit a tax offence effectively permit the Inland Revenue access to all of their clients' files. Section 20A applies whenever a 'tax accountant' has been convicted by a UK Court of any offence in relation to tax, or has had a penalty imposed under TMA 1970 s 99 (essentially for assisting in the preparation of incorrect accounts, information or returns – see **12.57**). The definition of a tax accountant set out at **5.60** applies for this purpose [TMA 1970 s 20D(2)].

5.76 The Revenue require consent to issue a s 20A notice. Because of the serious consequences of such a notice – which in practice is likely to seriously damage, if not destroy, the accountant's practice – consent must be obtained from a circuit judge (or a sheriff in Scotland or a county court judge in Northern Ireland) not from the Commissioners. The judge can give his consent only if he is satisfied that in all of the circumstances the Inspector is justified in issuing the s 20A notice [TMA 1970 ss 20A(3), 20D(1)].

5.77 It works in a similar way to s 20 in that the Inspector must first ask for voluntary production, before giving a formal notice in writing [TMA 1970 s 20B(1)]; it only applies to documents in the tax accountant's possession or power and even then only to those documents which (in the Inspector's reasonable opinion) contain information relevant to his clients and tax liability to which any client of his is, or has been (or may be or have been), subject [TMA 1970 s 20A(1)].

5.78 As with a s 20 notice an Inspector must be specifically authorised by the Board for the purpose of the section to be able to issue a notice [TMA 1970 s 20A(1)]. The Revenue are not entitled to access to personal records or journalistic material [TMA 1970 s 20A(1A)]. A notice to a barrister, advocate or solicitor can be given only by the Board, not by an Inspector [TMA 1970 s 20B(3)] and such a notice cannot force the disclosure of any document to which a claim for legal professional privilege could be raised [TMA 1970 s 20B(8)]. A notice cannot require the production of documents relating to the conduct of a pending appeal by any of the clients [TMA 1970 s 20B(2)]. Copies of documents can be delivered, provided that, if required, the original is made available for inspection [TMA 1970 s 20B(4)].

5.79 Where a notice is issued the notice itself must specify or describe the documents that have to be delivered to the Revenue and the time within which they must be delivered (which must not be less than 30 days after the date of the notice) [TMA 1970 s 20A(1B)].

5.80 It should be noted that s 20A applies only to papers in relation to clients of the tax accountant. Where he is a partner in a firm it cannot extend to clients of other partners. In theory, of course, in most firms the clients are clients of the firm not of an individual partner, although a specific partner may be responsible for looking after specific clients, but such an argument is unlikely to be successful.

5.81 An Inspector's power to issue a s 20A notice ceases 12 months after the day on which he first becomes entitled to exercise it [TMA 1970 s 20A(4)]. This date depends upon the appeal position. The section cannot be applied while an appeal against conviction or the imposition of a penalty is pending. In the absence of an appeal the power is treated as becoming exercisable from the date when the expiration of time to bring an appeal (and any further appeal) expires, or, in Scotland, 28 days from conviction. An appeal against the amount of a penalty (as opposed to whether a penalty is exigible at all) is ignored though, ie the 12-month period which the Inspector has in which to decide whether or not to issue a s 20A notice starts to run from the time that it is no longer possible to appeal against the imposition of any penalty at all [TMA 1970 s 20A(2)].

Production orders (TMA 1970 s 20BA)

5.82 A client can obviously become involved in a tax fraud, or suspected fraud, without the knowledge of his agent. This can cause the agent many problems, especially if search warrants are involved, as a search is at the very least disruptive. They are distressing to those who are totally innocent of any suspicion of an offence. To cater for this there is an alternative to serving a search warrant on third parties such as accountants, solicitors and banks.

5.83 Under s 20BA, on application on oath, a senior Revenue official can apply to a circuit judge (or in Scotland, a sheriff, or in Northern Ireland, a county court judge) for a production order against the accountant or other third party. The judge has to be satisfied that there is a reasonable ground for suspecting that an offence involving serious tax fraud has been, or is about to be, committed and that documents which may be required as evidence for the purpose of a prosecution are, or may be, in the power or possession of the accountant or other person against whom the order is sought [TMA 1970 s 20BA(1)].

5.84 It is interesting to note that s 20BA does not allow the judge to grant an order to assist an investigation by the Revenue. They must convince the judge that they are likely to need to produce the document or documents in question in any proceedings that may be instigated for the offence. This may well require them to have identified the specific document or documents that they think they need. An order, for example, to hand over the client's file may be invalid as it is hard to conceive that the entire file might be needed as evidence.

5.85 The person against whom the order is sought must have been notified of the intention to apply for it. He is entitled to attend and speak at the application hearing, unless the judge considers that doing so could seriously prejudice the investigation [TMA 1970 Sch 1AA para 3(1)].

5.86 The Revenue have power by regulation to expand on the obligation to give notice [reg 3(2); TMA 1970 Sch 1AA]. They have done so by the Order for the Delivery of Documents (Procedure) Regulations 2000, SI 2000/2875. This provides that the decision to apply for an order needs to be approved by a member of the Senior Civil Service in either SCO or the Revenue's Cross-Cutting Policy branch [reg 3]. The notification of the application needs to show the date, time and place of hearing of the application, the specifications or descriptions of documents which are the subject of the application, a description of the suspected offence, and the name of the person suspected of committing it (or being about to commit it) [reg 4(2)].

5.87 Notice must be given to the person entitled to it at least five working days before the hearing of the application [reg 4(2)]. If the notice is delivered to a person or left at his proper address it is deemed to have been given on the day it was delivered or left (unless that day is not a working day, when it is deemed to have been given on the next working day). A faxed notice is deemed to be given when the text is received in a legible form. A person's proper address for this purpose is his usual or last known place of residence, the place of his employment or, in the case of a company, its registered office or, if it is in liquidation, the liquidator's address for the purpose of the liquidation [reg 5].

5.88 The Regulations contain a procedure to resolve disputes as to whether a document, or part of a document, is subject to legal privilege [TMA 1970 Sch 1AA para 6; reg 7]. The person against whom the order is made has to apply to the court to resolve the dispute and lodge the document with the court. The court then notifies the Revenue of the application and fixes a hearing date, which has to be at least five working days after the Revenue are notified. At the hearing the court will resolve the dispute after hearing both parties [reg 7(1)–(5)]. It must order costs against the Revenue if it holds that any of the disputed documents (or if any part of a document) is subject to legal privilege [reg 7(5)(b)]. Provided that the application is made within the time allowed for by the order producing the document, that order is treated as having been complied with until the court resolves the dispute [reg 7(6)]. The Revenue and the person subject to the order can alternatively resolve the dispute themselves by agreement (whether in writing or otherwise) [reg 7(7)].

5.89 Once a person has been told that an application for an order is being made he must not conceal, destroy alter or dispose of any document to which the application relates. Nor may he disclose to any other person information likely to prejudice the investigation of the offence to which it relates unless he does so with leave of the judge or the written permission of the Revenue. These restrictions lapse once the order has been complied with or if the application is dismissed or abandoned [TMA 1970 Sch 1AA para 4(1), (2)]. This does not, however, prevent a professional legal adviser from disclosing information to his client (or the client's representative) in connection with the giving of legal advice, or to any person in contemplation of, or in connection with, legal proceedings, unless it is disclosed with a view to furthering a criminal purpose [TMA 1970 Sch 1AA para 4(3)].

5.90 The order must allow the person ten working days to provide the documents to the Revenue, but a period shorter or longer than this may be given if so specified in the order. Working days means any day except a Saturday, Sunday or public holiday [TMA 1970 s 20BA(2)].

5.91 The order is regarded as complied with if the documents are produced to the Revenue (by either delivering them to the officer or leaving them for him at the address specified in the order) within the time specified by the order or such further time, if any, as may be agreed with the officer [TMA 1970 Sch 1AA para 7; reg 6(1)(2)]. Where documents are sent by post they are deemed to be delivered on the second working day after posting if sent by first class post or the fourth working day if second class post is used (reg 6(3)).

5.92 Section 20BA cannot apply to items subject to legal professional privilege. For the purpose of s 20BA this is defined as:

(*a*) communications between a professional legal adviser and his client (or someone representing him) in connection with the giving of legal advice;

(*b*) communications between the adviser and his client (or someone representing him, or between the adviser, his client or any other person) in connection with or contemplation of legal proceedings and items enclosed with such communications while they are in the possession of a person who is entitled to possession of them [TMA 1970 Sch 1AA para 5].

5.93 Failure to comply with any of the provisions are dealt with as a contempt of court [TMA 1970 Sch 1AA para 9].

Preservation of documents (TMA 1970 s 20BB)

5.94 Once a person has been notified that an order under ss 20, 20A or 20BA is being considered, or indeed has been made, it becomes a criminal offence to intentionally falsify, conceal, destroy, or otherwise dispose of a document that is or may be required to be delivered or made available for inspection. It is also an offence to permit the falsification, concealment, destruction or disposal of any such document.

5.95 No offence is, however, committed if:

(*a*) the person is acting with the written permission of an Appeal Commissioner or the Revenue; or

(*b*) the document has been delivered or inspected;

(*c*) a copy of the document has been delivered and a copy inspected;

(*d*) two years have elapsed since the order was made, unless the Revenue have notified the person in writing that it is not satisfied that the order has been complied with;

(*e*) in the case of an opportunity to deliver the documents without an order under s 20B(1):

- (i) the application for consent to issue the order has been refused; or
- (ii) six months have elapsed since the Revenue first gave the opportunity for the documents to be delivered,

[TMA 1970 s 20BB(2)–(4)].

5.96 The offence is a criminal one and carries a maximum penalty on summary conviction of a fine up to the statutory maximum (£5,000), or a two year jail sentence and an unlimited fine or both on conviction on indictment [TMA 1970 s 20BB(5)].

Search warrants (TMA 1970 s 20C)

5.97 In very serious cases the Revenue have the power to obtain and execute search warrants. The legislation permits the Revenue to apply for a warrant only if there are reasonable grounds of suspecting that serious fraud is involved. The officer applying for the warrant has to give evidence on oath that there are such reasonable grounds and that evidence is likely to be found on the premises specified. He also has to swear on oath that he is acting with the approval of the Board of Inland Revenue in that particular case [TMA 1970 s 20C(1)]. The Board cannot approve an application for a search warrant unless they have reasonable grounds for believing that proceeding under s 20BA for a production order might seriously prejudice the investigation [TMA 1970 s 20C(1AA)]. The approval has to be given by the Board itself; it cannot delegate this to one of its officers [TMA 1970 s 20C(2)]. The application for the warrant must be made to a circuit judge (or in Scotland, a sheriff, or in Northern Ireland, a county court judge) [TMA 1970 s 20C(1)].

5.98 There is no definition of serious fraud. It is, however, specifically provided that an offence that involves fraud is a serious one if its commission has led, or is intended or likely to lead, either to substantial financial gain to any person or to serious prejudice to the proper assessment or collection of tax [TMA 1970 s 20C(1A)(a)]. An offence which on its own is not serious can nevertheless be regarded as such if there are reasonable grounds for suspecting that it forms part of a course of conduct which is (or but for its detection would be) likely to result in serious prejudice to the proper assessment or collection of tax [TMA 1970 s 20C(1A)(b)].

5.99 A warrant must be exercised within 14 days of it being granted. It will be granted to the named officer who applied for it. It can be made subject to conditions, which must be specified in the order as to the number of officers that are permitted to search the premises and the hours within which a search may be conducted. It can also specify that a uniformed police officer must be present at the search [TMA 1970 s 20C(1), (3)].

5.100 The warrant permits entry to the premises, if necessary by force, as well as a search of the premises, and permits the seizure and removal of documents or anything else that the officer to whom the warrant is issued has reasonable cause to believe may be required as evidence for the purpose of criminal proceedings, unless of course such documents attract legal privilege.

5.101 The officer also has power to search, or cause to be searched, any person found on the premises whom he has reasonable grounds to believe to be in possession of such documents or other things but the person who does the search must be of the same sex. The definition of legal privilege is the same as that at **5.92** above. The officer is entitled to take with him such persons as appear to him to be necessary. For example, he could take a locksmith if he believes he will need to break into the premises. Such other persons cannot join in the search unless they are amongst the number of officers listed in the warrant [TMA 1970 s 20C(3), (4), (4A), (4B)]. Where the officer has reasonable cause to believe that information that is contained in a computer may be required as evidence and the computer is accessible from the premises, the power of seizure includes a power to require the information in a form in which it can be taken away and in which it is visible and legible [TMA 1970 s 20C(3A)]. This appears to be wide enough that if, for example, the suspect uses internet banking, the Revenue can require him to log on to the bank's computer and download whatever information is accessible to him even though the warrant does not cover the bank's premises.

5.102 The officer in charge of the search must give a copy of the warrant to the occupier of the premises (or if he is not present the person on the premises who appears to be in charge) before starting the search. If there is no one on the premises the copy of the warrant must be left in a prominent place on the premises [TMA 1970 s 20C(5)]. The person handed the warrant clearly ought to immediately read it to ascertain what limitations it places on the Revenue's powers. It would be sensible to also try to arrange for the immediate attendance of a solicitor, particularly if the premises contain documents that might be subject to legal privilege.

5.103 Where documents are removed, the officer in charge of the search must attach to (or endorse on) the warrant (ie the original not the copy he gives the occupier) a list of the things seized. In England and Wales the Police and Criminal Evidence Act 1984 ss 10–12 (return, retention and inspection of warrants) apply in the same way as they apply to a warrant issued to a constable [TMA 1970 s 20C(7), (8)]. Once documents have been removed, the officer in charge of the search must provide a record of what has been taken. Documents taken can be retained only for as long as is necessary and must be returned if a photocopy will suffice.

5.104 Where documents (or anything else) are removed from the premises the occupier, or the person who had custody or control of the item immediately before its removal, is entitled to ask the officer in charge for a record of what was removed [TMA 1970 s 20CC(1)]. Such a list does not have to be given at the time of the search but must be provided within a reasonable time of the request [TMA 1970 s 20CC(2)].

5.105 If a photograph or photocopy of the item will suffice either as evidence at a trial or for forensic examination or for investigation in connection with an offence, the item itself cannot be retained by the Revenue for longer than is necessary to establish that fact and obtain the photograph or copy [TMA 1970 s 20CC(3)].

5.106 Access by the owner to the seized documents (or anything else that has been removed and retained) is permitted by the legislation, but only under Revenue supervision [TMA 1970 s 20CC(4)]. Copies of any document retained by the Revenue can be required subject to one proviso, namely that the Revenue can refuse copies and refuse access if they believe that this would prejudice the investigation (or any other investigation) or a trial [TMA 1970 s 20CC(5), (6), (8)]. The Revenue must provide copies of documents within a reasonable time of the request for copies being made [TMA 1970 s 20CC(7)].

Information for the purposes of Sch A (TMA 1970 s 19)

5.107 For the purpose of obtaining particulars of profits or gains taxable under Sch A an Inspector may, by notice in writing, require:

(*a*) any lessee or occupier of land (or former lessee or occupier), or anyone who has (or had) use of land, to give such information as may be prescribed by the Revenue as to the terms of any lease, occupation or use of the land and, if those terms are in writing, to produce the relevant document;

(*b*) any lessee (or former lessee) to give such information as may be prescribed as to any consideration he has given for the grant or assignment of the tenancy; and

(*c*) any person who as agent manages land or is in receipt of rent or other payments arising from land to give such particulars relating to payments arising from the land as may be specified in the notice,

[TMA 1970 s 19(1)].

5.108 The Revenue do not appear to have prescribed any information in relation to (*a*) and (*b*) above, so those provisions may be ineffective. It is only the Board that is empowered to prescribe information, an Inspector cannot simply decide what he would like in a particular case.

5.109 Information cannot be demanded in respect of a tax year ended more than three years before the date on which the information is requested [TMA 1970 s 19(4)].

5.110 Reference to a lessee includes an agreement for a lease and any tenancy and lessee must be construed accordingly [TMA 1970 s 19(3)]. The information demanded can also relate to charges to tax under Sch D Case VI in respect of premiums on leases [TMA 1970 s 19(2)].

Miscellaneous information powers

Dealers in securities

5.111 Any business involved with dealing in securities (which includes stocks and shares for this purpose) can be required by notice to make available for inspection by the Revenue all books accounts and other documents in its possession or power that in opinion of the Board contain information directly relating to securities transactions. This applies both to dealings by the business as principal and those carried out on behalf of other people [TMA 1970 s 21(1), (2), (7)].

5.112 The Revenue can similarly serve a notice on a stockbroker (or other member of a recognised investment exchange) requiring him to make available for inspection his own books and documents if the officer believes that these contain information relating directly or indirectly to securities transactions in the course of a business within **5.111** above which is carried on by someone other than the broker [TMA 1970 s 21(3), (7)].

5.113 Any person, not being a broker, who has directly or indirectly received payment from another person in the course of the business of a securities dealer within **5.111** above carried on by that other person, which is treated by the dealer as made in respect of interest (or dividends) on securities, can be required by notice in writing to furnish to the Revenue the name and address of the beneficial owner if he received the payment on behalf of someone else [TMA 1970 s 21(4)]. Similarly, they can require a person who directly or indirectly makes a payment to a securities dealer within **5.111** which is treated as a receipt of his business occurring in respect of interest on securities, to state whether his payment was (in whole or in part) received from, or paid on account of, a third party and if it was to supply that person's name and address [TMA 1970 s 21(4A)].

5.114 A person, in whose name securities are registered, can also be required, by notice in writing, to state whether he is the beneficial owner and, if not, to furnish the name and address of the beneficial owner of the securities. They can, however, ask for such information only if it is for the purpose of obtaining information in relation to securities transactions in the course of a business within **5.111** [TMA 1970 s 21(5)].

5.115 If it appears to the Revenue that a person may have incurred a liability to pay (or account for) tax under TA 1988 Sch 23A (manufactured payments) the Revenue can serve a notice on that person requiring him to supply them with information which is available to him and is (or may be) relevant to whether he has incurred such a tax liability and if so the extent of it [TMA 1970 s 21(5A)].

5.116 A notice under **5.111** must allow at least 28 days for the recipient to comply with it. There is no minimum period which must be allowed under the other provisions of s 21 but the notice needs to specify the period allowed for complying with it.

5.117 No information can be demanded in respect of transactions relating to a tax year that ended more than six years before service of the notice [TMA 1970 s 21(6)].

Details of sources of income

5.118 The Board can, by notice in writing, require any individual to give them particulars as to the several sources of his income and the amounts of each and the nature and amounts of any deductions therefrom as they may consider necessary. At least 28 days must be allowed to comply [TMA 1970 s 22]. This provision is now rarely used as the Revenue can obtain this information under s 19A. It could however be used where the enquiry windows had closed before the Revenue decide to investigate the individual's affairs. It could also be used to obtain information about payments made to, or received from, someone else where those payments constitute income or deductions of the individual.

Securities

5.119 The Revenue can require a company to deliver to them a certified copy of its securities register or any part of it, or any individual entry or entries in it containing the names of the holders. Securities for this purpose includes stock, shares, debentures and debenture stock. At least 21 days must be allowed for compliance with an order and, on delivery, the Board must pay 25p for every 100 entries. [TMA 1970 s 23]

5.120 The Revenue can, by notice in writing, require any person who is the registered holder of UK securities, and has received income arising from them on behalf of another person, to provide them with details of the payment and the name and address of the person on whose behalf they received it. The same information can be demanded from any person by, or through, income in respect of UK securities has been made on bearer securities where the securities belong beneficially to a third party [TMA 1970 s 24(1)]. At least 28 days must be allowed to provide the information. There is no need to provide details of payments to any person which do not exceed £15 in aggregate [TMA 1970 s 24(1)]. UK securities are any securities issued by the UK government or the government of Northern Ireland or by a company incorporated in any part of the UK [TMA 1970 s 24(4)]. The same information can be demanded from anyone who has acted as an intermediary (or as one of a series of intermediaries) between a person within **5.111** and the person beneficially entitled to the income in question. Such an intermediary can also be required to provide any other information that the Revenue may require for the purpose of enabling them to ascertain the names and addresses of the beneficial owners and the amounts receivable by them [TMA 1970 s 24(2)]. As the intermediary may not know the identity of the beneficial owner the Revenue need to be able to ask him, for example, for the name and address of the person with whom he dealt so that they can then serve a notice on that person.

5.121 A bank (within TA 1988 s 840A) cannot be compelled to disclose any details if the beneficial owner is not a UK resident. [TMA 1970 s 24(3)].

Chargeable gains

5.122 A general information gathering power for capital gains tax purposes is given to an inspector by TMA 1970 s 25. Issuing houses and other persons effecting public issues of shares or securities, or placings of shares or securities, on behalf of a company or on behalf of the holders of blocks of shares or securities which had not previously been the subject of an issue or placing can be required, by notice in writing, to give details of the persons to whom shares were issued in the course of its business, together with the number of shares/securities obtained by each [TMA 1970 s 25(2)]. A person who does not carry on such a business but effects a public issue or placing can similarly be required to give details of the issue, allotment or placing [TMA 1970 s 23(3)].

5.123 A number of specific types of business can be required by notice to give details of transactions effected by them.

(*a*) A member of a Stock Exchange (other than a market maker) can also be required to provide details of any transactions effected by him in the course of his business [TMA 1970 s 25(4)]. So can any other person who is not a member of a Stock Exchange but who acts as an agent or broker in the UK in transactions in shares or securities [TMA 1970 s 25(5)].

(*b*) A clearing house for any terminal market in commodities can be required to provide details of transactions effected through the clearing house [TMA 1970 s 25(6)].

(*c*) An auctioneer or a person carrying on a trade of dealing in any description of chattels can be required to provide details of transactions effected by or through him which result in the disposal of an asset by a person where the amount or value of the consideration in the hands of the recipient exceeds £6,000 [TMA 1970 s 25(7)].

In each case (other than (*c*) where only particulars of the transaction can be sought) the information that can be required are particulars of the parties to the transaction, the numbers or amounts dealt with in the transaction and the amount or value of the consideration. The notice must specify the period covered.

5.124 No information can be sought about transactions effected more than three years before service of the s 25 notice [TMA 1970 s 25(8)]. No time within which the information must be provided is specified in the legislation.

5.125 Again, for the purposes of capital gains tax, any person in whose name any shares of a company (including securities and loan capital) are registered can be required by the Revenue by notice in writing, to state whether he is the beneficial owner and if not to provide the name and address of the beneficial owner [TMA 1970 s 26].

5.126 The Revenue can, by notice in writing, require any person who is a party to a settlement to provide them with such information as they consider necessary for the purposes of capital gains tax. At least 28 days must be allowed to comply [TMA 1970 s 27].

5.127 A person holding shares or securities in a non-resident company can be required by the Revenue, in writing, to give such information as the Revenue consider necessary to enable them to determine whether the company is within TCGA 1992 s 13 and if that person is liable to capital gains tax under that section [TMA 1970 s 28].

Information power re transfers of assets abroad (TA 1988 s 745)

5.128 TA 1988 s 745 is a power specifically to support the anti-avoidance provisions at s 739 onwards, in relation to transfers of assets abroad. It permits the Revenue by notice in writing to require any person to provide such particulars as the Revenue think necessary for the purpose of these anti-avoidance sections.

5.129 A period of at least 28 days must be given to comply with the notice [TA 1988 s 745(1)]. The particulars that are required can in particular include those:

(*a*) as to transactions with respect to which the person is or was acting on behalf of others;

(*b*) as to transactions which the Revenue consider they should investigate, whether or not the recipient of the notice believes the anti-avoidance provisions apply; and

(*c*) as to whether that person has taken (or is taking) any part in any transactions of a description specified in the notice and if so what part in what transactions [TA 1988 s 745(2)].

5.130 The Revenue have been known to serve such a notice on firms of accountants asking for details of overseas settlements on which they have advised where the settlor is UK resident. A solicitor cannot be deemed to have taken part in a transaction for the purpose of (*c*) by reason only that he has given professional advice in relation to the transaction. A solicitor also cannot be compelled (except with the consent of his client) to do more than state that he is or was acting on behalf of a client and to give the name and address of the client, and the names and address of the transferor and transferee or of the persons concerned in any associated operations if he acted in connection with a transfer of assets, the name and address of the overseas company if he was involved in its formation or management, or the name and address of the settlor and trustees (or other recipient of the income) if he was involved in the creation of an overseas settlement [TA 1988 s 745(3)]. The reference to overseas companies means bodies corporate resident or incorporated outside the UK which would be close companies if they were UK resident and whose business does not consist wholly or mainly of the carrying on of a trade or trades [TA 1988 s 745(4)]. A solicitor cannot be required to disclose anything in relation to a company that does not satisfy those conditions.

5.131 A bank (within TA 1998 s 840A) cannot be required to furnish particulars of any ordinary banking transactions between it and a customer carried out in the ordinary course of banking business, unless it has acted on behalf of the customer in connection with the formation or management of an overseas company within s 745(4) (see **5.130**) or in connection with the creation of a settlement by virtue or in consequence of which income becomes payable to a person resident or domiciled outside the UK [TA 1988 s 745(5), (5A)].

5.132 TCGA 1992 s 98 similarly enables the Revenue by notice to require any person to furnish them within such time as they may direct (but not less than 28 days) with such particulars as they think necessary for the purposes of the anti-avoidance provisions in relation to those overseas trusts where a capital gain realised by the trust might be taxable on a beneficiary under TCGA 1992 ss 87–90 and Sch 4C [TCGA 1992 s 98(1)]. The details are identical to those set out at **5.128–5.131** above [TCGA 1992 s 98(2)].

Enterprise Management Incentives

5.133 The Revenue have specific enquiry powers under the Enterprise Management Incentive scheme. These broadly follow the self-assessment enquiry procedure. They can enquire into the option by notice to the employer. They can also enquire into whether the employee has met his working time commitment by notice to the employee. They can issue an enquiry notice up to a year after the end of the 92-day period within which the company is required to notify them of the grant of the option. They can open an enquiry at any time if any of the information given in the initial notification of the grant of the option was false or misleading in a material respect. If the Revenue issue a closure notice their decision in it is conclusive as to whether the requirements of the scheme are met in relation to the option. If they do not open an enquiry the closure of the enquiry window gives the same assurance. The normal rights of appeal apply [ITEPA 2003 Sch 5 paras 46–50].

Specific information powers

5.134 In addition to these information powers many provisions in the tax legislation contain their own information powers.

Arrangements for transferring relief, etc

5.135 If a company makes a claim for group relief, or is a party to a leasing contract and claims relief under TA 1988 s 395 (to carry forward a leasing loss of a predecessor) or claims relief under TA 1988 s 116 (arrangement for transferring partnership losses) and an inspector has reason to believe that any relevant arrangements exist (or may have existed at a time material to the claim) he can, at any time after the claim is made, require the company to furnish him with:

(*a*) a declaration in writing stating whether or not such arrangement existed at a material time; and

(*b*) such information as he may reasonably require for the purpose of satisfying himself whether or not any such arrangements exist (or existed at a material time).

He must allow at least 30 days to provide the information. Relevant arrangements are arrangements falling within TA 1988 s 395(1)(c) or 116(1), Sch 18 para 5(3), s 410(1) or (2), as the case may be. A notice relating to group relief can be served on the surrendering company as well as on the claimant company and one relating to s 116 can be served on the other partners as well as the company concerned. Arrangement means arrangements of any kind, whether in writing or not [FA 1973 s 32]. The Revenue tell their staff only to resort to this formal procedure where the company or its agent does not supply the necessary information under the normal enquiry procedure (Company Taxation Manual, para 2684)

Rules for ascertaining duration of leases

5.136 Where an Inspector believes that a person has information relevant to the ascertainment of the duration of a lease for the purpose of the special rules relating to premiums on lease he can require that person to give such information on the matters set out in TA 1988 s 38(1)–(4) as is in his possession. The legislation does not allow a minimum time to provide the information but the inspector must specify a time in his notice. A solicitor cannot be required to do more than state that he is (or was) acting on behalf of a client and give the name and address of the client [TA 1988 s 38(4)]

Appeals against determination under TA 1988 ss 34–36

5.137 Where an Inspector believes that a dispute in relation to the amount taxable under the rules on premiums will affect the tax liability of someone else, such as the person who pays the premium, he can notify the other person of the determination he intends to make and, unless he appeals against the notification, he will then be bound by it. The Inspector has power to require any person to give (within a time he specifies in the notice) such information as appears to the inspector to be required to enable him to decide whether to give such notification to any person [TA 1988 s 42(7)].

Non-residents and their responsibilities

5.138 The Revenue can designate any person who receives rent on behalf of a non-resident or acts in connection with the management or administration of the property business of a non-resident as a prescribed person [Taxation of Income from Land (Non-Residents) Regulations 1985, SI 1985/2902, reg 3]. They can then require that person to furnish them such information as they may reasonably require to satisfy themselves that that person has complied with the requirements of the Regulations. They must allow at least 14 days for the provision of such information [reg 13]. The Revenue can also require a prescribed person (again within not less than 14 days) to make available for inspection all such books, documents and other records in his possession or under his control as they may reasonably require to satisfy themselves that he has complied with the Regulations. Where records are computerised the prescribed person must also provide the officer making the inspection with all the facilities necessary for obtaining information from the computer [reg 15]. Once a person has been designated a prescribed person he is under an obligation to maintain and retain sufficient records to enable the Revenue to verify the above matters [reg 15]. Other than under FA 1989 s 182(5) (see **14.119**) the Revenue cannot use information obtained under these powers for the purpose of ascertaining the tax liability of any person other than a person whose usual place of abode is outside the UK, a person who accounts for rent to such a person or an agent of such a person [reg 16; TA 1988 s 42A].

Exempt distributions

5.139 If a distribution within TA 1988 s 213(3) (demergers) is made and the inspector has reason to believe that it might form part of a scheme or arrangement within s 213(11) he can require any relevant company under s 213(3) or any person controlling such a company (within the meaning of TA 1988 s 416) to furnish a declaration in writing stating whether or not, according to the information which the person has or can reasonably obtain, any such scheme or arrangement exists or existed, together with such other information as the Inspector may reasonably require for the purpose of s 213(11) which that person has or can reasonably obtain [TA 1988 s 217(1)]. If the Inspector has reason to believe that a chargeable payment has been made within five years after an exempt distribution he can ask the person making the payment for the same information [TA 1988 s 217(3)]. If the Inspector has reason to believe that a person has not delivered a return which he is required to make under TA 1988 ss 214(1)(b) or 216(2) or (3) in respect of a payment or transfer, he can require that person to furnish such information as the Inspector may reasonably require for the purpose of s 214 [TA 1988 s 217(2)]. In such case at least 30 days must be allowed to provide the information. An Inspector can also require any recipient of a chargeable payment (or any person on whose behalf such a payment is received) to state whether the payment is received on behalf of someone else and if so give his name and address [TA 1988 s 217(4)]. The inspector cannot impose any time limit on how quickly such information must be supplied though.

Purchase of own shares

5.140 If an Inspector has reason to believe that a purchase of own shares which was treated as a capital payment may form part of a scheme or arrangement of the kind referred to in, TA 1988 ss 219(1)(a) or 223(2), he can require the company or any person connected with it (within TA 1988 s 228) to supply a written declaration as to whether or not, according to information which the company has or can reasonably obtain, any such scheme or arrangements exist (or have existed) and, if it does, such other information as the Inspector may reasonably require for the purpose. He must allow at least 60 days to supply the information [TA 1988 s 226(3)]. The recipient of the distribution and any person on whose behalf it is received can also be required (without a time limit) to state whether the payment was received on behalf of another person and, if so, to give the name and address of that other person [TA 1988 s 226(4)].

Distributions

5.141 If it appears to an Inspector that a company has made a non-qualifying distribution for which a return ought to have been made under TA 1988 s 234(5)–(7), he can require the company to furnish him, within the time he specifies in the notice, with such information relating to that distribution as he may reasonably require [TA 1988 s 234(8)]. This does not apply to an amount applied by the trustees in acquiring dividend shares under an Approved Share Incentive Plan on behalf of a participant [ITEPA 2003 s 493(3)]. The Revenue have power by Regulation to modify, supplement or replace any of the provisions of s 234(5)–(9) for the purpose of requiring UK companies to make returns and give information to the Inspector in respect of non-qualifying distributions [TA 1988 s 253] but do not appear to have done so [TA 1988 s 253].

Stock dividends

5.142 If it appears to an Inspector that a company ought to have made a return under TA 1988 s 250 (but has not done so) he can require the company to make a return stating that no relevant share capital was issued in the period in question if such was the case [TA 1988 s 250(6)]. He can also require the company to provide such further information regarding stock dividends included in a return as he may reasonably require for the purposes of TA 1988 ss 230 and 249–251 [TA 1988 s 250(7)]. In both cases the Inspector must allow at least 30 days to supply the information.

EIS relief

5.143 If an Inspector has reason to believe that a person has not given a notice that he was required to do under TA 1988 s 310(1)–(3) (events triggering a withdrawal of EIS relief), has given or a received value which would have triggered a notice but for it being insignificant, or has made or received a repayment that would have triggered a notice but for TA 1988 s 303AA(1), an Inspector can require that person to furnish him with such information relating to the event or case as the inspector may reasonably require for the purpose of EIS relief [TA 1988 s 310(4)]. Where EIS relief has been claimed and the Inspector has reason to believe that it may not be due by reason of a scheme or arrangement, he can require any person concerned to supply a declaration stating whether or not, according to the information which that person has or can reasonably obtain, such an arrangement or scheme exists (or has existed) together with such other information as he may reasonably require for the purpose of the provision in question and as that person can reasonably obtain [TA 1988 s 310(5)]. The provisions concerned and persons that can be asked to supply information are:

s 289(6)	–	the claimant, the company and any person controlling the company
s 291B(5)	–	the claimant
s 293(8)	–	the company and any person controlling the company
s 299B(1)	–	the claimant, the company and any person connected with the company
s 308(2)(e)	–	the company and any person controlling the company

References to the claimant include any person to whom the claimant appears to have made a transfer within s 304(1) of the shares in question [TA 1988 s 310(6)]. At least 60 days must be allowed to supply the information. Where EIS relief has been given, any person who receives from the company a payment or assets which could constitute value for the purpose of TA 1988 ss 301–304(3) (and any person on whose behalf such a payment is received) can be required to state whether the payment or asset is received on behalf of someone else and if so to state that person's name and address [TA 1988 s 310(7)] Where EIS relief has been claimed the shareholder can similarly be required to state whether the shares were held on behalf of someone else and if so to give the name and address [TA 1988 s 310(8)].

TESSAs

5.144 The Tax-exempt Special Savings Account Regulations 1990, SI 1990/2361, require the TESSA provider to provide information to the Revenue if required to do so, and to keep records and make them available for inspection [regs 14–16; TA 1988 s 326C].

Life assurance companies

5.145 The Insurance Companies (Overseas Life Assurance Business) (Compliance) Regulations 1995, SI 1995/3237, contain rights to the Revenue to seek information and to inspect records [regs 22, 23; TA 1988 s 431E].

Unit trusts

5.146 The Income Tax (Authorised Unit Trusts) (Interest Distributions) Regulations 2003, SI 2003/1830, give the Revenue power to require the trustees or manager of an authorised unit trust to supply them with such information as they may reasonably request (including copies of any relevant books, documents or other records) for the purpose of determining whether interest distributions were properly made without deduction of tax. They must allow at least 14 days for the information to be provided [reg 7]. They also have power to inspect such records [reg 8]. Other than under FA 1989 s 182(5) (see **14.117**) the information so obtained cannot be used for the purpose of ascertaining the tax liability of any one other than the trust, a unit holder or the beneficiary of a trust which receives the distribution [reg 9; TA 1988 s 468PB].

Building societies

5.147 The Income Tax (Building Societies) (Audit Powers) Regulations 1992, SI 1992/10, similarly allow the Revenue to require a building society to furnish them with such information (including copies of books, documents and records) as they may reasonably require for the purposes of determining whether payments by the building society were properly made without deduction of tax [reg 3]. They must allow at least 14 days. They can also require the records in the society's possession or control to be made available for inspection [reg 4]. The information so obtained is not to be used (other than under FA 1989 s 182(5)) other than for the purpose of ascertaining the tax liability of any person other than the society or a person to whom the information relates [reg 12; TA 1988 s 477A].

Deposit takers

5.148 The Income Tax (Deposit-takers) (Audit Powers) Regulations 1992, SI 1992/12, contains identical provisions in relation to deposit takers [TA 1988 s 482(11)].

Chargeable events

5.149 The Revenue have power to make regulations including such provisions as they think fit for ensuring that they are able to ascertain whether there is likely to have been a contravention of the obligations of an insurance company to issue a chargeable events certificate and to verify any such certificate [TA 1988 s 552ZA]. They do not appear to have yet done so.

Non-resident entertainers and sportsmen

5.150 The Income Tax (Entertainers and Sportsmen) Regulations 1987, SI 1987/530, require any person who makes a connected payment or transfer (within reg 3) to furnish them with particulars of such payment or transfer, including the dates and amount or values of each payment or transfer, a sufficient description to enable any asset or money's worth transferred to be identified, the business and private name and address of the person to whom each payment or transfer was made, the name and address of the entertainer and the relevant activity to which the payment relates, including full particulars of all performances. They must specify in the notice the time within which the information is to be provided [reg 9(4); TA 1988 s 555(7)]. No obligation of secrecy, imposed by statute or otherwise, precludes the Revenue from disclosing to any person who appears to them to have an interest in the matter information which may be relevant to determine whether s 555(2) or (3) applies to a payment or transfer [TA 1988 s 558(4)].

Pension schemes

5.151 The Pension Scheme Surpluses (Administration) Regulations 1987, SI 1987/352, provide that if the Revenue have reason to believe that a surplus payment has been made to an employer in respect of which no return (or an incorrect return) has been made under reg 3 they can require the Administrator of the scheme to furnish a return or further return containing the particulars to which reg 3 refers [reg 7; TA 1988 s 602].

5.152 The Retirement Benefits Schemes (Information Powers) Regulations 1995, SI 1995/3103, allow the Revenue to require specified persons to furnish them with such particulars and furnish such documents as they may reasonably require relating to any monies received or receivable by an approved retirement benefits scheme or a relevant statutory scheme, any investments or other assets held by the scheme or any monies paid or payable out of funds held under the scheme. The specified persons are the scheme administrator (within TA 1988 s 611AA), any former scheme administrator, any person who is or has been a scheme employer or a scheme sponsor and any person who provides or has provided administrative services to the scheme. They must allow at least 28 days to comply with the notice. They cannot serve a notice on a former administrator or other person who on ceasing to act transferred to his successor all documents in his possession or under his control relating to the scheme [reg 12]. The Revenue can also require the insurance company or friendly society which issued an annuity contact (or in the case of an insurance company its chief executive and manager as defined in Financial Services and Markets Act 2000 ss 417(1), 423, or in the case of a friendly society its chief executive and secretary or any assistant or deputy chief executive or secretary) to provide them with such particulars and documents as they may reasonably require relating to any annuity contract issued by that person by means of which benefits provided under an approved scheme or relevant statutory scheme have been secured. They must allow at least 28 days to provide the information [reg 13; TA 1988 s 605]. The Personal Pension Schemes (Information Powers) Regulations 2000, SI 2000/2316, contain similar requirements in relation to personal pension schemes [TA 1988 s 651A].

Purchased life annuities

5.153 The Personal Pension Schemes (Relief at Source) Regulations 1988, SI 1988/1013, empower the Revenue to require any person who is or has at any time been either a Scheme Administrator to whom net of tax contributions have been paid, or any individual who has paid such contributions, to give them such information as they may prescribe in the notice. They must allow at least 14 days to comply and are entitled to prescribe the form in which the information is to be given [reg 14(1); TA 1988 s 639].

5.154 The Income Tax (Purchased Life Annuities) Regulations 1956, SI 1956/1230, empower an Inspector to require the payer of such an annuity to give him such particulars relating to the annuity as he may require (whether reasonably or not) including, if known, the age of the person during whose life the annuity is payable, the consideration given for the grant of the annuity and particulars of any other matters appearing to him (it is not clear if this refers to the Inspector or the payer – it is probably the Inspector) to be relevant for the purposes of TA 1988 ss 656–658 [TA 1988 s 658].

Settlements

5.155 An officer of the Board can require any party to a settlement to furnish him with such particulars as he thinks necessary for the purposes of TA 1988 ss 660G. He must allow at least 28 days to provide the information [TA 1988 s 660F].

Deceased estates

5.156 An Inspector can require any person who is or has been a personal representative of a deceased person, or any person who has or had an interest in the residue of the estate (whether absolute or limited) or in any part of such residue, to supply such particulars as the Inspector thinks necessary for the purpose of TA 1988 ss 695–702 [TA 1988 s 700(4)].

Transactions in securities

5.157 If it appears to the Revenue that by reason of any transaction or transactions a person may be a person to whom TA 1988 s 703 applies, they can require him to give them information in his possession with respect to the transaction (or any of the transactions) as to matters specified in the notice which are relevant to the question of whether a s 703(3) notice should be given to him. They must allow at least 28 days for the provision of the information [TA 1988 s 708]. In order to obtain, for the purposes of TA 1988 ss 710–727A, particulars relating to securities, the Revenue can also require any person in whose name any securities are registered to state whether or not he is the beneficial owner and if not to give them the name and address of the beneficial owner [TA 1988 s 728].

5.158 The Movements of Capital (Required Information) Regulations 1990, SI 1990/1671, empowers the Revenue to require a UK resident company which enters into a transaction within TA 1988 s 765A (movement of capital between residents of member states) to give them such particulars relating to the transaction, to related transactions, or to persons connected with the transaction or related transactions, as they may require [reg 4; TA 1988 s 765A(2)(b)].

Change in company ownership

5.159 If it appears to the Revenue that there has been a change in the ownership of a company and in connection with that change a person (the seller) may be (or may become) liable to be charged to tax under TA 1988 s 767A or 767AA, the Revenue can require any person to supply them with:

(*a*) any document in the person's possession or power which appears to the Revenue to be relevant for the purpose of determining specified matters; and

(*b*) any particulars which appear to them to be relevant for that purpose.

The specified matters are whether the seller is, or may become, liable to tax under those provisions and the extent of the potential liability, and whether the company (or an associated company) is, or may become, liable to tax and the extent of its potential liability. The Revenue must allow at least 30 days for the information to be provided. The information they require must be specified in the notice. The rules on copies in TMA 1970 s 20B(4) (see **5.29**), the protection for professional advisors in TMA 1970 s 20B(8)–(14) (see **5.55–5.68**) and the exclusion for personal records and journalistic material under s 20(8C) (see **5.30**) apply to such a notice [TA 1988 s 767C]. An Inspector can also require any person in whose name shares, stock or securities are registered to state whether or not he is the beneficial owner and, if he is not, give the name and address of the beneficial owner [TA 1988 ss 768(9), 768D(7), 768E(6)]. The notice requiring the information must state that the information is required for the purposes of s 768 (change of ownership: disallowance of trading losses), 768D (change in ownership of company carrying on a property business) or 768E (change in ownership of company with unused non-trading loss on intangibles) as the case may be.

Transactions between dealing company and associated company

5.160 If it appears to the Revenue that by reason of any transaction or transactions a person may have incurred a liability to tax by virtue of TA 1988 s 774, they can require him to give them information in his possession with respect to the transaction (or any of the transactions) as to matters specified in the notice which are relevant to the question of whether he may have incurred such a liability. They must allow at least 28 days for a response [TA 1988 s 774(5)].

Sale of income from personal activities and transactions in land

5.161 The Revenue can require any person to furnish them with such particulars as they think necessary for the purposes of TA 1988 ss 775, 776. They must allow at least 30 days to reply. The particulars they can ask for include particulars as to:

(*a*) transactions or arrangements with respect to which the person was acting on behalf of others;

(*b*) transactions or arrangements which in the opinion of the Revenue should properly be investigated for the purposes of s 775 or 776, notwithstanding that in the opinion of the person to whom the notice is given no liability to tax arises under those sections; and

(*c*) whether the person to whom the notice is given has taken (or is taking) any, and if so what, part in any transactions or arrangements of a description specified in the notice.

A solicitor cannot be deemed for the purpose of (*c*) to have taken part in a transaction or arrangement by reason only that he has given professional advice to a client in connection with it. In relation to anything done by a client, a solicitor cannot be required to do more than say that he is or was acting on behalf of a client and give the name and address of the client [TA 1988 s 778].

Pre-13 March 1984 life insurance policies

5.162 The Revenue can require any person who has or had a policy of life insurance or contract for a deferred annuity with a life office, or who pays or paid premiums under such a policy or contract, to furnish them with in such time as they may direct with such information (including copies of relevant documents) as they require for the purpose of TA 1988 s 266 or Sch 14 (life assurance premium relief) [TA 1988 Sch 14 para 7; Income Tax (Life Assurance Premium Relief) Regulations 1978, SI 1978/1159, reg 11]. They are also entitled to inspect the records of every person to whom such premiums are paid [reg 12]. As the relief applies only to policies taken out prior to 13 March 1984 it is unlikely that this power will ever be used.

Venture capital trusts

5.163 If an Inspector has reason to believe that a person has not given a notice which he is required to give of an event that triggers the withdrawal of VCT relief, he can require that person to give him such information relating to the suspected trigger event as he may reasonably require for the purpose of VCT investment relief [TA 1988 Sch 15B para 15]. The Revenue can require any company which is or has been a VCT or any person who holds (or has held) shares in such a company to furnish them with such information as they may reasonably require for the purpose of TA 1988 s 842AA or Sch 15B or the VCT regulations. They must allow at least 14 days to comply [VCT Regulations 1995, SI 1995/1979, reg 24; TA 1988 Sch 15B para 15(5); FA 1995 s 73]. They can also require any such person to make available for inspection such accounts, records and other information as are in that person's possession or under that person's control as they may reasonably require for such purposes. They must again allow at least 14 days to comply. If information is held on computer the person must also provide the Revenue with the facilities necessary to obtain the information [reg 25].

Employee share ownership trusts

5.164 An Inspector can require a return to be made by the trustees of an ESOT if they have at any time received a sum which the company has deducted (or has been treated as deducting) under FA 1989 s 67(2)(a) [FA 1989 s 73(1)]. Section 67 has been repealed in relation to payments by the company after 31 December 2002 [FA 2003 s 142(1)]. The Inspector must specify the information he requires to be contained in the return. This must be information needed for the purposes of FA 1989 ss 68–72, which can include information about sums received by the trustees (including borrowings), expenditure of the trustees, assets acquired by the trustees and transfers of assets by them [FA 1989 s 73]. An Inspector can also ask the trustees of an ESOT for a return containing such information as he may specify of shares acquired by them for which the vendor has claimed roll-over relief under TCGA 1992 s 229. The Inspector can only ask for information that he needs for the purposes of TCGA 1992 ss 232–234. This can include information about expenditure by the trustees, assets acquired by them and transfers of assets made by them [TCGA 1992 s 235(1)–(6)].

Close companies

5.165 An Inspector can require any company which appears to him to be close to furnish him with such particulars as he thinks necessary for the purposes of TA 1988 ss 13–13A, 231 and 419–422. He must allow at least 30 days for a response [FA 1989 Sch 12 para 2]. He can also require, for the purposes of the same provisions, any person in whose name shares or loan capital are registered to state whether or not he is the beneficial owner and, if he is not, give the name and address of the person on whose behalf he owns the shares [FA 1989 Sch 12 para 3]. For the purposes of the same provisions an Inspector can also require any company which appears to him to be a close company to supply particulars of any bearer securities issued by the company, the names and addresses of the persons to whom they were issued and the amounts issued to each. He can also require a person to whom such bearer securities were issued, or to or through whom they were subsequently sold or transferred, to give such further information as he may require, with a view to enabling him to ascertain the names and addresses of the persons beneficially interested in the securities. Securities for this purpose includes shares, stocks, bonds, debenture stock and any promissory note or other instrument evidencing indebtedness to a loan creditor of the company [FA 1989 Sch 12 para 4].

CGT: charge on settlor

5.166 An Inspector can require any person who is (or has been) a trustee, a beneficiary or a settlor in relation to a settlement to give him such particulars as he thinks necessary for the purpose of TCGA 1992 ss 77–79. He must allow at least 28 days to provide the information [TCGA 1992 s 79(6)].

CGT: attributions of gains of overseas settlement to beneficiaries

5.167 The Revenue can require any person to furnish them with such particulars as they think necessary for the purposes of TCGA 1992 ss 87–90. They must allow at least 28 days for this to be done. As indicated at **5.132**, much of TA 1988 s 745 applies for this purpose [TCGA 1992 s 98].

Attribution of gains of non-resident trusts to settlor

5.168 An Inspector can require any person who is (or has been) a trustee, beneficiary or settlor in relation to a settlement to give him such particulars as he thinks necessary for the purposes of TCGA 1992 Sch 5 and s 86. He must allow at least 28 days [TCGA 1992 Sch 5 para 10].

EIS reinvestment relief

5.169 If an Inspector has reason to believe that a person has not given a notice that he is required to give under TCGA 1992 Sch 5B, or has given or received value which would have triggered a requirement to give notice had it not been an amount of insignificant value, or has made or received a repayment which would have triggered a return had it not fallen to be disregarded under Sch 5B para 14AA, he can require that person to furnish him with such information relating to the event or case as the Inspector may reasonably require for the purpose of Sch 5B [TCGA 1992 Sch 5B para 16(5)]. If the Inspector has reason to believe that a claim for reinvestment relief under the Schedule may not be well founded by reason of any such arrangements as are mentioned in TA 1988 Sch 5B para 1(2)(d) or 11(1) or s 293(8) or 308(2)(e) he can require any person concerned to supply a declaration in writing stating whether or not, according to the information which that person has or can reasonably obtain, any such arrangements exist (or existed) together with such other information as the Inspector may reasonably require for the purpose of the provision in question and as the person has or can reasonably obtain. A person concerned for the purpose of para 1(2)(d) is the claimant, the company and any person controlling it, for the purpose of para 11(1) it is the claimant, the company and a person connected with the company, and for the purpose of ss 293(8) and 308(2)(e) it is the company and any person controlling the company. If the claimant appears to have made a no gain/no loss disposal of the shares to his spouse, a notice can also be served on the spouse [TCGA 1992 Sch 5B para 16(6), (7)]. In both cases at least 60 days must be allowed to comply with the notice. The Inspector can also require any person who receives a payment or asset from the company which may constitute value received for the purpose of Sch 5B para 13 and any person on whose behalf such a payment or asset was received to state whether it was received on behalf of someone else and, if so, give their name and address [TCGA 1992 Sch 5B para 16(8)]. Once a claim for relief has been made the Inspector can require any person who holds or has held shares in the company (and any person on whose behalf any such shares are or were held) to state whether the shares are held on behalf of someone else and if so give their name and address [TCGA 1992 Sch 5B para 16(9)].

Discretionary trusts

5.170 The Revenue can require any of the trustees of a trust to provide them with both information about any notifications given by any of the trustees for the purpose of TA 1988 s 481(5B) (certain deposit interest arising to a discretionary trust) and such information as they may reasonably require for the purpose of themselves giving a notification under s 481(5B) with respect to any income arising to the trustees [FA 1995 s 86(12)].

Corporate venturing scheme

5.171 If the Revenue have reason to believe that a company or other person has not given a notice that it is required to give under FA 2000 Sch 15 para 64 or 65 or has given or received value which would have triggered a requirement to give such a notice had it not been of insignificant value, they can require the person concerned to furnish them with such information relating to the event as they may reasonably require for the purpose of Sch 15 [FA 2000 Sch 15 para 66].

Retraining courses

5.172 If the Revenue have reason to believe that a person's employer or former employer who was required to give a notice under ITEPA 2003 s 312 (that the conditions of s 311(4)(a) or (b) have not been met, so relief is not due) has not done so, they can require the employer to provide such information as they may reasonably require for the purpose of s 312 about a failure to begin the course, the continuation of the employment or the re-employment. They must allow at least 60 days for the information to be supplied [ITEPA 2003 s 312(5), (6)].

Employee securities and options

5.173 The Revenue can by notice require any person to provide them with such particulars of any reportable event (see **4.65**) which takes place in the period specified in the notice and in relation to which that person is a responsible person (see **4.65**) as are required by the notice. If no reportable event has taken place in the period the person must state that fact. They must allow at least 30 days to comply with the notice. Once such a notice has been complied with (or the responsible person has made a return – see **4.65**) the Revenue cannot ask anyone else for the same information. A person need not provide particulars if they have already been given in a notice under ITEPA 2003 Sch 5 para 44 [ITEPA 2003 s 421J(4)–(11)].

Approved share incentive plans

5.174 The Revenue can require any person to provide them with information which they reasonably require for the purpose of their functions under the SIP code and which they believe that such person has or can reasonably obtain. In particular, they can ask for information to enable them to decide whether to approve a SIP or to withdraw an approval already given, or to determine the liability to tax (including CGT) of any person who has participated in a SIP, and information about the administration of a SIP and any proposed alteration of its terms. They must allow at least three months to provide the information [ITEPA 2003 Sch 2 para 93].

Approved SAYE option schemes and approved CSOP schemes and enterprise management incentives

5.175 The Revenue have identical powers to those in **5.174** in relation to the three types of approved share option schemes [ITEPA 2003 Sch 3 para 45, Sch 4 para 33, Sch 5 para 51].

Reliefs and clearances

5.176 There are a number of provisions relating to reliefs and clearances where the Revenue can require information in order to determine whether or not to grant the relief or clearances. A detailed consideration of these is outside the scope of this work. The main ones are:

TA 1988 s 79(8)	Contributions to local enterprise agencies
TA 1988 s 306	EIS relief
TA 1988 s 326C	TESSAs
TA 1988 s 326D	TESSAs: Tax representatives of European institutions
TA 1988 s 333	PEPs
TA 1988 s 477A	Building Societies (see SI 1992/10)
TA 1988 s 482(11)	Deposit takers (see SI 1992/12)
TA 1988 s 552A	Tax representatives of overseas insurer
TA 1988 s 555(7)	Overseas entertainers and sportsmen
TA 1988 ss 559–567	Subcontractors in the construction industry
TA 1988 s 604	Occupational pension schemes
TA 1988 s 631	Personal pension schemes
TA 1988 s 658	Purchased life annuities
TA 1988 s 707	Certain transactions in securities: clearance application
TA 1988 s 760	Non-qualifying offshore funds
TA 1988 s 765	Treasury consent for migration of company
TA 1988 Sch 23ZA para 3	Conversion of certain approved retirement benefit schemes
TA 1988 Sch 28B para 11B	VCTs – share exchanges
FA 1988 s 130	Company migration

FA 1990 s 25	Gift aid donations
F(No 2)A 1992 s 28	Charities
FA 1995 s 73	Venture capital trusts
FA 1999 s 85	Advance pricing agreements
FA 2000 Sch 15 para 89	Corporate venturing scheme: advance clearance
CAA 2001 s 118	overseas protected leasing
ITEPA 2003 s 690	application to apply tax to part only of the income of a person who is not resident or ordinarily resident in the UK
ITEPA 2003 s 715	payroll-giving schemes
ITEPA 2003 Sch 5 para 44	Enterprise Management Incentive options

Third party information

5.177 There are also provisions under which a person can be required to provide information to a third party, not to the Revenue, namely as follows.

(*a*) A company which makes a qualifying distribution must, if the recipient so requests in writing, give the recipient a written statement showing the amount or value of the distribution and the amount of the tax credit [TA 1988 s 234(1)].

(*b*) Where a dividend or interest is paid by a UK company it must, within a reasonable period, send an appropriate statement to that person. If the payment is made direct to a bank or building society account it can send the statement to either the bank or the account holder. If the recipient is a nominee he must then, within a reasonable time, send an appropriate statement to the beneficial owner (or to the beneficial owner's bank or building society). The appropriate statement must show the amount of the dividend and tax credit (or the gross interest, net amount paid and rate of tax deducted) and the date of the payment [TA 1988 s 234A(1)–(7)]. Curiously the statement must apparently be sent by post, not handed to the recipient [TA 1988 s 234A(8)]. Failure to comply attracts a penalty of £60 in respect of each offence, subject to a maximum of £600 for any one dividend or interest payment [TA 1988 s 234A(9)].

(*c*) Where allowable loan interest under TA 1988 s 353 is paid, the person to whom it is paid (other than a building society or local authority) must, if the recipient so requests in writing, furnish the recipient with a statement showing the date the debt was incurred, the amount of the debt when incurred, the interest paid in the tax year and the name and address of the debtor [TA 1988 s 366(3)].

(*d*) If at any time interest on a loan ceases to be relevant loan interest or the payer ceases to be a qualifying borrower, the borrower must give notice of that fact to the lender [TA 1988 s 375(1)]. If there is an unreasonable delay in doing so, the borrower is liable to a penalty equal to any tax that has been deducted from the payment [TA 1988 s 375(4A)]. If the lender has reason to believe that any interest has ceased to be relevant loan interest or the borrower is no longer a qualifying borrower, it must furnish the Revenue with such information as is in its possession with respect to the situation [TA 1988 s 375(5)]. Relevant loan interest is interest on a loan made before 9 March 1999 to a person over 65 at the time the loan was made in connection with a home income plan that qualifies for relief under TA 1988 s 365.

(*e*) An insurance company is required to provide information to the policyholder in relation to chargeable events [TA 1988 s 552].

(*f*) The personal representatives of a deceased person, if requested in writing to do so by a person who has (or had) an absolute or limited interest in the residue of the estate of the deceased (or a person who has received a discretionary payment out of the income of the residue), must provide that person with a statement setting out each amount paid or treated as paid to that person as income in the tax year and the amount of any tax at the applicable rate which any such payment has borne [TA 1988 s 700(5)].

(*g*) A life office can at any time, by notice in writing, require an individual who pays premiums on a life policy net of tax by virtue of TA 1988 s 266 to furnish to it a statement in a specified form to enable it to determine whether he is entitled to pay the premiums net [Income Tax (Life Assurance Premium Relief) Regulations 1978, SI 1978 No 1159, reg 3; TA 1988 Sch 14 para 7].

Chapter 6

Assessments and Claims

Income tax

Finality

6.1 Everything comes to an end at some point and although it may not seem like it will to those undergoing an enquiry there will come a point in time when the Revenue decide that they have completed their enquiry into a tax return under ss 9A or 12AC. At this point the Revenue must issue a 'closure notice' to advise the taxpayer that the enquiries have been completed [TMA 1970 ss 28A(1), 28B(1)]. This will either state that no amendment is required or make the amendments necessary to give effect to the Revenue's conclusions [TMA 1970 ss 28A(2), 28B(2)]. In the case of an amendment to a partnership return the Inspector is entitled, by notice to each of the partners, to also amend their individual returns to give effect to his amendment of the partnership return [TMA 1970 s 28B(4)]. A closure notice takes effect when issued [TMA 1970 ss 28A(3), 28B(3)]. There is a right of appeal both against the issue of a closure notice and against an amendment of the self-assessment by the Revenue in consequence of such a notice.

6.2 The legislation gives the taxpayer an important right. If he believes the Revenue have gone far enough with their enquiry he can apply to the Appeal Commissioners for a direction that the Revenue issue a closure notice within a specified period [TMA 1970 ss 28A(4), 28B(5)]. In other words the Revenue can be ordered to stop their enquiry within a specified time period. An application for a closure order is heard and decided in much the same way as appeals against assessments [TMA 1970 ss 28A(5), 28B(6)]. The Commissioners must give the direction applied for unless they are satisfied that there are reasonable grounds for not doing so [TMA 1970 s 28A(6), 28B(7)].

6.3 These provisions also apply for corporation tax purposes, as identical rules are contained in FA 1998 Sch 18 paras 31A–31D.

6.4 In practical terms, if the Appeal Commissioners do direct the Revenue to close their enquiry it does not follow that there will be no tax to pay, or that there is an end to the argument. What it means is that the Revenue will be barred from asking any further questions relating to the tax return under s 19A and will have to make a decision. That decision can of course be either that no amendment to the return is necessary, ie the tax return as submitted is accepted as correct, or that the return is wrong. In the latter case the Revenue will amend the tax assessment put forward by the taxpayer in the return to the figure they believe likely on the information to hand at that point in time.

6.5 In other words, it forces the Revenue make a decision. If this decision is to amend the assessment then this will be done and the appeal process can start if the figures are not agreed. This appeal process can of course involve further correspondence and dialogue in an attempt to settle matters without the costs and uncertainty involved with taking an argument before a tribunal, but this will have to take place outside the enquiry procedure. It is not necessarily sensible to apply for an order for a closure notice. Although it forces the Inspector to make a decision, that will probably be to disallow all contentious deductions and tax all contentious receipts. He will therefore have been forced to adopt a position which he subsequently feels bound to defend, whereas he might not have done so if the enquiry had been allowed to take its course.

Discovery assessments

6.6 The concept of the closure notice is to give the comfort of finality to the taxpayer. It provides a date by which he can be certain his tax affairs are settled and in order. This is a most welcome benefit, but the Revenue need to have a 'get out of jail' card to protect the Exchequer against those who are negligent, or even cheating, and would definitely avoid facing any consequences arising out of their behaviour. That counterbalance is provided by enabling the Revenue to open a year for enquiry if it 'discovers' that something has not been correctly assessed, or that tax relief has been given when it should not have been.

6.7 Because the discovery procedure undermines the finality principle, strict conditions need to be satisfied before the Revenue are able to make a discovery. If the taxpayer has submitted a tax return under TMA 1970 s 8 or 8A in respect of the year of assessment concerned (in the same capacity) they need to show either that:

(*a*) tax is due because of the fraudulent or negligent conduct by the taxpayer, or a person acting on his behalf, eg his accountant [TMA 1970 s 29(4)]; or

(*b*) at the time the 'enquiry window' closed, or the Revenue issued a closure notice, the officer could not have been reasonably expected, on the basis of the information made available before that time, to be aware that tax that ought to have been assessed had not been assessed (or a relief had become excessive) [TMA 1970 s 29(5)].

If the taxpayer has not submitted a tax return they merely need to show that income or capital gains tax that ought to have been assessed have not been assessed or that an assessment has become insufficient or that a relief has become excessive [TMA 1970 s 29(1)]. An objection to the raising of a s 29 assessment on the grounds that neither of the above conditions are met can be taken only on an appeal against the assessment [TMA 1970 s 29(8)].

6.8 Information must be regarded as having been made available to the Revenue if:

(*a*) it is contained in the tax return for the year or in any accounts, statements or document that accompanied the return;

(*b*) it is contained in any claim that has been made for that tax year or in any accounts, statements or document that accompanied the claim;

(*c*) it is contained in any documents, accounts or particulars that are produced to the Revenue for the purposes of any enquiry into the return or claim; or

(*d*) it is information, the existence and relevance of which to the person's tax liabilities, could reasonably be expected to be inferred by an officer from information that had been provided under (*a*) to (*c*) above or otherwise in writing by the taxpayer or his agent,

[TMA 1970 s 29(6)]. The protection for information provided in or with a return does not just cover the return for the year concerned, but also the returns for the two immediately preceding tax years (or accounting periods for a company) and where the taxpayer is a member of a partnership to the partnership returns for the three years [TMA 1970 s 29(7)].

6.9 TMA 1970 s 29 has, in effect, put the decision of the House of Lords in the case of *Scorer v Olin Energy Systems Ltd ((1985) 58 TC 592)* onto the statute books. Accordingly, similar considerations about the availability of information apply where the year concerned falls into the pre-self-assessment era.

6.10 The Revenue are concerned that people might attempt to overwhelm them with a volume of paper that may contain information relevant to the tax return. They reject such a tactic. Their view is that taxpayers have to be aware that the submission of documents may not provide them with protection against a discovery assessment. If they contain so much material that the offices 'could not have been reasonably expected, on the basis of the information made available to him … to be aware' [TMA 1970 s 29(5)] of the point being made, they consider it incumbent on the taxpayer to explain the relevance to them.

6.11 It is questionable to what extent this is right. It probably depends on the information concerned. It is unlikely that the Commissioners will be sympathetic to an Inspector who says 'I could not reasonably have realised that a dividend schedule, or a bank interest certificate, was relevant to the return'. On the other hand if you send the Revenue a 56 page share sale agreement and tucked away on page 54 there is something that makes the agreement conditional the Commissioners might well hold that the Inspector could not reasonably have been expected to infer that that particular clause was relevant. Even with such a long agreement, it is likely that he would be expected to infer that the clauses that refer to the identity of the parties or the amount of the consideration is relevant.

6.12 In other words the Revenue cannot hide behind the fact that they have been sent a lot of documents as an excuse for not even looking at them. Section 29(6) is designed to protect the taxpayer; the Revenue cannot water down that protection administratively by inaction. On the other hand a taxpayer cannot bind the Revenue by hiding relevant information so that it will not be apparent even on a quick skim through what has been sent.

6.13 There are different views as to whether it is sensible to send the Revenue a great deal of additional information with a tax return. They request that things are not sent unless they are necessary to explain an entry in the return. In the early days of self-assessment many Inspectors sent back enclosures, but the Revenue now accept that the taxpayer is entitled to attach whatever information he thinks appropriate. This clearly follows from s 29(6), which envisages enclosures. The main argument against attachments is that the more one gives the Revenue the more they have to ask questions about. A subsidiary argument is that there is no point in sending something that adds little if anything to the entries in the return. The argument in favour of attachments are, firstly, that the more information that is given the less likely it is that the Inspector will need to open an enquiry to ask for explanations of entries and, secondly, that as sending information protects against discovery it is sensible to seek to benefit as much as possible from that protection.

6.14 It is understood that, in practice, enclosures are separated from the return when it is processed. This procedure cannot undermine s 29(6), but it is nevertheless advisable to list the enclosures in the white space on the return so that it is apparent what enclosures were included in case the Revenue subsequently seek to raise an assessment under s 29.

6.15 Taxation is a complex subject which can be difficult to understand. It sometimes happens that both the Revenue and the public think that the law means one thing but it is subsequently found that everyone is wrong. In such circumstances the Revenue cannot make a discovery assessment simply because it changes its view on the applicable law, as there can be no discovery if a return contains an error or mistake that reflected what was the generally prevailing practice at the time [TMA 1970 s 29(2)].

Partnerships

6.16 If an Inspector discovers that something has not been correctly included on a partnership statement he can amend the partnership return to make good any omission or deficiency or eliminate any overstatement [TMA 1970 s 30B(1)]. He must then amend the returns of each of the partners (by notice to them) to give effect to his amendment of the partnership return [TMA 1970 s 30B(2)]. As with an individual's return, he can make such an amendment only if either:

(*a*) the situation discovered is attributable to fraudulent or negligent conduct on the part of the representative partner or any other person who was a partner at the time the return was made; or

(*b*) at the time the enquiry window closed he could not have been reasonably expected, on the basis of the information made available to him before that time, to be aware of the situation,

[TMA 1970 s 30B(4)–(6)].

6.17 Paragraphs **6.8–6.11** above again apply to determine what is available information [TMA 1970 s 30B(7)]. As with an individual's return, the Revenue cannot amend a partnership return if the situation discovered is attributable to an error or mistake as to the basis on which it ought to have been made and it was in fact made on the basis (or in accordance with the practice) generally prevailing at the time when it was made [TMA 1970 s 30B(3)].

Recovery of overpayments

6.18 On the other hand, it is obviously necessary for the Revenue to be able to recover an excessive repayment of tax. Where an amount of income tax or capital gains tax has been repaid to a person which ought not to have been repaid to him that amount can be assessed on him under Sch D Case VI and recovered as if it were unpaid tax [TMA 1970 s 30(1), (4)]. The rules in paras **6.7–6.11** above in relation to discovery assessments apply also to an assessment under s 30 [TMA 1970 s 30(1B)]. The Revenue obviously cannot raise both a discovery assessment and a s 30 assessment in relation to the same item [TMA 1970 s 30(1A)].

6.19 If the original repayment or set-off attracted repayment supplement the excessive supplement can of course also be clawed back by a s 30 assessment [TMA 1970 s 30(2), (3)].

6.20 A s 30 assessment can be made at any time up to the end of the tax year following that in which the amount assessed was repaid (or set-off) or, if later, up to the time that an enquiry into the taxpayer's return is closed (or where applicable the time given by s 36 (see **6.38**)) [TMA 1970 s 30(5), (6)].

Revenue assessments

6.21 A formal tax assessment by the Revenue is an uncommon event as assessments are now usually made by the taxpayer himself, ie by self-assessment. If, however, the Revenue decides that it does need to make an assessment then one can be made by any officer of the Board [TMA 1970 s 30A(1)]. Although differing rules apply to various sources of income, all of the tax chargeable may be included on one assessment [TMA 1970 s 30A(2)]. A notice of assessment has to be served on the person assessed, state the date of issue and the time limits for appealing, and once it has been served it cannot be altered except in the circumstances authorised by legislation [TMA 1970 s 30A(3)–(5)].

Right of appeal

6.22 A person has a right of appeal against:

(*a*) an amendment of a self-assessment by the Revenue under TMA 1970 s 9C (see **3.32**);

(*b*) a conclusion stated, or amendment made, by a closure notice under TMA 1970 ss 28A or 28B (see **6.1**);

(*c*) an amendment of a partnership return under TMA 1970 s 30B(1) (see **6.16**); or

(*d*) an assessment which is not a self-assessment (such as a discovery assessment – see **6.7**),

[TMA 1970 s 31(1)].

6.23 Notice of an appeal must be given in writing to the Inspector (or officer concerned) within 30 days of the date on which the notice of amendment, closure notice or assessment was made, and must specify the grounds of appeal – although on hearing the appeal the Commissioners may (and invariably, if not always, do) allow the appellant to put forward grounds not specified in the notice if they are satisfied that the omission was not wilful or unreasonable [TMA 1970 s 31A].

6.24 An appeal normally goes to the General Commissioners [TMA 1970 s 31B]. However, the taxpayer can elect to bring the appeal before the Special Commissioners instead [TMA 1970 s 31D(1)]. This right of election is not absolute. The Inspector is entitled to refer the election to the General Commissioners, who must override the election unless they are satisfied that the appellant has arguments to present or evidence to adduce on the merits of the appeal [TMA 1970 s 31D(3), (5)]. If the Inspector intends to refer an election to the Commissioners he must give notice to the taxpayer [TMA 1970 s 31D(4)]. Although the legislation does not set out how such a decision is to be made, the reference is probably 'proceedings' before the

Commissioners to which the normal appeal rules will apply. It is hard to envisage how the Commissioners can make a decision without hearing the applicant, so a right to attend a hearing and make representations seems implicit in the provision. There is no right of appeal against a decision of the General Commissioners to override an election [TMA 1970 s 31D(7)]. However, they can themselves revoke it if they subsequently become satisfied that there are arguments or evidence to put forward on the merits of the appeal [TMA 1970 s 31D(6)]. It is unclear whether this procedure is simply designed to weed out pointless appeals or if the Commissioners have a discretion to block an election even where they think that the appeal is meritorious.

6.25 If the appeal relates to a notice of enquiry under s 9A (jeopardy amendments) (see **3.32**) or 12AC (see **3.54**) and notice has been given under TMA 1970 s 28ZA (see **7.64**) referring a question to the Special Commissioners, the remainder of the appeal must be heard by the Special Commissioners unless they otherwise direct (even if the notice of referral was subsequently withdrawn) [TMA 1970 s 31C(1)]. If the assessment is made by the Board (as opposed to an officer of the Board) or if it is under TA 1988 s 350 (to recover tax that should have been deducted under TA 1988 s 349) and the assessment is not a self-assessment the appeal must be heard by the Special Commissioners not the Generals [TMA 1970 s 31C(2)]. There are also a number of other matters for which the Specials have sole jurisdiction (see **7.16**).

6.26 An appeal against a jeopardy assessment cannot be heard until the enquiry is completed [TMA 1970 s 31(2)]. There is no right of appeal against a determination under TMA 1970 s 9D or 12AE (Revenue choice between different cases of Sch D) [TMA 1970 s 31(3)].

6.27 The detailed rules in relation to appeals are considered in **CHAPTER 7**.

6.28 It may seem unnecessary to need legislation to give a remedy to someone who has been assessed more than once, but TMA 1970 s 32 provides for this. If it can be proved to the Board's satisfaction that a person has been assessed more than once for the same cause and for the same period, they must direct that any overcharge is vacated. Should the Board not agree that there has been a multiple charge an appeal can be made to the Appeal Commissioners.

Error or mistake

6.29 The Revenue's power to raise discovery assessments is counterbalanced by a right of the taxpayer to reopen an agreed position to correct an error or mistake. If a person who has paid income tax or capital gains tax under an assessment (including a self-assessment) alleges that it was excessive by reason of some error or mistake in a return he can make a claim to the Board (or in practice the inspector) for relief. Such a claim must be made by notice in writing within five years after the 31 January next following the year of assessment to which the return relates, ie a claim in relation to a 1999/00 return must be made by 31 January 2006 [TMA 1970 s 33(1)]. It was pointed out by the *Marsden v Gustor [2000] STC (SCD) 371* that it is a condition of s 33 that a claimant must have paid the tax in dispute. *Woodcock v IRC ((1977) 51 TC 698)* was a claim by a Schedule E taxpayer to admit expenses. The Revenue refused the claim on the basis that there had been no assessment (as the PAYE scheme does not require one) and this was upheld in the High Court. The Revenue do not appear to have taken the point that there was no return either. That point was taken in *R v IRC, ex p Tracy ((1995) 67 TC 547)*, which concerned a partnership continuation election under the pre-self-assessment legislation. The High Court held that 'it is simply not right or arguable that this letter of election counts as a return', in spite of the wording of TMA 1970 s 118 that a 'return', includes any statement or declaration under the Taxes Acts. The judge felt that this clearly means that any document which is put before the Revenue for the type of proposals for which all formal tax returns are intended counts as a return, and is therefore subject to all the obligations of the taxpayer with regard to making accurate returns.

6.30 On receiving a claim, the Revenue must enquire into the matter and give by way of repayment 'such relief in respect of the error or mistake as is reasonable and just'. They must have regard to all the relevant circumstances of the case. They must consider in particular whether the granting of relief would result in profits dropping out of charge to tax and for that purpose may take into consideration the liability of the taxpayer and assessment made on him for other years [TMA 1970 s 33(3)].

6.31 If the taxpayer's concept of what is reasonable and just differs from the Revenue's he can appeal to the Special Commissioners. It appears that they can consider the matter afresh, ie the taxpayer does not have to prove the Revenue decision is unreasonable but they must follow the principles that the section requires the Revenue to follow. There is no further right of appeal other than on a point of law arising in connection with the computation of income or chargeable gains [TMA 1970 s 33(4), (5)].

6.32 As with discovery, relief cannot be given for an error or mistake as to the basis on which the liability ought to have been computed where the return was in fact made on the basis, or in accordance with the practice, generally prevailing at the time the return was made [TMA 1970 s 33(2A)(a)]. It was held in *Rose, Smith & Co Ltd v IRC ((1933) 17 TC 586)* and again in *Carrimore Six Wheelers Ltd v CIR (26 TC 301)* that the generally prevailing practice is a pure question of fact to be decided by the Commissioners and does not involve any point of law in connection with the computation of profits; the fact that something may affect the amount of the profits does not make it a point affecting the computation of those profits (see *Arranmore Investment Co Ltd v IRC [1973] STC 195*. A claim cannot be made under s 33 in respect of an error or mistake in a claim which is included in the return [TMA 1970 s 33(2A)(b)] – but this is probably because claims have their own time limits, most of which coincide with that under s 33. The Special Commissioners held in *Howard v IRC [2002] STC (SCD) 408* that a BES claim form is not a return and is therefore not within the scope of s 33. Accordingly an error in a claim could only be remedied by making a further claim within the statutory time limit for that claim. At the time the tax return form did not include space for a BES claim. The current return does include a space for an EIS claim, so it is possible that the position is now different.

6.33 An error or mistake claim can similarly be made where a trade, profession or business is carried on by two or more persons in partnership and those persons allege that the tax charged by self-assessments of theirs was excessive by reason of some error or mistake in a partnership return [TMA 1970 s 33A(1)]. The claim must be made by one of the partners (the representative partner) within five years after the filing date under TMA 1970 s 12AA (see **3.51**) [TMA 1970 s 33A(2)]. The duties of the Revenue and the right of appeal mirror those at **6.29–6.32** [TMA 1970 s 33A(3), (5)–(8A)]. If the Revenue agree to amend the partnership return they must also amend the personal returns of the individual partners to give effect to the amendment [TMA 1970 s 33A(4)].

6.34 In *Eagerpath v Edwards (73 TC 427)* the Board refused the claim on the basis that the point in issue had been raised and discussed prior to the assessment being determined by agreement under TMA 1970 s 54(1) (see **7.78**) and TMA 1970 s 46(2) provides that a determination of an appeal 'shall be final and conclusive'. The Special Commissioners upheld the refusal as the point in issue had been aired (albeit only incidentally to the main issue). The taxpayer had conceded that the same tests applied to s 33 as had been applied to the pre self-assessment discovery provisions in *Cenlon Finance Co Ltd v Ellwood ((1961) 40 TC 176)* and *Scorer v Olin Energy Systems Ltd ((1982) 58 TC 592)*. Robert Walker LJ in the Court of appeal held that:

> 'whether that concession was rightly made is a question of law but in the light of Carrimore and Arranmore it cannot possibly be regarded as a question of law in connection with the computation of profits so the Court had no jurisdiction'.

Brooke LJ felt that s 33 is now virtually obsolete and that the taxpayer should have sought judicial review of the Commissioners' decision.

6.35 By contrast, in *Wall v IRC [2002] STC (SCD) 122* the Special Commissioners held that an agreement reached after an inspector has given an enquiry notice under s 9A and before the issue of a completion notice and the consequent amendment of the return did not preclude a claim for an error or mistake.

> 'In the absence of words equivalent to those in sections 54 and 46(2), it seems to me that an amendment of a self-assessment following enquiries has the same status as a normal self-assessment. In other words error or

mistake relief is available under section 33(1) as long as the claim is made within the stated time limit'.

Time limits

6.36 There is a general time limit imposed on the Revenue within which assessments to income tax or capital gains tax must be made. This is five years after the 31 January next following the tax year to which the assessment relates [TMA 1970 s 34(1)].

EXAMPLE

An assessment for the year 2002/03 must be made by 31 January 2009, ie the 31 January next following 2002/03 is 31 January 2004; five years from then is 31 January 2009.

6.37 An objection to an assessment on the grounds that it was made late can only be made on an appeal against the assessment [TMA 1970 s 34(2)].

6.38 This 'normal' time limit does not, however, apply to an assessment on a 'person in default' for the making good to the Crown a loss of income tax or capital gains tax attributable to the fraudulent or negligent conduct of such a person, or of someone acting on his behalf. Such an assessment can be made at any time up to 20 years after 31 January next following the tax year to which it relates [TMA 1970 s 36].

EXAMPLE

If a person puts in an incorrect tax return for 2002/03, fraudulently or negligently, he can only be sure that a demand will not be made after the 31 January 2024 passes, ie the 31 January next following 2002/03 is 31 January 2004; 20 years from then is 31 January 2024.

6.39 If the 'person in default' was a partner in a business this extended time limit also applies to the assessment on any of his partners [TMA 1970 s 36(2)]. Revenue Interpretation RI155 explains that this does not create a joint and several liability but that the purpose of the legislation is to permit each partner to be assessed on his revised profit share.

6.40 Similarly, an act of omission by an European Economic Interest Grouping is deemed to be an act or omission of each member of the grouping [TMA 1970 s 36(4)].

6.41 Where such an extended time limit assessment is made, in determining the tax chargeable the person assessed can require effect to be given to any relief or allowance to which he would have been entitled on a claim or application made within the time allowed by the legislation [TMA

1970 s 36(3)]. In other words, he can make any claims that he would have been able to make if the assessment had been raised at the normal time. The Revenue view is that s 36(3) extends the time limit for claims but not for elections (CGT Manual, paras 13720, 13761). However, it is hard to reconcile this with s 36(3A), which states that in s 36(3) 'claim or application' does not include an election under TA 1988 s 257BA (election to transfer married couples allowance) or under TA 1988 Sch 13B (elections as to transfer of children's tax credit). This suggests that s 36(3) normally covers elections but these two elections, which affect another taxpayer, are disapplied.

6.42 The meaning of 'negligent conduct' was considered in *Hurley v Taylor ((1998) 71 TC 268)* where the judge commented:

> 'I should mention that the expression "fraudulent or negligent conduct" replaced "fraud, wilful default or neglect" in 1989. It is generally assumed, and I assume in this judgement, that this was a change of terminology rather than of substance, and that the large body of case law about fraud, wilful default or neglect is applicable to the new concepts of fraudulent or negligent conduct.'

He later says:

> 'Honest inadequacy is not "fraudulent conduct". It is probably "negligent conduct". The Commissioners had there described the records as unreliable but at least as consistent with honest inadequacy as with dishonest diversion of cash. In *King v Walden (74 TC 45)* the judge commented, "As to whether Mr King was 'negligent', I have no doubt that he was". Mr Woolf argued that the benefit of any doubt should be given to the taxpayer. With that, I agree. But when one finds a taxpayer offering a variety of improbable stories … one is compelled to the view that his conduct in making tax returns and supplying information has at the very least, been negligent.'

In the *Last Viceroy Restaurant v Jackson ((2000) 73 TC 322)* the judge said:

> 'To me it is entirely plain that the Appellants were negligent. A duty falls on everyone in business to conduct their tax affairs with the Inland Revenue properly and to make accurate returns, in particular to assure that the proper returns are made by the entity which is conducting the business that gives rise to assessable tax. In the present case it emerges … that it was not until 1995 that the Revenue was in possession of facts from which it could properly identify the taxable entity … That sprang from the failure by the partners of the Appellant firm to make proper returns to the Revenue'.

6.43 In *King v Walden ((2001) 74 TC 45)* the Commissioners derived, from past cases:

> 'the principle that neglect exists where there has been a failure to give any notice, or to make any return, or to produce or furnish any document

> or other information required by or under the Taxes Act. Neglect also exists where inadequate returns are made by a taxpayer of matters within his own knowledge unless the taxpayer shows that his inadequate return was due to some reason other than neglect. In our view the words "neglect" and "negligent conduct" have the same meaning.'

In *Robertson v IRC [2002] STC (SCD) 182* the Revenue contended that a solicitor acting as an executor was negligent in undervaluing two properties in an IHT return as the executors had not fulfilled their obligation under IHTA 1984 s 216, which required them to make the fullest enquiries that were reasonable practicable, which resulted in an incorrect return being submitted. Mr Robertson actually obtained informal valuations from local valuers which he described as 'estimated value' in the IHT return. The properties were subsequently sold for substantially more than these values. The Special Commissioners had no hesitation in holding that there was no negligence.

> 'The explanations … were reasonable in the circumstances. The course of action taken by Mr Robertson … was reasonable in the circumstances … Mr Robertson did not negligently fail in his capacity as executor. On the contrary, he acted prudently throughout and exercised reasonable care in his capacity as executor. In so far as he was acting in his capacity as a solicitor, he conducted himself throughout at least in the manner and with the skill of a solicitor of ordinary skill exercising ordinary care in relation to executory work'.

6.44 Where an assessment is made on a person for the purpose of making good a loss of tax wholly or partly attributable to fraudulent or negligent conduct, the fact that a person's liability to income tax, or his total income for any tax year, is assessed as greater than it was previously taken to be is not to affect the validity of any income tax reduction made to that person's spouse or partner by virtue of TA 1988 s 257BB (transfer of married couples allowance), 265 (transfer of blind persons allowance) or Sch 13B para 4 (transfer of child tax credit) [TMA 1970 s 37A]. Instead the entitlement to such relief of the person in default must be reduced to reflect the transfer.

6.45 Death alters all of the time limits for raising assessments. For income tax or capital gains tax arising before the death the executors or administrators of a deceased person can only be assessed within three years beginning with the 31 January next following the tax year in which the death occurred [TMA 1970 s 40(1), (3)].

Example

> If the death occurred on 1 December 2002 this was in the tax year 2002/03. The next following 31 January is the 31 January 2004. Three years from then is 31 January 2007.

6.46 If the deceased had been fraudulent, or negligent, an assessment for the purpose of making good to the Crown any loss attributable to such conduct can be made only in relation to tax years that ended within six years before his death and such assessment must again by raised within the three years beginning with the 31 January next following the tax year in which the death occurred [TMA 1970 s 40(2)]. This significantly curtails the normal 20 year limit that applies to live persons. This limit also applies to a default by an EEIG of which the deceased was a member [TMA 1970 s 40(4)].

EXAMPLE

If death occurred on 1 December 2002, ie the 2002/03 tax year then the six years that ended before then are those ending before 1 December 1996:

2001/02	
2000/01	
1999/00	
1998/99	
1997/98	
1996/97	ended 5 April 1997 + 6 = 5 April 2003, so in time
1995/96	ended 5 April 1996 + 6 = 5 April 2002, so out of time

So assessments can be made for all years from 1996/97 provided they are made by 31 January 2007.

Determinations

6.47 If the Revenue have required the submission of a tax return under s 8 or 8A and this is not done by the filing date the Inspector can make a determination, to the best of his information and belief, of the amounts chargeable to income tax and capital gains tax for the year and the amount of income tax payable on those estimated figures [TMA 1970 s 28C(1), (2)]. This reads a bit odd in that it appears that the Revenue can determine the amount of income taxable and the amount of tax due on that income but seem only to be able to determine the amount chargeable to capital gains without then being able to determine the amount of capital gains tax payable! Clearly that would be nonsense. The explanation is that TMA 1970 s 9 (see **3.9**) requires the return to show capital gains but only to calculate the amount of income tax – presumably because there are often too many uncertainties in self-assessing capital gains – and s 28C seeks to reflect the s 8 and 9 obligations.

6.48 Notice of any such determination has to be served on the person on whom it is made and state the date of issue [TMA 1970 s 28C(2)]. It stands until superseded by a self-assessment made by the person, ie he puts in his tax return [TMA 1970 s 28C(3)].

6.49 A determination has the same effect for the purposes of payment, collection and recovery (but not appeals) as if it were a self-assessment, ie the Revenue can sue for the tax they have determined [TMA 1970 s 28C(4)]. If proceedings to collect the tax on a determination are commenced, but before they are concluded the determination is superseded by a self-assessment the proceedings still continue but for the amounts shown in the self-assessment, so the devious cannot prevent a court judgement by filing a return minutes before the hearing; the amount being claimed would merely be replaced by that shown on the return [TMA 1970 s 28C(5)].

6.50 If the Revenue decide to make a determination they must do so within five years of the filing date under s 8(1A) (see **3.17**) or 8A(1A) (see **3.49**) [TMA 1970 s 28C(5)(a)]. If the taxpayer files a tax return to displace the determination he must do so within the same period or, if later, within 12 months of the date of the determination [TMA 1970 s 28C(5)(b)].

Lloyds underwriters

6.51 An Inspector also has power to determine the profits of a Lloyds syndicate [FA 1993 Sch 19 para 3; FA 1994 s 221]. If he is satisfied that the return by the managing agent (see **4.59**) affords correct and complete information, he must determine the profit as loss accordingly. If he is not so satisfied, he must determine the syndicate's profits to the best of his judgement. If he subsequently discovers that a determination understates the profits or overstates the loss, he can vary his original determination. The inspector must serve notice of the determination on the syndicate's managing agent [FA 1993 Sch 19 paras 3, 5].

6.52 Where such a determination is made, varied or modified (whether on appeal or otherwise) the Inspector can ask the managing agent for a return apportioning the profit or loss so determined between the members of the syndicate [FA 1993 Sch 19 para 6]. The amount determined is conclusive against members of the syndicate that the syndicate's profit or loss is in the stated amount [FA 1998 Sch 19 para 7(1)]. It does not appear to be conclusive as to the amount allocated to a particular member.

Corporation tax

6.53 The discovery provisions for corporation tax broadly mirror these at **6.6–6.9** above, the main difference being that fraudulent or negligent conduct of a person who was a partner of the company can also trigger the assessment, provided that some of the conditions in para **6.7** above are met, if they discover that a corporation tax return for an accounting period incorrectly states an amount that affects (or may affect) the tax payable for a different accounting period or that payable by another company [FA 1998 Sch 18 para 41(2)]. This will enable them to then make a discovery assessment for the other accounting period or on the other company to give effect to the determination. The Revenue obviously do not need to show either fraud or negligence or new information that they could not necessarily expect to have been aware of in order to make such a discovery assessment [FA 1998 Sch 18 para 42(2)].

6.54 The comments at **6.10–6.12** above concerning the need to explain the relevance of information where it is not reasonably apparent, also apply equally to companies. Corporate tax self-assessment started from 1 July 1999. The principles established by the House of Lords in *Scorer v Olin Energy Systems Ltd ((1985) 58 TC 592)* apply in relation to earlier periods.

6.55 As with income tax, the Revenue must issue a closure notice. The rules broadly follow those considered at **6.1** onwards, with the exception that it is left to the company to amend its return in accordance with the closure notice and to amend the returns of any other companies affected by the amendment [FA 1998 Sch 18 para 34(1)]. A company can of course make such an amendment even where the normal time limit for an amendment has expired. If the company does not make the amendment within 30 days the Revenue can make it (subject to the normal rights of appeal against an amendment) [FA 1998 Sch 18 para 34(2)–(4)]. If the Revenue conclude that the return was made for the wrong period, the closure notice must specify the accounting period for which it ought to have been (or the first such period if there is more than one ending in the period covered by the return) and the company must amend the return to reflect that period [FA 1998 Sch 18 para 32]. If the effect is that this leaves a period for which no return has been delivered (including none that could be amended so as to become one for the outstanding period), the company must submit a return for that period within 30 days from the date that the Revenue determine the period for which a return should be made (or if later by the filing date specified in the original notice) [FA 1998 Sch 18 para 35]. The power to ask the Commissioners to direct the closure of an enquiry (see **6.2**) again applies [FA 1998 Sch 18 para 35].

6.56 The normal time limit for the making of an assessment or a discovery determination on a company is six years from end of the accounting period to which it relates. However, if fraud or negligence on the part of the company, its agent, or a person who was its partner at the relevant time is involved, the time limit is extended to 21 years after the end of the accounting period to which it relates. An objection to an assessment on the basis that the time limit has elapsed can only be made on an appeal against the assessment [FA 1998 Sch 18 paras 46, 49].

6.57 A notice of assessment has to be served on the company and state the date on which it was issued and give the time limits for any appeal. Once made it cannot be altered except under the provisions of the Taxes Acts [FA 1998 Sch 18 paras 47, 49]. An appeal can of course be brought against any assessment (other than a self-assessment) within the normal 30-day period [FA 1998 Sch 18 para 48].

6.58 Paragraphs **6.28** (relief in cases of double assessment) and **6.29–6.35** (error or mistake claims) also apply to companies, although the time limit for an error or mistake claim is six years from the end of the accounting period to which the return relates and in deciding whether to give relief the Revenue can obviously take into account the tax position of another company which may have benefited under a group relief or similar claim [FA 1998 Sch 18 paras 50, 51]

6.59 If the Revenue believe that certain amounts paid to a company (or allowed by any of set-off) ought not to have been paid they can raise an assessment to recoup the overpayment. The amounts concerned are payments by way of repayment of corporation tax or income tax or payment or a tax credit, repayment supplement, research and development tax credits under FA 2000 Sch 20, land remediation tax credit or life assurance company tax credit under FA 2000 Sch 22, or interest on tax overpaid [FA 1998 Sch 18 para 52(1)–(3)]. The rules in relation to discovery assessments apply to such an assessment. The assessment is under Sch D Case VI and is treated as an assessment to corporation tax for the accounting period in which the unjustified relief was given [FA 1998 Sch 18 para 51(1), (4), (5)]. Such an assessment can be made at any time before the end of the accounting period following that in which the amount was initially repaid or, if later, within three months from the completion of the Revenue's enquiry into the company's tax return for the period concerned [FA 1998 Sch 18 para 53(1)]. If the overpayment was due to fraud or negligence within para **6.56** above, the 21-year time limit under that paragraph instead applies [FA 1998 Sch 18 para 53(2)]. Such an assessment covers interest at the prescribed rate under TMA 1970 s 87A, from the date when the payment being recovered was made until payment of the assessment that recovers it [FA 1998 Sch 18 para 52(6)].

6.60 The provisions considered at **6.47–6.50** in relation to Revenue determinations where a return is not completed, also broadly apply to corporation tax returns [FA 1998 Sch 18 paras 36–43]. A determination can be made if no return is delivered by the filing date (12 months after the end of the accounting period) or if a filing date cannot be ascertained by the later of 18 months of the end of the period specified in the notice requiring a return to be made or three months from the date on which that notice was served on the company [FA 1998 Sch 18 para 31(2)].

6.61 The accounting periods for which a determination can be made are:

(*a*) if there is only one accounting period ending in or at end of the period, that period;

(*b*) if there is more than one accounting period ending in, or at the end, of the period, each of those periods; or

(*c*) if the Revenue have insufficient information to identify the accounting period, such period as the Revenue may determine,

[FA 1998 Sch 18 para 36(3)].

6.62 A determination cannot be made more than five years after the day on which power becomes exercisable. It has no effect if the company can show either that it has no accounting period ending in the period specified in the notice, that it has delivered a return for the accounting period, or that no return is yet due for that period [FA 1998 Sch 18 para 36(5), (6)].

6.63 If a return is delivered but it appears to the Revenue that there is another accounting period ending during the period covered by the notice to make a return that may also be an accounting period but for which no return has been made, they can make a determination to the best of their information and belief for that 'outstanding period'.This power is exercisable both if a filing date for the outstanding period can be ascertained and no return has been delivered, and if a filing date cannot be ascertained, and no return has been made 30 months from the end of the period specified in the notice to make the return or, if later, three months from the date on which that notice was served [FA 1998 Sch 18 para 37(1), (2)]. Such a determination has to be served on the company, state the date of issue, and cannot be made more than five years after the day on which power becomes exercisable. It has no effect if the company can show either that the outstanding period is not an accounting period or that it has delivered a return for the accounting period [FA 1998 Sch 18 para 37(3)–(5)].

6.64 Where the Revenue make a corporation tax determination they can determine not only the tax payable but also any amount forming part of the calculation of the tax payable. They can also determine the dates on which the tax becomes due and payable under TMA 1970 s 59D or 59E [FA 1998 Sch 18 para 38]. For enforcement purposes a determination is treated as a self-assessment [FA 1998 Sch 18 para 39].

Claims and elections

Income tax

6.65 TMA 1970 s 42 sets out the rules which govern claims for tax reliefs and elections other than where a specific relief has its own provisions. All claims for relief, allowances or repayments of tax must be quantified at the time of making the claim [TMA 1970 s 42(1A)]. Where a notice to complete a tax return was issued, the claim or election can only by made by including it in the tax return, or an amendment to it, unless either it could not, at the time of the claim or at any subsequent time, be included in a tax return (eg it is made later than the time allowed to amend the return) or it relates to the PAYE system [TMA 1970 s 42(2), (3)]. Claims and elections on behalf of incapacitated persons may be made by their trustee, guardian, tutor or curator [TMA 1970 s 42(8)].

6.66 In the case of a trade, profession or vocation being carried on in partnership, a claim under TA 1988 ss 84, 91B, 101(2), 471, 472, 504, 531,

570, 571(4), 723(3), 732(4), or Sch 5 paras 2, 6 and 11, or FA 1989 s 43(5), CAA 2001 ss 3, 83, 89, 129, 131, 135, 177, 183, 266, 268, 290. 355, 381 or 569, or F(No 2)A 1992 ss 40B(5), 40D, 41, or 42, must be made by including it in the partnership return if it is possible to do so. If it is not it must be made by one of the partners [TMA 1970 s 42(6), (7)].

6.67 If a claim or election has been made but it is later found that an error or mistake was contained in it, a supplementary claim can be made within the time limit for the original claim [TMA 1970 s 42(9)].

6.68 The general time limit for claims is five years after the 31 January next following the tax year to which it relates, but many provisions contain their own, shorter, time limit. If a claim could not have been allowed but for making an assessment after the end of the tax year to which it relates, the time limit is extended so that the claim can be made up to the end of the tax year following that of the assessment year [TMA 1970 s 43].

6.69 If a discovery assessment is made under TMA 1970 s 29 but it is not made for the purpose of collecting tax lost due to fraud or neglect, any claim, election, application, or other notice which was not timeously made can then be made within a year from the end of the tax year in which the assessment is raised. Any claim or election previously made can also be varied or revoked within that extended time limit, unless the legislation under which it was made makes it irrevocable. A late claim cannot be made for the transfer of aged married persons allowance or children's tax credits. A claim is relevant to a tax year if it relates to that year or is made by reference to an event occurring in that tax year. If the application of this section would alter the income tax liability of another person it cannot be made without that person's consent. Such a late claim cannot exceed the income tax charged on the further assessment [TMA 1970 ss 43A, 43B]. Similar provisions apply where the discovery assessment is raised to cover tax lost by fraud or negligence (see **6.44**).

6.70 Special rules apply to claims and elections which it is not possible to make in a return [TMA 1970 Sch 1A and s 42(11)]. Such claims must be made to an inspector [TMA 1970 Sch 1A para 2(1)]. A claim requiring the repayment of tax must not be made unless the taxpayer holds documentary proof that the tax has been paid (by deduction or otherwise) [TMA 1970 Sch 1A para 2(2)]. If the Board specify the form of a claim it must be made in that form. Such a form must contain a declaration that the particulars given in the form are correctly stated to the best of the taxpayer's information and belief [TMA 1970 Sch 1A para 2(3)–(5)]. If the claimant is non-UK resident (or claims to be non-resident or not ordinarily resident) the Revenue can require a statement or declaration in support of the claim to be made by affidavit [TMA 1970 Sch 1A para 2(6)].

6.71 A person who may wish to make a claim outside a return must keep and preserve the records needed for the purpose of enabling him to make a correct and complete claim. The record keeping requirements mirror those considered at **3.70–3.83** [TMA 1970 Sch 1A para 2A]. The right for the Revenue to amend a return to correct obvious errors considered at para **3.32** also applies to claims [TMA 1970 Sch 1A para 3(1)(a)]. As with a tax return, the taxpayer can amend a claim within 12 months of making it, but if at that stage the Revenue have issued an enquiry notice the amendment cannot be made until after the enquiry into the claim has been completed [TMA 1970 Sch 1A para 3(1)(b), (2)].

6.72 As with tax returns, the Revenue have power to enquire into a claim. They must issue the enquiry notice within the later of the quarter day (31 January, 30 April, etc) following the first anniversary of the date the claim was made or the first anniversary of 31 January following the end of the tax year to which it relates (or the first anniversary of the end of the period to which the claim relates, if that is not a tax year) [TMA 1970 Sch 1A para 5(1), (2)]. If the Revenue enquire into a claim (or amendment) and the claim is subsequently included in a tax return they cannot enquire into the claim again if they enquire into the tax return [TMA 1970 Sch 1A para 5(3)].

6.73 The Revenue's powers under TMA 1970 s 19A to call for information for the purpose of an enquiry (see **5.1**) also apply to an enquiry into a claim [TMA 1970 Sch 1A para 6]. So does the taxpayer's right of appeal against a notice requiring the production of such information (see **5.15**) [TMA 1970 Sch 1A paras 7–11]. The provisions considered at **6.1** and **7.17** in respect of closure notice and appeals against amendments following such a notice apply equally to claims [TMA 1970 Sch 1A paras 7–11]. If the issues on an appeal include any question arising under TA 1988 s 278 (personal reliefs for non-residents), or any question of residence, ordinary residence or domicile, or the question whether TA 1988 s 615(3) (pension funds for service abroad) applies, the time limit for appealing is three months from the date of the closure notice instead of the normal 30 days [TMA 1970 Sch 1A para 9(2)]. On an appeal against the Revenue's amendment to a claim or election, the Commissioners have power to vary the amendment both upwards and downwards [TMA 1970 Sch 1A para 9(3)]. Section 46C(1) and (3) (see **7.16**), which require certain matters to be determined by the Special Commissioners, also apply to claims made under Sch 1A. An appeal on a claim which relates to the administration of an estate must also be heard by the Special Commissioners [TMA 1970 Sch 1A para 10]. Subject to that the taxpayer can elect for the appeal to be heard by either the General or Special Commissioners (subject to the rules considered at **7.16**) [TMA 1970 Sch 1A para 11].

6.74 The Revenue must, as soon as practicable after a claim (or amendment) is made (or after the completion of their enquiry if they decide to enquire into it), give effect to the claim by discharge or repayment of tax (or if the claim relates to PAYE they can give effect to it in some other way). In the case of a partnership claim they must of course give the relief to the individual partners [TMA 1970 Sch 1A para 4]. Obviously, if the claim or amendment is not one for the discharge or repayment of tax this does not apply [TMA 1970 Sch 1A para 4(4)].

6.75 A curious position arises in relation to claims for negligible value under TCGA 1992 s 24. The Revenue's view is that a claim that an asset is of negligible value in the year of claim can be made under Sch 1A. If, however, a claim is made to carry the loss back a year it must be made in the return for the previous year and a claim to carry the loss back two years must be made by amending the previous year's return if that is still in time, or under Sch 1A if it is not. It is difficult to discern the logic of the Revenue's position. Section 24(2)(a) states that where the owner of the asset makes the claim the Act is to apply as if he had sold and immediately reacquired the asset at the time of the claim or at any earlier time specified in the claim. Clearly a claim for the current year can never be made in a return, ie a claim in May 2004 deems the disposal to occur in 2004/05 and the 2004/05 return will not be issued to the taxpayer until after 5 April 2005. If the claim is delayed until after that date it will no longer be a 2004/05 claim but becomes a 2005/06 one. But what if an earlier time is specified in the claim, eg the claim made in 2004/05 is to treat the asset as having been disposed of in 2003/04? The Revenue view is based on the assumption that it is now a 2003/04 claim. However, the legislation seems to be framed in such a way that the claim is still a 2004/05 claim, albeit that it is a claim made in 2004/05 to treat an event as having occurred in 2003/04. It is not a claim for relief; it is a claim to deem a transaction to have occurred.

6.76 Special rules apply if a claim for relief (or an election or notice) involves two or more tax years [TMA 1970 Sch 1B]. Schedule 1B deals with three specific situations. Presumably these are the only cases in which the Revenue believe that a claim can involve more than one year.

6.77 The first is where a person makes a claim for relief for a loss incurred (or payment made) in one tax year (the later year) to be carried back to an earlier year. Such a claim is deemed to be a claim for the later year but need not be included in the tax return for that year [TMA 1970 Sch 1B para 2(1)–(3)]. Effect is to be given to the claim in relation to the later year, whether by repayment or set-off or by treating it as an increase in the self-assessment payments an account or otherwise [TMA 1970 Sch 1B para 2(6)]. This means that the taxpayer is not entitled to simply take relief for the claim by reducing his tax payable for the earlier year. Instead, the tax for that year has to be computed, ignoring the carry back claim, although the tax repayable on the carry back claim (which will be a Sch 1A claim) can be set against the tax due on the self-assessment for the earlier year. The reason for the procedure is that the government want the payments on account for the later year to be based on the tax payable for the previous year, not on that tax reduced by the carry back claim. The claim for relief is for an amount equal to the difference between the sum on which the taxpayer is chargeable for the earlier year and what that would have been if it had been possible to treat the carry back claim as a claim for that earlier year [TMA 1970 Sch 1B para 2(4)]. Where there are associated claims, ie two or more claims of the type covered by Sch 1B or an averaging claim in respect of creative artists, the amount of each claim has to be determined on the assumption that relief had been given for the associated claim in the year [TMA 1970 Sch 1B para

2(5)]. A carry back of capital losses by the personal representatives of a deceased taxpayer is deemed to be made for the purpose of para 2 in pursuance of a claim requiring relief to be given in respect of the loss.

6.78 The second situation dealt with by the Schedule is farmer's averaging. Again the claim is deemed to relate to the later year. The calculation of the claim is the same as under para 2(4), (5) [TMA 1970 Sch 1B para 3(1)–(4)] In so far as the claim results in some profits of the later year being deemed to arise in the earlier, effect is to be given to it by an increase in the tax payable for the later year – which seems to result in also increasing the payments on account due for the year after that [TMA 1970 Sch 1B para 3(5)]. If it results in an overpayment for the earlier year the overpayment is treated as an additional payment on account in respect of the later year. If the paragraph applies twice in relation to the same year of assessment (ie the profits of year two are averaged with those of year one and in the following year are averaged with those of year three) the adjustment in the first year is ignored in determining the amount of the claim in the second [TMA 1970 Sch 1B para 3(6)].

6.79 If, as a result of a farmer's averaging claim, the taxpayer becomes entitled to make or amend under TA 1988 s 96(9) some other claim that would otherwise be out of time that other claim (or amendment) is also deemed to relate to the later year. The amount claimed is again calculated under para 2(4), (5) (see **6.77**) [TMA 1970 Sch 1B para 4(1)–(4)]. If the claim or amendment relates to the earlier year, effect is again to be given to it in relation to the later year by increasing the tax payable for the later year [TMA 1970 Sch 1B para 4(5)].

6.80 Curiously, Sch 1B does not cover a claim for averaging for creative artists. However, the situation in such circumstances is the same as for farmer's averaging. For some reason best known to the draftsman, the detailed rules are contained in TA 1988 Sch 4A para 7.

6.81 The third situation dealt with by the Schedule is the carry back of post-cessation receipts to the date of discontinuance of the trade under TA 1988 s 108. The claim is again deemed to relate to the later year (ie the one in which the receipt arises). The calculation again mirrors that at para 2(4), (5), with the exception that calculating the amount that would have been chargeable if the claim could have been given effect to in the first year, expenses and capital allowances which can be set against the receipt under TA 1988 s 105, are ignored [TMA 1970 Sch 1B para 5(1)–(5)]. It is unclear why such expenses are ignored. It is presumably because the law assumes that such expenses were claimed in the year in which they were incurred, so that an enquiry into the allowability of such expenses would already have been considered and, if necessary, taken place. In practice, in the past, many people have not bothered to make a claim for post-cessation expenses on the off chance that they might subsequently get post-cessation receipts. It may be unwise to adopt that procedure under self-assessment, particularly if post-cessation receipts are still possible more than six years later, so that the time limit for an error or mistake claim for the year in which the expenditure was incurred will have expired. Effect is to be given to the claim in relation to the later year by increasing the tax payable, ie the extra tax payable for the year of cessation is added to the tax payable for the year of the claim [TMA 1970 Sch 1B para 5(6)]. This does not affect the payments on account for the following year though.

Corporation tax

6.82 The rules for claims and elections by companies are contained in FA 1998 Sch 18 paras 54–65. As with income tax claims a corporation tax claim for relief, an allowance or a repayment must be quantified at the time that it is made [FA 1998 Sch 18 para 54]. A claim for any corporation tax relief must be made within six years from end of the accounting period to which it relates, unless any specific relief provides for a longer or shorter period [FA 1998 Sch 18 para 55]. If a company makes a claim or an election but subsequently discovers that a mistake was made in the original claim or election, it can make a supplementary claim within the time limit allowed for the original claim [FA 1998 Sch 18 para 56].

6.83 If a company's claim affects only one accounting period and a company tax return has been demanded for that period, any claim or election that can be made in the return (or by an amendment to it) must be so made [FA 1998 Sch 18 para 57(1)–(3)]. Where the claim cannot be made in a return (for example because it is made before a notice to make the return was issued, or at a time when it is too late to amend the return for the period to which it relates), TMA 1970 Sch 1A (see **6.70**) applies to provide the machinery for the claim and enquiries into it [FA 1998 Sch 18 para 57(4)].

6.84 If a claim or election involves more than one accounting period (ie the event given rise to the claim arises in one accounting period but the claim affects another, in whole or in part) the claim or election is treated as an amendment to the return by the company if a return for the other accounting period has been submitted and is still able to be amended. In any other case it is treated as a claim under TMA 1970 Sch 1A [FA 1998 Sch 18 para 58]. Schedule 1A also applies to any other claim or election not within FA 1998 Sch 18 para 57 or 58. Where Sch 1A applies, the provisions of that Schedule obviously exclude those of Sch 18 [FA 1998 Sch 18 para 59].

6.85 Under certain circumstances corporation tax claims, elections, applications and notices may be made late or revoked or varied, namely where:

(*a*) a company tax return is amended under para 34(2)(b) (see **6.55**), following a closure notice after an enquiry into the company's returns for a different period, and the effect is to increase the tax payable;

(*b*) a discovery assessment is made; or

(*c*) an assessment is made to recover excess group relief,

[FA 1998 Sch 18 para 61(1)]. This does not, however, give a right to revoke a claim or election which is specifically stated to be irrevocable [FA 1998 Sch 18 para 62(1)].

6.86 Any such claim that could have the effect of reducing a relevant liability of the company can be made (or revoked or varied) within a year from the end of the accounting period in which the closure notice is issued or the assessment is made as the case may be [FA 1998 Sch 18 para 62(1), (2)]. A relevant liability for this purpose is the increased liability to tax resulting from the amendment or assessment or any other tax liability of the company for the accounting period to which the amendment or assessment relates, or for a later accounting period ending not later than 12 months after that to which the amendment relates [FA 1998 Sch 18 para 62(3)]. If such a claim affects the tax liability of another person it can be made only with the consent of that person [FA 1998 Sch 18 para 63(1)]. There is no knock on right to the other person to in turn claim reliefs late under para 61 or under TMA 1970 s 43A (the corresponding income tax provision) [FA 1998 Sch 18 para 63(2)]. The reduction in tax liabilities as a result of a claim or claims made late by virtue of para 61 is limited to the amount of the additional liability arising from the assessment or amendment of the self-assessment. If this restriction limits the reduction in a company's tax liability for more than one accounting period, or the reduction of tax liabilities of more than one company, the limited relief must be apportioned in such manner as the Revenue specify (by notice in writing). The person concerned (or persons concerned jointly) can specify a different method of apportionment if they prefer, but must do so (by notice in writing) within 30 days of the Inspector notifying them of his apportionment [FA 1998 Sch 18 para 64]. The Revenue obviously have power to make all such adjustments as are required to take account of the effect of such claims, etc [FA 1998 Sch 18 para 62(4)]. The normal appeal procedures in relation to claims, apply to late claims under this provision [FA 1998 Sch 18 para 62(5)].

6.87 The above rules do not apply where an assessment is made on a company in a case involving fraud or negligent conduct on the part of the company, its agent or a person who was a partner of the company. Instead, if the company so requires, effect must be given to any relief or allowance that the company would have been entitled to (had it made a claim within the time allowed for that claim) in determining the amount of tax to be assessed [FA 1998 Sch 18 para 65].

Group relief

6.88 A claim for group relief must be made by including it in the claimant company's tax return for the period to which it is relevant or by any amendment to that return [FA 1998 Sch 18 para 67]. The claim must specify the amount of the relief claimed and the name of the company surrendering the relief. The amount claimed must be quantified when the claim is made. If any of the claimant company, the surrendering company or any other company by virtue of which the two are members of the same group (or entitled to consortium relief) is non-UK resident in either the accounting period of the surrendering company to which the surrender relates or the corresponding accounting period of the claimant company, it must also state that fact [FA 1998 Sch 18 para 68]

6.89 A group relief claim can be for less than the maximum amount that is available for surrender at the time the claim is made. The claim is, however, ineffective if the amount claimed exceeds the amount that is available for surrender at the time the claim is made [FA 1998 Sch 18 para 69(1), (2)]. For this purpose the amount available for surrender is the amount so available under TA 1988 s 403 (ignoring any part that is deferred by para 31(3), ie that has been claimed by an amendment to the return made during the course of an enquiry that has not yet been completed) less all amounts for which consents to surrender have been given by the company and not withdrawn. Where one or more claims are withdrawn and new claims made on the same day, effect is given first to the withdrawals. If more than one claim is made on the same day and those claims together exceed the amount available for surrender, the Revenue are entitled to determine the one that should be treated as ineffective – but can treat it as ineffective only so far as is necessary to bring the total claimed down to the amount available for surrender [FA 1998 Sch 18 para 69(3)–(6)].

6.90 A group relief claim requires the consent of the company that is surrendering its relief. Such consent must be given by notice in writing to the Revenue office to which the surrendering company makes its corporation tax returns at or before the time that the claim is made. The claim must be accompanied by a copy of the surrender notice. If any of these conditions are not adhered to the claim is ineffective. A consortium relief claim additionally requires the consent of each member of the consortium and a copy of such notice must also be submitted with the claim [FA 1998 Sch 18 para 70]. The notice of consent must contain the name of the surrendering company, the name of the company to whom relief has been surrendered, the amount surrendered, the accounting period of the surrendering company to which it relates and the tax district references of both the surrendering and claimant companies. Otherwise the notice is ineffective [FA 1998 Sch 18 para 71(1)]. A consent notice may not be amended but it can be withdrawn (by notice in writing to the Revenue) and replaced by a fresh consent. A notice of withdrawal of a consent must be accompanied by a notice signifying that the claimant company consents to the withdrawal. The claimant company also has to amend its corporation tax return to reflect the withdrawal of the consent if it is still in time to do so [FA 1998 Sch 18 para 71(2)–(5)].

6.91 If consent to a surrender is given after the surrendering company's tax return has been submitted it must, at the time it gives consent, amend its return to give effect to the consent. It can do this even if the normal time limit for amending the return has expired. If it had carried the loss forward to a later accounting period prior to consenting to surrender it, it must also of course amend its return for that later accounting period. Failure to make such amendment renders the consent notice ineffective [FA 1998 Sch 18 para 72].

6.92 A group relief claim can be withdrawn, but only by amendment to the claimant company's tax return. A group relief claim cannot be amended, so to make a change the original must be withdrawn and a fresh claim made [FA 1998 Sch 18 para 73].

6.93 A group relief claim can be made, or withdrawn, at any time up to the last of the following dates:

(*a*) the first anniversary of the company tax return filing date of the claimant company for the accounting period to which the claim relates;

(*b*) 30 days after any enquiry into that company tax return has been completed;

(*c*) if after any enquiry into the company tax return the Revenue amend the return, 30 days after notice of such amendment is issued;

(*d*) if any amendment to a company tax return is appealed, 30 days after the appeal is finally determined; or

(*e*) any later time that the Revenue may allow,

[FA 1998 Sch 18 para 74(1), (2)]. The normal time limits for amending a return do not apply to an amendment to the extent that it makes or withdraws a claim for group relief. Heads (*b*)–(*d*) above do not apply to an enquiry which is limited to enquiring into a previous amendment making or withdrawing a claim by it for group relief [FA 1998 Sch 18 para 74(3), (4)].

6.94 A claimant company which receives a notice of withdrawal or of a direction by the Revenue must amend its own return (if it is in time to do so) to reflect the new position (including any new consent to surrender). The surrendering company has a right of appeal, within the normal 30-day time limit, against a direction given by the Revenue [FA 1998 Sch 18 para 75].

6.95 If a company has given a surrender notice but the total amount available for surrender is later reduced, it must withdraw its notice of consent (or, if more than one, as many as are necessary to bring the total surrendered within the new limit) within 30 days but can then give a new notice or notices to reflect the reduced amount. It must give notice of withdrawal both to each of the companies affected and to the Revenue. Should it fail to do this the Revenue may give such directions as it sees fit as to which notice or notices are to be ineffective or to be treated as being effective for a reduced amount. The Revenue must notify such a direction to all of the companies affected.

6.96 If a group relief claimant company owes extra tax as a result of a notice of withdrawal of consent or of a Revenue direction, under para 75, and any tax remains unpaid as a consequence for more than six months after the time limit for making or withdrawing group relief claims by the claimant company, the Revenue can assess the tax (in the name of the company in default) on any other company that obtained group relief as a result of the same surrender. Any such assessment cannot be made more than two years after that time limit and the amount assessed cannot exceed the lower of the unpaid tax or the tax that the company that is assessed saves by virtue of the surrender. The company assessed has a right of recovery of the tax (and any interest on overdue tax on it) against the company in default [FA 1998 Sch 18 para 75A].

6.97 If the Revenue discover that excess group relief has been given they can make an assessment to correct the matter [FA 1998 Sch 18 para 76(1)]. This power is without prejudice to their power to raise discovery assessments or to make adjustments by way of discharge or repayment of tax or otherwise where a claimant company has obtained too much relief or a surrendering company has forgone too much. If a para 76 assessment is made because a claimant company does not amend its tax return (including if it is out of time to do so) the Revenue can raise the assessment outside the normal time limits provided that they do so within 12 months of the date on which the surrendering company notifies the withdrawal of its consent or, if later, sends a copy of a new notice of consent to the claimant company (or within 12 months of the Revenue sending the claimant company a notice of a direction under para 75(4)) [FA 1998 Sch 18 para 76(2), (3)].

6.98 The Treasury are given power by regulation to simplify some of the above provisions [FA 1998 Sch 18 para 77]. They have done so by the Corporation Tax (Simplified Arrangements for Group Relief) Regulation 1999, SI 1999/2975. These allow an 'authorised company' on behalf of itself and its 'authorising companies' to apply in writing to the Revenue to be allowed to enter into a simplified arrangement with the Revenue [reg 6(1)]. An authorising company for this purpose is a member of a group of companies (or a consortium company) which is either one of the companies named in the application under reg 6 or is subsequently treated as such a company by agreement with the Revenue [reg 5]. The authorised company is the member of the group that the other companies authorise to act on their behalf in relation to the arrangement [reg 4]. The application for an arrangement must specify the names and tax office references of the authorised company and each of the authorising ones and give sufficient details of their relationship to demonstrate that they qualify as members of the same group (or as a consortium company). It must also contain a statement by each of the companies that they agree to be covered by the arrangements and to be bound by claims, surrenders and withdrawals made under the arrangements. It must be signed on behalf of each of the companies concerned and sent to the tax office dealing with the tax affairs of the authorised company. It must be accompanied by a specimen copy of the statement referred to in reg 10(2) (see **6.102**). In the case of a consortium company, it must also be accompanied by an agreement signed by all of the members of the consortium, and by the consortium company, consenting to the authorised company acting on their behalf in relation to the arrangement [reg 6].

6.99 The Revenue have three months to accept the application, to accept it in relation to only some of the companies or to refuse it. If they do none of these things the authorised company is entitled to enter into the arrangements with the Revenue at any time after the expiry of the three months period. The Revenue can accept the application in relation to only some of the companies only if they believe that a company that they decide to exclude either has failed to comply with its corporation tax obligations in relation to any accounting period or is in liquidation or otherwise in the hands of an insolvency practitioner.

6.100 They can refuse an application completely only if:

(*a*) they believe that one or more of the companies named in the application is not a member of the group (or a consortium company);

(*b*) they believe that one or more of the companies named in the application has failed to comply with its corporation tax obligations for any accounting period;

(*c*) the tax affairs of all, or substantially all, of the companies are not dealt with by the same tax office; or

(*d*) the specimen copy of the statement is not adequate to enable the Revenue to deal with claims for group relief,

[reg 7].

6.101 Once an agreement has been entered into the Revenue can at any time exclude a company from it if they believe that they would have been entitled to exclude it for the reasons in **6.99** or if it ceases to satisfy the conditions to be an authorising company [reg 9]. They can exclude a consortium company if there is a change in the members of the consortium unless a fresh agreement is entered into by the companies in the consortium and sent to the Revenue [reg 8]. They can also agree to add new authorising companies as from the date that they agree to do so [reg 7(5)].

6.102 Where such an agreement is entered into:

(*a*) group relief claims do not need to be accompanied by a copy of the notice of consent by the surrendering company under FA 1998 Sch 18 para 70(4) provided that the surrendering company gives authority for the claim to be made in its tax return or an amendment to its tax return [reg 9A]; and

(*b*) the authorised company can from time to time send the Revenue (in accordance with the specimen sent with the application or another subsequently authorised by the Revenue) a statement containing the information necessary for the amendment of the company tax returns of itself and the authorising companies for the purpose of making and withdrawing claims and surrenders of group relief. This statement must include the information specified in Sch 18 paras 68 and 71 and, where applicable, details showing the effect of the claim on each company's self-assessment, and details showing which, if any, of the returns are under enquiry [reg 10].

6.103 The authorising company remains liable in accordance with the provisions of Sch 18 for any incorrect claim or incorrect company tax return arising from a statement provided under reg 10 even though it did not provide the statement [reg 10(6)].

6.104 Either the Revenue or the authorised company can at any time terminate the arrangement, by notice in writing, with effect from the date of issue of the notice [reg 11(1)]. The authorised company can at any time, by notice in writing to the Revenue, exclude an authorising company from the arrangements with effect from the date of issue of the notice.

6.105 The idea is that, where the Revenue agree that a group can adopt such arrangements, the authorised company will simply send the Revenue a spreadsheet showing all of the group relief claims of the group and the adjusted profits of each company as a result of such claims, and the Revenue will treat that spreadsheet as a notice of amendment of the individual returns of each of the companies to reflect such claims. This should substantially reduce the administrative costs of both large groups of companies and the Revenue.

Capital allowances

6.106 Claims to capital allowances under the Capital Allowances Act 2001 for corporation tax purposes must also be included in the corporation tax return, or an amendment to it, for the accounting period concerned [FA 1998 Sch 18 para 79; CAA 2001 s 3]. The claim must specify the amount claimed, which must be quantified at the time it is made [FA 1998 Sch 18 para 80]. A claim may be withdrawn or amended only by amendment of the tax return [FA 1998 Sch 18 para 81].

6.107 A company's capital allowances claim can be made, amended or withdrawn at any time until the latest of:

(*a*) the first anniversary of the company tax return filing date of the claimant company for the accounting period relating to the claim;

(*b*) 30 days after any enquiry into that company tax return has been completed;

(*c*) if after an enquiry into the company tax return the Revenue amend it, 30 days after notice of such amendment is issued;

(*d*) if any amendment to a company tax return is appealed, 30 days after the appeal is finally determined; or

(*e*) any later time that the Revenue may allow,

[FA 1998 Sch 18 para 82(1), (2)].

6.108 The normal time limits for amendment of a tax return are replaced by the above to the extent that the amendment makes, changes or withdraws a claim for capital allowances. Heads (*b*)–(*d*) above do not apply to an enquiry that is restricted to a previous amendment making, changing or withdrawing a capital allowance claim [FA 1998 Sch 18 para 82(3), (4)].

6.109 If a claim has the effect of reducing the amount of capital allowances available for another accounting period, the company has to make any necessary amendments within 30 days. If it does not do so the Revenue may make its own amendment to make it consistent with the amount available for capital allowances. Such a Revenue amendment is subject to the usual 30-day right of appeal [FA 1998 Sch 18 para 83].

Other claims

6.110 Any claim by a company for R&D tax credits under FA 2000 Sch 20, land remediation credits under FA 2001 Sch 22 para 14, life assurance company credits under FA 2001 Sch 22 para 24 or tax credit for vaccine, etc, research under FA 2002 Sch 13, must be made in its corporation tax return for the accounting period, or by an amendment to that tax return. Such a claim must specify the amount, which has to be quantified at the time the claim is made. A company can amend, or withdraw such a claim only by amending its tax return and only until the first anniversary of the corporation tax return filing date for the relevant accounting period (or any later date that the Revenue may permit) [FA 1998 Sch 18 paras 83B, 83E, 83H–83K, 83M–83Q].

6.111 If a company fraudulently or negligently makes a claim for one of the above tax credits, or discovers that a claim honestly made by it is incorrect and does not remedy the error without unreasonable delay, it becomes liable to a penalty of up to 100 per cent of the excessive amount claimed [FA 1998 Sch 18 paras 83F and 83L].

Telephone claims

6.112 The Board can, by publishing them in whatever manner they choose, give such general directions for the purpose of income tax as they consider appropriate with respect to the circumstances in which, and the conditions subject to which, claims can be made by individuals by telephone or otherwise without a written claim [FA 1998 s 118(1)]. Such claims are valid notwithstanding any enactment requiring a claim to be in writing [FA 1998 s 118(2)]. The Board can use such directions to modify any requirement by which, or under any enactment as to the period within which, a claim is to be made, or the content of a claim, and can provide how any requirement as to the contents of a claim is to be fulfilled where it is not made in writing [FA 1998 s 118(6)]. The directions can also cover elections, the giving of notifications or notices, the amendment of any return and the amendment or withdrawal of any claim, election, notification or notice [FA 1998 s 118(8)]. The Revenue can revoke or vary any such direction [FA 1998 s 118(7)].

6.113 The power of the Board to give directions under s 118 does not extend to the making of any claim, etc, by an individual in his capacity as a trustee, partner or personal representative, but can cover a claim made by an individual through another person acting on his behalf [FA 1998 s 118(4)]. Nor can the directions cover claims under TMA 1970 Sch 1B (claims affecting more than one year) or claims under the Capital Allowances Act 2001 [FA 1998 s 118(5)].

6.114 The current directions are contained in two statements of practice, SP2/03: Business by Telephone–Services Non-Contact Centre Customers and SP3/03: Business by Telephone–Inland Revenue Contact Centres. The list of claims and elections that can be made by telephone are set out as annexes to these statements. Claims, etc, can be made by the individual himself or by an agent, although not all claims can be made through an agent and the Revenue will accept claims from an agent only if they have been able to check his identity and hold evidence that the taxpayer has given his consent for that representative to act on his behalf.

Chapter 7

Appeals and Other Proceedings

7.1 As indicated in **CHAPTER 1** appeals can be heard in the first instance by either the General or Special Commissioners. There is then normally a right of appeal, on a question of law only, to the High Court.

Allocation to the relevant Commissioners

7.2 There are a large number of bodies (or divisions) of General Commissioners. The legislation accordingly sets down rules as to which has jurisdiction [TMA 1970 s 44(1)]. These provide that appeals by an individual should be heard by the General Commissioners for the division which covers:

(*a*) the taxpayer's usual place of residence (provided that there is one in the UK);

(*b*) the taxpayer's place of business in the UK (the head office or place where it is mainly carried on if he has more than one); or

(*c*) the taxpayer's place of employment in the UK,

[TMA 1970 Sch 3 para 2(2), (4)].

7.3 Except where proceedings are brought by the Revenue, the taxpayer can elect in which of the above jurisdictions he wants the appeal heard [TMA 1970 Sch 3 para 2(1)]. The election is made by notice in writing to the Revenue. It must be made at the time that the notice of appeal is given (or in the case of other proceedings, when the taxpayer commences the proceedings) or by such later date as the Revenue allows, and is irrevocable [TMA 1970 Sch 3 para 5]. If the taxpayer does not elect, the Inspector becomes entitled to do so, by notice in writing served on the taxpayer [TMA 1970 Sch 3 para 2(3), 6]. If neither party elects, in practice, the Revenue chooses when it first lists the appeal for a hearing.

7.4 The above rules do not apply to appeals under the PAYE regulations. In this case it is the place specified in the regulations, unless the taxpayer elects for one of the places in 7.2 instead. The Regulations do not in fact specify a place. The relevant regulation (Income Tax (Employments) Regulations 1993, SI 1993/744, reg 100) was repealed by the Income Tax (Employments) (Amendment No 3) Regulations 1996, SI 1996/1312. Accordingly, the position seems to be that the taxpayer, but not the Revenue, has a choice out of the three places in **7.2** but if he does not choose his appeal will, by default, be heard by the Commissioners before which the Inspector chooses to list it for hearing.

7.5 Many accountants and other advisors overlook the opportunity to elect when they make an appeal – probably partly because the appeal form that used to be produced by the Revenue did not contain a space for doing so and partly because few appeals in practice have to be settled by the Commissioners. It needs to be appreciated though, that by the time it becomes apparent that a contentious hearing is necessary it is too late to exercise this choice. In practice the Revenue are normally prepared to accept a late election but cannot do so after proceedings have commenced before the Commissioners, which is probably when the appeal is first listed for a delay hearing.

7.6 For corporation tax (or an income tax appeal in which a UK company chargeable to corporation tax is a party or a TA 1988 s 419 or 420 appeal) the choices are:

(*a*) the place where the company carries on its trade or business;

(*b*) the place where the head office or principal place of business is situated; or

(*c*) the place where the company resides.

Again, it is for the company to elect at the time of its appeal (or such later time as the Revenue may allow) and if the company does not elect the Inspector can do so. If the proceedings are commenced by the Revenue only they have the right to choose the relevant division of Commissioners [TMA 1970 Sch 3 para 4].

7.7 In the case of a partnership appeal, there is no right of election. The relevant division is that for the place where the partnership business is carried on or, if it is carried on in more than one place, where it is mainly carried on [TMA 1970 Sch 3 para 7].

7.8 The Board of Inland Revenue can overrule the above rules by direction in relation to any class of proceedings specified in the direction. Notice of the direction has to be served by the Inspector on the taxpayer, who is then entitled to object to it by notice given to the Revenue within 30 days [TMA 1970 Sch 3 para 8]. Where the taxpayer so objects it appears that the normal rules will apply.

7.9 The Board also has power to direct which division of Commissioners should hear the appeal if either the normal rules do not provide an answer or they would point to a place outside the UK. Again, the Inspector must serve notice of the direction on the taxpayer, but in this case there is obviously no right to object to the direction [TMA 1970 Sch 3 para 9].

7.10 Notwithstanding the above rules, if the parties to the proceedings agree, whether before or after the institution of the proceedings, that the appeal or other proceedings should be brought before the General Commissioners for a division specified in the agreement the proceedings are to be brought before those Commissioners [TMA 1970 s 44(2)].

7.11 Once the General Commissioners have determined an appeal their decision cannot be challenged on the grounds that they were not the appropriate division to hear the appeal, unless, in the course of the proceedings leading to the determination, an objection to their hearing was made before them by the party wishing to challenge it [TMA 1970 s 44(4)].

7.12 The taxpayer normally has a right to elect that a case should be heard by the Special Commissioners not the General Commissioners.

7.13 In addition, the General Commissioners before whom proceedings are brought can themselves arrange with the Special Commissioners for transfer of the proceedings to them (and vice versa). They can do so if they think fit on an application by either party to the appeal, etc (but only if the proceedings are competent to be heard by either body) [TMA 1970 s 44(3)]. The General Commissioners also have power to arrange to transfer the proceeding to the Special Commissioners if those Commissioners agree (even apparently an appeal which the parties have no right to be heard by the Special Commissioners) if they consider that they should do so either because of the complexity of the appeal or the length of time likely to be required for hearing it. The General Commissioners must consider any representations made to them by the parties before deciding on such a transfer [TMA 1970 s 44(3A)].

7.14 A right to bring an appeal or other proceedings under the Taxes Acts (or the NIC legislation) before the Special rather than the General Commissioners is exercised by notice in writing to the Revenue, which must either be given with the appeal notice or by a separate notice given within the same time limit as the appeal. If no such notice is given the appeal must be heard by the General Commissioners [TMA 1970 s 46(1)].

7.15 A decision of the General Commissioners must normally be made by at least two people [TMA 1970 s 44(5)]. A single Special Commissioner can act alone [TMA 1970 s 45(1)]. Specific legislation can of course override this general rule [TMA 1970 ss 44(5), 45(1)]. The Presiding Special Commissioner has power to direct that two or more Special Commissioners should hear a particular appeal. If he does so, any continuation of the appeal can be determined by one provided that the parties to the proceeding consent and after such consultation as is practical with the absent Commissioner. This can be done only if the continuing Commissioner or Commissioners is satisfied that to continue without the absent one will avoid undue delay in the hearing of the appeal [TMA 1970 s 45(1), (3)].

7.16 The following matters are outside the jurisdiction of the General Commissioners; any question involving them must be decided by the Special Commissioners:

(*a*) the value of shares or securities in a UK-resident company (other than shares or securities quoted in the Stock Exchange Daily Official List), which arises in relation to the taxation of capital gains (including corporation tax on chargeable gains);

(*b*) the application of the settlement provision;

(*c*) the administration of estates;

(*d*) liability under TA 1988 s 740 or 743(1) (transfer of assets abroad) – but curiously not apparently s 739;

(*e*) CFCs;

(*f*) The application of TA 1988 s 830 or TCGA 1992 s 276 (territorial sea and the continental shelf);

(*g*) any claim made to the Board (as opposed to one made to an Inspector; including claims by non-residents for personal allowances under TA 1988 s 278, clearance for demergers under TA 1988 s 215, whether a qualified lender under TA 1988 s 376A, Board's direction in relation to friendly societies under TA 1988 s 461, 461C or 465, tax representative of overseas insurer under TA 1988 s 552A, approval of personal pension schemes under TA 1988 s 651, counteraction of a tax advantage under TA 1988 s 703, claim for exemption from TA 1988 s 739 or 740, Board's direction in relation to dual resident investing company under TA 1988 Sch 17, distributor states of offshore funds under FA 1988 s 130, advance clearance of company reorganisation under TCGA 1992 s 135, advance clearance under corporate venturing scheme under FA 2000 Sch 15 para 92, decisions in relation to tonnage tax under FA 2000 Sch 22 para 43 or 126, disposals of oil licences under CAA 2001 Sch 3 para 91, accreditation of community development finance institutions under FA 2002 Sch 16 and various decisions in relation to corporation tax gains on intangible fixed assets under FA 2002 Sch 29 para 88);

(*h*) a claim under TA 1988 s 121 (management expenses of owner of mineral rights);

(*i*) a claim under TA 1988 s 459 or 460 (exemption for certain friendly societies);

(*j*) a claim under TA 1988 s 467 (exemption for certain trade unions and employers' associations);

(*k*) a claim under TA 1988 s 527 or 536 (relief in respect of royalties);

(*l*) double tax relief claims (to the extent they fall within TA 1988 ss 788–791);

(*m*) management expenses claim [TA 1988 s 75(5)];

(*n*) transfer of part only of an insurance business [TA 1988 s 444A];

(*o*) whether overseas income unremittable [TA 1988 s 584];

(*p*) taxable portion of purchased life annuity [TA 1988 s 658];

(*q*) transfer pricing [TA 1988 Sch 28AA para 12; FA 1988 s 111];

(*r*) certain transactions in relation to insurance companies [FA 1989 s 83AB(4); TCGA 1992 ss 211ZA(9), 213(8) and 214A(11)];

(*s*) attribution of gains of non-resident company [TCGA 1992 s 13(15)];

(*t*) transitional relief for charities [F (No 2) A 1997 s 35];

(*u*) referral of questions during corporation tax enquiry [FA 1998 Sch 18 para 31A];

(*v*) questions whether plant and machinery has become part of a building if it affects two or more persons [CAA 2001 s 204(2)];

(*w*) employment income disputes concerning ordinary residence or domicile [ITEPA 2003 s 43];

(*x*) approval of bodies whose subscriptions attract relief against employment income [ITEPA 2003 s 345];

(*y*) approval of payroll given agents [ITEPA 2003 s 715]; and

(*z*) approval of employee share schemes [ITEPA 2003 Sch 2 paras 82 and 85, Sch 3 paras 41 and 44, Sch 4 paras 29 and 32].

[TMA 1970 s 46C(1), (3)].

7.17

Where one of the questions in dispute on:

(*a*) an appeal against an amendment of a self-assessment under TMA 1970 s 9C or FA 1998 Sch 18 para 30 (ie a jeopardy assessment – see **3.32** and **3.64**);

(*b*) an appeal against a conclusion stated in, or amendment made by, a closure notice under TMA 1970 s 28A or 28B or FA 1998 Sch 18 para 34(2) (see **6.1**, **6.3** and **6.55**);

(*c*) an appeal against a discovery assessment or any other assessment that is not a self-assessment; or

(*d*) an appeal against a closure notice or decision in respect of a claim under TMA 1970 Sch 1A (see **6.1** and **6.73**),

relates to one of the above matters that matter has to be determined by the Special Commissioners, although the remainder of the dispute can in theory be decided by the Generals. In practice it normally makes sense for the Special Commissioners to hear the entire appeal if they have to decide one of the issues [TMA 1970 ss 46B(1), 46C(8)].

7.18 To the extent that the question in one of the types of proceeding set out in **7.17** relates to the value of land or a lease of land, that has to be determined by the Lands Tribunal [TMA 1970 s 46D]. So does any question of the value of land in relation to an appeal against a refusal of EIS relief [TMA 1970 s 47B].

7.19 An Inspector can agree to accept a late notice of appeal if he is satisfied that there was a reasonable excuse for not bringing it on time and the application to accept the late notice was made without a reasonable delay. If he is not so satisfied he must refer the application for determination by the General Commissioners (unless an election to have the appeal heard by the Specials has already been exercised) [TMA 1970 s 49].

Procedures on appeals

7.20 The Lord Chancellor has power to make Regulations concerning the jurisdiction of the Commissioners and the practice and procedure before them [TMA 1970 ss 46A, 56B–56D]. He has done so by the Special Commissioners (Jurisdiction and Procedure) Regulations 1994, SI 1994/1811, and the General Commissioners (Jurisdiction and Procedure) Regulations 1994, SI 1994/1812. Except where otherwise indicated the rules set out below apply to both bodies of Commissioners. The first reference below is to the Special Commissioners Regulations and the second to the General Commissioners Regulations.

7.21 Any party to proceedings can serve notice on the Clerk to the Commissioners that he wishes a date for the hearing to be fixed. The Clerk must then fix a meeting and send notice to each party of the place, date and time of the meeting. Unless the parties otherwise agree (or the Commissioners otherwise direct) the date of the hearing must be at least 28 days after the date on which the notice is sent to the parties [SI 1994/1811 reg 3; SI 1994/1812 reg 3]. In the case of an appeal to the Special Commissioners the Clerk has to be satisfied that they have jurisdiction over the proceedings and that he has sufficient particulars of the proceedings and the issues for determination before he need fix a meeting. The Presiding Special Commissioner has power to direct that notice of the meeting should not be sent to each party. It is unclear why or in what circumstances he might be tempted to do so. On the face of it such a notice would be a breach of the human rights of the party concerned.

7.22 Prior to the hearing of the proceedings and for the purpose of enabling the parties to prepare for the hearing or assisting the Tribunal to determine any of the issues in the proceedings, a Special Commissioner can, either on the application of a party or on his own motion, give such directions as he thinks fit. Such an application must be made in writing to the Clerk and must be served by the Clerk on the other parties. The Special Commissioner must consider any objection to the application raised by the other party and, if he thinks it necessary, give the parties an opportunity to be heard. The Tribunal itself can similarly give directions during the course of a hearing [SI 1994/1811 reg 4]. The General Commissioners do not have such a power. It is becoming increasingly common for the Special Commissioners to make such an Order to speed up the hearing of the substantive appeal.

7.23 A party to the appeal can apply for a witness summons where he requires the attendance of a person at the hearing to give evidence or to produce any document in his possession, custody or power. The witness summons requires the attendance of the person at the hearing (or the production of the documents) if he is in the UK. The witness summons must state the name and address of the person to be served and must be signed by the Commissioner issuing it. It is issued to the party who asked for it, leaving it to him to serve it on the person concerned. A witness summons on an individual is served by leaving a copy of the summons with him. One on a UK company or other body corporate is served by leaving a copy of the summons with the secretary (or Clerk) and one on an overseas company with a place of business in the UK is served by leaving a copy of it with a person authorised to accept service of process on the body corporate [SI 1994/1811 reg 5(1)–(5); SI 1994/1812 reg 4(1)–(3)].

7.24 A person who, in obedience to a witness summons, attends the hearing is treated as a witness of the person on whose application the summons was issued and cannot be cross-examined by that person without the leave of the Tribunal hearing the proceedings – which can be given only if the Tribunal decides that he can be treated as a hostile witness. A person cannot be required to attend the hearing unless the summons is served on him at least seven days before the hearing (or he has informed the Clerk that he accepts service). Nor can he be required to attend if, when the summons is served on him, the person serving the summons did not pay him a sum sufficient to cover his reasonable expenses of travelling to and from the hearing or his attendance at the hearing (or agree with him to pay such expenses) [SI 1994/1811 reg 5(6), (7); SI 1994/1812 reg 4(6), (7)].

7.25 A person so summoned cannot be compelled to give any evidence or produce any document that he could not be compelled to give in a court of law. Similarly, an auditor or tax advisor cannot be compelled to produce any document that he could not have been required to produce in response to a TMA 1970 s 20(3) or (8A) notice (see **5.57**), and if he could have been compelled to produce part of a document he need do no more than make a photocopy of that part available for inspection by the Tribunal [SI 1994/1811 reg 5(8)–(10); SI 1994/1812 reg 4(8)–(10)].

7.26 A person served with a witness summons can, by notice in writing to the Clerk, ask for it to be set aside in whole or in part by a Commissioner.

The person who sought the summons is entitled to be heard on such an application [SI 1994/1811 reg 5(11); SI 1994/1812 reg 4(11)].

7.27 If the person fails to attend in obedience to the summons, or attends but refuses to be sworn or to affirm, or refuses to answer any lawful questions, or refuses to produce a document required by the summons (and none of the above exceptions apply) the Tribunal hearing the proceedings can summarily determine a penalty against him of up to £1,000, in the case of the General Commissioners, or £10,000, in the case of the Specials [SI 1994/1811 reg 24(2); SI 1994/1812 reg 4(12)]. Such a penalty can be enforced as if it were tax due and payable [SI 1994/1811 reg 24(3); SI 1994/1812 reg 4(13)].

7.28 It is not necessary to serve a witness summons in order for a witness to be called at a hearing. This procedure is intended to compel the attendance of a person who will not attend voluntarily.

7.29 If a party agrees a document for the purpose of an appeal (unless he states otherwise in the agreement) he is deemed also to admit that the document was written and signed or executed by the person by whom, and on the date on which, it purports to have been done, and if it purports to be a copy of another document that it is a true copy of it. However, in the absence of an express admission or agreement he is not deemed to admit the truth of the content of the document [SI 1994/1811 reg 6; SI 1994/1812 reg 5].

7.30 If two or more appeals have been brought before the General Commissioners for one or more divisions and it appears to two or more of the Commissioners for one of those divisions that some common issue arises in both or all of them, or that both or all are relevant to some common issue, those Commissioners can direct that all of the proceedings should be heard by the same Tribunal in their division either at the same time or consecutively. The Presiding Special Commissioner can direct that, in such circumstances, appeals should be consolidated and heard by the Specials even if one or more has been brought before the General Commissioners [SI 1994/1811 reg 7(1); SI 1994/1812 reg 6(1)]. This power to consolidate hearings can be exercised on an application by a party or on the Commissioners' own motion but cannot be exercised once a hearing has started. Before making a direction, notice must be given to all the parties who are entitled to be heard. Notice of the direction, once made, must be given to all of the parties and to the Clerk of the division whose proceedings have been taken over [SI 1994/1811 reg 7; SI 1994/1812 reg 6].

7.31 If it appears to the Commissioner (on the application of a party or otherwise) that it is desirable that any person other than the Revenue be made a party to an appeal (or other proceedings), they can order that person to be joined as a party and can give such directions to give effect to that order as they think fit. Where the question that affects such a joined party is only one of the issues in the main appeal, he is not entitled to be present at the remainder of the appeal unless all of the other parties consent (unless of course it is a hearing in public). The party who is joined in the proceedings can ask for the proceedings to be transferred to the General Commissioners for the division in which he ordinarily resides (unless the matter is within **7.16** above) or to the Special Commissioners, and the Commissioners can agree if they satisfied that it would be to the convenience of the parties to do so [SI 1994/1811 reg 8(3), (4); SI 1994/1812 reg 7(3)].

7.32 The Special Commissioners (but not the Generals) have power to direct that a preliminary hearing should take place. The Clerk must give at least 14 days notice of such a hearing to the parties. At the preliminary hearing the Commissioner can given such directions as he thinks necessary or desirable to enable the appeal to be disposed of expeditiously, effectively and fairly. Alternatively, if the parties agree, he can determine the appeal without any further hearing [SI 1994/1811 reg 9].

7.33 A Tribunal has power to postpone or adjourn the hearing of an appeal. If it does so the Clerk must give notice of the new place, date and time to the parties (unless this is announced before an adjournment in the presence of the parties). If a hearing is adjourned, so that further information or evidence can be obtained, the Tribunal can give directions regarding the disclosure of such information or evidence to the parties prior to the resumption of the hearing [SI 1994/1811 reg 11; SI 1994/1812 reg 10].

7.34 If it is wished to adduce expert evidence at a hearing the party intending to do so must either:

(*a*) agree with the other party or parties that the substance of the evidence must be disclosed in the form of a written report or opinion in advance of the hearing and not later than such date as is specified in the agreement (and must of course actually make such disclosure); or

(*b*) must apply to the Tribunal for permission to adduce the evidence within 21 days from the date that notice of the hearing is sent to him (or such later time as the Tribunal may permit) stating whether he is willing to disclose the substance of the evidence prior to it being given at the hearing and, if not, the reasons for his objection.

The Tribunal has power to override these rules. If it grants permission under (*b*) it must direct that the substance of the evidence be disclosed to the other party unless it considers that there are special reasons for not doing so [SI 1994/1811 reg 12; SI 1994/1812 reg 9].

7.35 In practice it is normal to reach agreement with the Revenue under (*a*) and send them either the expert's witness statement or the expert's report a few days prior to the hearing. It needs to be realised that the role of an expert witness is to assist the Tribunal, not one of the parties. Accordingly, whilst he will be called by one of the parties he has a duty to give his opinion in a neutral manner.

Hearing and determination of proceedings

7.36 The Tribunal, on hearing an appeal (or in the case of Special Commissioners, on a preliminary hearing), can serve notice on any party, other than the Revenue, at any time before the final determination of the proceedings, directing him within the time specified in the notice:

(*a*) to deliver to it such particulars as it may require for the purpose of determining any of the issues in the appeal; and

(*b*) to make available for inspection by it, or a Revenue officer, all such books, accounts or other documents in his possession or power as are specified in the notice and which, in the opinion of the Tribunal, contain or may contain information relevant to the subject matter of the appeal.

A Revenue officer can, at all reasonable times, inspect and take copies of, or extracts from, any particulars delivered under (*a*) above and he or the Tribunal can take copies of, or extracts from, records delivered under (*b*). Such a notice is commonly referred to as a 'precept'. If a person fails to comply with a precept issued by the General Commissioners they can impose a penalty of up to £300 and if the failure continues after such a penalty has been determined a further penalty or penalties of up to £60 a day for each day on which the failure continues after the day on which the penalty was determined. It appears that failure to comply with a precept issued by the Special Commissioners attracts a penalty of up to £10,000 [SI 1994/1811 regs 10, 24(1); SI 1994/1812 reg 10].

7.37 It should be noted that the Commissioners have power to issue a precept only for information that they believe they require in order to determine an issue in the appeal, or for records that they believe contain information relevant to the subject matter of the appeal. Many Inspectors of Taxes seem under the misapprehension that the Commissioners can issue a precept to assist the Revenue. Indeed the Revenue's Enquiry Manual states (at para 2035):

> 'You may list a case for hearing because you require information ... If it is not [sent in prior to the meeting] then you can ask the Commissioners to determine the assessments, [or] remind them of their powers to issue a precept under Regulation 10.'

Where the Revenue notify the taxpayer that they intend to ask for the issue of a precept, consideration needs to be given as to whether it might be advisable to attend the hearing and object if the information requested does not appear relevant to the appeal. Often it is the answer to an outstanding letter, in which case the relevance of the questions ought to be considered item by item. In many cases General Commissioners seem to readily issue precepts on request without knowing anything at all about the case. It is hard to see how such a precept can be valid. The Commissioners cannot reasonably believe that they require information to decide an issue in the appeal if they do not know what the issues are. Any such objection clearly needs to be raised politely and in a reasoned manner to avoid any risk that taking such procedural points might prejudice the Tribunal against the client.

7.38 In *Campbell v General Comrs of Income Tax for Rochdale and IRC (50 TC 411)* the Commissioners issued a precept for the production of books. Mr Campbell did not produce them and in proceedings for a penalty he contended that the statutory requirements

> 'do not require him to do anything more than sit tight and that if the Inspector of Taxes or the Commissioners ring up and say "Come on, what about these documents" he is entitled to say "They are here, and if you would like to come along I will let you look at them".'

Not surprisingly Templeman J, as he then was, did 'not take that view'. He opined

> 'I believe the boot was on the other foot and that it was up to the taxpayer to say to the Inspector, "I have the documents referred to in item 1", and at least where and when they could be inspected.'

In *Johnson v Blackpool General Comrs and IRC ((1996)70 TC 1)* Mr Johnson did just that. He told the Inspector:

> 'Our books and records will be available at exactly 23.59 hours on the thirtieth day allowed at this address. The time will be regulated by the atomic clock and I shall insist upon being present while you conduct your shameful investigation.'

Robert Walker J felt that:

> 'this gesture towards compliance with the notices was thoroughly unreasonable. Mr Johnson must have known that inspection on the conditions which he sought to lay down would be so highly inconvenient as to be totally unreasonable'.

7.39 At least two, but 'where possible' three and not more than five, General Commissioners can hear an appeal. They must decide which of them is to preside. One, two or three Commissioners form a Tribunal. The Presiding Special Commissioner nominates who is to preside if there is more than one. Once the appeal has started it can be continued before one or more of the Commissioners if the parties consent [SI 1994/1811 reg 13; SI 1994/1812 regs 11, 2].

7.40 At the hearing, the Revenue can be represented by a barrister, advocate, solicitor or any Revenue officer. The taxpayer (and any other party) can be represented by any person whether or not legally qualified. If the Tribunal is satisfied that there are good and reasonable grounds for doing so, they can, however, refuse to permit a particular person to represent a party at the hearing unless that person is legally qualified or has been admitted a member of an incorporated society of accountants [SI 1994/1811 reg 14; SI 1994/1812 reg 12].

7.41 Proceedings before the General Commissioners are now heard in public. The change is apparently to protect the taxpayer as the government consider that a private hearing infringes the taxpayer's human right for justice to be seen to be done, not dispensed in secret. It seems doubtful whether many taxpayers would themselves regard having to expose their tax affairs to the public gaze as a protection. In practice as General Commissioners hearings are not advertised it is improbable that members of the public are likely to appear. Hearings before the Special Commissioners have been in public for many years. However, before either body, any party can apply for the hearing (or part of the hearing) to take place in private. Such an application by the taxpayer must itself be held in private. Where the Commissioner directs that a hearing is to take place in private the following persons are nevertheless entitled to attend:

(*a*) the Clerk and other staff of the General Commissioners;

(*b*) a member of the Council on Tribunals in the capacity of member;

(*c*) any of the Special Commissioners; and

(*d*) a member of the Judicial Statutes Board or any of its committees in the capacity of member,

and the Tribunal can allow any other person to attend with the consent of the parties [SI 1994/1811 reg 15; SI 1994/1812 reg 13].

7.42 The Commissioners can agree to a private hearing only if either they are satisfied that a private hearing is necessary in the interests of morals, public order, national security, juveniles or for the protection of the private life of the party, or they consider that publicity would prejudice the interests of justice. They must give all the parties to the appeal an opportunity to make representations before making a decision, and have to consider whether it would be sufficient for only part of the hearing to be heard in private

7.43 If a party fails to attend or be represented at a hearing of which he has been duly notified the Tribunal can hear and determine the appeal in the absence of that party, unless it is satisfied that there is a good and sufficient reason for such absence. Before deciding to do so they must consider any representations in writing, or otherwise submitted by or on behalf of that party in response to the notice of hearing, and must give any party present at the hearing an opportunity to be heard in regard to those representations. Alternatively, the Commissioners can postpone or adjourn the hearing [SI 1994/1811 reg 16; SI 1994/1812 reg 14].

7.44 Where a taxpayer does not receive notice of the appeal hearing the Commissioners have power to re-open the hearing (or to rehear the matter afresh) (see **7.48**) but the onus is on the taxpayer to show that he did not receive the notice. In *R v General Comrs of Income Tax for Tavistock, ex p Adams ((1969) 46 TC 154)* the Court of Appeal pointed out the difficulties of proving that an individual notice had either been sent out or received and held that, on balance, it had probably not been received by Mr Adams. They seem to have been impressed by the fact that the copy that the Revenue said had been sent to his accountants had not been received either.

7.45 In most cases, notices of a hearing before the General Commissioner are not sent out by the Clerk. They are sent out by the Revenue as agent for, and in the name of, the Clerk. The Revenue are unlikely to be able to prove in most cases that a notice was sent out; they can do no more than explain the system that they operate and point out that if the system worked properly the notice must have been delivered. The Revenue generally seem to place great emphasis that a letter is not returned via the Post Office's dead letter office. It is unclear why. In the real world many letters do not get returned, particularly where they are addressed to a former occupant of part of a multi-tenanted building. It is obviously helpful to the client's case if he has a system for dealing with incoming post – or his accountant to whom a copy of the notice would have been sent does so – for him to give evidence as to the system adopted by the recipient to seek to demonstrate that the notice was not received, rather than received and mislaid. Even if a notice is mislaid it is worth asking the Clerk that the Commissioners consider re-opening the matter. Many will do so as a matter of natural justice if they are convinced that the accountant and his client were not aware of the hearing rather than simply ignored it. If the Commissioners are prepared to do so they will normally fix a hearing to consider whether to rehear the case. Common sense indicates that you should attend such a hearing, not merely make written representations, but also that any outstanding information holding up the agreement of the true position is supplied to the Revenue prior to that hearing and, if possible, the taxable profit or other issue in the appeal agreed with the Inspector.

7.46 At the beginning of the hearing of an appeal the Tribunal must, unless it considers it unnecessary to do so, explain the order of proceeding which it proposes to adopt [SI 1994/1811 reg 17(1); SI 1994/1812 reg 15(1)]. The Tribunal must conduct the hearing in such manner as it considers most suitable to the clarification and determination of the issues before it and generally to the just handling of the proceedings. So far as appears to it appropriate it should seek to avoid formality in the procedure. It is for the Tribunal to determine in which order the parties are to be heard. The parties are entitled to give evidence, call witnesses, question any witnesses (including other parties who give evidence) and address the Tribunal both on the evidence and generally on the subject matter of the proceedings [SI 1994/1811 reg 17(2), (3); SI 1994/1812 reg 15(2), (3)]. In assessing the truth and weight of any evidence the Tribunal can take account of its nature and source and the manner in which it is given. Evidence can be given orally or, if the Tribunal so directs, by affidavit or a written statement. Where it is given in writing the maker of the document can be required to give oral evidence. The Tribunal can require a witness to give evidence on oath or affirmation. It cannot refuse to admit any evidence which would be inadmissible in a court of law but can admit evidence even if it would be inadmissible in a court [SI 1994/1811 reg 17(4)–(7); SI 1994/1812 reg 15(4)–(7)].

7.47 Decisions are made by majority, with the Presiding Commissioner having a casting vote. The decision can be given orally at the end of the hearing or can be reserved and notified later. It must be recorded in a document dated and signed by the Tribunal and notice of the final determination must be sent by the Clerk to the parties. If the decision is not announced at the hearing it is deemed to have been made on the date that the Clerk sends the notice to the parties [SI 1994/1811 reg 18(1)–(4), (8), (9); SI 1994/1812 reg 16]. The Special Commissioners must include in the document recording the decision, a statement of the facts found by the Tribunal and the reason for the determination. The Generals do not need to do so as they can be called upon to state a case. The Specials also have power to reserve the final determination and give a written decision in principle on one or more issues arising in the proceedings and adjourn making the final determination until the further matters arising from that decision have been agreed or determined by the Tribunal at a further hearing. Such a decision in principle must contain a statement of the facts found in relation to it and the reason for the decision. The final determination need not then restate those matters [SI 1994/1811 reg 18(5)–(7)].

7.48 The Commissioners have power either on an application of a party or on their own volition to review and set aside or vary a final determination if they are satisfied that either:

(*a*) the final determination was wrongly made as a result of an administrative error on the part of the Clerk, or any of the staff of the Commissioners, or a party;

(*b*) a party who was entitled to be heard but failed to appear or be represented at a hearing had good and sufficient reason for having failed to do so; or

(*c*) accounts or other information relevant to a party's case had been sent to the Clerk or to the appropriate Revenue officer prior to the hearing but had not been received by the Tribunal until after the hearing.

An application for a review must be made in writing to the Tribunal within 14 days of the notice of the determination having been sent by the Clerk to the party seeking it (or such later time as the Tribunal may allow) and must state the grounds in full. If the review is initiated by the Tribunal it must serve notice on the parties within the 14-day period. The parties have a right to be heard on an application for a review [SI 1994/1811 reg 19; SI 1994/1812 reg 17]. In the case of the Special Commissioners an application can be made to review a decision in principle as well as a final determination.

7.49 Many accountants and other agents seem reluctant to argue an issue before the Commissioners because they are unsure of the procedure. If a large amount of tax is involved it is probably sensible in most cases to engage a barrister, who is a trained advocate. However, for small disputes, particularly those where the client feels strongly about an issue, but cannot afford (or does not wish to afford) legal fees, it is often more sensible for an accountant to take a case than to simply let the Revenue win by default.

7.50 The General Commissioners usually sit in threes. The layout of the room is likely to depend on its shape. Normally the Commissioners will either sit at the end of a T-shaped table with the Revenue on one side of the long end and the taxpayer on the other or the Commissioners will sit on one side of an oblong table with the Revenue and the taxpayer opposite. Their Clerk will either sit next to the Commissioners or on a table of his own to the side. If the hearing is at a normal meeting, where the Commissioners dispose of a long list of appeals, the Revenue will be called in first and will remain in the room throughout the whole list, with taxpayers and/or their agents being called in when their case is reached. Where a hearing is likely to take more than an hour or so the Commissioners will usually arrange a special meeting on a date that is convenient to everyone. In such a case the Revenue representative and the taxpayers will normally be called in together. If it is clear that the matter will take a half-day or a day to argue, it is sensible to tell the Clerk when it is first listed that the appeal is a contentious one and a special meeting will be required. However, it may be necessary to attend the general meeting at which it is listed to ask the Commissioners to fix a date for a contentious hearing. Take your diary, as some Commissioners like to fix the date there and then. Witnesses generally sit with the person who is calling them, ie the taxpayer's witnesses will sit in the taxpayer's party and the Revenue witnesses in the Revenue's party.

7.51 The procedure at the hearing is down to the Commissioners. Normally the taxpayer opens the case, the Revenue respond and the taxpayer is then given an opportunity to comment on new issues raised by the Revenue. There are significant advantages in opening. Not only does this entitle you to the last word but it also allows you to explain the facts. Increasingly, on contentious matters the Revenue are being represented by a specialist inspector who is unlikely to have the full understanding of the facts that you do (or at least should do). If the Revenue open, you may therefore find yourself having to challenge incorrect facts put forward by the Revenue, which could put you off your stride. However, an accountant should not argue a case if he does not feel competent to do so. The case of *Parmar (t/a Ace Knitwear) v Woods [2002] EWHC 1085 (Ch), [2002] STC 846* is a salutary warning. The case was argued before the Special Commissioners by the business's accountant. They appealed to the High Court for a rehearing on the ground that the Appellants did not have a fair hearing before the Commissioners because of the accountant's incompetence. This was refused, except on one issue, but the judge commented:

> 'I should add that I am seriously troubled by the case made on behalf of the Appellants … If Mr Saujani is incompetent, as he says in his evidence, to conduct appeals before the Special Commissioners, it is most unfortunate that his professional body allows him to do so',

and he ordered copies of the papers to be sent to the ICAEW with an invitation to it 'to give consideration to taking remedial action.'

7.52 Assuming that you open, you first explain the issue in dispute, then set out the agreed facts and any unagreed ones, making clear that they are unagreed, then set out your case and arguments and finally say that you are calling the client (and/or whoever else is to give evidence), ask him to state his name and occupation and put to him the questions that you have prepared to draw out the issues you want him to cover. You are not supposed to ask leading questions, ie those the answer to which is 'Yes' or 'No' or otherwise obvious. You should ask neutral questions. The Special Commissioners tend to be a lot stricter on this than the General Commissioners. After you have finished, the Inspector can cross-examine the witness and you can re-examine him on new issues raised by the Inspector.

7.53 Once you call a person as a witness the Revenue can ask him questions on anything they think relevant to the case, not just the issues you have raised with the witness, so calling a person as a witness can be a two-edged sword.

7.54 You then call your next witness, if you have more than one, and go through the same process. After all the taxpayer's witnesses have been called the Revenue then present their case and call any witnesses they have. After the Revenue have finished their case you then have the opportunity to comment on the points raised by the Inspector. The Commissioners will then either ask you and the Inspector to wait outside while they deliberate or will say that they need to consider the issues and will deliver a judgement in writing at a later date. The procedure is fairly informal. You normally remain seated where you are to present your case and the witnesses, similarly, to give evidence. The Commissioners may throw in questions to seek to help them understand your case. If you are not sure of the procedure they are normally happy to help you should you ask.

7.55 The Special Commissioners are generally more formal. The layout is like a court, with the Commissioners on a raised bench and you and the Revenue seated side by side in the well of the court, with space behind for the public and your witnesses. Witnesses go into a witness box near the bench to give their evidence.

7.56 It is sensible to try to agree on a statement of agreed facts with the Revenue in advance of the hearing. The Special Commissioners in particular expect this. A statement of agreed facts saves time as you do not then have to bring evidence to prove such facts. It is also helpful to try to agree with the Revenue a common 'bundle' or file of documents to which either of you wish to refer. Each page of this ought to be numbered consecutively, rather than individually numbering the documents, so that you can refer the Commissioners to the particular page you want them to look at. It is far easier to say, 'You will see from page 46' than, 'You will see from the fifth page of document 11'. You can if you wish also prepare in advance a skeleton argument that you can give to the Commissioners, setting out the bones of your case. However, if you do, you have to give this to the Revenue in advance. It is therefore not necessarily a good idea because it allows them more time to think of counteracting arguments. You can similarly prepare in advance a witness statement and ask the witness to read it out rather than putting a succession of questions to him. Though again, if you do so it becomes part of the case papers and has to be given to the Revenue in advance. Using a witness statement does not bar you from asking the witness additional questions not covered by the statement.

7.57 Some common mistakes are as follows.

(*a*) Forgetting that the Commissioners are primarily arbiters of fact. No matter how erudite your advocacy may be, if you do not present evidence to prove the facts you are likely to lose the case, as if no facts are proved (or agreed) the Commissioners will have difficulty in making any finding. In particular, it is not sufficient to assert something as a fact when you present your case. You need to bring evidence to prove it. Evidence is not necessarily a document. It can be the oral testimony of your client or another witness.

(*b*) Forgetting that the Commissioners know nothing about the case. They have not seen the Revenue's file and know nothing of the background. You need to explain everything that you consider relevant. It is common to put the correspondence with the Revenue into the bundle as this will have set out the main facts and arguments, so referring the Commissioners to the relevant letter and taking them through it is likely to help to bring out the issues.

(*c*) Worrying about how to address the Commissioners. Sir or Madam will do for both sets of Commissioners.

(*d*) Looking at the Revenue all the time. You should be addressing your remarks to the Chairman of the Commissioners

(*e*) Relaxing after you have completed your case. You need to have a pad with you, listen carefully to the Inspector's case and make notes of issues that you want to challenge later or question his witnesses about.

7.58 There is a legal principle that, where there is a written agreement the courts should in general merely interpret that agreement and not look beyond it. The leading case is a Privy Council case, *Narich Pty Ltd v Pay-Roll Tax Comr [1984] ICR 286* at 291. In that case Lord Brandon said (at 291):

> 'The first principle is that, subject to one exception, where there is a written contract between the parties whose relationship is in issue, a court is confined, in determining the nature of that relationship, to a consideration of the terms, express or implied, of that contract in the light of the circumstances surrounding the making of it; and it is not entitled to consider also the manner in which the parties subsequently acted in pursuance of such contract. The one exception to that rule is that, where the subsequent conduct of the parties can be shown to have amounted to an agreed addition to, or modification of, the original

written contract, such conduct may be considered and taken into account by the court.'

Although Privy Council cases are not binding in the UK, the members of the Privy Council are or course the same as those of the House of Lords, so the case has strong persuasive authority. The case was referred to with approval in *Barnett v Brabyn ((1996) 69 TC 133)* and in the VAT case of *Nasim (t/a Yasmine Restaurant)v Customs and Excise Comrs [1987] STC 387.*

7.59 If the market value of an asset on a particular date, or the apportionment of an amount or value, is a material question in a capital gains tax appeal, either party can require the Commissioners to record in its final determination (or decision in principle in the case of the Specials) that market value or apportionment. That value or apportionment can then be proved in any other proceedings relating to capital gains tax (including corporation tax on chargeable gains) by a certificate stating the material particulars and signed by the Inspector (if the appeal was settled by agreement) or the Clerk to the Commissioners or the clerk or registrar of another Tribunal which determined the material issue under TMA 1970 ss 46D or 47B (ie the Lands Tribunal to whom a question was referred) [SI 1994/1811 reg 22; SI 1994/1812 reg 18]

7.60 The Commissioners must refer to the appropriate Tribunal any question that is required to be determined in accordance with TMA 1970 ss 46D or 47B (see **7.18**). The Revenue can alternatively refer the matter to the appropriate Tribunal before the hearing of the appeal starts. Where this happens, the Commissioners hearing the main appeal do not wait for a decision of the other Tribunal. They must finally determine the remaining issues but hold up finally determining the appeal until they are notified of the decision of the other Tribunal [SI 1994/1811 reg 23; SI 1994/1812 reg 19]. In the case of the General Commissioners they can (and should) also be asked to state a case if an appeal is contemplated once they have determined the issues within their remit.

7.61 As stated at **7.47**, the Special Commissioners must set out in their decision the facts found and reasons for their decision. The Generals are not required to do so. Indeed, they are not required to give any explanation of their decision when they hand it down. This is because they can be required to state a case. Any party to the case who is dissatisfied with the determination or decision as being erroneous in point of law can, by notice served on the Clerk within 30 days after the final determination of the appeal, require the General Commissioners to state a case for the opinion of the High Court. A fee of £25 needs to be sent to the Clerk with the notice [TMA 1970 s 56(3)]. The case stated will set out the facts found by the Commissioners, their final determination and usually (although it is not a statutory requirement) their reasoning. The Commissioners can ask the party requiring the case to be stated to identify the question of law on which he requires the case to be stated. They must allow him at least 28 days to do so [SI 1994/1812 reg 20].

7.62 The Clerk must send a draft of the case to all of the parties in the appeal within 56 days of it having been requested (or within 56 days of the question of law having been identified to the Commissioners). The parties then have 56 days to make written representations on the draft to the Clerk (but must copy those representations to the other party). After the expiry of the 56-day period the parties then have a further 28 days to make further representations in response to representations made by other parties. Failure to comply with these time limits does not invalidate the case [SI 1994/1812 reg 21]. At the end of that 28-day period the Commissioners who heard the appeal must state and sign the case. Before doing so they must consider any representations made but do not have to adopt them. If one of the Commissioners had died in the interim the case can simply be signed by the others – or if all have died, by the Clerk. The Clerk then sends the case to the party that asked for it and must tell the other parties that he has done so (he is likely to do this by sending them a copy). The party requesting the case then has 30 days to decide whether or not to appeal. If he wishes to do so he must transmit the case to the High Court within that 30-day period [SI 1994/1812 reg 22]. In Scotland and Northern Ireland the case is transmitted to the Court of Session or the Court of Appeal as the case may be [SI 1994/1812 reg 23].

7.63 This is a somewhat odd procedure. It effectively requires the Clerk to draft a case before the parties know enough about the decision to decide whether to appeal. Accordingly, if a question of law is involved it is almost inevitable that the taxpayer will want to request a case if he the loser, as even if he does not intend to appeal he is likely to want to know why he lost. Clearly, if on receipt of the draft it is obvious that an appeal is inappropriate, it is courteous to tell the Clerk (and the Revenue) as soon as possible so that they do not need to spend time on finalising the case.

Referral of questions during enquiry

7.64 At any time during the course of an enquiry, under TMA 1970 ss 9A(1) (see **3.35**) and 12AC(1) or FA 1998 Sch 18 para 24, any dispute arising in connection with the subject matter of the enquiry can be referred to the Special Commissioners (but not to General Commissioners) for their determination [TMA 1970 s 28ZA(1); FA 1998 Sch 18 para 31A(1)]. The referral has to be jointly by the taxpayer and the Revenue [TMA 1970 s 28ZA(2); FA 1998 Sch 18 para 31A(2)]. The notice of referral must specify the question or questions being referred [TMA 1970 s 28ZA(3); FA 1998 Sch 18 para 31A(3)]. More than one referral can, if necessary, be made in respect of the same enquiry [TMA 1970 s 28ZA(4); FA 1998 Sch 18 para 31A(4)]. The idea of a referral is so that, in a lengthy enquiry, decisions can be made on issues of principle, which may, for example, also affect other years, without waiting for the enquiry to be completed, and hopefully in some cases without a lot of unnecessary work being done that is necessary only if the technical issue is resolved in a particular way.

7.65 Either party can withdraw a request for referral [TMA 1970 s 28ZB(1); FA 1998 Sch 18 para 31B(1)]. This is done by notice to both the other party and the Special Commissioners. The request cannot be withdrawn after the first hearing by the Commissioners in relation to it [TMA 1970 s 28ZB(2); FA 1998 Sch 18 para 31B(2)].

7.66 The Lord Chancellor is empowered by regulation to make provisions with respect to referrals [TMA 1970 s 28ZC]. He does not appear to have done so yet.

7.67 Once a referral has been made (and not withdrawn) the Revenue cannot issue a closure notice in relation to the enquiry, and the taxpayer cannot ask the Commissioners to require them to do so, until the question referred has been finally determined, ie it has been determined by the Special Commissioners and there is no further possibility of its being varied or set aside (disregarding any power to give permission to appeal out of time) [TMA 1970 s 28ZD; FA 1998 Sch 18 para 31C].

7.68 Such a determination by the Special Commissioners is binding on the parties to the same extent as a decision on a preliminary issue on an appeal. It must be taken into account by the Inspector in reaching his conclusions on the enquiry and in formulating any consequent amendment of the return [TMA 1970 s 28ZE(1), (2); FA 1998 Sch 18 para 31D]. If an appeal is made against the Inspector's amendment or the closure notice, the issue determined cannot be re-opened in that appeal except to the extent, if any, that it could have been re-opened if it had been determined as a preliminary issue in the appeal [TMA 1970 s 28ZE(3), FA 1998 Sch 18 para 31D(3)].

Other matters

7.69 An irregularity resulting from a failure to comply with the regulations or a direction of the Tribunal does not of itself render the proceeding void. The Tribunal has to decide what to do to cure or waive the irregularity if it considers that someone has been prejudiced by it [SI 1994/1811 reg 25(1), (2); SI 1994/1812 reg 24(3)]

7.70 Notices required by the Regulations must be given in writing unless the Tribunal authorises otherwise [SI 1994/1811 reg 26; SI 1994/1812 reg 25]. A notice or other document (other than a witness summons) can be sent or delivered to (or served on) any person by post at his normal address or in the other usual specified ways [SI 1994/1811 reg 27; SI 1994/1812 reg 28]. If the person on whom a notice or document (other than a witness summons) is to be served cannot be found or has died or is out of the country the Tribunal has power to dispense with service of the document or can make an order for substituted service (such as by a newspaper advertisement) [SI 1994/1811 reg 28; SI 1994/1812 reg 27].

7.71 Decisions of the General Commissioners are private. The Presiding Special Commissioner can make arrangement for the publication of such of the decisions and determinations of the Specials as he thinks appropriate. Where the hearing was held in private he must ensure that the report is in a form which, so far as possible, prevents the identification of any person whose affairs are dealt with in the decision [SI 1994/1811 reg 20]. The policy of Stephen Oliver QC, the current Presiding Special Commissioner is to publish all decisions.

7.72 The General Commissioners have no power to award costs. The Special Commissioners can make an order awarding the cost of (or costs incidental to) the hearing against any party (including one who has withdrawn his appeal) if they consider that party has 'acted wholly unreasonably' in connection with the hearing. They must give that person an opportunity to make representations against the making of the order. If the amount of the costs is not agreed it must be taxed in the county court by reference to such scales of costs as the Commissioners may order [SI 1994/1811 reg 21].

7.73 In practice, the risk of costs being ordered against the taxpayer seems slight. The Revenue unsuccessfully asked for costs of an adjourned hearing in *Clark (executor of Clark decd) v Green [1995] STC (SCD) 99*. They sought costs without success in *Homeowners Friendly Society Ltd v Barrett [1995] STC (SCD) 90*, *Salt v Young [1999] STC (SCD) 249* (where the Commissioner seemed unwilling to award costs against a taxpayer in person, albeit that he would have been very tempted to do so had he been a lawyer) and *Salt v Buckley [2001] STC (SCD) 262* (where the Commissioner said that the taxpayer should count himself lucky that the Revenue had not warned him that they intended to apply for costs). They did succeed in *Phillips v Burrows [2000] STC (SCD) 112*, where the taxpayer made an application for the decision to be set aside on grounds of ill-health but did not supply the medical report that the Tribunal directed to support this, did not comply with other directions of the Tribunal, even after they had imposed a penalty for such failure, and finally failed to attend or be represented at the hearing of the appeal. The test that costs can be awarded only if the person acts wholly unreasonably is a very hard one to meet. On a number of occasions, such as in *Carter v Hunt [2000] STC (SCD) 17*, the Commissioners have bemoaned the very narrow scope of the power to award costs.

7.74 The taxpayer has not fared much better in obtaining costs. He did so in *Scott (t/a Farthings Steak House) v McDonald [1996] STC (SCD) 381*, where the Commissioner felt not only that the Revenue had acting wholly unreasonably but that they had shown bad faith. However, he held that 'the costs incidental to the hearing' could not cover all of the costs from the date of the appeal. Whilst the costs of preparation for the hearing would be allowable, the costs of the long drawn out pre-trial negotiations would not. The taxpayer also succeeded in *Robertson v CIR (No 2) [2002] STC (SCD) 242*, where the Commissioner could 'detect no rational nor logical or evidential basis for proceeding against Mr Robertson' for penalties.

Onus

7.75 The onus of proof on an appeal is on the taxpayer. The legislation provides that, if the majority of the Commissioners present at the hearing consider, by examination of the appellant or by other evidence, that the appellant is overcharged by an assessment (or any accounts contained in a partnership statement are excessive), the assessment or amount should be reduced accordingly 'but otherwise the assessment or statement shall stand good' [TMA 1970 s 50(6)]. If it appears to them that the taxpayer has been undercharged, the assessment or amount must be increased accordingly [TMA 1970 s 50(7)]. If an amount contained in a partnership statement is reduced or increased, the Revenue must amend the returns of the individual partners to give effect to the change [TMA 1970 s 50(9)]. The burden of proof is the civil burden, ie on the balance of probabilities.

7.76 The position may be different on a discovery assessment under TMA 1970 s 29 (see **6.7**), particularly where it involves an allegation of 'fraudulent or negligent conduct' or an extended time assessment under TMA 1970 s 36 (see **6.38**) Thus, in *Rowland v Boyle [2003] EWHC 781 (Ch), [2003] STC 855* the judge commented:

> 'It is accepted that where, as here, the findings in question involve fraudulent and therefore criminal conduct although the burden of proof is the balance of probabilities there is a degree of inherent unlikelihood that a professional man otherwise of good character would commit such acts, and that such a finding should therefore be regarded as requiring correspondingly stronger evidence before the balance shifts in favour of the Revenue'.

7.77 In *Last Viceroy Restaurant v Jackson ((2000) 73 TC 322)* the Revenue accepted:

> 'that s 36 places on the Revenue the burden of showing that the taxpayer, or any person acting on his behalf, has acted fraudulently or negligently, that there as been a loss of tax to the Crown and that that loss is attributable to fraud or negligence on the part of the taxpayer or person acting on his behalf'.

Although the wording of s 36 (see **6.38**) is not identical to that of s 29 it seems probable that the same onus on the Revenue to show fraud or negligence applies before the onus shifts to the taxpayer to disprove the assessment. In *Hurley v Taylor ((1998) 71 TC 268)* the judge said in relation to s 36:

> 'This requires the Revenue to show (1) fraudulent or negligent conduct by the taxpayer, and (2) a loss of tax attributable to it. On appeal to the Commissioners the burden rests on the Revenue of establishing 1 and 2. If they do not discharge the burden the appeal should be allowed … The burden does not rest on the Revenue to any greater extent than the section 36 burden. If they establish some fraudulent and negligent conduct and some loss of tax attributable to it they have satisfied section

36. From then on section 50(6) takes over and applies as it does for in-date assessments: that is to say, thereafter the burden rests on the taxpayer to establish that the assessment is wrong'.

Settling of appeals by agreement

7.78 If the appellant (or his agent) and the Inspector come to an agreement, before the appeal is determined by the Commissioners, that the assessment or decision under appeal should be treated as upheld without variation, or as varied in a particular manner, or as discharged or cancelled, the same consequences ensue as if the Commissioners had determined the appeal at the time of the agreement [TMA 1970 s 54(1), (5)]. If the agreement is not in writing this applies only if the fact that an agreement was entered into and the terms agreed are confirmed in writing (and the agreement is then deemed to be reached when that confirmation is given) [TMA 1970 s 54(3)].

7.79 The taxpayer (but not the Revenue) can repudiate or resile from the agreement by notice in writing to the Revenue given within 30 days of the agreement being reached. If he does so, the agreement has no effect [TMA 1970 s 54(2)].

7.80 If after giving notice of an appeal, a taxpayer no longer desires to proceed with it, he can give written notice of that fact to the Revenue. They then have 30 days in which to give written notice to the taxpayer that they are unwilling that the appeal should be treated as withdrawn. If they do not do so the appeal is deemed to have been settled at the date of the taxpayer's notice by an agreement that the decision under appeal should be upheld without variation [TMA 1970 s 54(4)].

Recovery of tax not postponed

7.81 Where an appeal is made against an assessment or an amendment to a self-assessment (or a closure notice or a notice under TA 1988 s 753(1) or (3)) the tax charged by the assessment or amendment remains due and payable as if there had been no appeal [TMA 1970 s 55(1), (2)]. This is subject to an important proviso. If the taxpayer has grounds for believing that he is overcharged to tax by the assessment or amendment, he can apply to the Commissioners for a determination of the amount of tax the payment of which should be postponed pending the determination of the appeal. Such an application must be made by notice in writing to the Inspector within 30 days of the issue of the notice of amendment or assessment (or the closure notice), stating the amount by which the taxpayer believes he is overcharged and his grounds for that belief [TMA 1970 s 55(3), (10A)]. An application can be made outside the 30-day time limit if there is a change in the circumstances of the case as a result of which the taxpayer believes he is overcharged [TMA 1970 s 55(3A)]. Curiously there appears to be no time limit at all for such a claim, eg it does not need to be made within 30 days of the change of circumstances.

7.82 The application to postpone is to be heard and determined by the Commissioners in the same way as an appeal [TMA 1970 s 55(5)]. The amount of tax to be postponed is the amount which appears to the Commissioners, having regard to the representations made and any evidence adduced, there are reasonable grounds for believing that the taxpayer is overcharged [TMA 1970 s 55(6)].

7.83 If the circumstances change after the Commissioners have determined the amount of tax to be postponed, the taxpayer can make another application for postponement of a further amount – and the Revenue can similarly apply for part of the tax previously postponed to become payable (they must notify the taxpayer setting out the amount they think should be paid and their grounds for doing so) [TMA 1970 s 55(4)].

7.84 Where a postponement determination is made by the Commissioners the date on which the tax determined is payable must be ascertained as if it were tax charged by an assessment, notice of which was issued on the date of the determination [TMA 1970 s 55(6)(a)]. If the determination relates to the variation of a previous determination the date on which any tax which ceases to be postponed is due is similarly ascertained by reference to the date of the new determination, and if the new determination reduces the tax payable any tax overpaid becomes repayable [TMA 1970 s 55(6)(b)].

7.85 If an appeal is brought against an amendment under TA 1988 s 747(4)(a) (CFCs) as well as against a notice under s 753 the two issues must be dealt with together [TMA 1970 s 55(6A)]. Section 753 was repealed from 1 July 1999, so this provision is no longer current.

7.86 If the taxpayer and the Inspector come to an agreement as to the amount to be postponed it is treated as equivalent to a determination by the Commissioners on the date the agreement was reached (or in the case of an oral agreement was confirmed in writing) [TMA 1970 s 55(7), (8)].

7.87 When the substantive appeal is determined, the due and payable date of tax that was postponed but has become payable is to be ascertained as if it were tax charged by an assessment issued on the date that the Inspector issues to the taxpayer a notice of the total amount payable as a result of the determination. Of course, any tax overpaid becomes repayable [TMA 1970 s 55(9)].

Appeals to the courts

7.88 When a case stated by the General Commissioners is transmitted to the High Court (or the Court of Session) that court hears and determines any question of law and must either reverse, affirm or amend the determination of the Commissioners or remit the matter back to them with the opinion of the court thereon, or can make any other order that it thinks fit [TMA 1970 s 56(6)]. It can also send the case stated back to the Commissioners for amendment if it thinks that appropriate, and deliver judgement after it has been amended [TMA 1970 s 56(7)].

7.89 There is a further right of appeal from a decision of the High Court to the Court of Appeal and thence to the House of Lords [TMA 1970 s 56(8)].

7.90 Where the appeal is initially heard by the Special Commissioners the taxpayer can similarly appeal to the High Court, both in relation to a final decision (other than one which merely incorporates a decision of the Lands Tribunal) and a decision in principle [TMA 1970 s 56A(1)]. Alternatively, the appeal can go direct to the Court of Appeal if all of the parties to the appeal consent, the Special Commissioners certify that the decision involves a point of law relating to the construction of an enactment which was fully argued before them and fully considered by them, and the leave of the Court of Appeal is obtained [TMA 1970 s 56A(2)]. If a decision is varied or set aside by the Commissioners under SI 1994/1811 reg 19 (see **7.48**), any pending appeal against that decision is treated as withdrawn [TMA 1970 s 56A(3)]. The duty and powers of the High Court (or the Court of Appeal) are the same as at **7.48**.

7.91 There is a further right of appeal to the Court of Appeal (if the case was heard by the High Court) and the House of Lords [TMA 1970 s 56A(5), (6)].

7.92 If a decision of either body of Commissioners is appealed the tax is nevertheless payable in accordance with the determination of the Commissioners [TMA 1970 ss 56(9), 56A(8)]. If the High Court judgement (or Court of Appeal judgement in the case of a direct appeal) alters the tax payable and as a result too much tax has been paid, the excess must be refunded with such interest, if any, as the court may allow. If too little tax has been charged the additional tax becomes due and payable 30 days after the date on which the Inspector issues to the taxpayer a notice of the total amount payable in accordance with the order or judgement of the Court [TMA 1970 ss 56(9), 56A(9)].

7.93 In Northern Ireland, appeals go to the Court of Appeal in Northern Ireland, and thence to the House of Lords [TMA 1970 s 58].

Chargeable gains

7.94 The Board of Inland Revenue have power to make regulations as respects the conduct of capital gains tax appeals [TMA 1970 s 57]. They have done so by the Capital Gains Tax Regulations 1967, SI 1967/149. Much of these have since been revoked, but some are still relevant.

7.95 If the market value of an asset on a particular date, or the apportionment of an amount or value, is a material question in any appeal, any other person whose liability to capital gains tax for any period may be affected by that market value or apportionment can apply to be joined as a party to the appeal by writing to the Inspector giving his name and address and setting out the question which may affect his capital gains tax liability, how his liability may be affected and his contention with regard to the question [SI 1967/149 reg 8(1), (2)]. The Inspector must send a copy of the application to the parties to the appeal. If the application is received by the Inspector at least 30 days before the date of the appeal hearing (or when he receives it no date has yet been fixed) and he is satisfied it is proper to join the applicant as a party to the appeal he must do so. If he receives it less than 30 days before the hearing (but before the appeal has been determined) or if he is not satisfied that it is proper to join the applicant he must refer the application to the Commissioners who have discretion to allow or refuse the application [reg 8(3)–(5)]. At the hearing the third party has the same rights (and the same rights of appeal) as the appellant [reg 8(7)].

7.96 If the market value of an asset on a particular date, or the apportionment of any amount or value, may affect the liability to capital gains tax (for any period) of two or more people, either of them can apply to the Commissioners to determine the value or apportionment (unless it has already been determined on an appeal). Such an application is made in writing to the Inspector stating the question for determination and (to the best of the applicant's knowledge) the names and addresses of the other persons whose liability might be affected. The rules for appeals including the right to elect for the application to be heard by the Special Commissioners, will apply to such proceedings [SI 1967/149 reg 9].

7.97 Where a market value at a particular date or an apportionment is finally determined on an appeal that determination is conclusive for capital gains tax purposes between the Revenue and both the parties to the appeal and any person who was entitled to apply to be joined as a third party and did not do so (provided that he had notice of the appeal in reasonable time for making such application and this specified the question in the appeal entitling him to apply) [SI 1967/149 reg 11(1)]. A person who applied to be joined as a third party but whose application was denied is not bound [reg 11(1)(b)]. A value or apportionment is deemed to have been determined on an appeal even if there was no dispute at the hearing in relation to it, if it was a material question in the appeal [reg 11(2)(b)].

7.98 A third party is not bound where an appeal is settled by agreement unless the agreement is between the Revenue and all of the parties to the appeal whose liability may be affected by it. If that is done a third party who could have asked to be joined in the appeal (within **7.95** above) but did not do so is bound by the agreement [SI 1967/149 reg 12].

7.99 A determination or agreement which, under the Regulations, is conclusive against, or in favour of, any person, is similarly conclusive in relation to his personal representative and trustee or assignee in bankruptcy or under a deed of arrangement [SI 1967/149 reg 13(1)]. Something which is conclusive in relation to trustees is also conclusive in relation to a beneficiary who becomes absolutely entitled to the property as against the trustees, and something which is conclusive in relation to personal representatives is also conclusive in relation to a legatee [reg 13(2), (3)]. If an issue is conclusive in relation to a person it is also conclusive in relation to his spouse if the asset is transferred to the other or to any person to whom the asset is transferred under TCGA 1992 s 258 (works of art, etc, under a no gain, no loss transfer) [reg 13(4)].

7.100 A determination or agreement is not, however, conclusive in favour of any person if it is shown that any form of fraud or wilful default committed by (or on behalf of) that person contributed to procure the determination or agreement [SI 1967/149 reg 14].

7.101 For the above purposes:

(*a*) A market value or an apportionment is a material question in an appeal if the adoption of a different value or different apportionment might produce a different determination to the appeal [SI 1967/149 reg 15(a)].

(*b*) A person is one whose liability to CGT may be affected at a particular time only if, on or before that time, there has been (or is deemed to be) a disposal or acquisition of the asset in question by him (or by personal representatives from whom he might acquire the asset as legatee, or by an overseas company or trust whose chargeable gains can to any extent be treated as accruing to him) and he is at that time, or at some time within the tax year in which a disposal or acquisition was made, resident or ordinarily resident in the UK or carrying on a trade in the UK (ie he is within the scope of CGT) [reg 15(b)].

(*c*) If the same persons are personal representatives or trustees in relation to more than one estate or trust they are treated as separate persons in respect of each [reg 15(c)].

(*d*) If it appears to an Inspector that a person is entitled to apply to be joined as a third party in an appeal he can give him notice of the appeal and disclose to him the market value of any asset or the apportionment of any amount or value used in making the assessment or decision from which the appeal is brought – and must do so if that person so requests [reg 16].

(*e*) The Revenue view is that a person is not an interested party merely because he owns a similar asset (eg the owner of a neighbouring similar piece of land is not an interested party) or even if he owns an identical holding of shares in the same company as that held by the appellant [CGT Manual, paras 16434, 16435].

Capital allowances

7.102 Where a question arises as to:

(*a*) the way in which a sum is to be apportioned for the purposes of industrial buildings allowances, agricultural buildings allowances, flat conversion allowances, mineral extraction allowances, research and development allowances, patent allowances, assured tenancy allowances, contributions or the capital allowances supplementary provisions;

(*b*) the market value of any property which is to be determined for the purpose of plant and machinery allowances or of CAA 2001 ss 423 (disposal value for mineral extraction allowances), 559 (effect of successions), 568 or 569 (sales treated as being for alternative amount) or 573 (transfers treated as sales);

(*c*) any determination of the amount of any sums paid, or proceeds, for the purpose of CAA 2001 s 357 (IBA: arrangements having an artificial effect on pricing); or

(*d*) for the purpose of determining any question of apportionment, or the tax liability of either company, under CAA 2001 s 561 (transfer of a UK trade to a company in another EC country),

and it appears that the determination is material to the determination of the tax liabilities (for whatever period) of two or more persons the Commissioners who are to hear and determine the questions are:

(i) if a single body of General Commissioners has jurisdiction over all the persons concerned (and those persons do not agree that the determination is to be made by the Special Commissioners), that body;

(ii) if different bodies of General Commissioners have jurisdiction (and the persons concerned do not agree that the determination is to be made by the Special Commissioners), such of those bodies of General Commissioners as the Board may direct; and

(iii) in any other case, the Special Commissioners,

[CAA 2001 ss 563(1)–(5), 564]. The Commissioners determine the question in the same way as an appeal, but all the persons concerned are entitled to appear before the Commissioners and be heard by them and to make written representations to them [CAA 2001 s 563(6)].

7.103 If a person who is entitled to a capital allowance for income tax purposes enters into an agreement in writing with the Revenue for the tax year in which the allowance would be given effect (eg, following a back duty investigation) and as a result no assessment giving effect to the allowances is made for the year, the allowance must be treated (to the extent set out in that agreement) as if it had been included in an assessment for the year for capital allowances purposes [CAA 2001 s 565].

Chapter 8

Payment of Tax

Income tax

8.1 Income tax for a year is normally payable in three instalments. The first two (the interim payments) are due on 31 January in the tax year and 31 July following the end of the tax year and are normally 50 per cent of the tax liability for the previous year less any tax deducted at source in that year [TMA 1970 s 59A(2)]. The third (balancing payment) is payable on 31 January following the end of the tax year and is of course the tax due for that year less the two interim payments.

The interim payments

8.2 Not every taxpayer has to make interim payments. These are due only if in the preceding tax year:

(*a*) the person was assessed to income tax under TMA 1970 s 9;

(*b*) the amount to which he was assessed exceeded the total tax deducted at source for that year;

(*c*) that excess was at least £500; and

(*d*) that excess was at least 25 per cent of the tax assessed,

[TMA 1970 s 59A(1) and The Income Tax (Payments on Account) Regulations 1996, SI 1996/1654]. The £500 de minimis figure has remained unchanged since the start of self- assessment in 1996/97. The 25 per cent de minimis figure has remained unchanged since 1997/98 (no percentage de minimis applying for 1996/97).

8.3 In other words no interim payments are required if:

(i) the taxpayer had no UK taxable income in the previous year so that there was nothing to be assessed;

(ii) the income was wholly taxed under PAYE and either he was not required to submit a self-assessment tax return or the PAYE wholly satisfied his tax liability (or largely did so, within the de minimis exceptions);

(iii) the taxpayer had UK taxable income in the previous year but was not asked to submit a tax return (but if this was because he had failed to notify chargeability volunteering the interim payments could reduce the penalty for failure to do so);

(iv) the taxpayer was required to submit a return but did not do so and the Revenue have not determined an amount of tax payable (but again, a failure to volunteer interim payments could aggravate the penalties for late filing of the return); and

(v) the excess of the tax payable for the previous year over that deducted at source for that year fell within one of the de minimis limits at (*c*) and (*d*) above.

8.4 If the taxpayer believes that the amount on which he will be assessable to income tax for the current year is less than the 'relevant amount' for the previous year, ie the tax assessable for that year after deducting tax deducted at source, the interim payment can be reduced to 50 per cent of the tax payable (less tax deducted at source) for the current year. This relief must be claimed. There is no statutory form of claim. It can be made by letter. It must, however, state the amount by which the taxpayer believes his interim payments should be reduced (or that he believes that his liability for the current year will be wholly covered by income tax deducted at source) and must state the grounds for that belief. The claim must be made before 31 January following the end of the tax year, because for practical purposes interim payments cease to apply at that stage as the whole of the tax for the year then becomes due [TMA 1970 s 59A(3), (4)].

8.5 If the preceding year's assessment is amended (or is first made) after the first interim payment becomes due (ie after 31 January in the current tax year) the amount of the interim payment due for the following year is also altered to reflect that revised figure [TMA 1970 s 59A(4A)]. Similarly, if a discovery assessment (see **6.7**) is made in relation to the preceding year under TMA 1970 s 59, the following year's interim payments must reflect the sum of the original assessment and the discovery assessment [TMA 1970 s 59A(4B)].

8.6 When the amount of the interim payment due is revised under any of the provisions set out in **8.4** and **8.5** above, such adjustments must be made as are necessary to give effect to the revision, either by making further payments or by the Revenue repaying the excess payment [TMA 1970 s 59A(5)]. In practice, the Revenue tend not to make the repayment unless the taxpayer specifically requests it, but merely credit the overpayment on the taxpayer statement.

8.7 If a taxpayer fraudulently or negligently makes any incorrect statement in connection with a claim to reduce his interim payments he becomes liable to a penalty of up to 100 per cent of the difference between the tax that would have been payable had he not made the incorrect statement and the interim payment actually made by him [TMA 1970 s 59A(6)]. The tax that would have been payable is not necessarily that which would have been due had no claim been made. If the taxpayer can show that a lesser reduction than that actually made would have been justified it appears that the maximum penalty is limited to that amount. It is not clear whether the taxpayer can avoid the penalty by making the interim payment in arrears. There appears to be nothing to stop him doing so even after the Revenue have levied the penalty – but it is probably too late to make an interim payment after the balancing payment has been made.

8.8 It should particularly be noted that the interim payments are based not on the tax liability of the previous year but on that liability as reduced by tax deducted at source. This includes not only actual tax deductions but also amounts treated as deducted or treated as paid on any income for that year [TMA 1970 s 69A(8), (9)]. It also includes any amounts which 'are to be deducted at source' under PAYE and tax credits attaching to UK dividends under TA 1988 s 231 [TMA 1970 s 59A(8)(b)]. The Revenue are given power to provide in the PAYE regulations that, for the purpose of determining the excess under s 59A(1)(c) (see **8.2**), any necessary adjustments in respect of matters prescribed by those regulations is to be made to the amount of tax deducted at source under PAYE [TMA 1970 s 59A(10)]. They do not appear to have yet done so.

8.9 It should be particularly noted that the PAYE to be taken into account seems to be not that actually deducted but the amount which ought to have been deducted under the PAYE regulations. In most cases this will of course be the same amount, but if the taxpayer's employer has not properly applied PAYE it will not be. It needs to be borne in mind that SI 2003/2682 reg 72 (the PAYE Regulations) allows a Collector of Taxes to switch the liability for any under-deduction under PAYE from the employer to the employee if the Collector is satisfied that the employer took reasonable care to apply the PAYE rules and the under-deduction was due to an error made in good faith. The Revenue can similarly switch the liability to settle an underpayment of PAYE to the employee if it considers that the employee received emoluments knowing that the employer had wilfully failed to deduct the tax [SI 2003/2682 reg 81]. From 12 April 2004 a right of appeal has been introduced [SI 2003/2682 regs 72B, 72C and 81A, inserted by the Income Tax (PAYE) (Amendment) Regulations 2004, SI 2004/851]. Prior to 12 April 2004 there was no right of appeal against such directions, nor even any right for the employee to put his side of the story to the Collector or the Board as the case may be. The only remedy was by way of judicial review. This is an expensive procedure and to succeed the taxpayer would probably need to show bad faith on the part of the Revenue, which is likely to be virtually impossible to do. Seeking to reduce the interim payments to reflect PAYE not actually paid risks triggering action by the Revenue under one of these provisions.

8.10 An Inspector of Taxes or other officer of the Board can direct that a taxpayer is not required to make interim payments for a particular year of assessment. Such a direction cannot be made after 31 January following the end of the year of assessment. Where a direction is made, any interim payment already made becomes recoverable [TMA 1970 s 59A(9)]. It appears that such a direction is intended to apply to an individual taxpayer, not to a class of taxpayer, as the legislation requires the person concerned to be specified in the direction. The purpose of this provision is unclear. It is unlikely that Parliament intended to allow an Inspector to pick and chose who should have to make payments on account. Curiously it is an all or nothing provision. The Inspector can absolve a taxpayer from the need to make any payments on account but he cannot permit him to make payments of a lesser amount than required by the statute.

8.11 Interim payments apply only to income tax. If the individual realised capital gains in the preceding year of assessment the tax on such gains is not brought into account in calculating the interim payments for the following year.

Balancing payment

8.12 The balance of the tax is payable on 31 January following the end of the year of assessment [TMA 1970 s 59B(4)]. The amount payable is normally the amount of income tax and capital gains tax calculated in the taxpayer's self-assessment less the aggregate of any payments on account made by him in respect of that year of assessment (including of course interim payments) and less any income tax deducted at source [TMA 1970 s 59B(1)]. Where tax in respect of an earlier year is deducted under PAYE that amount obviously needs to be excluded in determining the tax deducted under PAYE for the year [TMA 1970 s 59B(2)]. Conversely, where tax due for the year of assessment is to be collected under PAYE in a subsequent year it is treated as having been deducted at source in the year to which it relates [TMA 1970 s 59B(2)(b)]. For example, if the Revenue agree to collect the balance due for 2002/03 by amending the taxpayer's PAYE coding for 2004/05, the tax is treated as having been paid in 2002/03. Tax credits in relation to dividends and other distributions are also of course treated as if they had suffered tax deduction at source during the year of assessment [TMA 1970 s 59B(2)(b)].

8.13 If the aggregate of the payments on account and tax deducted at source exceed the tax due for the year of assessment the excess is repayable [TMA 1970 s 59B(1)]. A taxpayer is, however, not entitled to repayment of tax treated as deducted under:

(*a*) TA 1988 s 233(1) – tax credit in respect of non-qualifying distributions.

(*b*) TA 1988 s 246D(1) – foreign income dividends (this provision was repealed by F(No 2)A 1997).

(*c*) TA 1988 s 249(4) – stock dividends.

(*d*) TA 1988 s 421(1) – deemed tax at the Sch F ordinary rate on the release of a loan to a participator within s 419.

(*e*) TA 1988 s 547(5) – tax at the basic rate deemed to have been paid on gains on certain life assurance contracts.

(*f*) TA 1988 s 599A(5) – tax at the basic rate deemed to have been deducted from an unauthorised receipt from an approved superannuation scheme.

[TMA 1970 s 59B(1).] Tax credits in relation to UK dividends or other distributions are not repayable either [TA 1988 s 231(3)]. Such credits were repayable up to 1998/99.

8.14 If a person gave a notice of chargeability under TMA 1970 s 7 by 5 October following the end of the tax year (as that section requires) but the Revenue did not issue him with a tax return (or otherwise require him to complete a return) until after 31 October following the end of that year the due date for the balancing payment is three months after the date of issue of the tax return, instead of the normal 31 January date [TMA 1970 s 59B(3)]. In such a case the balancing payment will normally be the full tax due, as it is unlikely that a return would have been issued in the previous year, so there would be no requirement to make interim payments.

8.15 Obviously, if the Revenue enquire into a return that shows a repayment due they do not have to make the repayment until they have completed their enquiries and issued a closure notice, but they can make a provisional repayment of such amount as they think fit pending the completion of those enquiries [TMA 1970 s 59B(4A)]. If the enquiry is an aspect enquiry and there is likely to be a repayment even if the items under enquiry cannot be substantiated, it is worth requesting an interim repayment.

8.16 If a person's self-assessment is amended following an enquiry into the taxpayer's return or a partnership return (or otherwise corrected or amended by either the Revenue or the taxpayer under TMA 1970 s 9(4)) any additional tax due or repayable as a result of the amendment is payable or repayable 30 days after the notice of the amendment is given if this is later than the normal due date [TMA 1970 s 59B(5) and Sch 3ZA]. In the case of an amendment by the taxpayer under TMA 1970, the 30-day period starts from the day on which the notice of amendment is given [TMA 1970 Sch 3ZA para 2]. If the return is amended by the taxpayer under TMA 1970 s 9B(3) (amendment during an enquiry) and the amendment is not taken into account by the Inspector in his own amendment following the enquiry, it instead runs from the day on which the closure notice is given [TMA 1970 Sch 3ZA para 2(3)]. If the return is amended by the Inspector under TMA 1970 s 28A, the 30 days runs from the day on which the closure notice is issued (or in the case of an amendment during the enquiry to prevent a loss of tax from the day on which the notice of amendment is given) [TMA 1970 Sch 3ZA para 45]. If the return is corrected by the Revenue under TMA 1970 s 9ZB (ie without opening an enquiry) the 30 days runs from the day on which the notice of correction is given [TMA 1970 Sch 3ZA para 3].

8.17 When a partnership return is amended by the taxpayer, the Revenue have to give notice to each of the partners amending his personal return [TMA 1970 s 12ABA(3)(a)]. In such a case the 30 days runs from the date that such notice is given [TMA 1970 Sch 3ZA para 6]. If the Revenue correct a partnership return, it runs from the date the correction is notified by the Revenue to the partner who made the return [TMA 1970 Sch 3ZA para 7]. Where the Revenue enquire into a partnership return, the Revenue must not only issue a closure notice but must notify each individual partner of the amendment to his individual return [TMA 1970 s 28B(4)(a)]. It is the issue of those individual notices that start the 30-day period running [TMA 1970 Sch 3ZA para 8].

8.18 If an Inspector of Taxes makes a determination under TMA 1970 s 28C of the tax due from a person in the absence of a return, the tax so determined is payable as if it were a self-assessment [TMA 1970 s 28C(3)]. The due date for such tax appears to be the normal 31 January date (unless **8.14** above applies), even though the determination may not have been made at that time. Such a determination cannot be appealed against but is automatically displaced if and when the taxpayer submits his tax return (provided that he does so within five years from the filing date or, if later, within 12 months of the date of the Revenue's determination). Where this is done the normal due date applies, ie 31 January or the date given by **8.14** above. Filing the return does not create a later due date for any tax payable or repayable [TMA 1970 s 59B(5A)].

8.19 The due date for tax payable on an assessment (other than a self-assessment or Revenue determination) is 30 days after the notice of assessment is given [TMA 1970 s 59B(6)]. This will apply to discovery assessments and to special assessments, such as to recover from a non-taxpayer tax deducted at source. It should be noted that the 30-day period runs from the day on which the notice of assessment is given, not from the day on which the assessment is made. This is probably the date that the taxpayer receives the notice (or rather the date on which he would have done so in the normal course of post – two days after posting for first class post and four days for second class – unless he can prove that he actually received it on a later date), not the date that the Inspector sends it to him (*Wing Hung Lai v Bale [1999] STC (SCD) 238*). Although the *Wing Hung Lai* case dealt with the interpretation of 'given' in TMA 1970 s 9A there is no logical reason why the word should be interpreted differently in s 59B.

8.20 Where a discovery assessment is made in respect of a partnership statement the Revenue must notify each individual partner amending his individual return [TMA 1970 s 30B(2)(a)]. The tax arising from the amendment is payable within 30 days after the issue of that notification [TMA 1970 Sch 3ZA para 9]. A similar procedure applies on a partnership error or mistake claim, with the due date for repayment of the tax being 30 days after the issue of such individual notices [TMA 1970 Sch 3ZA para 10]. Such individual notices are also required where a partnership statement is amended following the determination of an appeal. In such circumstances the resultant tax is again payable or repayable 30 days after the issue of the individual notices [TMA 1970 Sch 3ZA para 11].

8.21 As with interim payments, the Revenue are given power under the PAYE regulations to provide in those regulations for any necessary adjustments in respect of any matter for the purpose of determining the amount of tax deducted at source under PAYE for the purpose of s 59B(1).

Surcharges

8.22 Where income tax or capital gains tax payable under s 59B or 55 (see **7.81**) is not paid within 28 days of the due date, the amount unpaid attracts a surcharge of five per cent of the unpaid tax [TMA 1970 s 59C(1), (2)] Any amount still unpaid six months after the due date attracts a further five per cent surcharge [TMA 1970 s 59C(3)].

8.23 If the taxpayer has incurred a tax-related penalty under s 7 (failure to notify chargeability), 93(5) (failure to file a return within 12 months of the due date), 95 (incorrect return) or 95A (incorrect partnership return) he is not liable in addition to a surcharge in respect of the same tax [TMA 1970 s 59C(4)]. This does not mean that once a surcharge has been imposed a penalty cannot later be assessed, but rather that if the Revenue choose to assess a penalty they must discharge the surcharge (and any interest thereon) (Enquiry Handbook, paras 632, 675).

8.24 A surcharge is imposed by the Revenue. Notice of its imposition must be served on the taxpayer. This must state the date on which it is issued and the time in which an appeal can be brought [TMA 1970 s 59C(5)]. An appeal against a surcharge can be brought within 30 days from the date of imposition of the surcharge [TMA 1970 s 59C(7)]. On such an appeal the appeal Commissioners can set aside the surcharge if it appears to them that the taxpayer had a reasonable excuse for not paying the tax throughout the period of default. Otherwise they must confirm it [TMA 1970 s 59C(9)]. The Commissioners have no power to reduce the surcharge. The Revenue, however, do; they can mitigate it and stay or compound any proceedings for the recovery of a surcharge [TMA 1970 s 59C(11)].

8.25 It is specifically provided that inability to pay the tax is not to be regarded as a reasonable excuse for the purpose of s 59C(9) [TMA 1970 s 59C(10)]. The Revenue do not in practice impose a surcharge where time to pay arrangements have been agreed and all payments have been made in accordance with the terms of that agreement (Enquiry Handbook, Chapter 1, para 30). They insist that the taxpayer must have made proposals before the due date for the surcharge that lead to an acceptable arrangement to pay the full liability by instalments (Self-assessment Manual, para A11). It is only the proposal that need be made before the surcharge becomes due; it does not have to have been agreed with the Revenue (Self-assessment Manual, para

A15). If such proposals are put forward after 28 February they can avoid the second surcharge even though the Revenue will still seek to collect the first. The Revenue have also indicated that they might reduce or not impose a surcharge in cases of hardship (SA/BK7 – Self-assessment and Surcharges for late payment of tax).

8.26 Where an appeal is made against a surcharge there is no right to make a formal postponement application. However, the Revenue have told their staff to informally stand over the full amount of the surcharge (Self-assessment Manual, para 1.17).

8.27 The Revenue's leaflet SA/BK7 – Self-assessment Surcharges for Late Payment of Tax, gives the following examples of what they might regard as a reasonable excuse.

(*a*) The cheque was lost in the post or lost by the Revenue or was destroyed by a fire or flood at the Post Office – but they will want evidence that the taxpayer tried to pay by the due date and that the non-payment was beyond the taxpayer's control, and would expect a replacement cheque to have been sent promptly once the taxpayer realised that the cheque had been lost.

(*b*) The cheque was dishonoured solely because of an error by the bank.

(*c*) The taxpayer had a serious illness. But it has to be so serious that it prevented the taxpayer from paying. Only a coma, major heart attack, stroke or other serious mental or life-threatening illness is likely to meet this test. The Revenue will only consider such an illness as a reasonable excuse if it began on, or shortly before, the due date for payment and the taxpayer could not have made arrangements to pay.

(*d*) A serious illness of a close relative or of the taxpayer's domestic partner which required his attention – but only if the taxpayer can show that he could not have arranged to pay the tax.

(*e*) The death of a close relative or domestic partner at around the due date for payment – but only if the tax is paid within a reasonable time.

(*f*) Although the booklet does not say so, it is likely that the Revenue will also regard the death of the taxpayer himself as a reasonable excuse, but probably only if the executors could not reasonably have got probate by the due date.

8.28 The Revenue do not regard as a reasonable excuse any of the following.

(*a*) Shortage of funds.

(*b*) A cheque made out incorrectly – 'it would not be fair to taxpayers who had completed theirs carefully'.

(*c*) A tax return not yet submitted.

(*d*) Pressure of work.

(*e*) Failure by a tax agent – but they point out 'you may have some recourse against your agent if he or she has been negligent'.

(*f*) Not knowing exactly what to pay – they say 'you should make a reasonable estimate of your tax and pay that'.

(*g*) Absence of reminders from the Revenue.

(*h*) The Revenue also say that they are unlikely to agree that a taxpayer had a reasonable excuse for not paying his tax at a time when he was able to pay other bills and manage the rest of his personal and finance affairs.

8.29 The Revenue say in SA/BK7 that in their view 'you have a reasonable excuse only where some exceptional event beyond your control has prevented you from paying by the due date'. However, at the end of the day it is not their view that matters. It is the view taken by the appeal Commissioners. It is a question of fact depending on the individual circumstances of each case what is reasonable. There are a great many decisions of VAT tribunals of what has and has not been regarded as a reasonable excuse for VAT purposes. Although that is a different tax and the interpretation of VAT law cannot automatically be assumed to be transposable to income and capital gains tax, the concept of a reasonable excuse is likely to be the same for both taxes. There is accordingly no reason why such decisions should not be drawn to the attention of the Commissioners. It would certainly be surprising if independent appeal Commissioners were to seek to rigidly apply the Revenue's published views, particularly as s 59B(9) clearly imposes an obligation on the Commissioners to form their own view as to what is a reasonable excuse.

8.30 The bigger problem is likely to be the requirement that the reasonable excuse must exist throughout the period of default. This means that for the first surcharge it must have began before the 31 January due date and persisted until at least 28 February (or 28 days after the due date where that is other than 31 January). For the second surcharge it must have begun before the 31 January and persisted until at least 31 July. Indeed, the period is longer than that because the reasonable excuse has to persist right through until the day before the tax is actually paid [TMA 1970 s 59C(12)]. Clearly very few excuses are likely in practice to extend for over six months. The Revenue have said that they recognise that taxpayers cannot be expected to pay their tax on the day the excuse ends and in practice will normally allow 14 days to pay the tax, but say that the appeal Commissioners may allow a longer or shorter period (Tax Bulletin 34, April 1998). It seems doubtful, however, whether the Commissioners have discretion to allow even an extra day, let alone 14.

8.31 Surcharges themselves carry interest. This runs from 30 days from the date on which the surcharge is imposed (not from the date it is notified to the taxpayer) to the date on which it is paid. The interest is at the rate applicable to interest on overdue tax, which is currently 6.5 per cent [TMA 1970 s 59C(6)].

National Insurance

8.32 Class 1 and 1A National Insurance contributions are payable by employers and collected in a similar manner to PAYE income tax. The relevant rules are contained in the Social Security (Contributions) Regulations 2001, SI 2001/1004, which are based on the PAYE Regulations. Class 2 (self-employment) and Class 3 (voluntary) contributions are payable quarterly. The Revenue issue a notice to the contributor within 14 days after the end of each contribution quarter showing the amount due, and the contributor then has 28 days after the date of notification (which is a date specified in the notice, not the date that the notice is actually either issued or received) to pay the amount due [reg 89]. The Revenue have power to approve alternative arrangements for payment [reg 90]. In practice most Class 2 and Class 3 contributions are paid by monthly direct debit.

8.33 Class 4 contributions (earnings-related contributions by the self-employed) are in contrast payable 'in the same manner as any income tax which is or would be, chargeable' in respect of the profits or gains on which the contribution is calculated [Social Security Contributions and Benefits Act 1992 s 15(2)]. The year of assessment for such National Insurance contributions is the same as the tax year [SSCBA 1992 s 15(2)]. It is specifically provided that all the provisions of the Income Tax Acts, including in particular provisions as to assessment, collection, repayment and recovery and the provisions of TMA 1970 Pt VA (payment of tax) and Pt X (penalties), are to apply to Class 4 contributions (with the necessary modifications) as if those contributions were income tax chargeable under Sch D Case I or II [SSCBA 1992 s 16(1)]. TMA 1970 Pt VA is ss 59A–59C and Pt X is ss 93–106.

8.34 The effect is that all of the above rules, both as to payment (including interim payments) and surcharges, apply to Class 4 National Insurance contributions as well as to income tax.

Corporation tax

Payment

8.35 The corporation tax for an accounting period is due and payable on the day following the expiry of nine months from the end of that accounting period [TMA 1970 s 59D(1)].

8.36 However, the Treasury can by regulation make provisions, in relation to companies of such description as may be prescribed, to treat corporation tax as becoming due and payable on earlier dates [TMA 1970 s 59E]. They have done so by the Corporation Tax (Instalment Payments) Regulations 1998, SI 1998/3175, as amended by the Corporation Tax (Instalment Payments) (Amendment) Regulations 1999, SI 1999/1929.

8.37 These apply to accounting periods ending after 30 January 1999. They require large companies to make quarterly payments on account of their corporation tax. A company is a large one for this purpose if its profits in an accounting period exceed the 'upper relevant maximum amount' in force at the end of the accounting period [reg 3(1)]. The upper relevant maximum amount is currently £1.5m, the small companies rate limit, where a company has no associated companies and £1.5m divided by the number of associated companies (including the company itself) where it has associated companies [reg 3(4)]. The rules in TA 1988 s 13 (small companies relief) apply for this purpose but disregarding TA 1988 s 434(3A), (3B) and FA 1989 s 88(4) (which apply only to life assurance companies and exclude the policyholders' share of profits in determining whether the small companies rate applies).

8.38 There are a number of exceptions. A company is not a large company for an accounting period, and does not have to make instalment payments, if either:

(*a*) the amount of its 'total liability' for the accounting period does not exceed £10,000 (proportionally reduced for an accounting period of less than 12 months) [reg 3(2)]; or

(*b*) its 'profits' for the accounting period do not exceed £10m (reduced in the same way as under TA 1988 s 13 where the company has associated companies) and, apart from this rule, it was not a large company in the 12 months preceding the accounting period [reg 3(3)].

8.39 'Profits' means the aggregate of the profits chargeable to corporation tax and franked investment income received by the company (other than intra-group dividends as defined in TA 1988 s 13(7) – broadly, those from a 51 per cent subsidiary) [reg 2(2)]. The 'total liability' is the tax payable for the accounting period, calculated in accordance with FA 1998 Sch 18 para 8(1) reduced by any deductions from payments to sub-contractors which are set off against the corporation tax payable [reg 2(3)]. It should be noted that the para 8(1) calculation includes tax on loans to participators under TA 1988 s 419 and tax on profits of CFCs under TA 1988 s 747. It is not simply the company's corporation tax liability. For the purpose of (*b*) above the number of associated companies is determined by reference to the number existing at the beginning of the accounting period [reg 3(5)] and a company is treated as not being a large company in the 12 months preceding the accounting period if it did not exist, or did not have an accounting period, for the whole of that 12 months or if it was not a large company applying reg 3 (apart from para (3)) for an accounting period which falls within or ends in that 12-month period [reg 3(6), (7)].

8.40 Where a company is required to make instalment payments these are based on its total liability (as defined in **8.39**) for the accounting period. The four instalments are payable:

1 six months and 13 days from the start of the accounting period;

2 nine months and 13 days from the start of the accounting period;

3 12 months and 13 days from the start of the accounting period; and

4 three months and 14 days from the end of the accounting period [reg 5(3)].

For a company with a 31 December year end this will give due dates of 14 July and 14 October, during the accounting period, and 14 January and 14 April following the accounting period. Where the accounting period is less than 12 months the third instalment is omitted, and if it is less than nine months the middle two are omitted. If it is so short that the final instalment would be due before the first then only the final instalment is due [reg 5(3), (4)].

8.41 The amount of each instalment is: (3 / n) × the company's total liability for the accounting period, where 'n' is the length of the accounting period in months and decimals of months (to two places of decimals) calculated on a standard 30-day month [reg 5(5), (1)]. However, each instalment is limited to a maximum of the company's total liability for the accounting period less the instalments previously paid [reg 5(6), (7))]. The final instalment is the balance of the total liability for the accounting period [reg 5(8)]. At first glance it is hard to see how 3 / n can produce a figure in excess of the total liability. This can occur where the accounting period is less than three months. The cap can also apply where the estimated total liability at the time of an instalment is less than that estimated at the time of an earlier instalment.

8.42 The instalment payments were lower for accounting periods ending before 1 July 2002. For those ending in the year to 30 June 2000 the instalments were based on 60 per cent of the company's total liability only. This increased to 72 per cent for accounting periods ending in the year to 30 June 2001 and 88 per cent for those ending in the year to 30 June 2002. The balance was payable nine months after the end of the accounting period [reg 4].

8.43 As the instalments are based on the income for the accounting period, the first two, at least, will have to be based on estimated figures, and in most cases so will the third and often the fourth too. As there are penalties for 'recklessly' failing to pay the right amount this has generated a great deal of criticism and the Revenue have issued guidance indicating the steps that they expect companies to take.

(*a*) They expect a company to follow normal commercial practice and apply corporate governance and standards appropriate to its size and nature.

(*b*) They accept that each estimate can only be made on the basis of the information available at the time. An event which happens unexpectedly in month eight or later, cannot be taken into account in estimating the first instalment to pay in month seven.

(*c*) Companies should consider known transactions, events or factors that might make a significant difference to their liability, and should take a view on what that impact will be. The Revenue will not use hindsight to challenge that view.

(*d*) Companies should make use of their management accounts or other internal management information systems in estimating their tax liability. A full corporation tax computation is not required. If experience indicates a pattern to the company's effective rate of tax in relation to its management account figures it would be acceptable to apply that and adjust for any major changes.

(*e*) Account can be taken of group relief that is likely to be available from companies that are incurring losses.

(*f*) The Revenue recognise that it is difficult to estimate the timing and impact of one-off transactions, particularly capital gains. The fact that expected rollover relief has not materialised, or an expected loss has not been realised, or that it was not certain when a gain would occur, will be accepted by the Revenue as valid reasons for an underpayment of quarterly instalments. They also recognise that there will be occasions when information about intended transactions is confidential or market sensitive at the time an instalment payment falls due and therefore cannot be taken into account in estimating that instalment.

(*g*) Movements in the financial and other markets (particularly foreign exchange) can have a significant impact on some companies. Such movements will be accepted as the reason for fluctuating instalment payments. Any reasoned view on future market trends will be accepted as the basis for estimating instalments – although where a company's normal commercial forecasting includes expected market movements they would generally expect the same basis to be adopted.

(*h*) The Revenue will accept that payments have been properly made where companies take a view on the likely outcome of a case that is not final at the time. Where consultation is taking place on proposed legislation it 'is acceptable for companies to take a view on the timing and details of the new provisions'.

(*i*) Where an enquiry is open on the return for a previous year or years the Revenue accept that the company is entitled to take a view on the likely outcome of the enquiry.

[Tax Bulletin 60, Aug 2002, and guidance on Revenue website.]

8.44 If after paying an instalment a company believes that, by reason of a change in the circumstances of the company, it was excessive (by reference to the aggregate amounts due and payable up to the time the claim is made), it can claim repayment of the excess [reg 6(1), (2)]. The claim must specify the amount claimed and the grounds for considering that it has become excessive [reg 6(3)]. Such a claim is to be heard and determined in the same way as an appeal [reg 6(5)]. If the company has an open appeal, or application to postpone tax pending an appeal, it can ask for the claim to be heard at the same time [reg 6(4), (6)].

8.45 Where a tax refund falls to be made to a company which is a member of a group it can alternatively be surrendered to another group company under FA 1989 s 102 provided that either the surrendering company or the recipient company is a large company for the accounting period [reg 9(1)]. This includes a refund of instalment corporation tax.

8.46 There is an anti-avoidance provision where between 25 November 1997 and 30 June 2002 a company changed its accounting date or entered into any arrangements or transactions the effect of which was to transfer the amount of its taxable profits to another group company, and the result is that corporation tax that would have been payable for any part of an accounting period beginning after 1 July 1998 and ending on or before 30 June 2002 if that action had not been taken becomes due and payable on a later date than it otherwise would have done [reg 14(1)]. The company can be required to pay interest on the amount deferred for the period for which the due date was deferred [reg 14(2)–(4)].

8.47 There are a number of exceptions. A change of accounting date does not trigger the provision if:

(*a*) it derived from a decision made before 25 November 1997;

(*b*) the change of accounting date is because the company begins or ceases to trade or to be UK-resident or ceases to be within the charge to corporation tax (other than by the transfer of its activities to another group company);

(*c*) it arises from a change in the ultimate control of the company, giving rise to the alignment of its accounting date with that of its new ultimate parent (but only if the change is made in the accounting period in which the change of control takes place);

(*d*) it arises from choosing its first accounting date within nine months of incorporation, giving rise to an alignment of its accounting date with its parent company [reg 14(1)(b)].

The transfer of profits similarly does not trigger the provision if either:

(i) the accounting period of the transferee company is identical to that of the transferor (and the transferor has not itself changed its accounting date within the relevant period), and as a result of the transfer of profits the profits of the transferor for the accounting period in which the transfer takes place, or for any subsequent accounting period, are not reduced by more than £5m (reduced proportionately for an accounting period of under 12 months) [reg 14(7)]; or

(ii) the transferee company is resident outside the UK and not trading in the UK through a branch or agency (or if it is the transferred profits do not form part of the taxable profits of that branch) [reg 14(3)].

Claims for repayment

8.48 Where a company has paid an amount of corporation tax for an accounting period and circumstances change so that it has grounds for believing that the amount paid exceeds its probable tax liability, it can claim repayment of the excess even though the amount of the liability has not been finally established [TMA 1970 s 59DA(1), (2)]. Such a claim cannot be made before the material date for the purpose of TA 1988 s 826 (interest on tax overpaid) [TMA 1970 s 59DA(2)]. This is the date the tax was paid or, if later, it's due and payable date. If the claim relates to repayment of company instalment payments the material date is instead normally the date the first instalment became due [TA 1988 s 826A(2) and Corporation Tax (Instalment Payments) Regulations 1998, SI 1998/3175, reg 8].

8.49 The claim must specify the amount that the company considers should be repaid and the grounds for believing that the amount paid exceeds its probable tax liability [TMA 1970 s 59DA(3)]. The claim is to be heard and determined in the same way as an appeal [TMA 1970 s 59DA(5)]. If the company has appealed against an assessment or an amendment to an assessment relating to the tax liability in question and that appeal has not been finally determined it can apply to the appeal Commissioners for a determination of the amount that should be paid to it pending determination of the liability [TMA 1970 s 59DA(8)]. If the company has made an application to postpone any of the tax assessed, that application can be combined with the application to determine a provisional repayment [TMA 1970 s 59DA(6)].

8.50 If such a claim for repayment is made before the company submits its corporation tax return for the period in question any deductions it has suffered under TA 1988 s 559 (construction industry sub-contractors scheme) must be disregarded in considering whether the amount paid exceeds its probable tax liability [TMA 1970 s 59DA(7)]. In practice this is likely to eliminate the claim if the company is a sub-contractor. The reason for this restriction is presumably because the Revenue are reluctant to sanction any payment of sub-contractor deductions until they are satisfied that no tax is due from the company as they are fearful that the company might disappear in the interim.

Surrender of tax refund within a group

8.51 If a company which is a member of a group throughout the 'appropriate period' is entitled to a tax refund relating to an accounting period ('the relevant period') and another group company which is also a member of the group throughout that period has the same relevant period as an accounting period, the two can jointly elect that the refund (or such part of it as is specified in the notice) should be set against the other company's corporation tax liability [FA 1989 s 102(1), (2), (4)].

8.52 Such an election must be made before the refund is made [FA 1989 s 102(2)]. The Revenue have power to specify a form of election but have not done so [FA 1989 s 102(2)]. The 'appropriate period' is the period from the start of the relevant accounting period to the date of the claim [FA 1989 s 102(3)]. The legislation actually reads 'beginning with the relevant accounting period' so it is possible this might be interpreted as the end rather than the start of that period, but the start seems more consistent with the legislation.

8.53 The tax refunds that can be surrendered are:

(*a*) repayable corporation tax for the accounting period;

(*b*) a repayment of income tax in respect of a payment received by the company during the accounting period; and

(*c*) a repayment of the whole or part of the tax credit comprised in any franked investment income received by the company in the accounting period (but such tax credits ceased to be repayable from 6 April 1999),

[FA 1989 s 102(3)].

8.54 The recipient company is treated as having paid on the 'relevant date' an amount of corporation tax for the relevant accounting period equal to the refund surrendered. The surrendering company is similarly treated as having received its tax repayment on that date. If the refund is a repayment of corporation tax any interest relating to it which has been paid by the surrendering company is treated as having been paid by the recipient company [FA 1989 s 102(4)]. The 'relevant date' is the date on which the corporation tax became due and payable under either TMA 1970 s 59D (general rule) or 59E (instalment payments by large companies). If the repayment is of income tax it is the date on which corporation tax for the accounting period became due and payable [FA 1989 s 102(5)].

8.55 If the recipient company makes a payment to the surrendering company in relation to the refund in pursuance of an agreement between them, that payment cannot be taken into account in computing the profits or losses of either company, and is not to be regarded as a distribution or a charge on income, provided that the payment does not exceed the amount of the refund in question [FA 1989 s 102(7)]. It is not clear what happens if it does exceed that amount. The payment does not appear to be taxable under general principles.

Chapter 9

Collection and Recovery

Demand notes

9.1 The legislation provides that when tax becomes due and payable the collector must 'make demand of the sums given to him in charge to collect' [TMA 1970 s 60(1)]. It is not wholly clear what this means. It probably means no more than the issue of a demand is the start of the collection procedure and that any action to recover the tax would be unlawful if that demand has not been made.

9.2 It is possible, but unlikely, that tax cannot be collected at all without such a demand. Certainly the Revenue do not interpret it in that way. The automated procedures for self-assessment do not result in the issue of a demand on or before the due and payable date and the Revenue believe that the taxpayer has an obligation to volunteer tax on the due and payable date even if they do not send him a demand notice. A collector is not involved in the issue of taxpayer statements. However, where tax is not paid by the due date it will sooner or later be referred to a collector at a local office. Their procedure is to write to the taxpayer demanding payment – and, generally, threatening prosecution. That is probably the demand that will validate the future collection procedures.

9.3 The demand is to be made 'from the persons charged therewith, or at the places of their last abode, or on the premises in respect of which the tax is charged, as the case may require'. This somewhat obscure wording is of ancient language. It is identical to that used in of the Income Taxes Act 1918 s 158 and derives from of the Taxes Management Act 1880 s 85. The Revenue interpret it as giving a Collector a right to demand payment of tax from a taxpayer at his private or business address (Personal Contact Manual, para 320). The wording does not, however, seem apt to achieve this other than to the extent that to permit the Collector to make demand from the person charged seems to allow that demand to be made anywhere that the Collector can find that person. In particular, tax ceased to be charged in respect of premises in 1963, so the last part is probably now obsolete. 'At the place of their last abode' probably does no more than make clear that the Collector can simply leave a demand at the person's last residence and does not need to ensure that the taxpayer actually receives it. 'Last abode' probably means just that, not 'last known abode' but TMA 1970 s 115(1), which allows notices to be served on a person either by delivery to him or by leaving it at his usual or last known place of residence, may well be interpreted as expanding on s 60(1), rather than conflicting with it.

9.4 On payment of the tax the Collector must, if so requested, give a receipt [TMA 1970 s 60(2)]. The Revenue interpret 'on payment' rigidly. It is not their practice to give a receipt if this has not been requested prior to payment. They will write a letter declining to give a receipt but confirming that they have received the money. This is probably because they regard the receipt as evidence to support a claim to repayment and do not want to risk issuing more than one receipt for the same amount, so will only issue a receipt at the time of payment.

Distraint

9.5 The Revenue have two main courses open to them to enforce payment of tax: court proceedings and distraint. The word distress is also used as alternative to distraint. They seem to use the two interchangeably. Distraint is defined as the act of seizing goods to compel payment of a debt. In addition to describing the emotional state of the taxpayer when distraint is levied, 'distress' used as a noun has the same meaning as distraint.

9.6 The following provisions do not apply to amounts payable under a contract settlement. Such an amount is not tax, interest or penalties; it is a sum to be paid in lieu of such imposts. Accordingly, it is not a tax debt; it is an ordinary civil debt, albeit one due to the Crown, and can be enforced only in the manner generally applicable to such debts.

9.7 If a person neglects or refuses to pay upon demand made by the Collector, the Collector is entitled to distraint upon the goods and chattels of that person [TMA 1970 s 61(1)]. 'Goods' and 'chattels' are both defined in the dictionary as moveable property, the former normally being used to describe business property and the latter personal property, although the distinction, if any, between the two is probably unimportant. Distraint cannot be levied (imposed) on land (real property) or on intangible property such as leases, copyrights, etc.

9.8 The Revenue's instructions tell Collectors that they cannot levy distraint on:

(*a*) goods which belong jointly to a husband and wife where the tax is owed by one spouse only (as will almost always be the case now that tax is no longer a partnership debt);

(*b*) goods in which the defaulter has a life interest only;

(*c*) goods belonging to an individual partner cannot be distrained on to satisfy a partnership debt;

(*d*) goods subject to a hire purchase agreement – but goods subject to a credit sale agreement can be seized, as under such an agreement title to the goods passes immediately to the buyer;

(*e*) goods hired out to a defaulter;

(*f*) goods hired out by a defaulter – as distraint cannot be levied at the hirer's premises and any attempt to levy distraint would interfere with the contract between the hirer and the debtor;

(*g*) goods subject to a retention of title clause;

(*h*) goods subject to a fixed charge in favour of a third party;

(*i*) furniture and furnishings which do not meet the requirement of the Furniture and Furnishing (Fire) (Safety) Regulations 1988, SI 1988/1324 – as the purpose of levying distraint is to raise money by auctioning the goods and it would be illegal for an auctioneer to sell such goods;

(*j*) electrical equipment for domestic use which does not meet the requirements of the Low Voltage Electrical Equipment (Safety) Regulations;

(*k*) other goods to which special safety conditions apply unless they can be sold – for example much second-hand electrical equipment can be sold only if it is first checked by a qualified electrician, although the costs of such a check need to be met from the proceeds as well as the tax, so it is not worthwhile to carry out checks on low value items,

(Enforcement Manual, para 2.405).

9.9 Although there is no legal restriction on distraining on the following, the Revenue tell their staff that they 'must not seize':

(*a*) perishable goods, such as frozen food or dairy products, which cannot be retained at the end of six days in the same condition as when seized;

(*b*) such tools, books, vehicles and other items of equipment as are necessary to the defaulter for use in their work (but they regard such an item as necessary only if it is so essential that without it there would be no way the defaulter could continue his work);

(c) furniture, household equipment and provisions necessary to satisfy the basic domestic needs of the defaulter and his family (staff are told not to seize a cooker, a microwave oven if that is the only means of cooking, a refrigerator, beds, bedding and clothing of the defaulter and his family, and at least one table and a sufficient number of chairs; conversely they are told not to treat stereo equipment, televisions, video recorders or microwave ovens as necessary);

(*d*) livestock or growing crops;

(*e*) loose money (coins or notes), which cannot be sold at public auction – but a coin collection is distrainable;

(*f*) meters, fittings and other apparatus which belong to the gas, electricity or water authorities;

(*g*) safety equipment, such as a fire extinguisher, fire blanket, safety gate or fire guard;

(*h*) fixtures and fittings which, if removed, would cause damage to the fabric of the building,

(Enforcement Manual, para 2.405). The first four of these items are things that the common law does not allow to be seized under the law of distraint. However, the Revenue right to distrain is statutory; they do not need to rely on the common law. Accordingly, such restrictions probably do not apply. They have been accepted by the Revenue on a voluntary basis, probably to avoid the risk of a distraint being challenged as unlawful.

9.10 A motor vehicle is a chattel. The Revenue are entitled to obtain information from the DVLA under TMA 1970 s 18A so can check ownership with the DVLA. The Revenue will regard a motor vehicle as a necessary tool of the debtor's trade only in exceptional cases (Enforcement Manual, para 2.405).

9.11 A Collector can only levy distraint on goods which are in his Collection area (Enforcement Manual, para 2.402). Unfortunately, the Revenue do not publish a map showing Collection areas. However, if the premises at which distress is being levied do not appear to fall within the geographical area of the Recovery (or Tax Collection) Office concerned (as Collectors' offices are now called) it might be sensible to ask the Collector for confirmation that the premises are indeed in his Collection area.

9.12 A Collector is not entitled to force his way into premises to levy distraint (unless he has a warrant authorising him to do so). He is told that when calling at a private house he must 'enter the premises by the door and at the invitation of the defaulter or their representative'. When calling at business premises he is told to use the main entrance (Enforcement Manual, para 2.403). However, it is not necessarily wise to refuse entry to the Collector. It is up to him what he distrains on and if he has to go away and get a warrant to break open the premises he can hardly be expected to be over co-operative with requests by the taxpayer not to distrain on certain items. In an old case, *Long v Clark ([1894] 1 QB 119)*, it was held that although a bailiff had no right to break into premises he was entitled to climb over a wall or fence from adjoining premises.

9.13 His ability to obtain a warrant derives from TMA 1970 s 61(2). A justice of the peace (JP) can issue a warrant in writing, authorising a Collector to break open, in the daytime, any house or premises and call to his assistance any constable, for the purpose of levying distress. The JP has to be satisfied by information on oath that there is reasonable ground for believing that a person is neglecting or refusing to pay a sum charged. If the Collector calls for help from the police they are required to assist him both in the execution of the warrant and in levying the distress.

9.14 In practice the Revenue rarely resort to such action. Their instructions as to what to do in such cases have been withheld from the published version of the Enforcement Manual. What they are more likely to do is to bring along a bailiff or possibly, if they fear violence, ask for a police presence to prevent a breach of the peace. In the past the Revenue almost always used bailiffs, but are now increasingly dispensing with them. In law they do not need a bailiff. Indeed the legislation provides that a levy (or a warrant to break open) must be executed by, or under the direction of, and in the presence of, the Collector [TMA 1970 s 61(8)]. Accordingly, even if they use a bailiff the Collector must also attend and must take charge of the proceedings. Indeed, Collectors are warned that they must not in any circumstances allow the bailiff to conduct any part of the actual distraint proceedings, persuade the Collector to levy distraint against his better judgement, have possession of the taxpayer's papers at any time or correspond directly with the defaulter (Enforcement Manual, para 2.104). The bailiff is presumably there to add weight to the proceedings and to use his skill to defuse aggression and to advise on how best to remove goods or which are the most appropriate to remove.

9.15 Where distraint is levied by the Collector the goods must be kept for five days at the cost of the defaulter [TMA 1970 s 61(4)]. In practice the Collector does not normally immediately remove the goods, he takes 'walking possession' of them, that is he leaves them on the debtor's premises (and thus available for use by the debtor but not for him to dispose of) provided that the debtor signs an agreement that he holds them as agent of the Collector and acknowledges that the Collector is entitled to remove them at any time. The Collector is told to ask the debtor (or responsible person in the case of a company) to read the terms of the walking possession agreement and to explain to him what it means if asked to do so. If the debtor agrees to walking possession he must sign and date the form (form C 204B). If the debtor is not present at the distraint, the Collector can accept a signature from some other person who is able to accept responsibility. They may do this if they levy distraint at business premises, but in other cases they are more likely to defer their distraint action until the debtor is present. They will not simply remove goods in the absence of someone to accept a walking possession order. They are specifically told that they cannot accept the signature of a receptionist, shop assistant or waiter on form C 204B, as such a person cannot accept responsibility for distraint action. Accordingly, they cannot levy distraint at all if no responsible person is present.

9.16 If the Revenue decide to physically remove goods (either immediately or after a period of walking possession) they cannot carry them in their private car, or even an Inland Revenue vehicle (Enforcement Manual, para 2.416). They must therefore either have arranged for a removal van to be available or must be accompanied by a bailiff – as a bailiff's car is authorised to transport seized goods. Alternatively, they will have to stay on the premises and ask someone else to make arrangements for a removal van. They could also take what is called 'lose possession' which involves leaving someone on the premises (such as the bailiff) until the goods can be removed.

This procedure is rarely used, particularly as it relies on the hope that the Collector will be invited back on the premises when he returns with the removal van the next day.

9.17 There is no limit on the period for which goods can be held. However, as the purpose of distraint is to collect the tax, and distraint is of itself a last resort in the collection process, this is unlikely to be prolonged. If the goods are physically removed the Collector will not wait to build up storage costs that he could be called on to justify. If he takes walking possession he will be wary of the possibility of the debtor absconding with the goods or becoming bankrupt (which would thwart the distraint), or of other creditors seeking to seize the goods. Collectors are told to 'bear in mind also that any failure to complete your distraint promptly diminishes the effectiveness of distraint as a recovery process and reduces your efforts to improve the payment performance of taxpayers' (Enforcement Manual, para 2.508). Accordingly, extra time to pay is likely to be granted only if the Collector is convinced that genuine efforts are being made to raise the money elsewhere to obviate a sale of the goods and that such efforts have a good chance of succeeding, or if he believes that serious hardship would be caused by removing the goods. If the goods are not removed the Collector will call on the debtor frequently to remind him both of the tax due and the existence of the walking possession order.

9.18 The Treasury are empowered by regulation to specify the fees chargeable in connection with levying distress and the costs and charges recoverable from the defaulter when distress is levied [TMA 1970 s 61(6)]. They have done so in the Distraint by Collectors (Fees, Costs and Charges) Regulations 1994, SI 1994/236. The fee for visiting the premises is a sum not exceeding £12.50 with a further £12.50 chargeable if the value of goods actually seized is £100 or less. Fees are on a graduated scale where the value of goods seized exceeds that figure. Where walking possession is taken, a fee of 0.45p per day can be charged, but only for up to 14 days. If close possession is taken the fee is £4.50, but the individual left in possession must provide his own board; it is not up to the debtor to feed him. The debtor can also be charged the reasonable costs and charges of removal and storage and the reasonable fees, charges and expenses of a valuer called on to appraise the goods. If the goods are sold, the auctioneer can charge 15 per cent (or 7.5 per cent, plus out-of-pocket expenses if the auction is held on the debtor's premises) plus the reasonable costs of advertising, removal and storage. All of these fees are exclusive of VAT where that is chargeable. The Collector is authorised to deduct these fees from the sums received on or in connection with the levying of the distress. If any dispute arises as to the amount of the fees they must be taxed by the district judge of the County Court for the district in which the distress is levied. The fees are of course totals, not per person, so if the Collector uses a bailiff the additional costs of doing so are down to the Revenue (or the bailiff himself) not the debtor. Bear in mind that VAT is chargeable on a bailiff's fees only if he is a taxable person and VAT should not be chargeable on the Revenue's fees if they do not use a bailiff, as the Revenue are not supplying a service to anyone. The debtor is entitled to look for evidence that VAT is properly charged. In practice the Revenue themselves absorb any VAT on bailiffs fees unless the goods are removed (Enforcement Manual, para 2.203).

9.19 When the Revenue call to levy distraint remember the following.

(*a*) A debtor is entitled to inspect:

- (i) the Collector's warrant card;
- (ii) any break-open warrant; and
- (iii) if a bailiff is used, his general certificate (issued by a County Court) or Sheriff's Officer's identity card (issued by the Sheriff of a County).

He is entitled to read these, not merely have them flashed at him.

(*b*) The Collector cannot come onto a taxpayer's premises unless either they are open to the public or the occupier invites him onto the premises.

(*c*) Under common law, distraint can be levied only between sunrise and sunset and cannot be levied on a Sunday or on a bank or public holiday (Enforcement Manual, para 2.402). It is unclear to what extent this applies to statutory distraint but the Revenue clearly think it does, so it can be quoted at a Collector who does not comply with it.

(*d*) The debtor is entitled to know the amount of the debt. In practice the Collector will request payment in full before levying distraint.

(*e*) The debtor, like any taxpayer, is entitled to confidentiality. The Collector should not disclose the existence of the debt to anyone else on the premises in advance of levying distraint (when obviously he may need to explain what he is doing).

(*f*) If the debtor offers payment in full before the distraint starts, eg when the Collector starts his visit by demanding immediate payment, the Collector will normally accept a cheque, unless previous cheques from the debtor have been dishonoured. If he offers part payment the Collector is instructed to take the money but to levy distraint for the balance (Enforcement Manual, para 2.303). If the funds can be raised, paying at this stage avoids the costs; paying once the distraint has formally started will not stop the process but, assuming that the cheque is met, will stop the sale. If part only can be raised consider whether the reduction in costs and the risk of sale justify a part payment. Consider also offering a part payment conditional on the Collector not levying distraint – although he will clearly want to know when and how the balance will be paid.

(*g*) It is understood that a motor vehicle can be seized if it is parked outside the premises but not if it is parked elsewhere.

(*h*) The debtor is entitled to a copy of the Distraint Notice and Inventory of goods distrained on (form C 204A) irrespective of whether or not goods are removed. The inventory needs to be prepared in sufficient detail to enable the goods seized to be identified. It is sensible to check it before the Collector leaves the premises.

(*i*) If any damage occurs while goods are being removed (either to the goods or the property) make a note of it and ask the Collector to sign a copy of the note, as the damage might give rise to a claim against the Revenue.

(*j*) If the Collector cannot leave the premises if he feels threatened or is assaulted, his instructions are to raise the alarm for assistance, for example by breaking a window to attract attention (Enforcement Manual, Appendix 1).

9.20 If, after distraint has been levied, the debtor does not pay the sum due (together with the costs and charges) the Collector must:

(*a*) appoint one or more independent persons to appraise the goods;

(*b*) arrange for them to be sold by public auction; and

(*c*) refund to the debtor any excess of the sale proceeds over the tax, interest, costs and charges,

[TMA 1970 s 61(8)]. The appraisal is normally made by the auctioneer (Enforcement Manual, para 2.509).

9.21 If goods are auctioned, a reserve price will not be set. If they do not sell, they will be re-auctioned. If the goods are damaged, they will be auctioned in that state, not put into good repair to achieve the maximum price. If the goods seized are insufficient to settle the debt, interest and charges, the balance is still owed by the debtor. The Collector could distrain on further goods to pay this but, as the courts do not like multiple distraints, is more likely to issue a summons for the balance. It was held in *Herbert Berry Associates Ltd v IRC ((1978) 52 TC 113)* that if the company goes into liquidation before the goods have been sold, the Collector is entitled to complete his distraint by selling the goods.

9.22 If a third party has already levied distraint but the goods have not yet been removed, the Collector can claim from that third party the net amounts of PAYE (but not National Insurance) and sub-contractor deductions deducted by the debtor in the 12 months immediately prior to the date of the third party's seizure [TMA 1970 s 62(1), (1A)]. The third party cannot then sell or remove the goods without first paying that amount to the Collector. If such payment is not made within 10 days of the claim by the Collector the Revenue are entitled to distrain on sufficient of the goods to settle that PAYE and sub-contractor debt [TMA 1970 s 62(2)]. To the extent that the tax debt is for other taxes the prior distraint takes precedent. If the third party is the landlord, or a bailiff executing a judgement on behalf of a landlord, and the landlord's debt is for rent, the landlord's distraint takes precedence even if there is unpaid PAYE.

9.23 Distraint does not apply in Scotland. It's nearest equivalent is the execution of a Summary Warrant. This is a legal document issued by a Sheriff allowing recovery by poinding (seizing or impounding removable goods) and sale, arrestment (requiring a third party to pay to the Revenue money that is or will become due to the debtor) and arrestment of earnings (requiring an employer to deduct a fixed sum each week or month from the debtor's salary and pay it to the Revenue). It will be seen that this is wider than distraint insofar as it extends to debts and other intangible assets. A salary can be arrested only if the payer is in Scotland. Poinding and arrestment is not carried out by the Collector. It must be done by a Sheriff Officer. A Sheriff Officer is an Officer of the Court but is not employed by it; he is a self-employed person.

9.24 A Collector applies to the Sheriff for the issue of a Summary Warrant. The application must be accompanied by a certificate stating that the tax has not been paid, the Collector has demanded payment, 14 days have elapsed since the date of the demand (unless it relates to PAYE or sub-contractors' deductions) and specifying the amount due [TMA 1970 s 63(1)(b)]. The Sheriff does not apparently need to be convinced that the tax is due; he merely checks that the application meets the statutory requirements. The Sheriff Officer will normally try poinding first. This must be carried out in the presence of a witness and cannot commence before 8am or continue after 8pm. No poinding can be done on a Sunday or public holiday. If poinding does not raise sufficient funds the Sheriff Officer can proceed to arrestment.

9.25 The Sheriff Officer's fees and outlays in connection with the execution of a summary warrant are chargeable to the debtor. However, he cannot charge the debtor a fee if the debtor pays him the debt to obviate poinding [TMA 1970 s 63A]. As in England and Wales (see **9.22**), if another creditor has taken possession of the goods but not removed them from the premises, the Collector can demand payment of up to 12 months PAYE and sub-contractors' payments from that creditor, and if it is not paid within 10 days the creditor cannot proceed with his poinding but the Revenue's summary warrant will be executed in its place [TMA 1970 s 64].

Court proceedings

Magistrates Court

9.26 The Revenue can recover summarily as a civil debt any amount due as income tax, capital gains tax or corporation tax if it does not exceed £2,000 [TMA 1970 s 65(1)]. The Treasury have power by statutory instrument to increase that figure but have not yet done so [TMA 1970 s 65(5)]. There are a number of other provisions that enable an amount to be recovered as if it were tax, namely:

(*a*) TMA 1970 s 59A(7): self-assessment interim payments.

(*b*) TMA 1970 s 69: interest, penalties and surcharges.

(*c*) SSCBA 1992 s 16(1): Class 4 NIC.

(*d*) PAYE Regulations, SI 2003/2682 reg 84: PAYE and related interest.

(*e*) Sub-contractor Regulations, regs 16, 19: deductions for sub-contractors and related interest and their Northern Ireland equivalents.

Summary proceedings are taken in the Magistrates Court before Justices of the Peace. It is normally a fast, cheap and simple procedure. Proceedings need to be taken in the court for the area in which the defaulter resides or carries on business. Proceedings must be brought within one year from the time when the matter complained of arose [TMA 1970 s 65(3)].

9.27 Proceedings are commenced by the issue of a summons. The Revenue normally serve this on the debtor by post. It needs to be served at least 10 clear days before the hearing date. If the debtor does not accept a summons by post the Revenue will serve it by hand. The Revenue instructions says that this should be done by handing it to the debtor but not enclosed in an envelope. They go on to say that if it cannot be served on the debtor personally it should be left with a responsible adult at the debtor's last known or usual place of abode (Enforcement Manual, para 3.101). This enables the Collector as a litigant in person to present the case without the need for a lawyer to represent the Revenue. Proceedings are adversarial as in any court hearing.

9.28 However, the Revenue do not need to present background evidence to support the debt. A certificate of the Collector stating that payment of the tax has not been made to him or, to the best of his knowledge and belief, to any other Collector, or to any person acting on his behalf or on behalf of another Collector 'is sufficient evidence that the sum mentioned in the certificate is unpaid and is due to the Crown'. Moreover, a document that purports to be such a certificate shall be deemed to be one until the contrary is proved [TMA 1970 s 70(1)].

9.29 In *R v Epping and Harlow General Comrs, ex p Goldstraw (57 TC 536)* the taxpayer sought to use a hearing before the Commissioners for the issue of an interest certificate under s 70 to reopen the prior determination by them of his appeal. On judicial review it was held that the Commissioners had no power to reopen the appeal once it had become final. It is no longer necessary for the Revenue to get an interest certificate from the Commissioners, the Collector now has power to issue it himself.

9.30 Similarly, a certificate in the same terms by a Collector stating that a penalty is payable under TMA 1970 ss 7–12B, 59A–59D, or 93–107 or FA 1998 Sch 18, or that a surcharge is payable under TMA 1970 ss 59A–59D, is sufficient evidence that the amount is unpaid and due to the Crown [TMA 1970 s 70(2)].

9.31 If the taxpayer is likely to dispute that he has received earnings, a written statement as to the wages, salaries, fees and other emoluments paid for any period to the taxpayer, purporting to be signed by his employer or any responsible person in the employment of the employer, is prima facie evidence in proceedings before the Magistrates Court or a County Court (or a Scottish Inferior Court) that the wages, etc, therein stated to have been paid have in fact been paid [TMA 1970 s 70(4)].

9.32 The fact that something is sufficient evidence does not mean that the court has to accept it, but merely that it cannot reject it as not constituting acceptable evidence. It is still open to the debtor to challenge its accuracy and to put forward his own evidence to seek to demonstrate that the amount claimed is incorrect, that he does not owe the tax or that he has paid the amount in question. Collectors are told that if the debtor attends the hearing 'it will always be to your advantage if before the hearing you have been able to interview the debtor' (Enforcement Manual, para 3.309). If the Collector requests such an interview consideration needs to be given as to whether to accede to the request. The Collector will obviously be interested in establishing what the debtor intends to dispute so as to be ready to counter the arguments that he puts forward. That is not necessarily in the debtor's best interest – although it is possible that such a meeting might head off the proceedings entirely and it is likely that if at the hearing the Collector cannot refute the taxpayer's contentions he will seek an adjournment, so it may be in the taxpayer's best interest to put all of the issues that he intends to raise on the table before the hearing.

9.33 It should be borne in mind that all of the sums due from any one person payable to any one Collector, and which are recoverable summarily, can be included in the same complaint, summons or other document to be heard before justices or issued by justices; that such a document is to be construed as a separate document in relation to each such sum; and that its invalidity as respects any one item does not affect its validity in relation to others [TMA 1970 s 65(2)]. Accordingly, if the debtor brings evidence to cast doubt on one item the summons will not fall away but the court can give judgement on the remaining items.

9.34 As far as the Revenue are concerned the object of the hearing is to secure payment, but if this cannot be done to obtain an order for payment (Enforcement Manual, para 3.306). Payment between receiving the summons and the date of the hearing will obviate the need for the hearing.

9.35 The Collector is instructed at a hearing to ask the Magistrates to order payment of:

(*a*) the tax and interest as on the summons;

(*b*) interest on overdue tax from the date of the summons at the appropriate rate per day; and

(*c*) fees and costs.

He is also told to ask the Magistrate to order that in default of payment the sum is to be recovered by distress – but only if the debtor attends the hearing. If the Revenue ask for such an order the debtor should explain why he considers it inappropriate. Such orders are not routinely made. They are at the discretion of the Magistrates and Collectors are told not to challenge a refusal (Enforcement Manual, para 3.304). If the Revenue are granted such an order it will enable them to ask the court to issue a distress warrant to a bailiff without the need for a further court hearing.

9.36 If the Magistrates do not grant a distress warrant the Revenue must use a judgement summons. They do not like to do so if this can be avoided as the procedure may be protracted if the debtor does not co-operate (Enforcement Manual, para 1.408). They must first apply to the court for the issue of a judgement summons. This must be served on the debtor. It requires him to appear in court on a specified date and explain why he should not be imprisoned for failing to pay as ordered. If the debtor fails to attend the hearing the Revenue have to apply to the Court for a witness summons. If he still does not attend they have to apply for a witness warrant and then a committal hearing. Some Magistrates are reluctant to imprison for civil debt and those that are prepared to do so may well look for a very high standard of evidence that the debtor has the means to pay.

9.37 If either party is aggrieved by an order of the Magistrates on the grounds that it is wrong in law or the Court has exceeded its powers, they can ask the Court to state a case for the opinion of the High Court. This must be done within 21 days after that on which the Court's decision is given. Such appeals are rare (Enforcement Manual, para 3.314). There is no right of appeal on a question of fact.

9.38 If the debtor does not pay and the Magistrates decline to send him to prison the Revenue's only other remedy is to initiate bankruptcy or winding up proceedings against the debtor in order to recover from the debtor's assets the debt subject to the Magistrates' order.

County Court

9.39 As an alternative to the Magistrates Court the Revenue can take proceedings in a County Court commenced in the name of a Collector [TMA 1970 s 66(1)]. Revenue staff are specifically authorised to address the court in such proceedings, even though not legally qualified [TMA 1970 s 66(2)]. There is no limit on the amount that can be sued for in a County Court (High Court and County Courts Jurisdiction Order 1991, SI 1991/724). However, the tax must be due and payable under an assessment [TMA 1970 s 66(1)]. As indicated at **9.26** above some statutory provisions provide that an amount can be recovered as if it were tax, and where such amounts are assessed or treated as assessed they will accordingly also be actionable in the County Court. In Scotland, the Revenue can similarly themselves bring proceedings in the Sheriff Court [TMA 1970 s 67].

9.40 The Revenue do not like to take County Court proceedings. They regard them as lengthy and expensive. Their preferred action is by summary proceedings (see **9.26**) for small debts and distraint (see 9.5) for larger ones. In Scotland it is the use of a Summary Warrant, whatever the size of the debt. They do, however, tell staff that 'use of CCP against professional taxpayers who would not ordinarily welcome a County Court Judgement against them can be very effective. Simply starting an action can often provoke payment' (Recovery Manual, para 1221).

9.41 There is no time limit for initiating proceedings for unpaid tax in the County Court. For NIC, proceedings must be initiated within six years of the tax becoming due – or if later, six years from the last occasion on which the person liable, or his agent, acknowledges the debt in writing or makes part payment (Recovery Manual, para 1305). If NIC is outstanding for over six years great care may need to be taken to avoid resurrecting the Revenue's ability to take action to recover it.

9.42 The Revenue issue County Court proceedings by way of a default action. Such action is initiated by applying for a default summons. This is then served on the debtor, normally by the court by first class post. If the debtor does not deliver an admission or a written defence within 21 days of service of the summons the court may well enter judgement by default without a hearing taking place. The Revenue can commence proceedings in the court for the district in which the Collector's office is situated. However, if a hearing is to take place the court will transfer the case to the defendant's home court, ie the one for the address he shows on his defence. Accordingly, the Collector is told that if the taxpayer lives outside his area he should transfer the papers to the Collector in that area and leave him to issue the proceedings (but not for a limited company) (Enforcement Manual, para 4.108).

9.43 If the taxpayer files a defence he can ask for further and better particulars. He can also ask for discovery of documents. If he admits the debt in whole or in part he can ask for time to pay. If the debtor does this he has to send details of his income and expenditure and his proposals for settling the debt to the Revenue. The Revenue must then tell the court if they accept or reject the proposal. If they reject it the court will decide whether the amount should be paid by instalments and if so the timing and size of those instalments. The Revenue tells it's staff, 'Unless you think that you can convince the court that the proposals are unreasonable, accept them' (Enforcement Manual, para 4.305). It is worth bearing this in mind when formulating the offer. If the debtor admits only part of the claim but does not comment on the balance, the Revenue tells its staff that they should reject the amount admitted and attend the hearing and prove the claim in full (Enforcement Manual, para 4.306).

9.44 If the debtor files a defence the case will need to proceed to a hearing. If the claim is over £3,000 the court will normally arrange a pre-trial review. If it is less, the papers will be referred to the District Judge, who will decide how best to proceed. He will normally order an arbitration hearing.

Where a defence appears irrelevant, or seems to be a disguised counterclaim against the Revenue, the Collector can apply to have it struck out. This will require a hearing at which the debtor is obviously entitled to attend. The rules in respect of evidence, considered at **9.28–9.30** above, apply equally to County Court (and, indeed, High Court) proceedings.

9.45 The Revenue rely heavily on *IRC v Pearlberg ((1953) 34 TC 57)*. Mr Pearlberg was served with a notice stating that it was intended to proceed against him for the recovery of tax under old-style Sch A (which was assessed on the owner of the property). He did not appeal against either the notice or the assessment, but when proceedings for recovery of the tax commenced he sought leave to defend on the grounds that he was not in fact the owner. Leave was refused and judgement given against him. He appealed to the Court of Appeal. Dismissing his appeal, Denning L J said:

> 'The right way for him to have challenged any of these matters was by appeal to the Commissioners in the way provided by the Income Tax Acts, and, as he did not raise the matter by way of appeal, he is not allowed to raise them now. If we were to allow Mr Pearlberg to raise these matters, it would mean that the High Court would become the tribunal to decide questions of fact and law on tax assessments, whereas they have been decided to the general satisfaction for a great many years now by the Commissioners, with an appeal on points of law by Case Stated to the High Court. That is the proper remedy and not this … Once there is an assessment duly made, and not appealed from them under section 169 of the Income Tax Act 1918 [which was virtually identical to TMA 1970 s 68 – see **9.50**] the tax charged may be sued for and recovered from the person charged therewith in the High Court as a debt due to the Crown. In my opinion, therefore, all issues on the merits of these cases, as to fact or law, should have been determined by appeal to the Commissioners and cannot be raised at this stage. If there has been no appeal to the Commissioners the debts become absolute and conclusive, and their legal effect cannot be denied.'

9.46 The Revenue will ask for the defence to be struck out on the basis of this 'finality principle' if the defence is one for which the taxpayer had a right of appeal to the Commissioners. They tell their staff that, in practice the *Pearlberg* case 'means that if the statutory requirements are met then the only defences to a claim for tax are those that relate to the tax itself and not the assessment, for example, disputes about payments or reliefs. Such defences are, of course, simply matters of evidence and easily answered' (Enforcement Manual, para 4.312). The Revenue consider that the finality principle applies equally to Class 4 NIC and reg 81 determinations, to penalty determinations and to PAYE claims against employees under the PAYE regulations, all of which are appealable. However, they say that the finality principle does not apply to a self-assessment (Enforcement Manual, para 4.313a). However, as a self-assessment return cannot be amended by either the taxpayer or the Revenue after the closure of the enquiry window it seems probable that the courts will take the same view as in *Pearlberg* and refuse to allow collection proceedings to be used as a route to bypass the statute. The finality principle does not apply to income tax deducted under the PAYE regulations 'as if' it 'had been charged on' the employer under Sch E. Accordingly, if the taxpayer disputes the amount of the emoluments, or the tax that his employer is liable to deduct or repay, the Revenue can be called on to prove these facts (Enforcement Manual, para 4.315).

9.47 Where the defence includes a counterclaim the Revenue will apply for this to be struck out. This is because Order 42, rule 9(1) of the County Court Rules states: 'In proceedings by the Crown for the recovery of taxes, duties or penalties the defendant shall not be entitled to avail himself of any set-off or counterclaims'.

9.48 If judgement is given against the debtor it will be entered by Registry Trust Ltd in the register of County Court judgements. If the debt is paid within one month of judgement the Court will ask for the entry to be deleted. If it is paid subsequently the order will remain on the register but will be marked 'satisfied' once the court has received evidence of payment.

9.49 There are six methods available to the Revenue to enforce a County Court judgement.

(*a*) Warrant of Execution – this is an order to the bailiff to seize and sell sufficient of the debtor's goods to satisfy the judgement.

(*b*) Garnishee – this is an order directed to someone who owes the debtor money directing him to pay it instead to the Revenue.

(*c*) Charging Order – this imposes a charge over land or securities so that they are not sold without first settling the tax debt.

(*d*) Attachment of earnings – this orders the debtor's employer to deduct a specified amount on each pay day from his salary.

(*e*) Bankruptcy/winding up.

(*f*) Judgement Summons – this requires the debtor to attend court to explain why the debt has not been paid. The judge will question the debtor about his financial circumstances and decide what action is appropriate, which can include committing the debtor to prison.

It is up to the Revenue to decide which of these actions to take. They are not mutually exclusive. They can take as many of them as they wish. In practice the Collector will normally seek a further interview with the debtor to try to persuade him that it is in his best interests to settle the judgement without the Revenue having to take enforcement action.

High Court

9.50 Any tax may be sued for and recovered in the High Court as a debt due to the Crown, or by any other means whereby any debt of record or otherwise due to the Crown can, or may at any time, be sued for and recovered, as well as by the other means specifically provided for in the Taxes Management Act. In Scotland, the action is taken in the Court of Session sitting as the Court of Exchequer [TMA 1970 s 68]. The Revenue do not normally institute proceedings for recovery in the High Court. However, the County Court has power to refer cases to the High Court where the sum involved is over £50,000. If action is pursued in the High Court the debtor clearly needs to obtain legal help.

Interest, penalties and surcharges

9.51 A penalty imposed under TMA 1970 ss 7–9A, ss 59A–59D, or ss 93–107 or under FA 1998 Sch 18, or a surcharge imposed under TMA 1970 ss 59A–59D and interest charged under TMA 1970 ss 86–92 or recoverable under TA 1988 s 826(8A) (see **11.12**) as if it were interest so charged, is to be treated as if it were tax charged, and due and payable, under the assessment to which it relates (or in the case of interest on tax which is not in fact assessed, or recovered under TA 1988 s 826(8A), as if it were tax charged and due and payable under an assessment). This deeming applies not only for the purpose of collection and recovery under the above provisions but also for the purpose of Crown Proceedings Act 1947 s 35(2)(g)(i) (rules of court to impose restrictions on set-off and counterclaim where the proceedings relate to taxes) (s 35(2)(b) in relation to Scotland) and for the purpose of any rules of court (including County Court rules) which impose such a restriction [TMA 1970 s 69].

9.52 In *Lord Advocate v Butt ((1991) 64 TC 471)* the taxpayers sought to defeat collection in reliance on the Prescription and Limitations (Scotland) Act 1973, the Scottish Equivalent of the Statute of Limitations. They claimed that the trigger was the earning of the profits and the statutory charging provision, as those created an obligation to pay tax. The making of the assessment merely provided a means to take court action. The Outer House of the Court of Session dismissed this on the basis that a statutory right to assess within six years pointed to a clear separation from the statutory obligation to pay tax. However, it felt that interest was different as the Prescription Act referred to interest 'due in respect of a particular period', so interest relating to periods earlier than the five-year interest period under that Act was not collectible. The Inner House felt that the judge had not given proper weight to s 69. This recategorises the interest as tax. Accordingly, if the tax is properly collectible it follows that the interest for the entire period is collectible too.

Insolvency action

9.53 If the Collector feels that local enforcement action is unlikely to be successful, or action has been taken but has failed to induce payment, the case will be referred to Enforcement Office. Collectors are told not to refer a case there unless the amount owing is at least £2,000 (£1,500 in Scotland). Although Enforcement Office will continue to seek to persuade the taxpayer to settle his tax, a transfer to Enforcement Office is generally a precursor to the Revenue seeking an order of bankruptcy or winding up.

Request for time to pay

9.54 A Collector can consider requests for time to pay at any time in the recovery process. They are told that, when considering offers of payment over a period of time, they should bear in mind that it takes about six months to wind up a company and 12 months to bankrupt an individual (Recovery Manual, para 1802). There is probably an inference that an offer to pay within such a timescale will be looked on reasonably favourably, but if an offer stretches beyond that the Collector will take a view on whether he can recover all of the tax fairly readily from a liquidator or trustee in bankruptcy.

9.55 Collectors are recommended to deal with time to pay arrangements in an interview. However, they are told that they should not refuse to consider such an arrangement where the request is made by post or telephone, although they should try to persuade the taxpayer to call in for interview (Recovery Manual, para 1809). They are also told not to give taxpayers the impression that such arrangements are a matter of routine and to make clear that it is concessionary treatment and cannot be taken for granted as a method of settling liabilities in the future. Also, they should not make arrangements that allow tax debts to accumulate with no realistic prospect of getting up to date (Recovery Manual, para 1812). The Collector is told to find out:

(*a*) why the taxpayer wants time to pay;

(*b*) what is the taxpayer's business (or source of income); and

(*c*) what does the taxpayer propose – and 'let the taxpayer make the first proposal as if you do you are unlikely to secure an improvement even if the taxpayer could pay more quickly' (Recovery Manual, para 1822 and 1825).

The Collector should then consider whether the proposals are justifiable and whether they are the best that can be achieved in the circumstances. If the taxpayer proposes settlement over a period of longer than six months the Collector is told to obtain full information about the taxpayer's financial situation – income, expenditure and assets – before deciding whether time to pay is appropriate. He should also do so if the taxpayer has requested time to pay in the recent past or if he believes that there is no valid basis for the request (Recovery Manual, para 1826). The Manual also warns (para 1828) that 'taxpayers often put their case for time to pay with less than total accuracy by understating their income, overstating their expenditure, or both'.

9.56 Collectors are also told that each case must be dealt with on its merits, using common sense, taking into account the interests of the Exchequer and at the same time being fair to the taxpayer. Some specific guidance is given.

(*a*) Someone with an uncommitted bank balance which exceeds the amount outstanding has no justification for requesting time to pay.

(*b*) Instalments of equal amount for the whole period are not justified if the taxpayer's income will increase as a result of seasonal effects on trading or when a personal loan or HP commitment clears.

(*c*) There is no point in turning down proposals spread over say three months if payment would have to be enforced by County Court proceedings which may take significantly longer.

(*d*) If the taxpayer's proposals 'are set at an unrealistic level, or are apparently more than the taxpayer can afford it is doubtful whether the taxpayer has given full and accurate information' (it is of course equally, if not more likely, that he has taken an unduly optimistic approach in trying to be as fair as possible to the Revenue or is trying to minimise the risk of his offer being rejected without realising that he probably will not be able to keep to it).

(*e*) If the taxpayer's proposals are less than he can apparently afford the Collector might suggest a rate of payment which he feels to be fair and acceptable and suggest tactfully to the taxpayer how he might make adjustments to his lifestyle to achieve it.

(*f*) Things like unemployment, ill-health or unforeseeable short-term business difficulties are good grounds for time to pay – but it is necessary to test their genuineness.

(*g*) If the taxpayer has assets that can be used to pay part of the liability he should be expected to do so even if withdrawal without notice incurs a penalty of lost interest on the amount withdrawn.

(*h*) If the taxpayer is expecting payment of an amount due, make arrangements so that on receipt the money is paid to the Revenue.

(Recovery Manual, paras 829 and 1832.)

9.57 Collectors are told that they should normally make it a condition of time to pay, that future debts will be paid in full as and when they fall due and should make clear that the concession may be withdrawn if the condition is not strictly observed (Recovery Manual, para 1829). Accordingly, if a proposed arrangement will stretch beyond the due date for payment of a later tax liability either the proposal ought to cover that liability as well or the need to pay that liability needs to be factored in when considering what funds will be available to settle the current liability. There is normally little point in making an instalment arrangement now if there is likely to be a need for another one in a few months time, as the Collector is likely to take a far harsher view second time round.

9.58 The Revenue also place emphasis on how quickly a request is made. They believe that a taxpayer who is genuinely conscious of his obligations will make a request for time to pay before or very shortly after the due date for the liability. A taxpayer who does not ask for time until immediately before the start of enforcement action may be deliberately stalling. Sadly, experience of acting for taxpayers suggests that many who genuinely need time to pay put off doing anything until things get desperate in the hope that something may come along. It is depressing to learn that the eventual approach to the Revenue is likely to be met with suspicion.

Payment by cheque

9.59 Where any payment to the Revenue is made by a cheque which is met on its first presentation to the banker on whom it is drawn, the payment is treated as made on the day on which the cheque was received by the Revenue for the purposes of the Taxes Management Act, TA 1988 ss 824–826 (repayment supplements and interest on tax overpaid) and FA 1992 s 283 (repayment supplement) [TMA 1970 s 70A].

Recovery from third parties

9.60 There are a number of provisions that enable the Revenue to recover tax from a third party if the person primarily liable does not pay it. If a company ceases to be UK-resident and any tax payable by it in respect of periods beginning before the date of its emigration is not paid within six months from the date of emigration the Revenue can require payment of the tax from any company which is a member of the same group as the migrating company or was a member of the group at any time in the 12 months prior to the date of the migration, or from any person who is (or was within the 12-month period) a controlling director of either the migrating company or a company which has control over it (or did so at some time in the 12-month period) [FA 1988 s 132(1), (3), (6)]. To do so the Revenue can serve notice on the person whom they wish to make liable for the tax, stating particulars of the tax payable, the amount remaining unpaid and the date it became payable, and requiring the person served to pay the tax within 30 days of the notice. They must serve the notice within three years from the time when the amount of the tax due is finally determined [FA 1988 s 132(2)]. The amount is then recoverable as if it were tax due and duly demanded of him. There is a right of recovery of the tax from the migrating company. The payer cannot of course claim a deduction for the payment in computing any income, profit or losses for any tax purposes [FA 1988 s 132(4), (6)]. There does not appear to be a right of appeal against such a notice.

9.61 If a chargeable gain accrues to a company which is resident in the UK at the time the gain accrues, and the whole or any part of the corporation tax assessed on the company is not paid within six months of the due date, the Revenue can recover the tax from the company which at the time of the gain was the principal company of the company's group or any other company which at any time in the 12 months before the gain was a member of the same group and owned the asset disposed of (or if the asset is an interest or right in or over another asset owned, either that asset or the other asset). If the gain arose in a UK branch of an overseas company within TCGA 1992 s 10(3), they can recover the tax from a controlling director of the company or of a company which has control over it (or a person who was such a controlling director at some time in the 12 months prior to the realisation of the gain) [TCGA 1992 s 190(1)–(3)]. The tax which can be sought is the lower of the corporation tax liability for the accounting period in which the gain arose or corporation tax on the amount of the gain [TCGA1992 s 190(4)].

9.62 The procedure (including the three-year time limit) is similar to that under s 132, but there is in this case a right of appeal as if the notice were a notice of assessment [TCGA 1992 s 190(5)–(7)]. If the unpaid tax is due under a Revenue determination in the absence of a return, the three-year period runs from the date of the determination [TCGA 1992 s 190(8)]. The time that tax is finally determined (from which the three-year period runs) is the end of the Revenue's enquiry window or 30 days after the latest of the completion of an enquiry, the amendment of the return or the final determination of any appeal. In the case of a discovery assessment it is the due and payable date for the tax, or if there is an appeal the date the appeal is finally determined [TCGA 1992 s 190(9), (10)]. As with s 130 there is a right of recovery from the company that realised the gain and if it cannot be recovered a prohibition on claiming tax relief for the payment [TCGA 1992 s 190(11), (12)]. It should particularly be noted that the provision applies even to a company that is and always has been resident in the UK.

9.63 There is also a right to recover from a third party corporation tax that has been assessed on a non-UK resident company and which is not paid within six months of it being due. The tax can be recovered from any company which was a member of the same group (51 per cent subsidiary) as the defaulting company at any time within a period starting 12 months before the beginning of the accounting period (or 1 April 2000 if later) and ending when the unpaid tax first became payable [FA 2000 Sch 28 paras 1, 2]. If the defaulting company was owned by a consortium the tax can also be recovered from any company which was a member of the consortium at any time during that period or any company which at such a time was a member of the same group of companies as one which was a member of the consortium [FA 2000 Sch 28 para 2(1)(c)].

9.64 The procedure and other rules are the same as under s 190 [FA 2000 Sch 28 paras 3, 4, 6]. In the case of a consortium company, only the proportion of the corporation tax liability attributable to the member's share can be recovered from a member (or another member of its group) [FA 2000 Sch 28 para 5].

9.65 Where a degrouping charge in relation to intangible fixed assets arises on a company leaving a group owning assets acquired intra-group and within the prior six years, the principal company and any other company which was a member of the group and owned the asset at any time in the 12 months prior to the taxpayer company leaving the group can be made liable for the tax if it is not paid within 12 months of the due date. If the taxpayer company is non-UK resident but trading through a UK permanent establishment, the tax can be recovered from anyone who was a controlling director of the taxpayer company or a company which controlled it during the 12-month period. The recoverable tax is the tax attributable to the asset. [FA 2002 Sch 29 para 68]. The procedure outlined at **9.60** and the rules at **9.62** again apply [FA 2002 Sch 29 paras 69, 70].

9.66 If the approval of a retirement benefit scheme is withdrawn and neither the scheme nor the employer pays the tax payable under TA 1988 s 591C as a result of that withdrawal, the tax can be collected from the employee for whose benefit the funds are held or from any person who is or has been a controlling director of the employer company. The assessment must be made within three years of the date on which the tax became due from the employer [TA 1988 s 606A]. Similarly, where approval of a personal pension arrangement is withdrawn the Revenue can recover the tax triggered by that withdrawal from the beneficiary if the scheme administrator does not pay it [TA 1988 s 650A(5), (6)].

9.67 Where there is a change in ownership of a company, any corporation tax assessed on the company for an accounting period beginning before the change which is not paid within six months of its due date can be collected from any person who controlled the company at any time within the three years prior to the change in ownership or any company of which that person had control within that three-year period [TA 1988 s 767A(1)–(3), (8), (9)]. This applies only if either:

(*a*) at some time during the three years prior to the change in ownership the activities of the company's trade or business ceased (or their scale of activities become small or negligible) and there was no significant revival of the activities before the change;

(*b*) such an event occurred at some time during the six years beginning three years before the change in ownership under arrangements made before the change; or

(*c*) at some time during the six years beginning three years before the change in ownership there was a major change in the nature or conduct of the company's trade or business, there was a transfer of assets of the taxpayer company to a person who controlled the company (or a connected person or to someone else under arrangements which facilitated a transfer to such a person), that transfer occurred in the three years before the change (or after it but in pursuance of prior arrangements) and the major change in the trade was attributable to that transfer,

[TA 1988 s 767(3)–(7)]. The assessment must be made within three years of the date that the tax liability of the company is finally determined [TA 1988 s 767A(10)]. The legislation does not attempt to define that date. It is likely that the rules in **9.62** above will in practice apply. It should be noted that tax avoidance does not need to be involved. The section will apply on an arm's length sale provided that one of the above three conditions apply.

9.68 Unpaid corporation tax of a company can similarly be recovered from a person who controlled the defaulting company (or controlled a company that controlled it in the prior three years) where:

(*a*) there is a change of ownership of the company;

(*b*) corporation tax relating to an accounting period of the company (or an associated company) ending on or before the change remains unpaid more than six months after it was assessed; and

(*c*) it would be reasonable to infer from either or both of the terms of the transactions entered into in connection with the change and the other circumstances of the change (and any such transactions) that at least one of those transactions was entered into by one or more of its parties on the assumption that a potential tax liability would be unlikely to be met, or met in full, if it were to arise [TA 1988 s 767AA(1), (2)].

A potential tax liability is a liability to corporation tax which, in circumstances which were reasonably foreseeable at the time of the change of ownership or the occurrence of which was a reasonably foreseeable risk at the time, might arise from an assessment made after the change of ownership on the transferred company or an associated company [TA 1988 s 767AA(3)–(5)].

9.69 If a chargeable event occurs which triggers a tax charge under FA 1989 s 68 on an employee benefit trust, and the trustees do not pay the tax within six months of the assessment becoming final and conclusive, the tax (and any accrued interest thereon) can be recovered from the company that established the trust or any company that paid a contribution to the trustees for which it obtained a corporation tax deduction under FA 1989 s 67(2)(a) [FA 1989 s 68(3)]. If the company does not pay the tax within three months the Revenue can thereafter proceed against both the company and the trustees [FA 1989 s 68(5)].

9.70 If there is a change of residence of a trust which triggers a capital gains tax charge on migration under TCGA 1992 s 80 and the tax thereon is not paid within six months of the time it becomes payable the tax can be recovered from any person who was a trustee of the settlement at any time within the 12 months prior to the migration (other than one who can show that when he ceased to be a trustee there was no proposal that the trustees might become either not resident nor ordinarily resident in the UK) [TCGA 1992 s 82].

9.71 If tax is triggered on a share exchange within TCGA 1992 s 135 or a scheme of reconstruction within TCGA 1992 s 136, because the Revenue are not satisfied that the transaction was carried out for bona fide commercial reasons and did not form part of a tax avoidance scheme, and the tax is not paid within six months of the time when the tax became due and payable (or was assessed on the chargeable person), it can be recovered from any other person who held all or any part of the shares or debentures that were issued to the chargeable person and acquired from him without there having been, since their acquisition by the chargeable person, any disposal (other than one between husband and wife or intragroup) [TA 1992 s 137(4), (4A)]. This convoluted language appears to be saying that, if the shares obtained on the share exchange have subsequently been transferred to the chargeable person's spouse, or another group company if it is a member of a group, the tax can be charged on the spouse or other group company. The spouse or company must be assessed within two years of the tax becoming payable [TCGA 1992 s 137(4)].

9.72 Similarly if, on a corporate reconstruction, a tax charge applies on the transfer of the whole or part of a company's business to another company and that tax is not paid within six months of the due date (or if later the date it was assessed), the tax (and any accrued interest) can be recovered from the transferee company or any other company that acquired the asset from it on an intra-group transfer if that company holds all or part of the assets transferred. The assessment must be raised within two years of the due and payable date (or the date of the assessment) [TCGA 1992 s 139(7)]

9.73 If a capital gain accrues to a person on a disposal of an asset by way of a gift (or sale at an undervalue), and he does not pay it within 12 months from the date on which it becomes due and payable, the tax can be recovered from the donee. An assessment must be made within two years of the time the tax became due. The amount assessed on the donee is not to exceed the lower of the chargeable gain on the gift or the unpaid tax grossed up at the donor's marginal rate of tax, ie an amount the tax on which will equal the amount of the unpaid tax [TCGA 1992 s 282].

9.74 If it appears to the Revenue that there may be tax payable for a tax year by an employer under PAYE the Revenue can determine the amount due to the best of their judgement and serve notice of the determination on the employer [Income Tax (Pay As You Earn) Regulations 2003, S1 2003/2682, reg 80]. If the tax so determined is not paid within 30 days of the determination becoming final and conclusive the Revenue can collect the PAYE from the employee (and release the employer from liability for it) if either:

(*a*) they consider that the employee in respect of whose earnings the determination was made received them knowing that the employer had wilfully failed to deduct the tax due under PAYE; or

(*b*) the unpaid tax represents an amount for which the employer was required to account and reg 62(5) (tax on notional payments where actual payments are insufficient to enable the full deduction to be made) applied.

Such tax carried interest. It cannot be treated as tax paid by the individual for the purpose of calculating the tax due on his self-assessment [reg 81].

9.75 The Revenue can similarly collect PAYE from the employee (instead of the employer) if it appears to them that the employer deducted too little tax and either:

(*a*) the employer satisfies the Revenue that he took reasonable care to comply with the PAYE regulations and the failure to deduct the right amount was due to an error made in good faith; or

(*b*) the employee has received the payment of earnings knowing that the employer wilfully failed to deduct the right amount of tax,

[reg 72]. If head (*b*) applies, the payment carries interest from 14 days after the end of the tax year concerned [reg 72(7), (8)].

Chapter 10

Interest on Overdue Tax

Income tax

10.1 If tax is not paid by the due date, interest is payable from that due date [TMA 1970 s 86(1)]. The rate of interest payable from time to time on overdue income tax and capital gains tax is fixed by the Treasury by statutory instrument [FA 1989 s 178]. It is currently 6.5 per cent and has been so since 6 November 2001. Interest runs from the due date even if it is a bank holiday [TMA 1970 s 86(3)].

10.2 Interest on tax payable under self-assessment of course runs from the due date under TMA 1970 s 59A(2) (see **8.1**), ie 31 January is the year of assessment in the case of the first interim payment, 31 July following the end of the year of assessment in the case of the second interim payment and the following 31 January for the balancing payment (including the whole of any capital gains tax). If the taxpayer gave notice of chargeability by 5 October following the end of the tax year but the Revenue did not issue him with a tax return until after 31 October, the interest runs instead from three months after the date of issue of the return [TMA 1970 s 86(2)]. If no return is issued by 31 October because notice of chargeability was not given, the interest runs from the normal 31 January date.

10.3 If the taxpayer makes a claim to reduce his interim payments (see **8.4**) and further tax is due, either as a balancing payment when the return is issued following an amendment or correction of the return or under a discovery assessment, interest is payable from the due date of each interim payment in relation to 50 per cent of that extra tax, but limited to interest on the amount by which the interim payment was reduced [TMA 1970 s 86(4), (5)].

EXAMPLE

Joe was due to make interim payments for 2001/02 of £20,000 each. He believed that his income had fallen significantly and applied to reduce the interim payments to £13,000 each. He paid the first £13,000 on 8 February 2002 and the second on 20 September 2002. When he submitted his return this showed tax payable for 2001/02 of £27,800. Joe paid the balance of £1,800 on 20 February 2003. The Revenue enquired into Joe's return. As a result of their enquiries the return was amended, the tax ultimately due being £46,000. The extra tax of £18,200 was paid on 19 December 2004.

10.3 *Interest on Overdue Tax*

Joe will have the following interest liabilities:

on	£13,000 paid	8.2.2002	from	1.2.2002 to 8.2.2002
on	£13,000 paid	20.9.2002	from	1.8.2002 to 20.9.2002
on	£1,800 paid	20.2.2003		
	on	£900	from	1.2.2002 to 20.2.2003
	on	£900	from	1.8.2002 to 20.9.2003
on	£18,200 paid	19.12.2004		
	on	£6,100 (ie £20,000 minus £(13,000 + 900))	from	1.2.2002 to 19.12.2004
	on	£6,100	from	1.8.2002 to 19.12.2004
	on	£6,000	from	1.2.2003 to 19.12.2004

10.4 It will be seen that the effect is to charge interest as if the interim payments had never been reduced (or as if they had been reduced only to the tax ultimately payable for the year). There are two points that particularly need to be watched. Although capital gains are ignored in determining the amount of interim payments they are brought into account for the purpose of the above calculations. If in the above example the tax for 2001/02 had been £25,600 on income and £2,200 on capital gains and the adjustment had been an additional capital gain, the capital gains would in effect carry interest from the due date of the interim payments even though Joe would have been entitled to reduce the interim payments if he had not anticipated realising any capital gains.

10.5 Secondly, although the additional tax payable as a result of an amendment to the return subsequent to the due date of the balancing payment is payable within 30 days of the date of the amendment [TMA 1970 s 59B(5) and Sch 3ZA] (see **8.16**), if it is not paid within that period interest runs from the normal 31 January date (or even earlier to the extent of any reduction in the interim payments). The interest on the late payment can accordingly be penal in such circumstances. It should particularly be noted that the 30-day period runs from the date that the amendment is notified to the taxpayer, not from the time that the Revenue issue a demand note for such tax. It can easily take 30 days before the demand note is issued.

10.6 In determining the interest payable on a balancing payment (or following an amendment or discovery assessment):

(*a*) it must be assumed that both of the interim payments were made (as if they were not, they themselves are already carrying an interest liability); and

(*b*) no account is to be taken of any amount which has been paid on account (other than in respect of the statutory interim payments).

It is not clear what head (*b*) is seeking to do. Suppose, for example, a taxpayer is due to make interim payments of £10,000 each for 2001/02 (and has not claimed to reduce them), he makes both payments on the due date but also pays a further £5,000 on 12 December 2002. The tax ultimately payable is found to be £28,000 and the balance of £3,000 is paid on 18 February 2003. Logically, interest should be payable from 1 February 2003–18 February 2003 on £3,000, not on £8,000. Undoubtedly parliament does not want the Revenue to have to pay interest on the £5,000 from 12 December 2002–31 January 2003, but as s 86 deals only with interest on overdue tax there seems no reason why the section should seek to deal with amounts paid early.

10.7 If the tax ultimately found to be due (including as a result of any adjustment or discovery assessment) is less than the interim payments, and either or both of the interim payments is paid late, 50 per cent of the interest applicable to each of the interim payments falls to be remitted [TMA 1970 s 86(8)]. Again no account is to be taken of any payments on account otherwise than as statutory interim payments [TMA 1970 s 86(9)].

EXAMPLE

Fred is due to make interim payments for 2001/02 of £15,000 each. He pays the first on 20 March 2002 and the second on 18 August 2002. Fred's tax liability for 2001/02 turns out to be £26,000.

Fred's interest payments will be:

on	£13,000	from	1 February 2002 to 20 March 2002
on	£13,000	from	1 July 2002 to 18 August 2002

The figure of £13,000 is the net figure. Fred is actually due to pay interest on the £15,000 with interest of £2,000 of that amount being remitted. It should be noted that interest is payable on £13,000 from 1 July 2002–18 August 2002 even though Fred paid £15,000 in March 2002; he is not given credit for the £2,000 excess when determining the interest due on the July payment.

10.8 Up to 1995/96 (1996/97 for partnership assessment) where tax was recovered to make good loss due to the taxpayer's default (which was the position on most discovery assessments) the interest was at a higher rate and in many cases ran from an earlier date than normal (the normal due date where this was earlier than 30 days from the issue of the assessment). This provision [TMA 1970 s 88] was abolished on the introduction of self-assessment by FA 1996 Sch 18 para 4(1), from 1996/97 (1997/98 for partnerships in existence at 6 April 1994) but still applies to interest for years up to 1995/96 (or 1996/97) where an assessment raised after 6 April 1997 relates to earlier years.

Corporation tax

10.9 Interest on corporation tax runs from the date when the tax becomes due and payable, normally nine months and a day after the end of the accounting period (see **8.35**). As with income tax, the rate is fixed from time to time by the Treasury by statutory instrument. Also, as for income tax, interest runs from the due date even if that is a bank holiday [TMA 1970 s 87A(1), (2)].

10.10 The rate is not the same as that which applies for income tax, and different rates apply to instalment payments. The current rates (from 6 November 2001) are:

on instalment payments	5 per cent (but where the amount is still unpaid nine months after the end of the accounting period the 6.5 per cent rate applies from that date).
on other payments	6.5 per cent
on pay and file liabilities (ie for accounting periods ending before 1 July 1999)	5 per cent

10.11 Companies, like other taxpayers, have to deduct income tax from certain annual payments and account for it to the Revenue. In the case of a company, such payments are accounted for in accordance with TA 1988 Sch 16 [TA 1988 s 350(4)]. This requires a return of payments due for each calendar quarter (after deducting any income tax suffered by deductions at source) to be made within 14 days after the end of that quarter. The same procedure applied under TA 1988 Sch 13 to advance corporation tax which was payable on dividends declared prior to 6 April 1999 when the impost was abolished. If tax due under Sch 16 (or Sch 13) is not paid by the due date, interest runs from that due date [TMA 1970 s 87(1)].

10.12 If tax is payable under Sch 16 for a quarter and the company suffers tax by deduction at source in a later quarter, the tax for the first quarter becomes repayable or, if not already paid, is discharged. When outstanding tax is so discharged interest is still payable on it but only up to the due date for the second quarter's return or, if earlier, the date of the return for that quarter [TMA 1970 s 87(2), (8)].

Example

Megacorp plc paid £100,000 of interest to an offshore bank on 14 February 2003 from which it deducted tax of £20,000. On 15 October 2003 it received a payment of interest under deduction of tax of £15,000. It overlooked submitting its Sch 16 return for the quarter to 31 March 2003. It submitted the return for the quarter to 31 December 2003 on 30 October 2003 when it also paid over the net amount of £5,000.

Megacorp will suffer interest:

on £15,000	from 15 April 2003–30 October 2003 (as it submitted the return prior to the due date of 14 January 2004)
on £5,000	from 15 April 2003–30 October 2003 (when it paid the tax)

Suppose that Megacorp did not submit its December return and pay the £5,000 until 30 January 2004.

It will suffer interest:

on £15,000	from 15 April 2003–14 January 2004 (the due date for the December return)
on £5,000	from 15 April 2003–31 January 2004 (the date of payment of the tax not discharged)

10.13 At least this seems to be the position. TMA 1970 s 87(3) does not seem to envisage the possibility of a return being made prior to the end of the calendar quarter, as it refers to the return being 'made earlier in those fourteen days'. Accordingly, it is possible that in the first example interest on the £15,000 would run to 14 January 2004 as there was no earlier payment during the 14 days 1 January 2004–14 January 2004.

10.14 Tax under Sch 16 is not normally assessed. If an assessment is raised in the absence of a return, the interest will run from the time the return ought to have been made, not by reference to the making of the assessment [TMA 1970 s 87(7)].

10.15 There are a number of provisions that allow corporation tax to be assessed or treated as assessed on someone other than the company, namely:

(*a*) TA 1988 s 346(2): which enabled tax on a chargeable gain to be recovered from a shareholder to whom it was distributed – but was repealed from 2002/03.

(*b*) TA 1988 s 347(1): which enabled tax on capital gains to be recovered from another group company – but was also repealed from 2002/03.

(*c*) TCGA 1992 s 137(4): which enables tax on capital gains arising on a company reconstruction to be recovered from a share or debenture holder if the reconstruction is not shown to have been carried out for bona-fide commercial reasons.

(*d*) TCGA 1992 s 139(7): which enables tax on capital gains arising on a reconstruction or amalgamation involving the transfer of a business to be recovered from the transferee.

(*e*) TCGA 1992 s 190: which enables tax on capital gains to be recovered from another group company or a controlling shareholder (and which replaced TA 1988 s 347).

(*f*) FA 1998 Sch 18 para 75A: which enables corporation tax due on the withdrawal of a group relief claim to be recovered from another group company.

(*g*) FA 2000 Sch 28: which enables tax payable by a non-resident company to be recovered by a member of the same group (51 per cent subsidiaries).

Where this happens interest runs from the date the tax originally became due and payable by the creditor company, not from the date that the Revenue raise the assessment on the other party from whom they seek to recover the tax [TMA 1970 s 87A(3)]. It should be noted that s 87A(3) does not refer to TCGA 1992 s 189 (the replacement for TA 1988 s 246(2)) which enables tax on chargeable gains to be recovered from a shareholder to whom a capital distribution is made.

10.16 If a company has a non-trading deficit on loan relationships for an accounting period and elects to carry it back to an earlier accounting period under FA 1996 s 83(2)(c), and as a result corporation tax for that earlier period which is unpaid ceases to be payable, interest on that tax remains payable for the period from the original due date until nine months after the end of the accounting period in which the deficit on loan relationships arises [TMA 1970 s 87A(4), (8)].

10.17 The same rule applies to losses carried back if the accounting period to which they are carried back does not fall wholly within 12 months prior to that in which the loss arose [TMA 1970 s 87A(6), (8)]. A carry back of a loss to the immediately preceding accounting period appears to eliminate the interest on the tax for that year.

10.18 If an Inspector raises an assessment on a company under s 252 to recover an excessive set-off of advance corporation tax or excessive payment of tax credit interest runs from the date of the set off or payment until the date that the sum assessed is paid. The assessment is treated for the purposes of TMA 1970 as if it were an assessment to income tax [TA 1988 s 252(5)]. Accordingly, the rate of interest is that applicable to unpaid income tax [TMA 1970 s 87A(5)].

10.19 TMA 1970 s 59E (see **8.36**) gives the Treasury power to vary the dates on payment of corporation tax – and is the authority for quarterly payments for large companies. The regulations under s 59E do not apply for the purposes of **10.16** and **10.17** above, ie the interest runs to the nine months anniversary even though the due date of payment for corporation tax for the later year is earlier [TMA 1970 s 87A(9)].

Disallowance of relief

10.20 Interest payable under TMA 1970 ss 86–88 must be paid gross. Interest paid by a company under s 87 or 87A for a period after 1 July 1999 is deductible as a deficit on loan relationships (the rate payable reflects the fact that it is deductible). Other interest on overdue tax is not deductible for any tax purpose [TMA 1970 s 90].

Effect of interest on reliefs

10.21 Where interest is payable under s 86 and the tax to which it relates is discharged, such adjustment is to be made to that interest as is necessary to ensure that the total tax and interest payable is the same as it would have been if the amount discharged had never been payable [TMA 1970 s 91(1)].

10.22 The same rule applies in general to corporation tax which is subsequently discharged, although is overridden by TMA 1970 s 87A(4A) and (6) (carry back of losses and deficits on loan relationships (see **10.16** and **10.17**) [TMA 1970 s 91(1A), (1B)].

10.23 If relief from tax paid for a chargeable period is given by repayment the taxpayer can require the amount repaid to be treated for the purpose of s 91 as if it were a discharge of the tax charged on him (whether alone or together with other persons) by an assessment for the same chargeable period [TMA 1970 s 91(2)]. This will enable him to claim repayment of any interest paid on the tax assessed. Such an election cannot be used to apply the repayment against an assessment made subsequent to the repayment. Although such an election can be used in relation to more than one assessment for the same accounting period to eliminate interest, it cannot partially reduce more than one; it must eliminate the whole of the first charge before any excess can be set against another [TMA 1970 s 91(2)]. It should be noted that the repayment need not be used against the assessment to which it relates. It can be used (subject to **10.25** below) to discharge the interest on any assessment for the accounting period.

10.24 If relief from corporation tax is given by repayment and that tax was paid for an accounting period ending after 30 June 1999 the company can require the amount repaid to be treated for the purpose of s 91 as if it were a discharge of the corporation tax charged on him for that accounting period [TMA 1970 s 91(2A)]. It is not clear what this provision is intended to do as s 91(2) seems to already achieve the same thing. It probably limits s 91(2), so that where it applies relief cannot be given against any other assessment for the accounting period.

10.25 However, notwithstanding the above general rules, no relief, whether by way of discharge or repayment, can be treated as:

(*a*) affecting tax charged by an assessment to income tax under Sch A or Sch D if it arises in connection with income taxable otherwise than under those Schedules (or relates to a source the income from which is taxable other than under those Schedules); or (*b*) affecting tax charged at a rate other than the basic rate (such as the lower rate or the starting rate) on income from which tax has been deducted at source (other than under PAYE) or treated as having been so deducted, unless it is a relief from the tax so charged,

[TMA 1970 s 91(3)].

10.26 A relief from corporation tax or capital gains tax cannot be used to affect the interest on tax charged by an assessment unless that assessment is to the same tax [TMA 1970 s 91(4)].

Recovery

10.27 Interest on overdue tax is recoverable as if it were an amount charged on the assessment to which it relates [TMA 1970 s 69].

Remission by reason of exchange restrictions

10.28 If the Board of Inland Revenue are satisfied that tax on income or chargeable gains arises in a country outside the UK, that as a result of action of the government of that country it is impossible for the income or gains to be remitted to the UK, and that having regard to such matters and to all the other circumstances of the case it is reasonable that the tax should for the time being remain uncollected, interest on such tax ceases to run as from the date on which the Board were first in possession of the information necessary for them to make that decision [TMA 1970 s 92(1), (2)]. If they are given such information within three months from the time the tax became due and payable the interest already accrued must also be remitted [TMA 1970 s 91(2)]. The interest starts to run again from the date that payment of the tax is demanded once the amount becomes remittable, but that interest must also be remitted if the tax is paid within three months from the date of that demand [TMA 1970 s 91(3)].

Remission in other cases

10.29 The legislation does not give the Revenue power to waive or mitigate interest. They can, however, do so under their general power of care and management. The Revenue see interest as commercial restitution. As such they are generally very reluctant to waive it. Code of Practice 1 states:

> 'when there is no good reason for a delay, and when we have taken more than 6 months in total – over and above the 28 day target we have set ourselves – we will give up interest on tax that was unpaid during the period of our delay'.

10.30 The Revenue say that:

> 'to qualify for consideration the responsibility for the progress of the case must have lain with the Revenue for at least 6 months over and above the 28 day turnaround target either as a single period or in total. The delay should have accrued after the notice of assessment was issued and at any time after the Inspector was first in a position to make progress with the case, eg following receipt of a return, accounts or other relevant information … Revenue delay prior to the issue of the notice of assessment or prior to the interest charging date is normally to be disregarded, mainly because it has not disadvantaged the taxpayer and is irrelevant to the accrual of interest.' (Accounts Office Review Unit Manual, para 3.3.)

10.31 It appears that this was written before the introduction of self-assessment, when interest normally ran from 30 days after the issue of the assessment if that was later than the normal due date. This no longer applies. Accordingly, relief should be claimed for a period of delay prior to the issue of the assessment if interest runs from such an earlier date.

10.32 Subject to that the Revenue tell their staff that:

> 'where a charge to interest is overlooked and then raised late a taxpayer's annoyance is understandable, and an apology for the Revenue's shortcomings is appropriate. It should be remembered that the late application for payment does not increase the amount of interest payable and, despite any delay, the taxpayer is not financially disadvantaged'.

10.33 They also say that:

(*a*) If an objection to interest is made on the grounds of non-receipt or late receipt of the original notice of assessment the interest charge must be cancelled if there is no evidence of service of the notice (including deemed service under TMA 1970 s 115, see **14.47**) or recomputed to a later date where the assessment had to be reissued (Accounts Office Review Unit Manual, para 4.2). However, where tax is due without assessment, interest charges are generally to be maintained (para 4.8).

(*b*) A taxpayer who is regularly absent, eg abroad, and wishes to avoid incurring an interest charge, is expected to make arrangements for payment of tax by the relevant dates. If they fail to do so and incur interest charges as a result then it can be argued that the interest is only reasonable recompense as in any other case (para 6.1).

(*c*) If a taxpayer is admitted to a mental institution before the due and payable date of the tax, delay may occur because of the need for an application to the Court of Protection. In such cases payment of the tax is normally required 30 days from the date of the order of the Court of Protection and interest is charged by reference to that date. If the taxpayer is admitted to the mental institution after the due and payable date the case will be considered on its merits (paras 7.1 and 7.2).

(*d*) If the Revenue overlook sending a copy of an assessment to an agent, 'whilst it is regrettable' there is no statutory requirement to do so and any interest charge is to be maintained (para 8).

(*e*) If a Notice of Assessment is correctly issued but does not indicate the amount of tax payable the interest charge is to be 'given up' (para 10).

(*f*) If a postponement application is made in relation to an appeal against an assessment and the application is not determined, interest is charged only from 30 days after the date of issue of the notice of revised liability. There is no longer a statutory basis for this in the self-assessment era but the Revenue have allowed their long-standing policy to continue as 'to do otherwise would be seen as an attempt by the Revenue to benefit from its own incompetence.' (Para 16.3.)

(*g*) If a taxpayer points out an arithmetical error by the Revenue which results in an assessment being increased and it is paid promptly interest in respect of the increase is to be given up (para 20.1).

(*h*) 'The absence of an interest warning is not considered to be grounds for giving up an interest charge. Interest accrues automatically, regardless of whether blame can be attached to the Department for its handling of the tax liability.' (Para 20.2.)

(*i*) Where a payment in advance of an increase is repaid in error, interest is to be given up from the original effective date of payment to the date of the repayment by the Revenue (para 35.1). Logically this ought also to apply where the Revenue incorrectly repay interim payments because they do not capture the return information properly. Indeed in such a case it is arguable that no interest should be payable if the amount repaid is returned promptly to the Revenue.

(*j*) 'Objections to interest sometimes takes the form of a plea for mitigation due to the taxpayer's circumstances, eg illness, old age, lack of funds etc. Such cases are usually maintained with expressions of sympathy.' (Para 42.)

Foot and mouth disease

10.34 The Revenue entered into agreements with farmers and other businesses in rural areas (under their power of care and management) to defer the collection of tax where the business would otherwise have suffered hardship. In such cases no interest on overdue tax is chargeable on the amount deferred from 1 January 2001 (or if the Revenue so direct the later date at which such an agreement took effect) until the date on which the agreement ceases to have effect. This is the date stated in the agreement, unless the Revenue agree to extend the deferment period by reason of circumstances arising as a result of the foot and mouth disease outbreak [FA 2001 s 107(1)–(3)]. Where the agreement provides for payment by instalments, interest starts to run on each instalment when it becomes due – but if an instalment is paid late the whole of the deferred tax is treated as becoming due at that time unless the Revenue agree to extend the period of deferment [FA 2001 s 107(4)]. If no agreement was made with the Revenue but they take the view that they would have made one had they been asked this interest holiday will apply [FA 2001 s 107(5)].

Setting of rate of interest

10.35 The rate of interest on overdue tax is in most cases, that provided for by regulations made by the Treasury [FA 1989 s 178]. The regulations are the Taxes (Interest Rate) Regulations 1989, SI 1989/1297. They provide for the rate of interest on unpaid tax and tax repayments and on repayment supplements to be fixed by a formula by reference to a reference rate, which is the average base lending rates of the major clearing banks on a reference date. The rates are reviewed periodically by reference to changes in the reference rate and amended rates promulgated by statutory instrument. The procedure for changing interest rates for instalments and early payments of corporation tax are contained in the Corporation Tax (Instalment Payments) Regulations 1998, SI 1998/3175.

Chapter 11

Interest Receivable and Repayment Supplements

11.1 The Inland Revenue do not in general pay interest on tax paid early or on repayments due from the Revenue. There are three circumstances in which interest or quasi interest can be earned:

(*a*) interest is payable in relation to certain overpayments by companies [TA 1988 ss 826 and 826A];

(*b*) a repayment supplement will be paid where a repayment is unduly delayed [TA 1988 ss 824 and 825; TCGA 1992 s 283]; and

(*c*) a taxpayer can purchase a certification of tax deposit which carries interest [FA 1995 s 157].

Corporation tax overpaid ('repayment interest')

11.2 Interest is payable from the 'material date' to the date that an order for repayment is issued in relation to either:

(*a*) a repayment of corporation tax for an accounting period ended after 30 September 1993;

(*b*) a repayment of ACT in respect of distributions made by the company in an accounting period ended after 30 September 1993;

(*c*) a repayment of income tax which falls to be made in respect of a payment received by the company under deduction of income tax in such an accounting period;

(*d*) a payment of all or part of a tax credit attaching to franked investment income received in such an accounting period;

(*e*) a payment of Research and Development tax credit under FA 2000 Sch 20; or

(*f*) a payment of land remediation tax credit or life assurance company tax credit under FA 2001 Sch 22,

[TA 1988 s 826(1)].

11.3 The material date for the purpose of (*a*) above is the date on which corporation tax was paid or, if later, the date on which it became due and payable (or would have become due) in accordance with TMA 1970 s 59D (see **8.33**), ie nine months and a day after the end of the accounting period [TA 1988 s 826(2)]. In practice this date never applies as it has been displaced by the Corporation Tax (Instalment Payments) Regulations 1998 (see **8.36**).

11.4 The Treasury have power by regulation to specify a different material date [TA 1988 s 826A(2)]. They have done so in the Corporation Tax (Instalment Payments) Regulations 1998, SI 1998/3175, which is of course the legislation requiring large companies to make quarterly payments on account (see **8.36**). Regulation 8 provides that the material date in relation to an overpayment of instalment payments is the date on which the first instalment payment for the accounting period is treated as becoming due or, if later, the date on which the excess amount arises [TA 1988 s 826(3A), inserted by reg 8(3)]. An excess amount arises when the total amount paid by a large company up to a point of time in respect of its total liability for the accounting period in accordance with reg 5 (see **8.40**) exceeds the amount that is treated as becoming due and payable by the company for that period at that time in accordance with that regulation [TA 1988 s 826(1)(d), inserted by reg 8(2)]. Instalment payments are recalculated each quarter on a cumulative basis, so an excess amount is likely to arise only if the estimated profits at the end of a quarter are less than the estimate at the end of the previous quarter. It should be noted that if a company were to pay more than it believes to be due for a quarter the interest is limited by reference to the amount that it believes to be due under the regulation.

11.5 Regulation 8 also provides that if a company that is not a large company in an accounting period makes a payment for that accounting period earlier than nine months and a day after the end of that period the material date is the date on which the first instalment payment would have become due had it been a large company (6 months and 13 days from the start of the accounting period) if the payment is made before that date. If it is made later it is the date of the payment [TA 1988 ss 826(3B) and 826(1)(e), inserted by regs 8(2) and 8(3)]. In other words the general rule for corporation tax is that interest is payable on tax paid early unless it is paid during the first half of the accounting period.

11.6 The material date in relation to the other items in para **11.2** above is:

(i) paras (*c*) and (*d*): the day after the end of the accounting period in which the item was received net of tax or the franked investment income was received;

(ii) paras (*e*) and (*f*): the later of the filing date for the tax return for the accounting period for which the tax credit was paid or the date on which the return (or amended return) claiming it was delivered to the Revenue,

[TA 1988 s 826(3)–(3B)].

11.7 Where tax becomes repayable under TA 1988 s 419(4) (repayment of loan to a participator), although that section treats it as if it were a repayment of corporation tax the material date is the later of:

(*a*) the date when the entitlement to relief in respect of the repayment accrued, ie nine months after the end of the accounting period in which the repayment took place (unless the repayment was made within nine months of the making of the loan, in which case it is nine months after the end of the accounting period in which the loan was made); and

(*b*) the date on which the tax was in fact paid,

[TA 1988 s 826(4)].

11.8 Interest under s 826 is payable without deduction of tax. If the company is within the charge to corporation tax it is taxable as a credit on loan relationships. If the company is not within the charge to corporation tax the interest is not taxable [TA 1988 s 826(5), (5A)].

11.9 Where a company pays corporation tax on different days the repayment must be treated for interest purposes as a repayment of the tax paid on a later rather than an earlier date [TA 1988 s 826(6)].

11.10 If the repayment arises from a claim to carry back a trading loss to an earlier accounting period, interest is payable only from the date from which corporation tax for the accounting period in which the loss arose became (or would have become) due and payable – which is deemed to be nine months and a day following the end of the accounting period [TA 1988 s 826(7A), (7D)]. This restriction also applies where the repayment is triggered by a claim to carry back to the previous accounting period a non-trading deficit on loan relationships, or to carry back unrealised overseas tax to an earlier accounting period under TA 1988 s 806D (including where the right to carry back the overseas tax is triggered by the carry back of a trading loss) [TA 1988 s 826(7BB)–(7D)].

11.11 The power of the Treasury under TMA 1970 s 59E (see **8.36**) to amend the date on which corporation tax becomes due and payable is not to affect this provision [TA 1988 s 826(7E)].

11.12 If after interest on tax overpaid has been paid to a company:

(*a*) there is a change in its corporation tax liability (or in the amount of tax credit due);

(*b*) that change does not in whole or in part correct an error (including a computational error or the allowance of a claim or election which ought not to have been allowed) made by the Board or an officer of the Board; and (*c*) as a result only of the change (and in particular not as a result of any error in the calculation of the interest) it appears to an officer of the Board that the interest should not have been paid (or should have been less),

the interest that should not have been paid can be recovered from the company as if it were an amount of corporation tax [TA 1988 s 826(8A)–(8C)]. It appears that if any part of the interest is attributable to Revenue error even the balance cannot be recovered.

Repayment supplement

Individuals and others

11.13 A repayment of:

(*a*) an amount paid on account of income tax under TMA 1970 s 59A;

(*b*) any income tax paid by or on behalf of an individual for a year of assessment;

(*c*) capital gains tax paid by an individual;

(*d*) a surcharge imposed under TMA 1970 s 59C; or

(*e*) a penalty incurred by an individual under any of the provisions of the TMA 1970,

is to be increased by a repayment supplement equal to interest on the amount repaid (at the rate applicable under FA 1989 s 178) for the period (if any) between the 'relevant time' and the date on which the order for the repayment is issued [TA 1988 s 824(1); TCGA 1992 s 283].

11.14 The relevant time depends on how the tax in question was originally paid:

(*a*) if it was a payment on account under s 59A it is the date of the original payment [s 824(3)(a)(i)];

(*b*) if it was other income tax paid for the year of assessment (as opposed to deducted at source) it is again the date of the original payment [s 824(3)(a)(ii)];

(*c*) if it was suffered by deduction at source it is 31 January following the end of the tax year to which it relates [s 824(3)(b)];

(*d*) if it was a gross payment of interest which ought to have been paid under MIRAS and the tax that could have been deducted is refunded by the Revenue under s 375(8), it is 31 January following the tax year in which the gross payment was made (5 April if it was made prior to 1996/97) [s 824(3)(aa)];

(*e*) if it was Sch D tax which has become repayable as a result of a claim to carry back loss relief, or for farmers' averaging or averaging relief for fluctuating profits of creative artists, it is 31 January following the end of the year that is the later year in respect of the claim, ie the year in which the loss arose or the second year to be averaged [s 824(3)(ab)]; or

(*f*) if the original payment was of a penalty or surcharge it is the date that the penalty or surcharge was paid [s 824(3)(c)].

11.15 Repayment supplement is also due on the payment of the whole or part of a tax credit (as if it were income tax paid in the year of assessment); a repayment made in consequence of a claim under TA 1952 s 228 (for personal allowances on reaching adulthood where income was accumulated under a trust, as if it were income tax paid for the year of assessment); a payment by the Board under TA 1988 s 375(8) (see **11.14**(*d*)) (as if it were a repayment falling within TA 1988 s 369(1)); or a payment by the Revenue following one of the claims referred to in **11.14**(*e*) (as if it were a repayment of tax paid by the taxpayer) [TA 1988 s 824(2)–(2C)].

11.16 Where the repayment is of income tax paid for a year of assessment it must be treated as far as possible as a repayment of the balancing payment for the year. Any excess is treated 50 per cent as repayment of part of the first interim payment and 50 per cent as repayment of part the second [TA 1988 s 824(4)(a), (b)]. Only if the repayment exceeds all three payments is the balance attributed to repayment of tax deducted at source [TA 1988 s 824(4)(c)]. Where any of the above payments are made in instalments, the repayment must be attributed to a later instalment before being attributed to an earlier one [TA 1988 s 824(4)(d)].

11.17 References above to income tax deducted at source means income tax deducted (or treated as deducted) from any income, or treated as paid on any income, in respect of the year of assessment concerned plus tax credits on qualifying distributions for that year under TA 1988 s 231 (which were repayable up to 1998/99 but cannot be repaid where the distribution was made after that date) [TA 1988 s 824(4A)]. It does not, however, include tax deducted under PAYE in respect of previous years, ie where additional tax was deducted to recoup an underpayment in respect of an earlier year [TA 1988 s 824(4B)].

11.18 No repayment supplement is payable in relation to the repayment of a post-war credit or in relation to a repayment made in consequence of an order or judgement of a court where the court had power to award interest [TA 1988 s 824(7)].

11.19 A repayment supplement is not income for any tax purpose [TA 1988 s 824(8)].

11.20 Section 824 applies to repayments to individuals, trustees and personal representatives. It does not apply to repayments to companies or other bodies corporate [TA 1988 s 824(1)(a)].

Companies

11.21 Repayment supplements are not payable to companies in relation to an accounting period ended after 30 September 1993 [TA 1988 s 826(8)]. This is because repayment interest (see above) applies.

11.22 Repayment supplement is payable to UK companies (but not non-resident ones even if within the charge to corporation tax) in relation to accounting periods ended before 1 October 1993, although a repayment for such a period can probably now only arise in the context of a back duty enquiry. The repayments which attract a supplement are:

(*a*) a repayment of corporation tax paid for the accounting period (including ACT paid in respect of distributions made in that period);

(*b*) a repayment of income tax suffered by deduction at source, in the accounting period; and

(*c*) a repayment of a tax credit comprised in franked investment income received by the company in the accounting period,

[TA 1988 s 825(1)].

11.23 A repayment supplement is, however, payable only if the repayment is made more than 12 months after the material date. It is calculated as an amount equal to interest (at the rate applicable under FA 1989 s 178) for each complete tax month (month ending on the 5th) in the period for the relevant date to the end of the tax month in which the repayment order is issued [TA 1988 s 825(2)].

11.24 For this purpose the 'material date' is the last day on which corporation tax on any of the profits of the company in question arising in the relevant accounting period could have been paid (nine months after the end of the accounting period, subject to a different rule for building societies) [TA 1988 s 825(8)].

11.25 The relevant date is the first anniversary of the material date unless the tax was paid on or after that date, in which case it becomes the first anniversary of the material date that follows the payment of the tax. Where the tax was paid on different dates the repayment is treated as far as possible as a repayment of the tax paid on a later rather than an earlier date [TA 1988 s 825(7)].

11.26 There are a few special situations:

(*a*) a repayment in consequence of a claim under TA 1988 s 239(3) to carry back surplus ACT to an earlier accounting period must be treated as a repayment of corporation tax paid for the accounting period in which the surplus arose;

(*b*) a repayment of tax under s 419(4) (loans to participants) is treated as a repayment of corporation tax for the accounting period in which the repayment of the loan was made; and

(*c*) a repayment of tax arising from a claim to carry back a loss is treated as a repayment of tax paid in the earlier accounting period if this falls wholly within the 12 months preceding that in which the loss arises but as a repayment of tax paid in the accounting period in which the loss arises in any other case.

[TA 1988 s 825(4)].

11.27 No repayment supplement is due in relation to a payment made in consequence of an order or judgement of a court if the court had power to allow interest on the payment [TA 1988 s 825(6)].

11.28 A repayment supplement is not income for the purposes of income tax or corporation tax [TA 1988 s 825(7)].

Capital gains tax

11.29 Repayment supplement also applies to an overpayment of capital gains tax by an individual (or a trust or the personal representative of a deceased person). The amount is equivalent to interest (at the rate applicable under FA 1989 s 178) for the period between the date on which the tax was paid and the date when the order for repayment is issued [TCGA 1992 s 283]. Repayment supplement is not payable if the repayment is made in consequence of an order or judgement of a court having power to allow interest on the payment [TCGA 1992 s 283(3)].

Certificates of tax deposit

11.30 The certificates of Tax Deposit scheme enables taxpayers to make payments to be held as deposits against future tax liabilities [FA 1995 s 157]. Interest is paid on the deposit. A certificate can be encashed instead of used to settle a tax liability, but the rate of interest is significantly reduced if this is done. Certificates purchased after 30 September 1993 cannot be used in settlement of corporation tax liabilities. As a Certificate ceases to accrue interest if it is not used or surrendered within six years, there are likely to be very few pre-1 October 1993 certificates still held by companies.

11.31 Deposits are made through the Revenue but the scheme is actually a Treasury scheme, with the Revenue acting as agent of the Treasury in issuing the certificate. The money is deposited by the Treasury in the National Loans Fund. The terms of the deposit are governed by a prospectus issued by the Treasury. There have been seven series of Certificates, the Seventh Series; the current one, relates to deposits made after 1 October 1993.

11.32 Deposits can be for any amount, but the initial minimum deposit must be at least £500. Once a deposit account has been opened additional deposits can be for £250 or more. Deposits of £100,000 or more must be remitted direct to an account of the Revenue at the Bank of England and a confirmatory letter sent to the Revenue's Financial Accounting Office at Worthing, giving the taxpayer's details. Deposits of under £100,000 are made to the Collector of Taxes.

11.33 Certificates can be used against the following liabilities:

(*a*) income tax and Class 4 NI (but not PAYE, Class 1 NI or sub-contractors deductions);

(*b*) capital gains tax; and

(*c*) income tax charged at the higher rate from which basic rate tax has been deducted.

A Certificate of Tax Deposit cannot be used to settle PAYE or sub-contractors liabilities at all. Neither can it be used to account for income tax deducted at source from payments to third parties. A certificate can only used to settle liabilities of the person to whom it was issued. In particular a certificate in the name of a partnership cannot be used to settle a liability of an individual partner. A certificate can also be used against inheritance tax and petroleum revenue tax.

11.34 Interest runs only to the due date of the liability being settled – but the liability is treated as settled on its due date, so the tender of the certificate will avoid interest on overdue tax. Interest is calculated on a daily basis. Where a person holds several certificates he needs to specify which is to be used against which liability. A certificate nearing its sixth anniversary ought normally to be used before a later one as it will stop accruing interest when it reaches that anniversary.

11.35 A certificate is used against a tax liability by sending it to the Collector of Taxes with appropriate instructions. If only part of the certificate (plus interest on that part) is required to settle a liability the Collector will issue a balance certificate for the difference. If this is for less than £500 (and the taxpayer has no other deposits) a further deposit can be made to bring the total up to £500 even if that deposit is less than £250. A balance certificate will bear the same date as the original deposit.

11.36 A certificate can be withdrawn for cash at any time by sending the certificate to the Inland Revenue Financial Accounting Office in Worthing. Repayment normally takes 10 working days. If a certificate is to be used partly to settle a tax liability with the balance being repaid, it must be sent to the Inland Revenue Accounts Office (Shipley or Cumbernauld). Interest runs to the date that the repayment order is issued. A withdrawal of £100,000 or more is made by bank transfer with interest ceasing on the day the Revenue instructs the bank to make the transfer.

11.37 The current interest rates are:

	To pay tax	*Encashed*
deposits of under £100,000	2.25 per cent	1.25 per cent
deposits of £100,000 or more		
held for under 1 month	2.25 per cent	1.25 per cent
held for 1–3 months	4.75 per cent	2.5 per cent
held for 3–9 months	2.25 per cent	4.25 per cent
held for 9–12 months	4 per cent	2 per cent

11.38 These rates are not particularly attractive. A Certificate of Tax Deposit is particularly useful where it is uncertain whether or not a tax liability will arise. The purchase of a certificate will avoid interest on overdue tax if the liability materialises. If it does not, the certificate can be used against other liabilities or encashed.

Chapter 12

Penalties

Criminal penalties

12.1 In general, direct tax penalties are civil penalties. There are only three specific criminal offence in the tax code. The first is TA 1988 s 766. Section 765 of that Act (migration of companies) makes it unlawful for a UK company to permit an overseas company over which it has control to create or issue any shares or debentures, or for a UK-resident company to transfer shares or debentures of a non-UK company over which it has control to anyone (even another UK-resident) without the consent of the Treasury.

12.2 Anyone who is a party to doing any act which to his knowledge amounts to or results in or forms part of a series of acts which together amount to or result in (or will amount to or result in) something which is unlawful under s 765 is guilty of an offence irrespective of whether that act takes place in the UK or abroad [TA 1988 s 766(1)]. In proceeding against a director of the UK company in question (or against any person purporting to act as a director):

(*a*) it must be assumed that he was a party to every act of the company unless he proves that it was done without his consent or connivance; and

(*b*) unless the contrary is proved, it must be presumed that any act which in fact amounted to or resulted in (or formed part of a series of acts which together amounted to or resulted in, or would amount to or result in) something which is unlawful under s 765 was to his knowledge such an act [TA 1988 s 766(2)].

12.3 The maximum penalty under s 766 is:

(*a*) imprisonment for up to two years, or a fine or both;

(*b*) if the person in question is a UK company, a fine of up to three times the corporation tax, capital gains tax and income tax which is attributable to the profits or gains arising in the three years immediately preceding the commission of the offence or, if greater, £10,000 [TA 1988 s 766(3)].

12.4 Proceedings cannot be brought for an offence under s 766 other than with the consent of the Attorney General [TA 1988 s 766(4)].

12.5 As far as is known no successful prosecutions have ever been brought under s 766 (or its predecessors) since what is now s 765 was introduced in 1951.

Fraudulent evasion of income tax

12.6 There is also a criminal offence of fraudulent evasion of income tax. A person commits this offence if he is knowingly concerned in the fraudulent evasion of income tax either by himself or by any other person [FA 2000 s 144(1)]. It does not apply to anything that happened before 1 January 2005 [FA 2000 s 144(3)]. The maximum penalty is on summary conviction imprisonment for up to six months or a fine of up to £5,000 ('the statutory maximum') or both, and on conviction on indictment imprisonment for up to seven years or an unlimited fine or both [FA 2000 s 144(2)].

12.7 It should be noted that this applies only to income tax. It cannot be used against the fraudulent evasion of capital gains tax or corporation tax or false claims for tax credits. It is primarily intended to provide a relatively quick means to enable the Revenue to prosecute simple cases in the black (or grey or shadow) economy and false claims for personal allowances.

12.8 It is also a criminal offence to destroy records once a person has been served with a notice under TMA 1970 s 20, 20A or 20BA (see **5.96**) or to provide information for tonnage tax purposes that he knows or has reasonable cause to believe is false in a material particular. The penalty is a fine of up to the statutory maximum (£5,000) on summary conviction or an unlimited fine on indictment [FA 2000 Sch 22 para 35].

12.9 In Scotland (but not in England and Wales) if a person, for the purpose of obtaining any allowance, reduction, rebate or repayment in respect of tax (either for himself for an other person) or in any return made with reference to tax, knowingly makes any false statement or false representation, he is liable on summary conviction to imprisonment for up to six months. Proceedings under the provision must be commenced within three years of the offence being committed [TMA 1970 s 107]. Although this provision relates only to Scotland, the Revenue consider that a statement or representation made in a return or letter is made at the Revenue office to which the return or letter is sent. Accordingly, this provision could well apply to an English taxpayer whose tax affairs are dealt with by a tax office in Scotland.

Other criminal conduct

12.10 The Revenue are a prosecuting authority, albeit that there are few specific criminal offences in the direct tax legislation apart from TMA 1970 s 766 and FA 2000 s 144. They prosecute fraud as the common law offence of cheat, normally Cheating the Public Revenue. They also prosecute for other common law offences such as making false statements, theft, forgery and whatever other such offence may be appropriate in a particular case.

12.11 In practice the Revenue do not prosecute in the vast majority of cases of fraud. There are many reasons for this. It is expensive to investigate and prosecute a case to criminal standards and a taxpayer facing prosecution is unlikely to volunteer a great deal of help to the Revenue. The standard of proof required for civil penalties, namely the balance of probabilities, is significantly less onerous than the criminal one of beyond reasonable doubt. Instead of seeking a criminal prosecution the Revenue are normally prepared to accept civil penalties on the basis of:

(*a*) full co-operation by the taxpayer; and

(*b*) the taxpayer paying for an independent person, such as an accountant or other tax advisor, to carry out an investigation and report to the Revenue, who are thus saved a great deal of work, as they merely need to question and verify the report.

This results in information being made available to the Revenue far more quickly than if they launch a criminal prosecution. If the Revenue use the criminal route they are still of course entitled to the tax and interest but in most cases cannot seek to recover this until after they have successfully prosecuted the taxpayer. In many cases a criminal investigation and prosecution can take many years whereas a civil settlement can be agreed in less than a year and it rarely takes more than three years to settle a case.

12.12 There are certain types of cases where the Revenue will tend to prosecute – and not even offer civil penalties as an alternative:

(*a*) where false accounts have been deliberately compiled (as opposed to the accounts omitting income that has been syphoned off from the business);

(*b*) documents have been altered or falsified;

(*c*) a solicitor, accountant or any tax advisor is a party to the suspected fraud;

(*d*) the taxpayer (or its director) have conspired with a third party to defraud the Revenue;

(*e*) a Certificate of Full Disclosure or Statement of Assets (see **12.27**) signed in relation to a tax investigation turns out to be false;

(*f*) further offences have occurred immediately or shortly after the conclusion of a tax investigation;

(*g*) the taxpayer is a member of either House of Parliament or has a special status in the administration of justice or tax;

(*h*) the suspected fraud or evasion uses the vehicle of an offshore company or other foreign entity to divert funds offshore;

(*i*) phoenixism;

(*j*) false claims to personal allowances;

(*k*) false claims in relation to the construction industry deduction scheme; and

(*l*) PAYE fraud,

(Investigation Handbook, paras 451, 3220). They will not always prosecute in such cases, particularly if the amount involved is comparatively small.

12.13 The Revenue have said that where they prosecute someone their practice is:

(*a*) not to also seek civil penalties in respect of any offence which has been brought before the courts;

(*b*) to seek civil penalties in respect of any offences which have not been brought before the court; and

(*c*) to reserve the right to seek a civil penalty in respect of negligence by a taxpayer who has been acquitted of criminal intent in respect of a prosecution for fraud,

(Statement of Practice 2/88). This statement was issued before the enactment of the Human Rights Act 1998. It is possible that head (*c*) infringes a person's rights under that act.

12.14 Where a prosecution is likely, the investigation will be carried out by one of the Revenue's Special Compliance Offices (SCO). The SCO works prosecution cases in accordance with the appropriate Civil Code, which is the Police and Criminal Evidence Act 1984 (PACE). The vast majority of SCO cases are not prosecution cases. They are dealt with as civil offences. It is easy to tell in most cases which route is being followed when SCO become involved in a case. If they are not contemplating a prosecution they will normally give the taxpayer a copy of their Code of Practice 9 and explain the Hansard procedure.

12.15 It is so named because it is enshrined in a parliamentary answer (or to be precise a series of parliamentary answers, as it is revised periodically) which was published in Hansard. The current answer is as follows:

> 'The practice of the Board of Inland Revenue in cases of suspected serious tax fraud is as follows.
>
> The Board reserves complete discretion to pursue prosecutions in the circumstances it considers appropriate.
>
> Where serious tax fraud has been committed, the Board may accept a money settlement instead of pursuing a criminal prosecution.

The Board will accept a money settlement and will not pursue a criminal prosecution, if the taxpayer, in response to being given a copy of this Statement by an authorised officer, makes a full and complete confession of all tax irregularities'.

12.16 It should particularly be noted that in the last paragraph the Revenue undertake not to prosecute if the taxpayer makes a full and complete confession. The previous statement did not give such a guarantee. It was altered, as it was felt not to be in conformity with human rights.

12.17 It should be stressed that being 'offered Hansard' is being given the opportunity to come clean without risk of prosecution and imprisonment. If the taxpayer accepts their offer the Revenue do not prosecute even, in practice, if the complete confession is not made immediately but is made gradually during the course of the enquiry. Refusal to accept the Hansard offer puts the Revenue in a degree of difficulty as they will then have to decide whether to incur the very heavy costs of a criminal investigation. Nevertheless, most people do not relish the thought of imprisonment and would prefer to accept the Revenue's offer. Accepting Hansard but not making full disclosure is highly likely to result in a prosecution should the hidden income subsequently be discovered by the Revenue.

12.18 Indeed, that is the worst possible approach, as the legislation provides that statements made or documents produced by or on behalf of a person are not to be inadmissible in:

(*a*) any criminal proceedings against the person in question for any form of fraudulent conduct in connection with or in relation to tax;

(*b*) any proceedings against him for the recovery of any tax due from him; or

(*c*) any proceedings for a penalty or an appeal against the determination of a penalty by reason only that it has been drawn to his attention that where serious tax fraud has been committed the Board can accept a money settlement and that the Board will accept such a settlement and not pursue a criminal prosecution if he makes a full confession of all tax irregularities, or that the extent to which he is helpful and volunteers information is a factor that will be taken into account in determining the amount of any penalty,

[TMA 1970 s 105]. Accordingly, what the taxpayer will have done is volunteer information to the Revenue to assist them in mounting a criminal prosecution against him.

12.19 Hansard interviews are tape-recorded and a criminal 'caution' is given to the client at the start of the interview:

> 'You do not have to say anything. But it may harm your defence if you do not mention when questioned something that you later rely on in Court. Anything you do say may be given in evidence.'

12.19 *Penalties*

This is a new procedure following the Court of Appeal decision in *R v Gill and Gill [2003] EWCA Crim 2256, [2003] STC 1229*. In that case the Gills submitted that what they had said in the Hansard interview ought to be excluded, in spite of s 105, as the Revenue ought to have followed Code C under the PACE 1984 and to admit evidence where they had failed to do so would have such an adverse effect on the fairness of the proceedings that the court ought not to admit it. Clarke L J, giving the judgement of the court, held that Code C applied to Hansard interviews and that 'the appellant should have been cautioned and a tape recording made of the interview'. He went on to hold that the Gills had not been prejudiced by this failure.

12.20 He also pointed out that:

> 'The purpose of Code C is to ensure that interviewees are informed of their rights, one of which is not to answer to questions, and to inform them of the use which might be made of their answers in criminal proceedings. It is clear from the Parliamentary statement that the SCO had the possibility of criminal proceedings in mind in respect of the fraud about which they were asking questions and we can see no reason why the Revenue should not have cautioned taxpayers suspected of fraud before asking them questions in these circumstances. We cannot see why a caution should reduce the chances of a taxpayer making a full confession which was the purpose of the process.'

12.21 Many practitioners would strongly disagree with that last sentence. It is unfortunate that at the time of the Gill Hansard interview the previous version of the parliamentary answer applied under which, to quote Clarke L J again:

> 'Since the Revenue expressly reserved the right to prosecute for fraud, it appears to us that one of the purposes of asking the questions must have been the "obtaining of evidence which may be given to a court in a prosecution" even if the Revenue's main aim was to arrive at a monetary settlement'.

The old version of the parliamentary answer indicated that a prosecution was unlikely; whether the court would have said the same thing in the light of the new version, which states that there will be no prosecution if the taxpayer performs his side of the bargain by making a full confession, seems questionable. Nevertheless, the Revenue felt that they had to adapt their procedures to reflect Code C of PACE 1984.

12.22 After the caution, at a Hansard meeting the taxpayer will normally be handed a copy of the Hansard statement and a copy of the five Hansard questions. He will normally have been sent in advance a copy of the Revenue's booklet COP9 'Special Compliance Investigations: Cases of suspected serious fraud'. This contains the five questions, so the taxpayer will have had an opportunity to consider them in advance. The questions are:

(*a*) Question 1
Have any transactions been omitted from or incorrectly recorded in the books of any business with which you are or have been concerned whether as a director, partner or sole proprietor?

(*b*) Question 2
Are the accounts sent to the Inland Revenue for each and every business with which you are or have been concerned whether as a director, partner or sole proprietor, correct and complete to the best of your knowledge and belief?

(*c*) Question 3
Are all the tax returns of each and every business with which you are or have been concerned whether as a director, partner or sole proprietor correct and complete to the best of your knowledge and belief?

(*d*) Question 4
Are all your personal tax returns correct and complete to the best of your knowledge and belief?

(*e*) Question 5
Will you allow an examination of all business books, business and private bank statements and any other business and private records in order that the Revenue may be satisfied that your answers to the first four questions are correct?

The answers the Revenue expect are obviously: yes, no, no, no and yes respectively. If they do not get these answers they will probably want to terminate the meeting and consider whether to investigate with a view to prosecution. Accordingly, if the client's answers are not the expected ones it is sensible to have an explanation ready. It is not necessary to answer the questions at the initial meeting, but the Revenue prefer this. They will in any event want the answers confirmed in writing. There is usually no reason not to answer at the meeting as the client will have already had ample time to consider them.

12.23 The Revenue are likely to want to ask further questions to ascertain the scope and extent of the defalcations. They will also invite the client to instruct an accountant or other professional advisor to prepare a detailed investigation report. When the investigation report is finished it has to be formally adopted (and signed) by the client. This is his full disclosure of the irregularities. It is a very important document. If something material is omitted from it the Revenue are likely to take the view that the taxpayer has not made a full and complete confession under the Hansard procedure. Although the Hansard procedure is not a statutory one it should be realised that it nevertheless needs to comply with the normal self-assessment enquiry procedures.

12.24 Local district enquiries are not conducted under the Hansard procedure and do not conform with PACE 1984. It is most unlikely that such an enquiry will result in a prosecution. Nothing disclosed by the taxpayer in the enquiry will be admissible in evidence so it would in practice be very difficult, if not impossible, for the Revenue to subsequently prosecute.

12.25 Because a Hansard investigation is a serious matter a practitioner needs to consider carefully whether he feels competent to handle it or ought to call for assistance either from a lawyer or a more experienced practitioner. However, the procedure is not difficult to pick up. The Revenue booklet COP9 is well written and helpful. It is sensible for the practitioner as well as the client to read it prior to the initial meeting. The Revenue normally only want to see the client twice during the course of the investigation, at the initial meeting and at the closure meeting when the settlement has been agreed. They are content to deal solely with the practitioner in between. The closure meeting is largely for the Revenue to satisfy themselves that the taxpayer understands the importance of the certificate of full disclosure and statement of assets and understands that he will be prosecuted next time round if he does not mend his ways.

12.26 The Revenue do not normally exact penalties as such at the end of an investigation where fraud is involved, whether by SCO or a local district. Instead they enter into a 'contract settlement'. This is an offer by the taxpayer to pay an agreed amount to the Revenue in consideration of their not prosecuting him. This is a contract between the Revenue and the taxpayer; although the amount payable is calculated as the sum of the tax, interest and penalties, it is not tax. The Revenue do not assess it. If the taxpayer does not pay the Revenue cannot use their tax enforcement powers but have to sue in the same way as any other creditor.

12.27 They also normally ask for a certificate of full disclosure and a reasonably up to date statement of assets. The certificate largely replicates that on the tax return but also confirms that all bank and building society accounts have been disclosed to the Revenue. The statement of assets is partly because a list of assets provides a broad check that everything has been disclosed and partly because it gives a starting point for the future. As such it is a very important document and needs to be completed with care. It is normally preferable to persuade the Revenue to accept that statement to reflect the position on the last day of your investigation as your investigation ought to have thrown up the significant assets owned by the client.

Civil penalties

Failure to make a return

12.28 Where a person has been given a notice to deliver a tax return under TMA 1970 s 8 (individuals) or 8A (trustees) and fails to comply with the notice he is liable for a penalty of £100 [TMA 1970 s 93(1), (2)].

12.29 In addition, if the General or Special Commissioners so direct he is liable to a further penalty of up to £60 for each day the failure continues after that on which he is notified of the direction of the Commissioners [TMA 1970 s 93(3)]. The daily penalty cannot be applied for any day after the return is filed [TMA 1970 s 93(6)].

12.30 If the failure continues for more than six months after the filing date for the return (and no application for the daily penalty is made) a further fixed penalty of £100 becomes due, ie normally, if the return is not filed by 31 July following the anniversary of the tax year concerned [TMA 1970 s 93(4)].

12.31 If the failure continues after the anniversary of the filing date the taxpayer becomes liable to a further penalty of an amount not exceeding 100 per cent of the tax due [TMA 1970 s 93(5)].

12.32 However, the two fixed £100 penalties at **12.28** and **12.30** are (together) limited to the 'liability to tax shown in the return' [TMA 1970 s 93(7)]. This is a misnomer. It is actually the amount which would have been payable under TMA 1970 s 59B if a property return had been delivered on the filing date. The amount payable under s 59B is the balancing payment. Accordingly, if the interim payments on account have been made before the 31 January filing date the penalty is limited to the excess. In practice the Revenue seem to treat every payment made on or before 31 January as if it were an interim payment, even if it exceeds the payment statutorily required under TMA 1970 s 59A. The result is that if a return is completed by 31 January but for some reason cannot be submitted – for example, the taxpayer is unable to sign it because he is abroad – paying the tax due by that date will in practice avoid the fixed penalties.

12.33 The above penalties also apply to partnership returns (other than that at **12.31** – which cannot apply as a partnership does not have a tax liability, but with some modifications [TMA 1970 s 93A]. The fixed penalties are £100 per partner [TMA 1970 s 93A(2), (4)]. The daily penalties of up to £60 are also per partner [TMA 1970 s 93A(3)].

12.34 The penalty for failure to deliver a corporation tax return is £100 if the return is up to three months late and £200 if it is more than three months late [FA 1998 Sch 18 para 17(1), (2)]. If the return is filed late for three consecutive accounting periods the penalty for the third is £500 if it is up to three months late and £1,000 if it is more than three months overdue [FA 1998 Sch 18 para 17(3)]. The penalties will then stay at the £500 and £1,000 level until a return is filed timeously.

12.35 If a corporation tax return is not filed within 18 months of the end of the accounting period, ie it is more than six months late, there is a further tax-related penalty of 10 per cent of the tax still outstanding at that date. If the return is filed more than a year after the end of the accounting period the penalty becomes 20 per cent of the outstanding tax. The outstanding tax for this purpose is the amount unpaid at the end of the 18 month period – but ignoring any relief under TA 1988 s 419(4), tax refundable on repayment of a participator's loan. If the filing date is later than 18 months after the end of the accounting period the 10 per cent tax related penalty applies if the return is late, ie even if it is a day late. As a separate return is required for each accounting period this can normally occur only if accounts are prepared for an exceptionally long period (as where a company prepares accounts covering a period of more than 18 months the filing date is 30 months from the beginning of that period of account – see FA 1998 Sch 18 para 14 [FA 1998 Sch 18 para 14].

12.36 A company is not liable to the flat-rate penalty if the period for which a return is required corresponds with one for which the company is required to file accounts with Companies House and the tax return is filed before the Companies House deadline for the accounts [FA 1998 Sch 18 para 19].

Incorrect return

12.37 If a person fraudulently or negligently:

(*a*) delivers a personal or trust tax return;

(*b*) makes any incorrect return, statement or declaration in connection with any claim for an allowance, deduction or relief in relation to income tax or capital gains tax; or

(*c*) submits any incorrect accounts in connection with the ascertainment of his liability to income tax or capital gains tax,

he is liable to a penalty of up to 100 per cent of the additional tax that would have been payable if the return, statement, declaration or accounts had been correct [TMA 1970 s 95(1), (2)].

12.38 The legislation actually defines the maximum penalty as the difference between:

(*a*) the amount of income tax and capital gains tax payable for the year of assessment concerned or the following year or any preceding year; and

(*b*) the amount which would have been the amount so payable if the return, statement, declaration or accounts as made or submitted had been correct,

[TMA 1970 s 95(3)]. The reason for the reference to other years is not clear. It is probable that it is intended simply to ensure that a penalty is payable if the incorrect information has an effect on the tax payable for other years.

12.39 Penalties similarly arise in the case of an incorrect partnership return (with the difference that **12.37**(*b*) above applies where the return statement or declaration is made in connection with the partnership return) [TMA 1970 s 95A(1)]. In the case of a partnership, however, each relevant partner (ie each person who was a partner during the period in respect of which the return is made) is liable for the penalty attributable to the additional tax payable in relation to his own return [TMA 1970 s 95A(2)]. In looking at whether the return has been made fraudulently or negligently it is fraud or negligence by the partner who signs the return that triggers the penalty. Furthermore, he is treated as having delivered the return fraudulently or negligently if his doing so is attributable to fraudulent or negligent conduct on the part of any relevant partner [TMA 1970 s 95A(2)].

12.40 If a return, statement or declaration referred to in s 95 (see **12.37**) is made or submitted neither fraudulently nor negligently and it subsequently comes to the notice of the taxpayer (or if he has died, that of his personal representatives) that it was incorrect then, unless the error is remedied without unreasonable delay, the return, statement, declaration or accounts must be treated as having been negligently made or submitted [TMA 1970 s 97(1)]. Curiously, s 97 does not appear to apply to a partnership return as that is governed by s 97A.

12.41 For the purpose of s 95 any accounts submitted on behalf of a person are deemed to have been submitted by him unless he proves that they were submitted without his consent or connivance [TMA 1970 s 97(2)]. Again, this does not appear to apply to accounts submitted in relation to a partnership return. The Revenue say that although s 97(2) ensures that accounts submitted by an agent without any direct evidence that they have been seen or approved by the taxpayer will be deemed to have been submitted by the taxpayer 'this is in itself not sufficient to establish conclusively that the TAXPAYER has been fraudulent or negligent' (Enquiry Handbook, chapter 9, para 670). They also say that the Board's Solicitor has advised that company accounts which include loans or advances to directors or other participators under general headings (such as sundry debtors) are not 'incorrect' for tax purposes (Investigation Handbook, para 4745).

12.42 If a company fraudulently or negligently either:

(*a*) delivers a company tax return which is incorrect; or

(*b*) discovers that a return that it delivered neither fraudulently nor negligently is incorrect and does not remedy the error without unreasonable delay,

it is liable to a penalty of up to the additional tax that would have been payable if the return had been correct (but ignoring any tax refundable under TA 1988 s 419(4) – repayment of loans by participators) [FA 1998 Sch 18 para 20].

12.43 If a company fraudulently or negligently makes an incorrect return, statement or declaration in connection with a claim for an allowance, deduction or relief in respect of tax, or submits incorrect accounts to either the Revenue or the Commissioners in connection with the ascertainment of its tax liability, it becomes liable to a penalty of up to 100 per cent of the tax understated as a result. For this purpose any relief due under TA 1988 s 419(4A) (relief in respect of loan repayments) is ignored. Accounts submitted on behalf of a company are assumed to have been submitted by it for the purpose of this penalty unless the company proves that they were submitted without its consent or connivance [FA 1998 Sch 18 para 89].

12.44 The Revenue say that a return which wholly omits an item of income or a gain does not comply with the TMA 1970 s 8 requirement to make a return (Investigation Handbook, para 4660). This seems of questionable validity. The wording indicates that the relevant paragraph was written pre self-assessment – indeed it appears to have preceded the previous amendment of s 8 by FA 1990.

12.45 There is no statutory definition of what is meant by negligence. The concept was considered by Pennycuick J in the High Court in *Salmon v Havering General Comrs ((1967) 45 TC 77)*. He said that:

> 'Where the Revenue puts before the adjudicating Commissioners returns made by a taxpayer of matters within his own knowledge … and assessments of a higher amount [are] confirmed by the General or Special Commissioners that must, I think, be at least sufficient prima facie evidence of neglect to throw upon the taxpayer the burden of rebutting this prima facie evidence – for example by showing that the inadequate return was due to some reason other than neglect.'

He also confirmed that 'where the Revenue bring a proceeding for a penalty, the burden lies upon the Revenue to establish fraud or neglect'.

12.46 In *A-G v Till ((1910) 5 TC 440))* Lord Atkinson thought that a person would be guilty of negligence if 'he did not estimate his gains and profits to the best of his judgement and belief'. In *Williams v Special Income Tax Comrs ((1975) 49 TC 670)* Walton J commented: 'I do not see how on any view of the matter it can be said that a person who deliberately omitted from his income tax return all reference to commissions which he had received can be said to be otherwise than negligent'.

12.47 In *King v Walden (No 2) [2001] STC 822* the Special Commissioners, after reviewing what little authority there was, commented:

> 'From these authorities we derive the principle that … neglect existed where there was a failure to give any notice, or to make any return, or to produce or furnish any documents or other information required by or under the Taxes Acts. Neglect also existed where inadequate returns are made by the taxpayer of matters within his own knowledge, and assessments in a higher amount are confirmed by the Special Commissioners, unless the taxpayer shows that his inadequate return was due to some reason other than neglect.'

12.48 If two or more tax geared penalties become chargeable by reference to any income or capital gains tax to which a person is chargeable for a tax year each penalty other than the first must be reduced so that the total penalties do not exceed the highest penalty that could be charged for any of the offences [TMA 1970 s 97A]. This also applies for corporation tax [FA 1998 Sch 18 para 90].

12.49 A company that fraudulently or negligently makes a claim for R & D tax credit, land remediation tax credit, life assurance company tax credit or vaccine, etc, research tax credit (see **6.110**), or discovers that such a claim is incorrect and does not remedy the error without unreasonable delay, becomes liable for a penalty of up to the amount of tax saved as a result of the claim [FA 1998 Sch 18 paras 83F, 83L, 83R]

Failure to produce documents under s 19A

12.50 The penalty for failure to comply with a s 19A notice (or a similar notice under Sch 1A or FA 1998 Sch 18 para 27) is a fixed penalty of £50 and if the failure continues after a penalty has been imposed further daily penalties of up to £30 per day if the penalty is determined by the Revenue or £150 a day if it is determined by the Commissioners. The Revenue can take penalty proceedings for such daily penalties before the Commissioners irrespective of whether or not the issue is one in which only the Commissioners can impose penalties. No penalty (even the fixed penalty) can be imposed once the failure has been remedied [TMA 1970 s 97AA; FA 1998 Sch 18 para 29].

Special returns

12.51 There are standard penalties for failure to deliver a return or other documents (under the provisions set out in column 1 of the table in TMA 1970 s 98(1)) or for failure to provide information (under the provisions set out in column 2 of the table). The basic penalty is up to £300. If the failure continues after that basic penalty has been imposed a further penalty of up to £60 per day for each day the failure continues (after the basic penalty was imposed) can be imposed [TMA 1970 s 98(1)]. No such penalty can be imposed for failure to make one of the specified returns in column 1 at any time after the failure has been remedied [TMA 1970 s 98(3)]. The basic penalty for failure to comply with a column 2 provision can be imposed in arrears but the additional amount of up to £60 a day can no longer be charged once the failure has been remedied [TMA 1970 s 98(4)]. In practice this means that if a person provides information when threatened with penalties he will escape the daily charge. The Revenue have to actually issue the penalty notice before the information is provided to be able to collect such a penalty.

12.52 If a person fraudulently or negligently furnishes, gives, produces or makes an incorrect information, certificate, document, record or declaration in relation to any of these special returns or requests for information a penalty of up to £3,000 can be imposed [TMA 1970 s 98(2)]. This appears to be in addition to any penalty for submitting the return late.

12.53 In some circumstances the penalty for failure to comply with TA 1988 s 350(1) (accounting for tax deducted from annual payments and annual interest) or Sch 16 (Collection of income tax or company payments completion of forms CT61), is increased to a basic penalty of up to £3,000 and a daily penalty of up to £600, namely:

(*a*) if the payment is made by a company or local authority (or a partnership of which either is a member) without deducting tax; at the time of the payment the company did not believe (or could not reasonably believe) that TA 1988 s 349B applied so as to exclude the obligation to deduct tax; and it ought to have deducted tax under TA 1988 s 349; or

(*b*) there is an obligation to deduct tax under TA 1988 s 349(1); the company does not deduct tax or deducts it at a lower rate, purporting to rely on TA 1988 s 349E(1) (power to take account of double tax treaty relief when paying royalties) and the company did not believe (or could not reasonably believe) that the payee was entitled to the benefit of the double tax agreement,

[TMA 1970 s 98(4)–(4D)].

12.54 These increased penalties of up to £3,000 plus £600 a day also apply to a failure to comply with, TA 1988 s 765A(2) (notice in relation to movement of capital between residents of EC countries, ie corporate migration, etc, within the EC) [TMA 1970 s 98(5)].

12.55 The penalties for failure to make an annual return under the PAYE or Construction Industry Sub-Contractor Regulations is a penalty of the 'relevant monthly amount' for each month or part of a month for which the failure continues (subject to a maximum of 12 months). The relevant monthly amount is £100 if the number of employees or sub-contractors that should have been included in the return is 50 or less plus a further £100 for each additional 50 employees and also for any remainder. For example, if a company has 461 employees the monthly penalty is up to £1,000 (£100 + 8 × £100 + £100 for the final 11 employees) and the maximum penalty if the default continues for 12 months is £12,000. If the failure does continue beyond 12 months there is also an additional penalty of up to the amount of the PAYE or sub-contractor payments for the year to which the return relates that was unpaid at 19 April after the year end [TMA 1970 s 98A(1)–(3)]. If the return is made but it is incorrect due to fraud or negligence there is a penalty of up to 100 per cent of the underdeclaration on the return [TMA 1970 s 98A(4)].

12.56 If an EEIG is required to submit a tax return under TMA 1970 s 12A (see **3.69**) it becomes liable to a penalty of up to £300 multiplied by the number of members of the EEIG at the time of the failure to comply. The General or Special Commissioners can then impose a further penalty of up to £60 times the number of members for each day the failure continues. If the EEIG had no taxable income or chargeable gains the penalty is limited to £100 though. The penalty for fraudulently or negligently delivering an incorrect return by an EEIG is up to £3,000 times the number of members of the EEIG [TMA 1970 s 98B]. Such an act or omission on behalf of the EEIG is treated as an act or omission by each of its members for the purpose of FA 1998 Sch 18 paras 43 and 46(2) (assessment in case of fraud or negligence) (see **6.56**) and para 61(2) and 65(1) of that Schedule (claims consequent on such an assessment) [FA 1998 Sch 18 para 91].

Assisting in the preparation of an incorrect return

12.57 A person who assists in, or induces, the preparation or delivery of an information, return, accounts or other document which:

(*a*) he knows will be (or is or are likely to be) used for any purpose of tax; and

(*b*) he knows to be incorrect,

is liable to a penalty of up to £3,000 [TMA 1970 s 99]. However, if, as is likely to be the case, the person who commits the offence is a tax accountant (the Revenue say that the main use of the section is against dishonest accountants – Enquiry Manual para 4860) the real penalty is that it also triggers the right of the Revenue to invoke TMA 1970 s 20A (see **5.75**).

12.58 A person who fraudulently or negligently gives a certificate of non-liability to income tax to a building society or deposit taker under the Regulations made under TA 1988 s 477A or 480B, or who fails to comply with any undertaking contained in the certificate (such as to tell the bank if he becomes UK-resident), becomes liable to a penalty of up to £3,000 [TMA 1970 s 99A].

Refusal to allow a deduction of income tax

12.59 A person who refuses to allow a deduction of income tax authorised by the Taxes Acts to be made out of any payment incurs a penalty of £50 [TMA 1970 s 106(1)]. However, it is probable that an agreement to pay such a sum as after deduction of income tax represents a specific amount is enforceable. Many overseas banks use such a formula in their loan agreements.

Administrative issues

12.60 The Board has power to mitigate any penalty, or stay or compound any proceedings for a penalty [TMA 1970 s 102]. In an effort to persuade an agent to accept a suggested penalty the Revenue have been known to point out that the Commissioners do not have power to mitigate penalties. This is true but largely irrelevant. Most penalties are 'up to' a particular amount. The Commissioners have power to decide what the penalty should be, ie to determine it at any amount between £1 or the statutory limit for the penalty. Accordingly, they have no need to mitigate a penalty. It is only with the fixed penalties where the Revenue's power to mitigate exceeds the Commissioners power to determine the amount, and in practice the Revenue are unlikely to mitigate a fixed penalty in any event.

12.61 Penalties must be determined, or penalty proceedings commenced before the Commissioners or a court, within six years after the date on which the penalty was incurred or, if later, within three years after the final determination of the amount of tax by reference to which the penalty falls to be calculated (but the three years extension does not normally apply where the taxpayer has died [TMA 1970 s 103]. A penalty under TMA 1970 s 99 (see **12.57**) can, however, be determined (or proceedings commenced) up to 20 years after the date on which it was incurred [TMA 1970 s 103(3)].

12.62 Penalties in relation to tax returns, enquiries and tax payments carry interest at the rate applicable under FA 1989 s 178 from the date on which the penalty becomes payable until payment [TMA 1970 s 103A].

12.63 These penalty provisions do not (unless other provided) affect any criminal proceedings for any misdemeanour [TMA 1970 s 104].

12.64 If two or more tax geared penalties become chargeable by reference to any income or capital gains tax to which a person is chargeable for a tax year, each penalty other than the first must be reduced so that the total penalties do not exceed the highest penalty that could be charged for any of the offences [TMA 1970 s 97A]. This also applies for corporation tax [FA 1998 Sch 18 para 90].

Company migration

12.65 Various statutory requirements have to be complied with if a company ceases to be UK-resident other than in pursuance of a Treasury consent [FA 1988 s 130]. A company that fails to comply with s 130 is liable to a penalty of up to 100 per cent of the tax which is (or will be) payable by it in respect of periods prior to the time of the failure to comply to the extent that such tax has not been paid prior to the time of the failure [FA 1988 s 131(1)]. Furthermore, any company which has control of the migrating company, or any director (as defined in TA 1988 s 163(8) or 417(5)), any person who does (or is party to) any act which to his knowledge amounts to, or results in (or forms part of a series of acts which together amount to or result in, or will amount to or result in), a migrating company failing to comply with s 130 is liable to a penalty of up to the same amount [FA 1988 s 131(2), (3)].

12.66 For the purpose of proceedings for such a penalty it must be presumed that the company or person concerned was party to every act of the migrating company unless he proves that it was done without his consent or connivance. Unless the contrary is proved, it must also be presumed that any act which in fact amounted to or resulted in the migrating company failing to comply with s 130 (or formed part of a series of acts which did so) was to that person's knowledge such an act [FA 1988 s 131(4)].

Determination of penalties

12.67 The Revenue are able to impose most penalties without recourse to the Appeal Commissioners. An officer of the Board authorised for the purpose can make a determination imposing a penalty and setting it at such amounts as he considers appropriate, under any provisions of the Taxes Act other than as follows.

(*a*) TMA 1970 s 93(1)(a) – this appears to be defective as that subsection does not impose a penalty following the replacement of s 93 by FA 1994. In the previous version it meant the £60 a day penalty, but the Revenue believe that they are now able to impose that without recourse to the Commissioners.

(*b*) TMA 1970 s 98(1)(i) – the basic penalty for special returns – see **12.51**.

(*c*) TMA 1970 s 98B(2)(a) – this also appears to be defective as that provision does not impose a penalty.

[TMA 1970 s 100(1), (2).] It is unlikely that the first and third of these three exceptions was intended by parliament. They were enacted in 1989 whereas the current versions of the provisions date from 1994 and 1990 respectively.

12.68 Notice of determination of a penalty under s 100 must be served on the person liable to the penalty. The notice must state the date of issue and the time within which an appeal can be made [TMA 1970 s 100(3)]. If the Revenue determine a penalty under s 93(2), (4) or (5) (failure to make income tax return) (see **12.28**) or FA 1998 Sch 18 para 18(2) (failure to make corporation tax return) (see **12.35**) and they later discover it is too high because the amount of tax on which it was based was too high they must reverse the determination to the correct amount (and repay any overpayment) [TMA 1970 s 100(6)]. Apart from that, the Revenue cannot alter a determination once it has been made [TMA 1970 s 100(4)].

12.69 A penalty determined under s 100 is due and payable 30 days after the date of the notice, and for collection and enforcement purposes is treated as if it were tax charged in an assessment [TMA 1970 s 100A(2), (3)].

12.70 There is a right of appeal to the Appeal Commissioners. The normal provisions in relation to appeals against assessments apply to such an appeal, save that there is no onus on the tax payer to displace the determination. Instead, the Commissioners must form their own view as to whether a penalty has been incurred and whether the amount determined is appropriate (or excessive or insufficient) and set the determination aside, uphold it, reduce it or increase it as appropriate [TMA 1970 s 100B(1), (2)]. There is a further right of appeal against the Commissioners' decision to the

High Court (or the Court of Session in Scotland). The Court must in turn form its own view as to what is appropriate in such an appeal. It is not an appeal solely on a question of law [TMA 1970 s 100B(3)].

12.71 For those penalties that the Revenue do not have power to determine, the Revenue need to bring penalty proceedings before the Appeal Commissioners. The Commissioners must then give notice to the taxpayers of the time and place when they intend to hear the appeal. The Commissioners then decide whether a penalty is due and the appropriate amount of such penalties. The taxpayer has a right of appeal to the High Court on both a question of law and the quantum of the penalty. On appeal, the Court form their own judgement as to what penalty is appropriate [TMA 1970 s 100C].

12.72 If the Board of Inland Revenue consider that the liability of any person for a penalty arises by reason of fraud (of the taxpayer or any other person) they can initiate penalty proceedings in the High Court (or the Court of Session) as civil proceedings. If the court does not find that fraud is proved but consider that a penalty ought to be imposed it has power to impose one of whatever amount it thinks appropriate [TMA 1970 s 100D].

12.73 An assessment which can no longer be altered on appeal is sufficient evidence for the purpose of penalty proceedings that the amounts in respect of which tax is charged in the assessment is correct [TMA 1970 s 101].

Confiscation orders

12.74 The tax penalty is not the end of the matter. The Revenue are increasingly also seeking confiscation orders under Criminal Justice Act 1988 s 71. This enables a Crown Court to make an order against an offender where he is found guilty of an offence and he has benefited from that offence. In *R v Foggon [2003] EWCA Crim 270, [2003] STC 461* the taxpayer diverted £1,007,034 from his company. He pleaded guilty to cheating the public revenue and was sentenced to two years imprisonment. The judge made a confiscation order for £1,068,441 with a further six years imprisonment in default. Mr Foggon contended that his benefit was the unpaid corporation tax, namely £450,398. The court of appeal upheld the order. It held that the full £1,068,441 was 'moneys obtained in connection with the offence of cheating the Revenue' and was therefore the benefit for which a compensation order could be made.

Chapter 13

The Revenue's Power of Care and Management

13.1 The Taxes Management Act 1970 begins: 'Income tax, corporation tax and capital gains tax shall be under the care and management of the Commissioners of Inland Revenue (in this Act referred to as "the Board")' [TMA 1970 s 1(1)]. What does this means? Section 1 goes on to require the Board to appoint Inspectors and Collectors to act under their direction [TMA 1970 s 162]. Such persons can be appointed for general purposes or for such specific purposes as the Board thinks fit [TMA 1970 s 1(2A)]. Where he is appointed for specific purposes he is deemed to have been appointed to be an Inspector or Collector for those purposes [TMA 1970 s 1(2B)]. Finally, it makes clear that any legal proceedings or administrative act relating to any tax begun by one Inspector of Collector may be continued by another and that any Inspector or Collector may act for any division or other area. Accordingly, on the face of it the opening sentence seems to do no more than to make the Board responsible for the administration of the three taxes acting through the Inspectors and Collectors that they appoint under s 1.

13.2 However, the power has been interpreted by the courts far more broadly than that. It in effect gives the Board a very wide discretion not to collect tax or not to enforce administrative rules.

13.3 The width of this power is emphasised in *R (on the application of Wilkinson) v IRC [2002] EWHC 182 (Admin), [2002] STC 347*. The Revenue there had explained to Mr Wilkinson their interpretation of the limited discretion that s 1(1) gave them.

> 'The Board's care and management powers allow us to make relaxations which give taxpayers a reduction in liability to which they are not entitled under the strict letter of the law. Most concessions are made to deal with what are, on the whole, minor or transitory anomalies under the legislation and to meet cases of hardship at the margins of the code where a statutory remedy would be difficult to devise or would run to a length out of proportion to the intrinsic importance of the matter … The care and management powers do not allow the Inland Revenue to contradict unambiguous, primary legislation.'

13.4 Mr Wilkinson was a widower. He had sought judicial review of the Revenue's refusal to grant him by concession a sum equivalent to widow's bereavement allowance. He claimed that it was a breach of Article 14 of the European Convention on Human Rights for them not to grant a concession where they have power to do so.

13.5 Unfortunately for Mr Wilkinson, whilst agreeing with him that the Revenue had power to make the discretion that he sought, Moses J held (not surprisingly) that he could not force the Revenue to exercise its discretion as, in principle, 'it is not possible to extinguish a power by converting it into a duty'. He did make a declaration of incompatibility under the Human Rights Act 1998 that TA 1988 s 262 (which grants the widow's bereavement allowance) offends Article 14 (that convention rights must be secured without discrimination on any ground such as sex or other status) in applying Article 1 (every natural or legal person is entitled to the peaceful enjoyment of his possessions – subject to the right of a State to enforce such laws as it deems necessary to secure the payment of taxes). Sadly this is not a great comfort, as such a declaration has no practical effect; it is no more than a hint to the government that it should consider changing the law.

13.6 But the significance of this decision is not so much the result as the thorough analysis of the Revenue's discretion under s 1. In addition to the statement quoted earlier, the Revenue told the court that 'the Board would consider it appropriate to use its power to make extra-statutory concessions where the result would be consistent with the intention of Parliament in passing the relevant legislation'. The judge noted that provisions of ESC A5 (removal expenses) 'cannot be regarded as minor or transitory and, it seems to me, contradicted the intention of parliament'. Similarly, under ESC A81 (termination payment) 'income tax liability has been reduced in a manner not provided for in primary legislation'. These demonstrate 'the wide scope of the power to issue extra statutory concessions'. He concluded:

> 'The essential quest ought, in my view, to be targeted on finding some principled distinction between extra-statutory concessions and the concession sought in this case. I can find none. Once it is accepted that there are extra-statutory concessions which are not merely temporary, are not merely of minor effect, but directly contradict the intention of Parliament expressed in statutory provisions, it becomes impossible to find any principle according to which in some cases the Revenue will grant a concession and in others they will not … It seems to me that Mr Brenman's reliance upon the fact that Parliament chose not to introduce retrospective legislation when it abolished WBA in 1999 may be relevant to issues arising under s 6 of the 1998 Act, but does not affect the question of the width of the power to issue extra-statutory concessions. I conclude that there is no principle which would prevent the Revenue from issuing an extra-statutory concession which contradicted the intention of Parliament to restrict the allowances to women … The power under s 1 is wide enough to permit the Revenue to grant an extra-statutory concession where failure to do so would lead to a violation of the taxpayer's convention rights.'

13.7 The judge later says:

> 'I accept … that s 262 of the 1988 Act is to be read as subject to the care and management power contained in s 1(1) of the 1970 Act. Section 262 contains no prohibition on the exercise of that power. It is in that respect similar to many other provisions of the 1988 Act on which must be grafted the power contained in s 1(1) of the 1970 Act'.

This seems to accept that the Revenue have power to grant a concession in relation to any provision that does not specifically prohibit them from doing so.

13.8 The first reference to the care and management powers in the Tax Cases is not to be found until 1977 in the case of *Nicholson v Morris ((1976) 51 TC 95)* where in response to a statement by the judge that:

> 'I have no power, I should have thought, to grant a stay, counsel says: "That is my submission my Lord, that there is no statutory power". Whether in a particular case the tax is actually required to be paid falls within the general discretion of the Board. They have the limited discretion, which is s 1 of the Act, that they are entrusted with the care and management of taxes generally.'

13.9 In *Lothbury Investments Corp Ltd v IRC ((1979) 53 TC 223)* the Special Commissioners point out that:

> 'The Board are entrusted with the care and management of the tax, and the Board's discretion must, we apprehend, be exercised with that function in mind; our discretion (if we have any) can only be judicial – the two things are different, as we know nothing of the general scene in which the Board has to make its decisions.'

13.10 In *Vestey v IRC ((1980) 54 TC 503)* Lord Edward-Davies was somewhat scathing of the Revenue's use of their care and management powers. In an earlier case, *Congreve and Congreve v IRC ((1946) 30 TC 163)*, the House of Lords had held that the anti-avoidance provision on the transfer of assets abroad (now TA 1988 s 739) applied whether or not the individual sought to be assessed was the person who transferred the assets. Applying this principle to the facts in *Vestey* would have resulted in multiple taxation, as the whole income of a settlement would have been apportionable to each and every beneficiary of that settlement. The Revenue told the court that under their care and management powers they would only collect the tax once but it was for them to decide which beneficiary they collect it from. Lord Edmund-Davies pointed out:

> 'The truth is that the strict application of Congreve to the facts of the present case leads to such extraordinary conclusions that the appellants have found themselves compelled to temper the wind to the (comparatively) shorn lamb. This procedure has been attacked as highly questionable, but, invoking the provision in s 5(2) of the Act of 1952, that they "may do all such acts as may be deemed necessary and

expedient for raising, collecting, receiving and accounting for the [income] tax in the like and as full and ample a manner as they are authorised to do with relation to any other duties under their care and management", the applicants claim to exercise dispensing powers and to make "extra-statutory concessions" in suitable cases. They submit that they have done no more than exercise those powers in the instant case by appointing "the estimated foreign income for each year … in the proportions in which the appointees had benefited, in the aggregate, by actually receiving accumulated income … My Lords, it is surely high time to consider the basis of this claim by the executive to make such extra-statutory concessions. It is, of course, well known that published lists of concessions have existed for many years. The first was in 1944, although in practice they have existed in one form or another for a much longer period … It has recently been pointed out … that Sir Stafford Cripps said in 1949 that they had come into existence "without any particular legal authority under any Act of Parliament but by the Inland Revenue under my authority" … And, despite the reliance sometimes placed upon the Income and Corporation Taxes Act 1970, s 115(2) [this reference appears to be wrong], the Taxes Management Act 1970, s 1 and the Inland Revenue Regulation Act 1890, s 1, the fact is that there exists no statutory support for the assessment procedure adopted in the present case. And, even were there some statutory or other basis for the published list of concessions Walton J [in the same case] made the important point that: " … they do represent a published code, which applies indifferently to all those who fall, or who can bring themselves, within its scope. What is claimed by the Crown now is something radically different. There is no published code, and no necessity for the treatment of all those who are in consimili casu alike. In one case the Crown can remit one-third, in another one-half, and in yet another case the whole, of the tax properly payable, at its own sweet will and pleasure. If this is indeed so, we are back in the days of the Star Chamber. Again, I want to make it crystal clear that nobody is suggesting that the Crown has, or indeed ever would, so utilise the powers which it claims to bring about unjust results … The root of the evil is that it claims that it has, in fact, the right to do so" … Judicial comment regarding extra-statutory concessions has been mixed … Even Lord Upjohn spoke with two voices. In 1968 he said in CIR v Bates: "The Commissioners … realising the monstrous result of giving effect to the true construction of the section, have in fact worked out what they consider to be an equitable way of operating it which seems to them to result in a fair system of taxation. I am quite unable to understand upon what principle they can properly do so". Yet in the following year he said in CIR v Korner of an unpublished concession: "This practice is very old, works great justice between the Crown and the subject and I trust will never be disturbed". Among the critics was Viscount Radcliffe who "never understood the procedure of extra-statutory concessions [when] at least the door of Parliament is opened every year for adjustment to the tax code" (CIR v Frere), and in another case Lord Wilberforce, in rejecting a concession, observed that administrative moderation … is … no real substitute for legislative clarity and precision" (CIR v Bates). And, my Lords, it should above all be remembered that none other than the Bill of Rights 1688 declared: "1. That the pretended power of suspending of laws, or the execution of laws, by regal authority, without consent of Parliament, is illegal. 2. That the pretended power of dispensing with laws, or the execution of laws, by regal authority, as it has been assumed and exercised of late is illegal". Wholly in line with such authoritative declarations were the observations of Scott LJ in Absolem v Talbot (26 TC 166): "No judicial countenance can or ought to be given in matters of taxation to any system of extra-legal concessions. Amongst other reasons it exposes Revenue officials to temptation, which is wrong, even in the case of a service like the Inland Revenue, characterised by a wonderfully high sense of honour. The fact that such extra-legal concessions have to be made to avoid unjust hardships is conclusive that there is something wrong with the legislation'.

13.11 Perhaps the leading case on the Revenue's care and management powers is *IRC v National Federation of Self-Employed and Small Businesses Ltd (FSB) ((1980) 55 TC 133)*. Casual workers in the printing industry had evaded tax for many years, with the tacit approval of their unions and their employers, by the expedient of filling in false or imaginary names on the forms that they signed to obtain their untaxed pay – these included names such as Mickey Mouse and Donald Duck that were so obviously false that it is hard to envisage why the newspapers concerned accepted them. The Revenue agreed with the relevant trade unions that if people regularised their position for the future and paid the arrears of tax for 1977–78 they would not investigate the loss of tax in earlier years. The FSB sought judicial review of this decision. It contended that the Board exceeded its powers in granting an amnesty.

13.12 The issue before the House of Lords was whether the FSB had 'sufficient interest' in the matter to seek judicial review, but Lord Wilberforce felt that 'this, in the present case, necessarily involves the whole question of the duties of the Inland Revenue and the breaches or failure of those duties of which the respondents complain'. He then goes on to say:

> 'The Commissioners of Inland Revenue are a statutory body. Their duties are, relevantly, defined in the Inland Revenue Regulation Act 1890 and the Taxes Management Act 1970. Section 1 of the Act of 1890 authorises the appointment of Commissioners for the collection and management of "inland revenue", and confers on the Commissioners "all necessary power for carrying into execution every Act of Parliament relating to inland revenue". By s 13 the Commissioners must "collect and cause to be collected every part of inland revenue and all money under their care and management and keep distinct accounts thereof". The Act of 1970 provides (s 1) that "income tax … shall be under the care and management of the Commissioners."'

13.13 He later recites that:

> 'Sir William Pile [the then Chairman of the Board of Inland Revenue] gives a general description of the scope and nature of the duties of the Inland Revenue with regard to the assessment and collection of taxes. He draws attention to the large number of potential taxpayers (about 25,000,000) the huge sums involved, and the limitations of the Board's manpower. His evidence is that it is impossible for the Board to collect all the tax that is due and that decisions have to be taken by way of "care and management" of the taxes to collect as much as is practicable, by cost-effective methods … As regards the "casuals" the Board approved the proposals made by Mr Hoadley [of the SCO] and considered that it had good and sufficient justification for doing so. This was clearly a "management" decision … On the evidence as a whole, I fail to see how any court considering it as such and not confining its attention to an abstract question of locus standi could avoid reaching the conclusion that the Inland Revenue, through Mr Hoadley, were acting in this manner genuinely in the care and management of the taxes, under the powers entrusted to them. This has no resemblance to any kind of case where the court ought, at the instance of a taxpayer, to intervene. To do so would involve permitting a taxpayer or a group of taxpayers to call in question the exercise of management powers and involve the court itself in a management exercise.'

13.14 Lord Diplock also expressed regret at the way that the application came on for hearing which has had the result of deflecting the lower courts from:

> 'giving consideration to the questions (1) what was the public duty of the Board of Inland Revenue of which it was alleged to be in breach, and (2), what was the nature of the breaches that were relied upon by the Federation … these two omitted questions need to be answered in the instant case before it is possible to say whether the Federation have "a sufficient interest in the matter to which the application relates", since, until they are answered, that matter cannot be identified … As respects the statutory powers and duties of the Board of Inland Revenue … all that I need say here is that the Board are charged by statute with the care, management and collection on behalf of the Crown of income tax, corporation tax and capital gains tax. In the exercise of these functions the Board have a wide managerial discretion as to the best means of obtaining for the national exchequer from the taxes committed to their charge, the highest net return that is practicable having regard to the staff available to them and the cost of collection. The Board and the inspectors and collectors who act under their directions are under a statutory duty of confidentiality with respect to information about individual taxpayers' affairs that has been obtained in the course of their duties in making assessments and collecting the taxes; and this imposes a limitation on their managerial discretion. I do not doubt, however, and I do not understand any of your Lordships to doubt, that if it were established that the Board were proposing to exercise or to refrain from

exercising its powers not for reasons of "good management" but for some extraneous or ulterior reason, that action or inaction of the Board would be ultra vires and would be a proper matter for judicial review.'

13.15 Lord Scarman states that TMA 1970 places income tax under the care and management of the Board:

> 'and for that purpose confers upon them and inspectors of taxes very considerable discretion in the exercise of their powers. It also imposes upon them the very significant duty of confidence in investigating, and dealing with, the affairs of the individual taxpayer … Indeed, the Lord Advocate … rightly observed that in the daily discharge of their duties inspectors are constantly required to balance the duty to collect "every part" of due tax against the duty of good management. This conflict of duties can be resolved only by good managerial decisions, some of which will inevitably mean that not all the tax known to be due will be collected … The analysis of the statutory provisions is clearly correct. They establish a complex of duties and discretionary powers imposed and conferred in the interest of good management upon those whose duty it is to collect the income tax. But I do not accept that the principle of fairness in dealing with the affairs of taxpayers is a mere matter of desirable policy or moral obligation. Nor do I accept that the duty to collect "every part of inland revenue" is a duty owed exclusively to the Crown … I am persuaded that the modern case law recognises a legal duty owed by the Revenue to the general body of the taxpayers to treat taxpayers fairly; to use their discretionary powers so that, subject to the requirements of good management, discrimination between one group of taxpayers and another does not arise; to ensure that there are no favourites and no sacrificial victims. The duty has to be considered as one of several arising within the complex comprised in the care and management of a tax, every part of which it is their duty, if they can, to collect. Authority for this view is plentiful, albeit only persuasive in character.'

13.16 In *Woolwich Building Society v IRC ((1988) 65 TC 265)* Ralph Gibson LJ, after reciting that the Revenue submitted that it has a general right outside statute to agree and settle disputed assessments and claims and, as part of its duty of care and management of the recovery of taxes imposed by Parliament, a discretion to make ex gratia payments, goes on to say:

> 'it seems clear to me that the Revenue must be held to have in law the capacity to make such an ex gratia payment. By that I mean a repayment of money, which has been paid to the Revenue in respect of an ultra vires claim to tax and which, because of the circumstances of payment, was in law a voluntary payment to recover which the payer has no cause of action. Such a power of repayment is, I think, a necessary part of the power of the management of the recovery of taxes. A decision by the Revenue whether or not to repay such a voluntary payment, must be made, as it seems to me, in the exercise of the discretion which the Revenue has been left by Parliament to use in the care and management of the recovery of taxes imposed by Parliament.'

13.17 It is clear that the care and management powers can enable the Revenue to extend any time limit even where the legislation does not specifically empower them to do so. For example, in *R v IRC, ex p Mattessons Wall's Ltd ((1996) 68 TC 205)*, which concerned a late loss relief claim, the Master of the Rolls points out:

> 'at the relevant time the Inland Revenue enjoyed no express statutory power to extend or waive that two-year time limit, which on its face bound both the Inland Revenue and companies seeking to set off losses against profits in the same accounting year. But s 1(1) of The Taxes Management Act 1970 provided that corporation tax should be under the care and management of the Commissioners of Inland Revenue, and it is common ground on these appeals that the Revenue had a discretion under that section to accept late claims for loss relief. Under what is now s 393A(10) of the Income and Corporation Taxes Act 1988, not in force at the material time, claims for loss relief must be made within two years of the end of the accounting period "or within such further period as the Board may allow" ... This express new statutory discretion is not said to vary the discretion which the Board already enjoyed under s 1 of the Taxes Management Act 1970.'

13.18 This was one of these fairly rare cases where the court held that the Revenue's decision not to admit the late claim was in the circumstances, in the words of the Master of the Rolls, 'so unreasonable as to be in public law terms, irrational' and in the words of Simon Brown LJ 'a plainly wrong exercise of discretion'.

13.19 The Revenue practice in relation to late claims is set out in SP4/92. However, this is not exhaustive. A letter from the Revenue quoted in *Liddell v IRC ((1997) 72 TC 62)* states:

> 'the Board are always prepared to exercise their discretion to extend the time limit in the circumstances set out in SP4/92. In addition the Board recognise that there may be other cases when, for good reason, the time limit is not met. The way in which the Board exercises its discretion under the general care and management provisions in s 1 of the Taxes Management Act 1970 was covered in a Ministerial Statement.
>
> That statement set out three general sets of circumstance where we permit the time limit to elect to be extended:
>
> - Where there has been a relevant error on the part of the Inland Revenue and the election is made shortly after the error has been drawn to the taxpayer's attention.
> - Where the taxpayer has given clear notice of intention to elect, but before the time limit expires has not completed any statutory requirement.
> - Where the reason for the delay in making the election was clearly beyond the taxpayer's control, eg because (s)he – or in the case of a company, the only individual who had the relevant information and experience – was seriously ill and there was no one who could

reasonably be expected to stand in their stead. We look to see that there had been no undue delays and that the election was made promptly after circumstances changed.

Basically, we are looking to see that either:

1 The taxpayer signalled an intention to elect before the time limit, or
2 There was a good reason for the time limit not having been met and that the election was made promptly after that reason ceased to apply.'

13.20 Decisions of the courts on the corresponding care and management powers of Customs may also provide some guidance on the extent of the Revenue's powers. In *Fine Art Developments plc v Customs and Excise Comrs [1994] STC 668*, counsel for Customs suggested that Customs could properly assess Express Gifts to tax on the basis that their direction applies to its supplies, and then by use of their care and management powers come to some accommodation with Express Gifts on what is an appropriate percentage of the total supplies in accordance with the direction. Peter Gibson LJ retorted:

> 'I have no hesitation in saying that that is or would be an abuse of the Commissioners' powers … I have never heard of the care and management powers of the Revenue authorities being used in conjunction with their assessment power in order to make taxable a proportion of what it has not established and cannot establish is taxable, and for my part I reject any suggestion that that is a proper use of these powers.'

However, in a dissenting judgement Neill LJ took a more relaxed view and thought it commendable that Customs 'have expressed their willingness to use their care and management powers to come to some accommodation with [Express Gifts]'.

13.21 In *Customs and Excise Comrs v Croydon Hotel & Leisure Co Ltd [1995] STC 855* the judge, Keene J, pointed out that VAT is under the care and management of the Commissioners and went on to say, 'accordingly the Commissioners (but not a person other than the Commissioners and therefore not the Tribunal) may by concession relieve a taxpayer of a tax liability imposed by law, subject to Judicial Review of any such concession.'

13.22 In *R v Customs and Excise Comrs, ex p Kay & Co Ltd* and others the judge says:

> 'It will be remembered that that subsection (1996 STC 1500) states that "VAT shall be under the care and management of the Commissioners." While it might be thought that that provision is first and foremost an identifying provision, establishing who is to have the care and management of VAT, the authorities establish that it does confer certain discretionary powers on the Respondents. It seems to be the source of their power to settle claims and compromise disputes. It has been held

by Hidden J in Customs and Excise Commissioners v. Arnold (1996) STC 1271 that it gives the Respondents the power to relieve by way of concession a taxpayer of a liability imposed by law, subject only to judicial review. That is not a surprising conclusion. The ability of the Inland Revenue to make similar extra statutory concessions as part of its managerial discretion was made clear in the Fleet Street casuals case, ie R. v. Inland Revenue Commissioners, exparte National Federation of Self-Employed and Small Businesses (1982) AC 617, and also in R. v. Inland Revenue Commissioners, ex parte MFK Underwriting Agencies Limited (1989) STC 873. Consequently Dr. Lasok submits that there is a power to manage VAT receipts in accordance with the principles of good administration and that, faced with the possibility of having to reclaim sums repaid to taxpayers if Parliament did approve the Paymaster General's proposal with retrospective effect, the Commissioners were entitled to decide to defer payment in the exercise of that power. The issue therefore becomes this: "do the Respondents, in the exercise of their powers of care and management of VAT, have the right to defer payment of sums which they have established are owed to a taxpayer?"'

13.23 He later says:

> 'The fact that Schedule 11, paragraph 1(1) [the VAT care and management powers] confers a power to make concessions to the taxpayer in no way implies that the respondents have the power to impose a heavier burden on the taxpayer than is sanctioned by statute.'

He also opined that:

> 'Had Parliament intended the Commissioners to have a power as important as the one now contended for it would have included that power in express terms. It is not in my view to be achieved by mere implication.'

He accordingly concluded that Customs 'do not have a discretion to defer payment of sums due from them to the taxpayer, once a claim by the latter has been established as well-founded'. This case concerned the three-year cap on retrospective refund claims, which the government announced in July 1996 would be imposed in the next Finance Bill. Customs had refused to make a repayment which was clearly due to Kay & Co under the then current law but would not be due once FA 1997 was enacted – and so if repaid would fall to be collected again by Customs a few months later.

13.24 In *R (on the application of Greenwich Property Ltd) v Customs and Excise Comrs [2001] EWHC Admin 230, [2001] STC 618* the judge says:

> 'I am prepared to accept that, since the Commissioners are relieving a taxable person of a liability imposed by law (something they are empowered to do by virtue of their "care and management" powers: see Customs & Excise Commissioners v Arnold [1996] STC 1271), the

taxable person must demonstrate that he has acted strictly in accordance with what the concession permits and has complied with all the conditions necessary to obtain the relief. Any doubt should be resolved in favour of the tax being payable according to the statutory provision since, if there is doubt, or the language of the concession is ambiguous, the taxpayer should inquire of the Commissioners whether what he intends to do falls within the concession.'

Revenue discretion and the Wednesbury principle

13.25 The care and management powers give a discretion to the Revenue. Is there any restriction on the exercise of that discretion? Yes, the courts will interfere if it is not exercised judicially or if its exercise is so unreasonable that no body of Commissioners properly apprised of the law could have made the decision under challenge.

13.26 There are a number of principles.

(*a*) 'A public officer vested with a discretion cannot bind himself ab ante as to the manner in which he will exercise that discretion. That would, as regards the future, be to surrender his discretion' (*Lord Sands in Riach v Lord Advocate ((1932) 18 TC 18)*). In that case an informer claimed that he had supplied information upon the terms that he should be paid 10 per cent of the sums recovered from the use of that information. He accepted that no payment out of public funds is recoverable from officers of the Crown unless the payment is authorised by Parliament, and relied on Inland Revenue Regulation Act 1890 s 32, which empowers the Revenue at their discretion to reward informers. Lord Sands felt that this authorised a reward only for a fait acompli. The Board could not take account of 'all of the relevant considerations if they were empowered to exercise their discretion by promising an award by way of commission to an informer who discloses no more than that he has something to disclose'. Lord Blackburn agreed:

> 'The fact that the expediency of making any award is left to the discretion of the Commissioners appears to me to require that the Commissioners shall not determine the amount to be awarded until the full information tendered has been put before them and the value of the result of the information has been satisfied … I do not think that to enter into a bargain with an informer ab ante that he should be awarded a percentage of the sums which might be recovered eventually would imply a proper exercise of the discretion … the statute does not give them power to make any such bargain.'

(*b*) The Revenue are required to at least consider whether they should exercise a discretion. Lord Greene, in *Jenkins Productions Ltd v IRC ((1944) 29 TC 142)*, said:

> 'It seemed to us that in considering, as they were bound to consider, whether the case is one in which they should make a direction, the

> Commissioners ought to bear in mind the paramount object of this machinery, which is to ascertain, as far as reasonably can be ascertained, what the real profits of the standard period were. Here they have to have had a method of ascertaining the profits of the standard period in respect of this Company, which would be absolutely accurate. That being so, we thought it right to point out that it seemed to us that that was a special circumstance … which the Commissioners ought to pay serious attention to in deciding whether they would exercise their discretion under this proviso. We also ventured to point out that, in our view, their duty, in deciding whether they should so exercise their discretion, ought to be performed in relation to the facts of each particular case, and not by reference to some supposed rule or precedent which they have thought convenient to adopt in order to guide them … Nothing that we say can bind the Commissioners to exercise their discretion one way or the other, but we did think it right in the circumstances to state what we thought was the way they might approach a question of this kind.'

This was an excess profit tax case. The profits of the standard period were expressed to be arrived at on a time apportionment basis 'unless the Commissioners, having regard to any special circumstances, otherwise direct'.

(*c*) The Revenue cannot properly exercise a discretion arbitrarily but must act judicially.

In *London and National Property Co Ltd v IRC ((1947) 29 TC 303)* another excess profits tax case, the Revenue made a direction on the basis that, owing to special circumstances, the basic rule should not apply. It was clear that there were no special circumstances; the Revenue had misread the agreement. The Revenue contended:

> 'Be that as it may, mistake or no mistake, the question whether there are special circumstances is exclusively a matter for the Commissioners of Inland Revenue; further that is a matter of discretion and, therefore, not appealable, and even if not strictly discretionary, none the less it is a matter solely for them.'

Atkinson J disagreed:

> 'It seems to me quite impossible to say that the determination of a question of fact or law can be a matter of discretion. A discretion connotes a choice of one of two or more courses of action, whether to do one thing or another … The Commissioners cannot be expressing a discretion when they hold that black is white or when they say an agreement means A when it means B, and unless the finding is an exercise of a discretion there is no provision in any Finance Act that I know of depriving the taxpayer of his right of appeal to the Special Commissioners.'

He then reviewed three cases in which the higher courts had reviewed a discretion vested in a lower court. In *Sharpe v Wakefield [1891] AC 173*, Lord Halsbury seems to lay down a very broad principle:

> 'Discretion means when it is said that something is to be done within the discretion of the authorities that that something is to be done according to the rules of reason and justice, not according to private opinion … according to law and not humour. It is to be not arbitrary vague, and fanciful, but legal and regular. And it must be exercised within the limit to which an honest man competent to the discharge of his office ought to confine himself … So a discretion which empowered justices to grant licences to innkeepers as … they deemed proper would not be exercised by coming to a general resolution to refuse a licence to everybody who would not consent to take out an excise licence for the sale of spirits.'

In *Jones v Curling ((1884) 13 QBD 262)* Brett MR said that:

> 'unless there is good cause shown the learned judge has no discretion as to costs … Whether there was a good cause or not is a question of fact, and the Court of Appeal must consider whether in their judgement that fact did exist and if they disagree as to this with the judge who tried the action they must allow the appeal'.

Atkinson J thought that there is no distinction in principle between good cause and special circumstances; both are conditions precedent to the exercise of a discretion. *Donald Campbell & Co Ltd v Pollak [1927] AC 732*, decided that even an absolute discretion must be exercised judicially. Viscount Case said: 'a discretion exercised on no grounds cannot be judicial. If however there be any grounds, the question of whether they are sufficient is entirely for the judge'.

(*d*) Ackner J in *Clinch v IRC ((1974) 49 TC 52)*, quoting Lord Wrenbury in *Roberts v Hopwood [1925] AC 578*, said:

> 'A person in whom is vested a discretion must exercise his discretion upon reasonable grounds. A discretion does not empower a man to do what he likes merely because he is minded to do so – he must in the exercise of his discretion do not what he likes but what he ought. In other words, he must, by use of his reason, ascertain and follow the course which reason directs … The words "as they think fit" do not mean as they choose. The measure is not the volition of the person vested with the discretion, it is the suitability or adequacy or fitness of the amount in the reasonable judgement of the person vested with the discretion.'

Ackner J went on to quote Lord Greene's words in the case of *Associated Provincial Picture Houses Ltd v Wednesbury Corp [1948] 1 KB 223* where a local authority was empowered to enable a cinema to open on a Sunday 'subject to such conditions as the authority think fit to impose'. It imposed a condition that no children under 15 should be admitted on a Sunday even if accompanied by an adult.

> 'Lawyers familiar with the phraseology commonly used in relation to exercise of statutory discretions often use the word "unreasonable" in a rather comprehensive sense. It has frequently been used and is frequently used as a general description of the things that must not be

done. For instance, a person entrusted with a discretion must, so to speak, direct himself properly in law. He must call his own attention to the matters which he is bound to consider. He must exclude from his consideration matters which are irrelevant to what he has to consider. If he does not obey those rules, he may truly be said, and often is said, to be acting unreasonably … The court is entitled to investigate the action of the local authority with a view to seeing whether they have taken into account matters which they ought not to take into account, or, conversely, have refused to take into account or neglected to take into account matters which they ought to take into account. Once that question is answered in favour of the local authority, it may be still possible to say that, although the local authority have kept within the four corners of the matters which they ought to consider, they have nevertheless come to a conclusion so unreasonable that no reasonable authority could ever come to it. In such a case, again, I think the court can interfere. The power of the court to interfere in each case is not as an appellate authority to over-ride a decision of the local authority, but as a judicial authority which is concerned, and concerned only, to see whether the local authority have contravened the law by acting in excess of the powers which Parliament has confided in them.'

This 'Wednesbury principle' is the basis adopted in most of the later cases. This principle was restated by Slade J in *Essex v IRC ((1979) 53 TC 720)* as follows.

'In essence … the court could interfere with the apparent exercise of an executive discretion entrusted by Parliament to an executive authority if, but only if, it was shown that the authority either –

i) had exercised its discretion dishonestly or in bad faith, or
ii) had taken into account matters which it ought not to have taken into account or had refused or neglected to take into account matters which it ought to have taken into account, or
iii) had come to a conclusion so unreasonable that no reasonable authority could ever have come to it.'

There is of course no right of appeal to the appeal Commissioners against an Inspector's or Collector's exercise of a discretion unless one or other of these conditions is met.

(*e*) Lawton J, in *R v IRC, ex p Preston ((1983) 59 TC 1)*, said:

'At whatever stage of the procedure the discretion arises, the Commissioners ought not to go ahead and utilise their powers having come to an agreement with the taxpayer whereby he has given consideration in order to finalise his tax affairs. Unless there is some compelling reason for not honouring such an agreement, not to do so is prima facie a wrongful exercise of discretion. Further, in deciding whether to go back on such an agreement the Commissioners must examine their own conduct.'

(*f*) Where a statute confers a power on an official to exercise his discretion only that official can exercise it. But once he has exercised that discretion he may delegate to others purely administrative tasks which flow from the exercise of that discretion (*Burford v Durkin (63 TC 645)*).

(*g*) Where Parliament confers a power or discretion on the Revenue only they can exercise it. The appeal Commissioners cannot impose their own discretion (except of course where Parliament gives them a specific power to do so) (*Steibelt v Paling (71 TC 376)*).

(*h*) The exercise of a discretion by the Revenue cannot normally even be reviewed by the appeal Commissioners. It can be challenged only by way of judicial review. Judicial review is a High Court proceeding. It is not a right but at the discretion of the court. The court will normally take a case only if the challenge is made fairly quickly after the making of the decision which it is wished to impunge.

Chapter 14

Miscellaneous

Persons chargeable in a representative capacity

14.1 Every body of persons is chargeable to income tax in like manner as a person is chargeable under the Income Tax Acts [TMA 1970 s 71(1)]. This is of course subject to the provisions of TA 1988, which charge the income of UK companies and UK branches of foreign companies to corporation tax instead of income tax. Nowadays the only bodies of persons that are likely to be chargeable to income tax are trustees (if indeed they constitute a body of persons) and overseas companies with UK rental income.

14.2 Subject to TMA 1970 s 108 (see **14.20**) (responsibility of company officers) the officer acting as treasurer, auditor or receiver for the time being is responsible for doing all such acts as are required to be done under the Income Tax Acts for the purpose of the assessment of the body and for payment of the tax [TMA 1970 s 71(2)]. Such person is entitled to be indemnified by the body for the tax he pays and to retain such tax out of any money coming into his hands on behalf of the body [TMA 1970 s 71(3)]. It is odd to see such burdens imposed on the auditor as he has no powers, and in many cases no ability, to carry out such tasks. The wording derives from ITA 1918 s 106 (ITA 1842 ss 40, 54), when the auditor's duties and the emphasis on auditor's independence were somewhat different to today.

14.3 The receiver (or trustee, guardian, tutor, curator or committee) of any incapacitated person having the direction, control or management of the property or business of that person is assessable and chargeable to income tax in the same way as the incapacitated person would be assessed and charged but for his incapacity [TMA 1970 s 72(1)]. The person so chargeable is responsible for all matters required to be done under the Income Tax Acts for the purpose of assessment and payment of income tax [TMA 1970 s 72(2)]. He is entitled to an indemnity for payments he makes in pursuance of the Income Tax Acts and to retain such tax out of money coming into his hands on behalf of the incapacitated person [TMA 1970 s 72(3)]. Income assessed under s 72 does not give rise to Class 4 NIC contributions (Inspector's Manual, para 6062).

14.4 An infant is of course an incapacitated person. The Revenue can collect the tax due by an infant from his parent or guardian if the infant does not pay. They can also take enforcement proceedings against the parent or guardian in the same way as with any other defaulter. If the parent pays the child's tax he 'shall be allowed all sums so paid in his account'. It is anyone's guess what that means. It is unlikely that it gives the parent a tax deduction for the child's tax. It probably gives the parent a right of reimbursement against the child [TMA 1970 s 73].

14.5 The executor or administrator of a deceased person is similarly liable for the tax chargeable on that deceased person and can deduct any such tax payments he makes out of the assets of the deceased. If the deceased estate is insolvent the executor still appears to be personally liable for the deceased's tax. It might therefore be dangerous to agree to act as executor for such a person. On the other hand it seems likely that the Revenue would normally use its care and management powers to forgo the tax in such circumstances. If the executor or administrator refuses to pay, the Revenue can take enforcement proceedings against him [TMA 1970 s 74].

14.6 A receiver appointed by a UK court which has the direction and control of any property in respect of which income tax is charged is similarly assessable and chargeable to tax as if the property were not under the control of the court, and is responsible for payment of the tax and doing everything else required by the Income Tax Acts [TMA 1970 s 75]. However, there is no specific power for the Revenue to take enforcement proceedings against such a person and no right of indemnity. It is not readily apparent why.

14.7 If a trustee authorises income from trust property to be paid direct to the beneficiary (or his agent), and that person actually receives the income, the trustee has no further responsibility towards the Revenue other than to make a return under TMA 1970 s 13 if so required [TMA 1970 s 76(1)]. Similarly, the only obligation on an agent or receiver for a UK-resident person, other than an incapacitated person, is to make a return under s 13 [TMA 1970 s 76(2)].

UK representatives of non-residents

14.8 A number of tax obligations are imposed on a branch or agency in the UK, which is the UK representative of a non-UK-resident. Such a branch or agency through which the non-resident carries on a trade, profession or vocation (whether solely or in partnership) is the non-resident's UK representative in relation to:

(*a*) such income from the trade, etc, as arises, directly or indirectly, from the branch or agency;

(*b*) income from property or rights which are used by (or held for) the branch or agency; and

(*c*) capital gains chargeable to tax under TCGA 1992 s 10,

[FA 1995 s 126(1), (2)]. The non-resident's UK representative continues as such even after ceasing to be a branch or agency through which the non-resident carries on the trade [FA 1995 s 126(3)]. The non-resident's UK representative must be treated as if he were a separate and distinct person from the non-resident [FA 1995 s 126(4)].

14.9 If the branch or agency is one carried on by persons in partnership, the partnership as such is the non-resident's UK representative [FA 1995 s 126(5)]. If the non-resident is himself a partner so that the trade or profession carried on through the UK branch is a partnership trade, the trade carried on through the UK branch is deemed to include the deemed trade or profession from which the non-resident's share in the partnership profits or losses is treated as deriving under TA 1988 ss 111–114 (partnerships) [FA 1995 s 126(6)]. If any member of the partnership is UK-resident the deemed trade under ss 111–114 is in addition treated as a trade carried on in the UK through the partnership as such [FA 1995 s 126(7)]. For the purpose of s 126 a branch or agency means any factorship, agency, receivership, branch or management [FA 1995 s 126(8)]. The section does not apply to income tax chargeable on income of a company other than as trustee.

14.10 The obligations (eg, to make returns and provide information) and liabilities of the non-resident, with respect to tax chargeable on, and interest payable by, him are treated as also being obligations and liabilities of the UK representative [FA 1995 Sch 23 para 1]. This will enable the Revenue to collect the tax from the UK representative. Obviously once one pays the tax that also discharges the liability of the other [FA 1995 Sch 23 para 2(a)]. The non-resident is bound by any act or omission of his UK representative in the discharge of his tax obligations as if they were his own [FA 1995 Sch 23 para 2(b)]. If an obligation or liability arises only on a notice or other document has been served on the taxpayer (or he has received a request or demand) it is not to be treated as having been imposed on the UK representative, unless the notice or document (or a copy of it) was served on the UK representative or he was notified of the request or demand.

14.11 Where the UK representative is the non-resident's 'independent agent' the obligations which are imposed by the Schedule on the non-resident's UK representative are not to require him to do anything except so far as it is practicable for him to do so by acting to the best of his knowledge and belief after having taken all reasonable steps to obtain the necessary information [FA 1995 Sch 23 para 4(1)]. An independent agent for this purpose is a person who is the non-resident's UK representative in respect of an agency from the non-resident in which he was acting on the non-resident's behalf in an independent capacity [FA 1995 Sch 23 para 7(1)]. A person cannot be regarded as acting in an independent capacity unless, having regard to its legal, financial and commercial characteristics, the relationship between the agent and the non-resident is one between persons carrying on independent businesses that deal with each other at arm's length [FA 1995 Sch 23 para 7(2)]. Where the obligation on the UK agent is limited under para 4, his performance of his limited obligation does not absolve the non-resident himself from the obligation to provide the full information. Conversely, the non-resident will not be bound by any error or mistake in information furnished by the UK representative on the basis of his limited knowledge, unless it arises from an act or omission of the non-resident himself or to which he consented or in which he connived [FA 1995 Sch 23 para 4(2)].

14.12 Neither the UK representative nor the non-resident can be guilty of a criminal offence unless he commits the offence himself or consented to or connived in its commission [FA 1995 Sch 23 para 5(1)]. An independent agent is not liable to any civil penalty or surcharge if the act or omission which gave rise to it is not one of the agent himself (nor one in which he consented or connived) and he can show that he will not be able to recover it out of any sums which he is entitled to retain [FA 1995 Sch 23 para 5(1)].

14.13 An independent agent is entitled to be indemnified by the non-resident in respect of any liability that he discharges on behalf of the non-resident. He is entitled to retain out of any sums that he is due to pay to the non-resident, or that he has received on behalf of the non-resident, amounts sufficient for meeting any liabilities which he has discharged as UK representative of the non-resident or to which he is subject [FA 1995 Sch 23 para 6].

14.14 None of the following persons is capable of being the non-resident's UK representative.

(*a*) An agent who does not act in relation to the transaction from which the income arises in the course of carrying on a regular agency for the non-resident [FA 1995 s 127(1)(a)].

(*b*) A broker where at the time of the transaction giving rise to the income the broker was carrying on a business of a broker, he carried out the transaction in the ordinary course of the business, the remuneration he received in respect of the transaction was at least at a rate which would have been customary for that class of business, and the non-resident does not otherwise fall to be treated as having the broker as his UK representative in relation to other income for the same tax year or accounting period [FA 1995 s 127(1)(b), (2)]

(*c*) An investment manager where the income arises from an investment transaction that he has carried out if at the time of the transaction he was carrying on a business of providing investment management services, the transaction was carried out in the ordinary course of that business, the manager acted for the non-resident in an independent capacity, his remuneration for the transaction was not less than is customary for the class of business concerned, the non-resident does not otherwise fall to be treated as having the investment manager as his UK representative in relation to other income for the same year or accounting period and the 20 per cent rule is met in relation to the transaction [FA 1995 s 127(1)(c), (3)]. This is that the investment manager and persons connected with him (within TA 1988 s 839) must not have a beneficial entitlement to more than 20 per cent of the non-resident's relevant excluded income arising from transactions carried out through the investment manager. The 20 per cent rule is treated as being met if the manager intending to meet it failed to do so, wholly or partly, for reasons outside his control despite his having taken such steps as might be reasonable to mitigate the effect of such matters [FA 1995 s 127(4)]. The relevant excluded income is the aggregate of those profits or gains of the non-resident for chargeable periods included in the qualifying period that derive from transactions carried out by the manager and which fall for the purposes of FA 1995 s 128 or 129 to be treated as excluded income (ie excluded from the charge to UK tax – FA 1995 ss 128(3), 129(2)). A qualifying period is a period of not more than five years comprising two or more chargeable periods including the one in question. In other words the 20 per cent test can be applied over a period of up to five years; it does not have to be met in the year concerned. It is not necessary to use five years. The test can be applied by reference to two, three, four or five years. The amount of relevant excluded income to which the manager has a beneficial entitlement means so much of any amount to which he has (or may acquire) a beneficial entitlement by virtue of any interest of his in property in which the whole or any part of the income is represented or any interest of his in other rights in relation to the non-resident as is (or would be) attributable to that income [FA 1995 s 127(5)–(7)]. The Revenue have given detailed guidance on the operation of the rules on investment managers, including examples, in Statement of Practise SP1/01. If the 20 per cent test is not met, the part of the income to which the manager and connected persons are beneficially entitled will be taxable on him as agent for the non-resident but the balance will not [FA 1995 s 127(8)]. Where the non-resident is a participant in a collective investment scheme the 20 per cent test is applied differently, by reference to the scheme as a whole [FA 1995 s 127(9)–(11)] as, if the scheme is a transparent vehicle to which the manager provides his services, it could never be satisfied under the normal rules as all the participants would be connected persons of the manager. For the purpose of s 127 investment transactions means transactions in shares, stocks, futures, options or securities of any description (but not futures or options relating to land), transactions consisting in the buying or selling of any foreign currency or in the placing of money at interest, and such other transactions as the Treasury may by regulation designate [FA 1995 s 127(12)].

(*d*) A managing agent or underwriting agent of a Lloyds syndicate of which the non-resident is a member where the income derives from his underwriting business [FA 1995 s 127(1)(d), (16)].

UK representative of non-resident companies

14.15 From 1 January 2003, a permanent establishment in the UK through which a non-resident company carries on a trade is treated as the UK representative of the company in relation to chargeable profits of the company attributable to that establishment. That establishment is to be treated as a distinct and separate person from the company. It continues as the UK tax representative in relation to those profits even after it has ceased to be a permanent establishment through which the company carried on a trade [FA 2003 s 150(2)]. The UK representative is jointly liable with the overseas company in connection with the assessment, collection and recovery of corporation tax to meet the tax obligations and liabilities of the company [FA 2003 s 150(1)].

14.16 The discharge of an obligation or liability by the company discharges the UK representative's obligation as well and vice versa [FA 2003 s 150(3)(a)]. As with non-residents generally (see **14.10–14.13**) an obligation or liability arising under a notice, etc, served on the company does not attach to the UK representative unless the notice or a copy of it was served on the UK representative or he has been notified of it. The company is not bound by mistakes in information provided by its UK representative unless the mistake results from an act or omission of the company itself (or to which it consented or in which it connived) and the UK representative cannot be proceeded against for a criminal offence unless it committed the offence itself or consented to or connived in its commission [FA 2003 s 150(4)–(6)].

Trustees

14.17 Anything done for the purposes of the Taxes Management Act by one 'relevant trustee' of a settlement satisfies the obligations of all of the trustees (and they are treated as having done it at the time it was done by that trustee) [TMA 1970 s 107A(1)]. The relevant trustees of a settlement are the people who are trustees when the income arises plus any subsequent trustees. For the purposes of capital gains tax (and of the income tax charge on gains from certain life assurance contracts) a person who was a trustee earlier in the tax year in which the gain arose is also a relevant trustee [TMA 1970 s 7(9)]. See also **14.7** in relation to income mandated to beneficiaries.

14.18 Where the relevant trustees of a settlement become liable to pay tax, or to a penalty, interest or surcharge, it can be recovered from any one or more of them – but only once [TMA 1970 s 107A(2)]. However, a penalty or surcharge (and interest thereon) cannot be recovered from a person who was not a trustee when the relevant act or omission occurred, with the exception that where a penalty accrues on a daily basis such a person is liable for the penalties that accrue from the start of the day on which he becomes a trustee [TMA 1970 s 107A(3)]. When considering whether trustees have a reasonable excuse under TMA 1970 s 93 for failure to deliver the trust return, or TMA 1970 s 59C (to avoid a surcharge), each of the trustees has to be looked at separately [TMA 1970 s 107A(4)]. The effect seems to be that all of the trustees are liable for the penalty or surcharge, even those who the Commissioners accept had a reasonable excuse, if any one trustee cannot show that he had a reasonable excuse.

14.19 Income tax chargeable in respect of income arising to the trustees of a settlement (or the personal representatives of a deceased person) can be assessed and charged on, and in the name of, any one or more of the relevant trustees or personal representatives. The relevant trustees are the person to whom any income arises and any subsequent trustees of the settlement. In relation to gains on life policies taxed as income it is the trustees in the tax year in which the gains arise and any subsequent trustees of the settlement [FA 1989 s 151].

Responsibility of company officers

14.20 Anything required to be done by a company under the 'Taxes Acts' is to be done through the 'proper officer' of the company or (unless a liquidator has been appointed) through any other person having the express, implied or apparent authority of the company to act on its behalf for that purpose [TMA 1970 s 108(1)]. The Taxes Acts are the Taxes Management Act 1970, the Tax Acts and the Taxation of Chargeable Gains Act 1992 and all other enactments relating to capital gains tax [TMA 1970 s 118(1)]. Unfortunately, the 'Tax Acts' does not appear to be defined anywhere. It is defined in TA 1988 s 831(2), as meaning the enactments relating to income tax and corporation tax, but only for the purpose of TA 1988. It is likely that the same interpretation will be placed on it for the purposes of the Taxes Management Act 1970.

14.21 The proper officer of a UK company is the secretary, or person acting as company secretary, except where a liquidator has been appointed in which case it is the liquidator [TMA 1970 s 108(3)(a)]. The proper officer of an unincorporated association or non-UK company (or of a UK company for which there is no company secretary) is the treasurer or the person acting as treasurer [TMA 1970 s 108(3)(b)]. In practice the Revenue seem content to accept the signature of a director on all tax documents. The Revenue view is apparently that, unless an officer has specifically been told that a particular person or class of persons does not have the company's authority, anyone who acts for the company under its apparent authority can do so (Corporation Taxation Manual, para 10897). Indeed, they conclude from this that if the sole director of a company is incapacitated at a critical time and so cannot make a claim a late claim should not be accepted if the company's claims are usually made by the accountant in submitting the corporation tax computations. This seems to take the principle much too far. There is a clear distinction between the managerial decision to make a claim and the clerical task of submitting it to the Revenue. The wide interpretation placed on implied authority by the Revenue is potentially worrying in the case of a non-UK company where the officers may not be unduly concerned about their tax obligations, on the basis that the country where they reside will not enforce the tax obligations of a foreign country. If the Revenue can look to a UK accountant, who perhaps submits only a non-residents landlords tax return, as having implied authority to act for the company generally, it becomes important to make clear to the Revenue the limited scope of the accountant's work for the company.

14.22 Service on a company of any documents under or in pursuance of the Taxes Acts can be effected by serving it on the proper officer [TMA 1970 s 108(1)].

14.23 Corporation tax or other tax chargeable under the Corporation Tax Acts on an unincorporated association or a non-UK incorporated company can be recovered from the proper officer (without prejudice to any other method of recovery) and that person can reimburse himself out of money coming into his hands on behalf of the company and is entitled to be indemnified by it [TMA 1970 s 108(2)].

Loans to close company participators

14.24 The provisions in TA 1988 ss 419 and 420 (charge in connection with loans by close companies to participators) directing that tax is to be assessed and recovered as if it were an amount of corporation tax must be taken as applying, subject to any necessary modification, to all enactments applying generally to corporation tax. This includes those relating to assessing, collecting and receiving corporation tax, those relating to appeals, and those concerning administration, penalties, interest on unpaid tax and priority of tax in cases of insolvency [TMA 1970 s 109(1)].

14.25 For interest purposes the due date of such tax is the day following the expiry of nine months from the end of the accounting period in which the loan or advance was made [TMA 1970 s 109(3); TA 1988 s 419(3)]. Where all or part of a loan is repaid, released or written off, interest on that amount is not payable in respect of any period after the date of repayment, release or writing off [TMA 1970 s 109(3A)]. However, TMA 1970 s 91 (see **10.21**) is not to apply in consequence of any discharge or repayment of tax under TA 1988 s 419(4), ie interest previously charged on late payment of the tax remains payable, and relief from tax under ss 419 or 420 is not to affect the tax charged by any assessment other than under that section [TMA 1970 s 109(4), (5)].

Valuation

14.26 Any person authorised to do so by the Board is entitled to enter on and inspect any land (which includes buildings) with a view to establishing its annual value where that annual value falls to be determined for the purposes of income tax or corporation tax. If so required he must produce evidence of his authority and he can only enter the land at a reasonable time [TMA 1970 s 110]. The only provisions which require an annual value of land to be determined are TA 1988 s 596B (cash equivalent of benefits from a non-approved pension scheme) and Sch 13 para 5 (deduction for pre-1963 Sch A payment) and ITEPA 2003 ss 103–113 (living accommodation provided for employee) and 205(3) (cash equivalent of benefits in kind). Any person will obviously include a valuer; in particular the District Valuer. It does not necessarily include an Inspector of Taxes, as it seems doubtful whether an Inspector can have 'a view to establishing' the annual value of land if he has no expertise in valuing it.

14.27 If the Board authorises an inspector or other officer of the Board to inspect any property for the purpose of ascertaining its market value for capital gains tax purposes the person having the custody or possession of that property must permit that officer to inspect it at such reasonable times as the Board may consider necessary. The penalty for wilfully delaying or obstructing the Officer is, on summary conviction, a fine of up to level 1 on the standard scale (£200) [TMA 1970 s 111]. This power is normally exercised only by the District Valuer or a specialist valuer engaged by the Shares Valuation Division. Any other person should be asked to demonstrate that he had been authorised by the Board for the purpose of s 111. The Capital Gains Manual tells local office staff:

> 'You should not in any circumstances insist on access to or require production of any asset which may later require inspection on behalf of the Revenue by the District Valuer or by any other person holding professional qualifications. These powers should only be exercised on authority from the Board and with great circumspection.' (Capital Gains Manual, para 16384.)

Documents

Loss, destruction and damage

14.28 If an assessment to tax (or duplicate of an assessment), a determination of penalties, or a return or other document relating to tax, is lost or destroyed (or is so defaced or damaged as to be illegible or otherwise useless) the Revenue and the Appeal Commissions can do all such acts and things as they might have done if the assessment had not been made or the return or other document had not been submitted or required to be submitted [TMA 1970 s 112(1)–(3)]. This appears to mean that if the Revenue lose a person's tax return they can charge the same penalties for non-submission as if he had never submitted it! In practice if they attempt to do this the taxpayer would undoubtedly complain very loudly. The provision is needed because without it if all copies of an assessment are lost the Revenue would not be able to collect the tax under it and would not be able to raise a new assessment for the same income. The section enables the lost assessment to be completely ignored. In practice if a return is lost or destroyed the Revenue are normally prepared to accept a photocopy of the return rather than insist on a new one being completed. It should be noted that the section is one-sided. The taxpayer has no rights in relation to a lost document!

14.29 If the taxpayer proves to the Board or the Appeal Commissioners that he paid tax on the basis of the original document he is entitled to relief for that payment either by abatement from the charge by the new assessment or by repayment [TMA 1970 s 112(1)]. Note particularly that it is for the taxpayer to prove that he has paid the tax if he is to avoid a double charge. The Revenue are not required to check their own records.

Form of returns, etc

14.30 Any returns under the Taxes Acts must be in such form as the Board prescribe. In prescribing income tax forms under this provision the Board must have regard to the desirability of securing, so far as possible, that no person shall be required to make more than one return annually of the sources of his income and the amounts thereof [TMA 1970 s 113(1)].

14.31 This provision does not entitle an individual inspector to prescribe a form in which he requires information. A form can be prescribed only by the Board. It is also likely that the reference to a return means only a statutory return, such as one under TMA 1970 ss 7–19, and does not extend to provisions which impose an obligation on a person to 'deliver' particulars or information to the Revenue.

14.32 It is of course the authority for insisting on the completion of an income tax return form. However, it needs to be borne in mind that the relevant charging legislation sets out the obligations of the taxpayer. For example, TMA 1970 s 8 states that:

> 'For the purpose of establishing the amount in which a person is chargeable to income tax and capital gains tax for a year of assessment and the amount payable by him by way of income tax for that year, he may be required … to make and deliver to the officer … a return containing such information as may reasonably be required in pursuance of the notice.'

Information reasonably required must relate back to the opening words of the sentence. Accordingly, information relating to, say, a different year of assessment which has no bearing on the current year's tax cannot be reasonably required within s 8. The Board's power to prescribe the form of the return required under s 8 must be limited to prescribing a form for supplying the information within s 8. If for convenience the Revenue ask for other information not relevant to s 8 to be given at the same time in the tax return the taxpayer cannot be required to supply that information. As a rough rule of thumb, where the Revenue use the word 'please' on a form they are almost certainly requesting non-statutory information.

14.33 The Revenue have confirmed that where a photocopy of an official return or an accurate facsimile are used these will satisfy the requirements of s 113(1) (Statement of Practice 5/78). For a substitute Tax Return to be acceptable the form need not be colour printed but must otherwise be an accurate facsimile of the official form in terms of the words which appear and the general layout. In their view (which seems questionable), it must also be readily recognisable as a return when it is received in Inland Revenue Offices and the entries of the taxpayer's details should be distinguishable from the background text. The Revenue go on to say that a facsimile return will be accepted if approval of the wording and design has been obtained in advance. However, if a return satisfies the requirement of s 113(1) it is hard to see on what basis they can purport to reject it. Not seeing it in advance is hardly a reasonable ground for doing so. It is sufficient that all of the pages are present and attached in the correct order if the facility to produce double sided photocopies is not available (SP 5/78).

14.34 Section 113 relates only to returns. However, various individual provisions of the Taxes Acts require notices to be given or claims to be made in such form as the Board may prescribe or for a relief to be subject to such conditions as the Board may prescribe, which obviously could include the form in which such relief is claimed. SP 5/78 states that the Revenue will accept such forms which are sent in as photocopies, but the requirement for all the pages to be present is important where one side of the form contains notes. Any copy which does not also duplicate the notes on the original will not be acceptable. This is because such elections may not be valid in the absence of the notes being before the signatories. This also seems of doubtful validity. A power to prescribe the form of a claim does not on the face of it include a power to dictate how it is signed. It is also unclear how the validity of a claim can be affected by whether or not accompanying notes are before the signatories. Indeed, a note on the back of a form is clearly not 'before' the signatory when he signs the front of the form.

14.35 Where the legislation does not empower the Revenue to prescribe the form of a claim or notice it can be made in any form that the taxpayer wishes provided that it contains the information required by the statute. If the taxpayer wants it to be acted on, common sense suggests that it also needs to include the taxpayer's name and tax reference and indicate the tax year to which it relates. Where the Revenue have power to prescribe a form but have not done so the taxpayer is similarly entitled to provide the necessary information in whatever format he wishes.

14.36 Every assessment, determination of a penalty, duplicate, warrant, notice of assessment, notice of determination, notice of demand or other document required to be used in assessing, charging, collecting and levying tax or determining a penalty must be in accordance with the forms prescribed from time to time in that behalf by the Board. A document in the form prescribed and supplied or approved by them is valid and effectual [TMA 1970 s 113(3)].

Mistakes

14.37 However, that appears to be irrelevant, as an assessment, determination, warrant or other proceeding which purports to be made in pursuance of a provision of the Taxes Acts is not be either:

(*a*) quashed or deemed to be void or voidable for want of any form; or

(*b*) effected by reason of a mistake, defect or omission therein,

if it is in substance and effect in conformity with (or according to the intent and meaning of) the Taxes Acts and if the person or property charged or intended to be charged or affected thereby is designated therein according to common intent and understanding [TMA 1970 s 114(1)].

14.38 In particular, an assessment or determination cannot be impeached by reason of:

(*a*) a mistake therein as to:
  (i) the name or surname of a person liable;
  (ii) the description of any profits or property;
  (iii) the amount of the tax charged; or

(*b*) any variance between the notice and the assessment or determination [TMA 1970 s 114(2)].

14.39 Megarry J considered s 114(1) in *Fleming v London Produce Co Ltd ((1968) 44 TC 582)*. An assessment had been raised on the company describing their business as 'agents' and addressed to the company 'as agents for Kaiapoi', an overseas company. London Produce said that Kaiapoi do not act as agents and have no income as such so the assessment must be bad. They claimed that what is now s 114 is not wide enough to treat the assessment as being on profits as meat salesmen. Megarry J said:

> 'I shall not attempt an exegesis of the subsections. I would be slow to accept that they provide an impervious cover for gross errors. One may observe the form of para (a) of sub [2]; what this saves from impeachment is a mistake in an assessment "as to" the name of surname of a person liable and so on. This suggests that, for example, something recognisable as the true name of the person liable must appear in the assessment, and only if it does is any mistake as to that name cured by the subsection. Faulty spelling is an obvious example. I think the subsection would apply if "McGarry" appeared in place of "Megarry" as in other contexts it often has: but it would be otherwise if the substitute were "Allen" or "Goff". The likelihood of the recipient being deceived or misled would be an important factor. One may ask whether an assessment of £80,000 on LP as agents for Kaiapoi is so gross and misleading an error as to be incapable of cure under [section 114] merely because the income assessable is described as "Agents". In my judgement, one has only to ask the question for it to answer itself.'

14.40 In *Murphy v Elders ((1974) 49 TC 135)* the boxes on a Sch E assessment for 'Particulars of Employment' and 'net tax deducted' were left blank. The judge felt that there was no statutory requirement to identify the employer concerned and if there were no deductions of tax there was nothing to put in that box, but if he were wrong was 'fully satisfied that the error, if there be one, is not a gross error but only a very minor defect covered by s 114(1) and (2)'. In *Bath and West Counties Property Trust Ltd v Thomas ((1978) 52 TC 20)* the Inspector raised an estimated assessment on short-term gains against which the company appealed. He subsequently agreed that the company had entered into an adventure in the nature of trade (which precluded these being short-term gains). The Revenue submitted that there had been a mistake – a genuine mutual mistake, common to taxpayer and Crown alike – as to the true nature for tax purposes of the undoubted profit which had been made and that this mistake should be corrected under s 114(1). Walton J retorted that there had been no mistake:

> 'That is the assessment which the Inspector of Taxes intended to make ... it is correct in every particular. He has not misunderstood the information with which he has been supplied by the taxpayer ... The assessment is exactly and precisely what he intended and, as drawn, it conveys to the outside world precisely and exactly what he intended to convey.'

As to 'common intent and understanding', the judge felt that the phrase does not mean the common intent and understanding of the taxpayer and the Revenue; rather it refers to the objective understanding of persons skilled in tax law. If that were not so the taxpayer could claim that he did not understand the first thing about the tax form and then there would be no common intent whatsoever. In *McGuckian v IRC ((1997) 69 TC 1)* an assessment was raised under TA 1988 Pt XVII Ch III (largely because the taxpayer did not provide the information to enable the Inspector to identify it properly) whereas the income fell within Chapter II. Carswell LJ observed that s 114(1) refers to a mistake, defect or omission 'therein', that is, in the assessment itself, 'which might be thought to point to a clerical type error rather than an assessment deliberately made under the provision selected, though the selection was caused by a misapprehension'. He thought that there was little authority from which assistance can be obtained on the ambit of s 114. In *Fleming v London Produce Co Ltd*, 'the error was obviously verbal and not one of substance'. He agreed with Walton J's view in *Bath and West Counties Property* that in this case, as in that, there had not been a mistake in the assessment which would permit its correction under s 114. He added that he 'should not wish to attempt to define the ambit of mistakes which may be so corrected'.

14.41 In *Baylis v Gregory ((1985) 62 TC 1)* an assessment purported to be for 1974/75 when it was intended to be for 1975/76. The taxpayer contended that s 114(1) does not provide for rectification of an assessment and that the relevant fiscal year of assessment is an integral, fundamental part of the assessment itself. Slade LJ commented: 'I, for my part, find it impossible to read the wording of s 114(1), wide though it is, as justifying in any circumstances the treatment of an assessment made for one fiscal year as an assessment made for another fiscal year'. He later commented that he did not derive great assistance from the authorities but felt that 'if, contrary to my view, this statutory right has any relevance in relation to an assessment which has been made for the wrong year, I think it unlikely that the legislative would have intended that it would be exercisable where the error was a gross one – as in the present case I think it must have been'.

14.42 The Revenue appear to rely on *Hart v Briscoe [1978] STC 89* as establishing that raising an assessment in a completely wrong name is not fatal (see Capital Gains Manual 37816). However, the facts in that case were unusual. An assessment had been made on three individuals 'as Trustees of Mrs L M Barne's Discretionary Settlement dated 6/1/1995'. In fact they were the Trustees of her 1972 Settlement. Both the Crown and the taxpayers wanted the court to hear the appeal from the Commissioners but the Crown had reluctantly submitted that because of the mistake the Court was bound to discharge the assessment and put the taxpayers and the Crown to the expense of starting afresh with a new assessment and appeal. Brightman J turned to s 114 to try to find a way out of this apparent impasse. He noted that the taxpayer's solicitors had said in a letter that the taxpayer regarded the precise identity of the trustees as somewhat technical. He was told that the real trustee of the 1995 settlement had instructed the trust's barrister to co-operate in any way possible to enable the matter to proceed. Brightman J having quoted the comments of Megarry J in *Fleming v London Produce Co Ltd* (see **14.39**), pointed out that:

> 'it is plain that no one has been in any way deceived or misled by the assessment in this case. It is perfectly clear that the assessment was intended to be on the trustees of Mrs Barne's discretionary settlement of 6 January 1955. An assessment in that form would be "in substance and effect in conformity with or according to the intent and meaning of the Taxes Acts".'

He accordingly felt able to take the view 'on the particular facts of this case' that s 114(1) cures the defect and thus to accede to the wishes of all of the parties and hear the appeal.

14.43 Where s 114 does not apply, all is not necessarily lost. In the Court of Appeal in *McGuckian v IRC ((1997) 69 TC 1)* (see **14.40**) Carswell LJ held that the final part of the wording of TMA 1970 s 56(6), 'The High Court … may make such other order in relation to the matter as the Court may seem fit', confers an authority on the court to uphold the assessment actually made under Part III as if it had been made under Part II. He affirmed that the Court has discretion whether to exercise that power, but he thought that 'section 56(6) is quite general in its terms … in my opinion it is a broad discretion, which the court is entitled to exercise when it considers it right and just in the circumstances of the case before it, taking into account the acts or omission of the parties and any other relevant matters'. His fellow judges agreed.

14.44 This is not a new principle. It derives from the decision of the House of Lords in *Pickles v Foulsham ((1925) 9 TC 261)*, Lord Cave said there that:

> 'Your Lordships were asked, in the event of your holding that the Respondent was not taxable under Case V, to send the matter back to the Special Commissioners with a view to their now assessing the Respondent in respect of the same income under Case II of Schedule D. My Lords, I am far from saying that the Respondent could not have been assessed under that case, or that the Court has no jurisdiction when Commissioners have proceeded under the wrong case to remit the matter to them under s 149(2) ITA 1918, with a view to their making a proper assessment; but I do not think that such a course should be taken in the present instance. The Revenue authorities have chosen deliberately to assess the Respondent under Case V and have persisted in that course notwithstanding the Respondent's objections. The time for assessing them under Case II has now expired and I do not think that it would be right now to require the Commissioners to make an assessment under that Case.'

The relevant part of s 149(2) read:

> 'The High Court … shall remit the matter to the Commissioners with the opinion of the court thereon, or may make such other order in relation to the matter … as the Court may seem fit.'

This is identical to the wording in TMA 1970 s 56(6). The other judges all agreed with Lord Cave's judgement. In reliance on *Pickles v Foulsham*, Walton J in the *Bath and West Counties Property* case had concluded that he had a discretion to change the assessment in that case from Case VII to Case I. He felt it right to do so as the taxpayer had 'unwittingly no doubt – seriously misled the Inspector'; and by the time the error had come to light in 1978 it was too late for the Inspector to make a fresh assessment.

Delegation of tasks

14.45 A notice or direction under the Taxes Acts requiring a return to be made to an Inspector or other Officer can be issued or given (in the name of that officer or in the name of the Board) by any officer of the Board and so as to require the return to be made to the first mentioned officer [TMA 1970 s 113(1A)].

14.46 Where the Board or an Inspector or other Officer have decided to make an assessment to tax and have taken all other decisions needed for arriving at the amount of the assessment, they can entrust to another officer responsibility for completing the assessing procedure (including serving notice on the person liable for the tax) (s 113(1B), TMA 1970). Similarly, where an Officer of the Board has decided to impose a penalty under TMA 1970 s 100 and has taken all other decisions needed for arriving at the amount of the penalty, he can delegate responsibility for completing the determination procedure [TMA 1970 s 113(1D)].

Delivery and service of documents

14.47 A notice or form which is to be served on a person under the Taxes Acts can either be delivered to him or left at his usual or last known address [TMA 1970 s 115(1)]. A notice or other document which is to be given, sent, served or delivered under the Taxes Acts can be served by post. If it is to be so given, etc, by the Board, by an officer of the Board or by or on behalf of any body of Commissioner's it can be so served addressed to that person at his usual or last known place of residence, or his place of business or his place of employment [TMA 1970 s 115(2)(a)]. In the case of a company it can alternatively be addressed to the company at any other place prescribed by the Board by regulations, or in the case of a liquidator at his address for the purpose of the liquidation [TMA 1970 s 115(2)(b)].

14.48 The Revenue instructions are to send notices to the address which determines the place of assessment (normally the principal trading address) (Assessment Procedures Manual, para 172). However, for s 20 notices, if the required documents are thought not to be held at the principle place of business but at a different address the notice will be sent to that different address (Investigation Handbook, para 8114).

14.49 Service by post is 'deemed to be effected by properly addressing, pre-paying and posting a letter ... and, unless the contrary is proved, to have been effected at the time at which the letter would be delivered in the ordinary course of post' [Interpretation Act 1978 s 7]. The onus is therefore on the Revenue to prove that a notice was not given timeously if the taxpayer says that it was sent by ordinary post in sufficient time to arrive by the due date (which is generally taken to be two working days for first class post and four for second class). The Revenue tell their staff to accept that a notice was given in time unless there is very good reason for doubt (Independent Taxation Manual, para 157). However, they also say that a claim that a timeous notice was sent should be accepted where:

(*a*) the Revenue's records for the relevant year have been mislaid or not kept;

(*b*) the taxpayer can produce photocopies of letters enclosing forms (or photocopies of timeously completed forms with a clear statement they were posted); or

(*c*) the taxpayer cannot produce copies but makes a clear statement he posted the notice on a particular date (a specified month would be acceptable) – but the Revenue may want to ask how the person is sure of the posting at the specific time.

The Revenue tell their staff, 'you should not accept a notice was lost where the taxpayer or agents simply say that some time within the time limit a notice was sent, even if they put their statement in an affidavit' (Relief Instructions, para 1415).

14.50 Notices to be given, delivered to, or served on, the General Commissioners are valid and effectual if given or delivered to or served on their clerk [TMA 1970 s 115(4)]. The General Commissioners Regulations 1994, SI 1994/1812, and Special Commissioners Regulations 1994, SI 1994/1811, contain their own rules in relation to delivery which override those in s 115.

Electronic lodgement of tax returns

14.51 TMA 1970 s 115A and Sch 3A contain the rules for electronic lodgement. The Schedule is to be repealed by FA 1999 s 133 from such date as the Treasury may by order direct. It provides the statutory backing for the Revenue's Electronic Lodgement Service (ELS). They have said that they will continue to support ELS until at least April 2004, so this Schedule had to remain in force at least until that time.

14.52 Where a person is required by a notice to which the Schedule applies to submit a tax return, that requirement will be treated as fulfilled if the information is transmitted electronically and the conditions in paras 4–7 are met (see **14.53**). The requirements that a return must be signed and include a declaration by the person making it that it is correct to the best of his knowledge and belief do not apply to electronically filed returns. The return is deemed to be filed at the end of the day in which the condition in para 7 (see **14.53**(*d*)) is met [TMA 1970 Sch 3A para 1]. Notices to file a return to which the Schedule applies are those under TMA 1970 ss 8 (personal return), 8A (trustee's return) and 12AA (partnership return) where the notice is given after 1 March 1997 (para 2 and the Electronic Lodgement of Returns Order 1997, SI 1997/57).

14.53 The conditions that must be met are:

(*a*) The transmission must be made by a person approved by the Board. This can be a taxpayer or agent. There is a limited right of appeal to the Special Commissioners against a refusal or withdrawal of approval [para 4].

(*b*) If the person who makes the transmission is notified by the Board of any requirements for the time being applicable to him as to the manner in which transmissions are to be made (including requirements as to hardware or software to be used) he must comply with such requirements [para 5].

(*c*) The transmission must signify in a manner approved by the Board that before the transmission was made a hard copy of the information proposed to be transmitted was made and authenticated in accordance with paras 8 and 9 [para 6]. A hard copy (ie, a printed out version of the information submitted electronically) is made in accordance with para 6 if it is made under arrangements designed to ensure that it contains the information in fact transmitted. A hard copy is authenticated where it is endorsed with a declaration by the taxpayer that the hard copy is to the best of his knowledge correct and complete [paras 8, 9].

(*d*) The information transmitted must be accepted for electronic lodgement, ie, accepted under a procedure selected by the Board for the purposes of Sch 3A [para 7].

14.54 If the notice requires supporting documents to be delivered with the return, that obligation is met if either those documents are submitted electronically and the conditions of paras 4–7 are met or they are not transmitted electronically but are delivered to the Revenue by the last day for the delivery of the return [TMA 1970 Sch 3A para 8].

14.55 Where a return is filed, or information transmitted, electronically, the Revenue have all the powers they would have had if it had been submitted by post. The taxpayer will also have the same power to amend the return and the same right to make an error or mistake claim as he would with a return delivered by post [TMA 1970 Sch 3A para 10]. A hard copy of the return shown to have been properly made and authenticated can be treated as if it were a return delivered for the purpose of any proceedings. If no such hard copy can be produced a hard copy certified by the Revenue to be a true copy of the information transmitted will be so treated and will be regarded as containing any declaration or signature that would have appeared on the hard copy (see **14.53**(*c*)). These rules also apply to documents other than a return, delivered in response to a requirement to deliver them [TMA 1970 Sch 3A para 11].

Other electronic communications

14.56 The Revenue have power by Regulation to provide more generally for the use of electronic communications:

(*a*) authorising taxpayers and others to use electronic communications to deliver information to the Revenue or to make payment to the Revenue;

(*b*) requiring taxpayers to use electronic communications for such purposes; and

(*c*) authorising the Revenue to communicate electronically with taxpayers and others,

[FA 1999 s 132(1)–(3)].

14.57 Furthermore, any power for either the Revenue or the Treasury to make Regulations in connection with the delivery of information or making of payment is deemed to include power to make such provisions as are permitted under s 132 even if the legislation itself specifies the form that such delivery must take, eg by notice in writing [FA 1999 s 133].

14.58 They have done so, in relation only to income tax returns, by the Income and Corporation Taxes (Electronic Communications) Regulations 2003, SI 2003/282. These permit the Revenue to use electronic communications in connection with the delivery of information the delivery of which is authorised or required by or under TMA 1970 ss 8–9D, 12AA–12AE, 59DA or 59DE or Sch 1A, or FA 1998 s 30 or 36 or Sch 18. They can also use electronic communications in connection with payment or repayment of tax or other sums in connection with the operation of those sections [regs 2(1), 3(1)]. However, the Revenue can communicate electronically in relation to such matters only if the recipient has indicated his consent to their doing so and has not informed them that he has withdrawn such consent [reg 3(1)]. The Revenue can also use intermediaries in connection with the electronic delivery of information or payments and the authentication or security of anything transmitted by electronic means, and can require other persons also to use intermediaries in connection with such matters [reg 4].

14.59 The Regulations allow taxpayers, their agents and other persons also to use electronic communications in relation to the above matters, but only if:

(*a*) that person is for the time being authorised by the Revenue (whether generally or specifically) to use electronic communications;

(*b*) he uses approved methods of authenticating his identity, of electronic communication and of authenticating information delivered by electronic means;

(*c*) any information or payment sent electronically is in a form and sent in a manner approved by the Revenue; and

(*d*) he maintains such records (in writing or electronic form) as may be specified by the Revenue,

[regs 2(1), 3(2)–(7)]. Prior to 5 March 2003 electronic communications could be used only for individual and trustee income tax returns.

14.60 Revenue authorisation can be given by means of Revenue directions. They have made the following directions under the provision.

21 August 2001

An agent who delivers information on behalf of another person which the other ('the taxpayer') is required to deliver by virtue of a notice under TMA 1970 s 8 is authorised to do so over the internet provided the following conditions are met—

(a) that the agent is authorised to act for the taxpayer to whom the return relates—
   (i) by means of a form 64–8 signed by the taxpayer; or
   (ii) by means of an on-line authorisation given by the taxpayer on the Government Gateway website;

(b) that—
  (i) the agent makes a copy of the information before it is sent; and
  (ii) the copy is authenticated by the taxpayer by means of a signature confirming that the information is correct to the best of the taxpayer's knowledge and belief before the information is sent by the agent; and
(c) that for the purpose of the electronic communication, the agent uses software approved by the Commissioners of Inland Revenue.

The Revenue further direct that—
(a) the methods approved by them for—
  (i) authenticating the identity of the individual sending the relevant information, and
  (ii) the delivery of the relevant information;
(b) the form approved by them in which the relevant information is to be delivered; and
(c) the software products approved for this purpose,

are the methods, form and software products set out, at the time of, and for the purposes of, the delivery of the relevant information, on the Inland Revenue website.

4 March 2003

A company that is required to deliver information in response to a notice under paragraph 3 of Schedule 18 to the Finance Act 1998 ('the relevant information') is authorised to do so over the Internet.

The Commissioners further direct that—

The methods approved by them for—
(a) authenticating the identity of the person sending the relevant information,
  (i) delivery of the relevant information, and
  (ii) authenticating the relevant information; and
(b) the form approved by them in which the relevant information is to be delivered;

are the methods and form set out, at the time of, and for the purposes of, the delivery of the relevant information, in the terms and conditions for use of the Internet Corporation Tax Service, on the Inland Revenue website (www.inlandrevenue.gov.uk).

Agents acting on behalf of companies—returns under paragraph 3 of Schedule 18 to the Finance Act 1998

The Commissioners of Inland Revenue hereby direct that on and after 5 March 2003 an agent who delivers information on behalf of a company, which the company is required to deliver in response to a notice under paragraph 3 of Schedule 18 to the Finance Act 1998 ('the relevant information'), is authorised to do so over the Internet provided that the following conditions are met.

The first condition is that the agent is authorised to act for the company to which the return relates by means of a form 64–8 signed by a proper officer of the company.

The second condition is that—

(a) the agent makes a copy of the relevant information before it is sent; and

(b) the copy is authenticated by a proper officer of the company, (or other person authorised to make the return of behalf of the company) by means of a signature confirming that the information is correct to the best of his knowledge and belief before the information is sent by the agent. This condition will not apply where the agent is a person authorised by the company to make the return on its behalf.

The Commissioners further direct that—

(a) the methods approved by them for—
    (i) authenticating the identity of the person sending the relevant information,
    (ii) delivery of the relevant information, and
    (iii). authenticating the relevant information; and

(b) the form approved by them in which the relevant information is to be delivered;

are the methods and form set out, at the time of, and for the purposes of, the delivery of the relevant information, in the terms and conditions for use of the Internet Corporation Tax Service, on the Inland Revenue website (www.inlandrevenue.gov.uk).

Other communications within the scope of the Income and Corporation Tax (Electronic Communications) Regulations 2003

The Commissioners of Inland Revenue hereby direct that—

– companies or their agents may use telephonic facsimile for other communications to which the regulations apply, and

– companies or their agents that are participating in the collaborative workspace trial may also use that facility for such communications.

14.61 Information which is delivered electronically is treated as having been delivered in the manner or form required by any provision of the Taxes Act or the Taxes Management Act provided that the above conditions are complied with and the other conditions (other than as to manner and form) of the relevant statutory provisions and any specific or general direction given by the Board are also met [reg 5(1)]. Information delivered electronically is regarded as delivered on the day on which the last of these conditions is satisfied (unless the Board directs that a different date should apply) but information cannot be regarded as having been delivered to an official computer system (ie, one maintained by or on behalf of the Revenue for the purpose of sending or receiving information or payments or processor storing information) unless it is accepted by that system [regs 1(2), 5(2)–(4)].

14.62 A document that is certified by a Revenue officer to be a printed out version of any information delivered electronically under these Regulations is evidence, unless the contrary is proved, that such information was delivered electronically at the time stated in the certificate and constitutes the entirety of what was delivered on that occasion. A document purporting to be a certificate under this Regulation must be presumed to be such unless the contrary is proved [reg 6]. The identity of the sender or recipient of an electronic communication is also presumed, unless the contrary is proved, to be the person recorded as such on an official computer system [reg 7].

14.63 Information delivered by an agent by an approved electronic method is deemed to have been delivered by the person on whose behalf he was acting unless that person proves that it was delivered without his knowledge or connivance [reg 8].

14.64 The use of an authorised method is presumed, unless the contrary is proved, to have resulted in the making of a payment or the delivery of information if the payment or delivery (whether by or to the Revenue) has been recorded in an official computer system (see **14.61**). Conversely, if it is not recorded on a Revenue computer it cannot be regarded as having been paid or delivered unless the contrary is proved. The time of receipt of the information or payment is presumed (unless the contrary is proved) to be that recorded on the Revenue's computer [reg 9].

14.65 If information within reg 2 (see **14.58**) is supplied electronically to the Revenue in a form or manner that does not satisfy the requirement of reg 3 (see **14.59**) it must be conclusively deemed not to have been delivered to the Revenue – even if it can be shown that they in fact received it [reg 10]. This does not of course apply to information supplied by electronic lodgement (see **14.51**) [reg 2(2)]

14.66 The Revenue also have power by Regulation to provide incentives to use electronic communications. These can in particular take the form of discounts, allowing additional time to comply with any tax obligation and the facility to deliver information or make payments at more convenient intervals [FA 2000 s 143 and Sch 38].

14.67 The relevant regulations are the Income Tax (Electronic Communications) (Incentive Payments) Regulations 2001, SI 2001/56. They require the Revenue to make an incentive payment of £10 to any individual who delivers a personal tax return under TMA 1970 s 8 electronically and satisfies the condition specified in any direction by the Revenue under the Regulations [reg 3(1), (2)].

14.68 On 19 February 1991 they directed that the conditions to be satisfied are that the return relates to 1999/2000, it is filed using the Internet Service for Self-Assessment, the individual is authorised to use that service, at least one of his 1999/00 payment is made electronically, and the tax return and tax payments made are filed by the due date. This incentive is not available for a subsequent return.

14.69 If a Revenue officer considers that the individual does not satisfy one or more of the specified conditions he must notify the individual [reg 3]. If the incentive payment has already been authorised or made the Revenue can give notice to withdraw it and can make an assessment under TMA 1970 ss 30 and 30A to recover the £10 as if it were an amount of income tax repaid in error to that person [reg 3(4), (5)]. The Revenue have power to give a direction relating to appeals against such notices [reg 3(3), (6)].

14.70 The regulations also require the Revenue to make an incentive payment of £50 to any employer who electronically makes a return under reg 73 of the PAYE Regulations (ie, the P35) and satisfies the conditions given in a direction by the Board [reg 4(1), (2)]. The provisions at **14.69** in relation to wrongly made payments again apply [reg 4(3)–(6)].

14.71 They also require the Revenue to make an incentive payment of £50 (in addition to that at **14.70**) to any employer who files his P35 electronically, during the tax year has paid tax credit to one or more of his employees (and recorded it on the P35) and satisfies the conditions given in a direction by the Board. [reg 5(1), (2)]. The provisions of **14.69** in relation to wrongly made payment again apply [reg 5(3)–(6)].

14.72 The Revenue made a direction under reg 4(2), but only in relation to P35s for 2001/02.

14.73 The Revenue also made a direction under regs 3(6), 4(6) and 5(6). Notice of an appeal must be in writing, not given electronically! It must be given within 30 days of the date of the notice or assessment (or later if the Revenue, or the Commissioners, are satisfied that there was a reasonable excuse for not having done it in time).

14.74 The carrot having proved largely ineffective, in 2002 the government changed to the stick. It gave the Revenue power by regulation to require 'the use of electronic communications for the delivery by specified persons of specified information required or authorised to be delivered by or under legislation relating to a taxation matter' [FA 2002 s 135]. Any power for the Revenue or the Treasury to make regulations in connection with the delivery of information in relation to any taxation matter includes a power to provide for it to be delivered electronically (notwithstanding anything in any enactment that provides otherwise or which precludes the use of an intermediary in connection with its delivery) [FA 2002 s 136]. Although this gives the Revenue power to require everybody to deal with them wholly electronically, it is understood that they currently have no intention to do so except in relation to forms P35 (PAYE annual return).

14.75 The Revenue were next given a specific power by regulation, to require large employers to use electronic means for making specified payments under legislation relating to any tax under their care and management. A large employer for this purpose is a person paying PAYE income to 250 or more employees [FA 2003 s 204]. It is understood that the Revenue have no current intention of using this power except in relation to PAYE. Again, there is power to override anything in any enactment that would otherwise allow payment to be made by some other means [FA 2003 s 205].

14.76 The Income Tax (Employment) (Amendment) Regulations 2003 amend the PAYE Regulations to reflect the use of the Revenue's powers under both FA 2002 s 136 and FA 2003 s 208. The relevant regulations are now contained in Income Tax (Pay As You Earn) Regulations 2003, SI 2003/2682, regs 199–216. These provide that a large employer to whom an e-payment notice in respect of a tax year has been issued must use an approved method of electronic communication to make specific payments, namely payment under reg 6 (periodic payments to and recoveries from the Revenue) in respect of tax months in the tax year to which the e-payment notice relates [reg 199(1), (2)]. The approved methods for 2004/05 are BACS direct credit, CHAPS, debit card over the internet ('BillPay'), Paymaster, Bank Giro and Alliance and Leicester Commercial Bank (Board Direction 21.10.2003). The Revenue have power by direction to override this requirement for any period [reg 199(3)]. An e-payment notice must be issued by 31 December following the specified date for the tax year [reg 200(2)]. This is a date to be announced each year by the Revenue on or before 30 November 2003 [reg 190]. For 2004/05 it is 20 October 2003. There is a right of appeal against an e-notice but only on the ground that the employer is not a large employer. Notice of appeal must be given within the usual 30 days [reg 200(3)–(6)].

14.77 An employer who is in default is liable to a surcharge. For this purpose an employer is in default only if his payment does not reach the Revenue on or before the due date (normally the 19th of the following month). A person who pays by cheque instead of electronically is not in default. Nor is one who had a reasonable excuse for failing to secure that the payment was received in time, provided that the payment was received by the Revenue without unreasonable delay after the excuse ceased. Inability to pay is not a reasonable excuse. Sending a cheque which although received by the due date cannot be cleared by them is a default [reg 201].

14.78 The Revenue must issue a default notice to the employer. There is aright of appeal against this (within 30 days) but only on the grounds that either the employer is not in default or is not a large employer [reg 203]. The employer is not liable to a surcharge for one default; he must commit three or more defaults during the surcharge period. This starts immediately after the first default and continues until such time as the employer shows a full tax year without a single default [regs 203(5), 204(1)]. The Revenue must issue a surcharge notice which shows the total surcharge liability for the tax year (ie, they do not issue it at the time of the third or subsequent default but must wait until after the end of the tax year). There is a right of appeal (within 30 days) but only on the grounds that either the number of defaults stated in the notice is incorrect or the amount of the surcharge is incorrect. A default that was appealed under reg 202 cannot be appealed again though. A surcharge notice must be issued within six years of the end of the tax year concerned (or if earlier, within six years of filing the forms P35 and P14) [reg 204(2)–(6)]. On appeal the Commissioners must make their own decision as to what, if any, the surcharge liability should be.

14.79 The amount on which the surcharge is calculated is the total tax due for the year less the total payments in respect of Working Tax Credit, Statutory Maternity Pay, Statutory Paternity or Statutory Adoption Pay and Construction Industry Sub-contractors deductions set against the sub-contractors PAYE liability [reg 203(3), (4)]. The surcharge for each default is the following percentage of the total tax due for the year.

3rd, 4th or 5th default:	0.17%
6th, 7th or 8th default:	0.33%
9th, 10th or 11th default:	0.58%
subsequent defaults:	0.83%

It will be apparent that once an employer has made three late payments he could face a surcharge of up to 9.9 per cent of his annual PAYE liability if he always pays late.

14.80 From 2004/05 a large employer is also required to deliver specified information by an approved method of electronic communication. So, from 2005/06, must a medium-sized employer if the Revenue issue an e-filing notice to him [regs 205, 206(1)]. A medium-sized employer is one who is treated as paying PAYE income to 50 or more employees at the specified date (see **14.76**) [reg 191(2)]. An individual who is a practising member of a religious society or order whose beliefs are incompatible with the use of electronic communication (or a partnership all the members of which is, or a company all the directors and the secretary of which is) is excused from the requirement [reg 206(2)]. The specified information is the P35 and P14 and accompanying information [reg 207]. The only methods of electronic communication approved for this purpose for delivering information either by the employer or by an agent on his behalf are the internet services provided through PAYE Online for Employers and PAYE Online for Agents (Board's Direction of 21.10.2003).

14.81 There is a right of appeal where an employer does not believe he is a large or medium-sized employer or that he is exempted under reg 206(2) [reg 203]. The information filed electronically must meet the standards of accuracy or completeness set by direction given by the Board. If it does not, it is treated as not having been delivered [reg 209]. These are those set out in the 'Quality Standard Validation Specification from April 2004' published on the Revenue's website (Board's Direction of 21.10.2003)

14.82 The penalty for not filing electronically for 2004/05 to 2008/09 (or only filing part electronically) depends on the number of employees for whom particulars should have been delivered but were not. It is nil for less than 50 employees, £600 if there are 50–249 employees (except for 2004/05 when it is nil), £900 (including for 2004/05) for 250–399 employees and £900 plus a further £300 for each additional 100 employees thereafter subject to a maximum of £3,000 [reg 210(2)(c)]. There is no penalty if the employer had a reasonable excuse. There is the normal right of appeal [reg 210(3)–(5)]. The penalties carry interest under TMA 1970 s 103A [reg 210(6)].

14.83 An employer can if he wishes file many other PAYE forms electronically, namely forms P12, P37, P45 Part 1 (but only on the death of an employee or pensioner), P45, Part 3, P46, P160, P35 and P14, P38A, P11D, P11D(b) and P46(car) [reg 21(4)]. Information is taken to have been filed electronically only if it is delivered to an official computer system by an approved method of electronic communication and accepted by that system [reg 192]. The presumptions at **14.61–14.65** apply to such information [regs 192–198].

Computer records

14.84 Any provision which requires a person to produce, furnish or deliver any document or to permit the Revenue to inspect any document has effect as if any reference in it to a document were a reference to anything in which information of any description is recorded (and as if any reference to a copy of a document were a reference to anything onto which information recorded in the document has been copied by any means and whether directly or indirectly) [FA 1988 s 127(1)].

14.85 A tax officer is entitled at any reasonable time to have access to, and inspect and check the operation of, any computer and any associated apparatus or material which is (or has been) in use in connection with any document which a person is (or can be) required to produce to the Revenue or permit the Revenue to inspect. The officer can require the person by whom (or on whose behalf) the computer is, or has been, so used, or any person having charge of the computer, apparatus or material (or who is otherwise concerned with its operation) to afford to the officer such reasonable assistance as he may require for the purpose of such access [FA 1988 s 127(1)–(3)]. Any person who obstructs the officer in the exercise of these powers, or fails within a reasonable time to comply with a requirement to afford assistance, is liable to a penalty of up to £500.

Action of ejectment in Northern Ireland

14.86 An action of ejectment in Northern Ireland (ie eviction) for non-payment of rent is not to be defeated on the ground that the person liable to pay the rent is entitled to deduct tax from it under the Income Tax Acts, reducing the amount due by him to the landlord below a year's rent [TMA 1970 s 117].

Time limits

14.87 For the purposes of the Taxes Management Act a person is deemed not to have failed to do anything required to be done within a limited time if he did it within such further time, if any, as the Board or the Commissioners or Officer concerned may have allowed. For such purposes:

> 'where a person has a reasonable excuse for not doing something required to be done, he shall be deemed not to have failed to do it unless the excuse ceased and, after the excuse ceased, he shall be deemed not to have failed to do it if he did it without reasonable delay after the excuse had ceased' [TMA 1970 s 118(2)].

These words are quoted verbatim because the provision can provide a very useful escape for taxpayers who do not comply with a time limit.

14.88 The first part of s 118(2) effectively allows the Revenue to extend any time limit. If they decline to do so the taxpayer is entitled to ask the appeal Commissioners to extend the limit. The Commissioners appear to have a wide discretion to do so. In many cases, such as late appeals, the Revenue will extend a time limit fairly readily. However, they will not normally do this where Parliament has laid down a special time limit and not given the Revenue a specific power to extend it. The Revenue's Corporation Tax Manual points out that an Inspector can allow further time for delivering a return. However, it tells Inspectors to apply the 'reasonable excuse' criteria, ie, to extend the time only if the company has a reasonable excuse for its anticipated delay and then to extend the limit up to the date when the reasonable excuse is expected to cease (para 10413). Under ESC B46 the Revenue do not charge a late filing penalty for a corporation tax return if they receive it within seven days of the statutory filing date. This concession is not given where further time is allowed (para 10416). The Investigation Handbook also points out that under s 118(2) an Inspector can extend the time limit for compliance with a TMA 1970 s 20 notice if he thinks the circumstances justify it (para 8120).

14.89 The second leg deals with reasonable excuse. What is reasonable is clearly a question of fact dependent on the circumstances of each individual case. The Revenue say that all claims should be considered on their merit. 'Honesty of purpose is a preliminary condition that a company always needs to fulfil', whatever that may mean. Account also needs to be taken of the circumstances of the person making the claim. A higher standard is expected from an experienced controlling director than of a newly appointed director with no previous business experience (Corporation Tax Manual, para 10414). In the Investigation Handbook they similarly say (para 5062):

> 'There are no absolute standards by which the words "reasonable excuse" can be defined. Generally, it can be said to be an excuse which sounds reasonable in the mouth of the person giving it, that is, the

standard of reasonableness can vary according to the type, education, background etc of the taxpayer concerned.'

14.90 The Revenue give examples of things that might constitute a reasonable excuse for filing a corporation tax return late:

(*a*) one director runs the company and he (or an immediate family member) dies or suffers a sudden and serious illness close to the filing date;

(*b*) such a director has a prolonged and serious illness throughout much of the return period;

(*c*) unavoidable and unexpected absence abroad of the responsible director close to the deadline because of business commitments and domestic emergency;

(*d*) accidental destruction of the records through fire or flood;

(*e*) exceptional postal delays due to a strike by postal workers or other civil disruption;

(*f*) the District did not receive a return but the company claims to have posted it in good time;

(*g*) an inexperienced director fails to comply with the regulations, perhaps on incorrect or misleading advice from an agent, and he rectifies the fault as soon as he recognises it (Corporation Tax Manual, para 10414).

14.91 They do not accept that the following can constitute a reasonable excuse:

(*a*) simple ignorance of the law;

(*b*) failure due to a dilatory agent;

(*c*) information relevant to the return is not available at the filing date;

(*d*) the affairs of the company are too complicated to enable the return to be completed on time;

(*e*) the responsible director is too busy running the company's business;

(*f*) there is no intention of avoiding tax, or deferring payment of tax;

(*g*) the company is not liable to tax for the period for which the return is required or has unpaid tax;

(*h*) the company is not a commercial enterprise,

(Corporation Tax Manual, para 10415).

14.92 The above is merely the Revenue's published views. The appeal Commissioners may well apply a different test. As mentioned at **8.29** there are a great many VAT Tribunal cases on what is and is not a reasonable excuse. There is no obvious reasons why the circumstances in those cases should not be decided in the same way for income and corporation tax purposes. But remember that s 118(2) contains an additional test, namely that when the reasonable excuse ceases, the failure must be remedied without unreasonable delay.

14.93 Reliance on one's accountant who failed in his duty has been held not to be a reasonable excuse where the taxpayer knew long before that the accountant was incompetent (*Mankowitz v Special Comrs ((1971) 46 TC 707)*). The argument that a s 20 notice may put a burden on the recipient, and objecting to the notice on a point of law that turns out to be ill-founded, were both said not to be a reasonable excuse in *B and S Displays Ltd v Special Comrs ((1978) 52 TC 318)*. In *Moschi v General Comrs for Kensington ((1980) 54 TC 403)* the judge felt that the excuse of a combination of the time taken by the taxpayer's accountants and his own continuing ill health was not put forward in evidence in sufficient detail to persuade him that it formed a reasonable excuse. In *Thorne v General Comrs for Sevenoaks ((1989) 62 TC 341)* the judge commented:

> 'There appears to be no authority on what may constitute a reasonable excuse. The taxpayer relied on four matters: overwork at his business, the death of his father and divorce from his wife. I find it difficult to see how any of these matters could give rise to a reasonable excuse [for incorrect tax returns]. But the fourth matter was reliance on information provided by his own bank … It seems to me that it is at least arguable that if the taxpayer genuinely reasonably believed and relied on what his bank told him, this could constitute a reasonable excuse within s 118(2).'

14.94 In *Kingsley v Bellingham [1992] STC 132* the Special Commissioners commented:

> 'Nor did Mr Kingsley have a "reasonable excuse" for the failure in question. It was not sufficient for him to blame his accountants then acting. Mr Kingsley had received the return forms; he knew that he had not signed them after completion by his accountants; and he must therefore have known that they had not been delivered to the Inspector. Nor can Mr Kingsley reasonably have believed that the information about the disposals had been regularly reported to the Inspector by the accountants in some other form; for Mr Kingsley knew that no assessments to capital gains tax had been made although the amounts of the gains were substantial.'

This probably illustrates the risks inherent in arguing 'reasonable excuse' before the Special Commissioners. The level of knowledge that lawyers presume clients to possess often seems far greater than accountants' experience would regard as credible! In *Creedplan v Winter [1995] STC (SCD) 352* the Commissioner clearly did not believe the taxpayer's contention that the return received by the Revenue on 3 May had been posted on 18 March. He dismissed the taxpayer's contention that he had a reasonable excuse for not having submitted a complete return by 31 March as the

Revenue had not told him that it was incomplete until 10 May, saying that even if the return had been posted on 18 March there was no excuse for sending a return which was less than was required.

14.95 In *Orakpo v Lane [1996] STC (SCD) 43* the taxpayer contended that his claim that the basis of assessment should have been Sch D could have been discovered from the correspondence and such claims had not been put forward sooner than they had, or had not been pursued as they could have been, because of the Revenue's error in dealing incorrectly with the taxpayer's affairs, which was outside his control especially since he was at a number of points not professionally advised. The Special Commissioner felt that that could not constitute a reasonable excuse, adding 'whether the taxpayer has been dealt with fairly is not a matter for me to consider.' That is somewhat surprising as most people would probably consider fairness a significant factor in deciding the reasonableness of an excuse.

14.96 The taxpayer did succeed in *Akarimsons Ltd v Chapman [1997] STC (SCD) 140*. The excuse put forward for not having submitted a tax return and accounts by 30 November 1996 was that the director of the company, who died in December 1996, suffered a stroke in 1995 which left him virtually paralysed and without speech, and the company secretary had suffered chronic ill health for many years, culminating in his undergoing serious surgery in June 1995. The Special Commissioner commented, 'in those circumstances I do not find it surprising that the company did not comply precisely with the requirements of the statute'. Some would think it surprising that the Revenue did not accept that such a combination of misfortunes amounted to a reasonable excuse, particularly as the company secretary had told the Revenue in November 1995 that preparation of the accounts was delayed due to the illness of the director.

14.97 In *Nunn v Gray [1997] STC (SCD) 175* the Inspector submitted that a taxpayer can rely on s 118(2) if he sends in a late return but not if the return is incomplete, or complete but erroneous, since then the only question is whether it is correct and complete. The Special Commissioners rejected that:

> 'In my opinion the defence in s 118(2) is available to a taxpayer who has put in an incorrect or incomplete return. As I see it, the duty of the taxpayer is to put in one correct and complete return. I decline to construe s 118(2) in so restricted a fashion as to preclude a taxpayer advancing a reasonable excuse for his failure to put in a return which is correct and complete, having put in a return which in some respects is incorrect or incomplete.'

In the event he held that:

> 'It appears to me that the taxpayer was very unwise to sign an incomplete return, leaving it to his accountant to complete and despatch the return. Thereby in practical terms, he put the completion of the return out of his own direct control … In the circumstances I am very

doubtful whether abrogation of his personal responsibility can amount to a reasonable excuse.'

This seems another example of the standards assumed by lawyers being far removed from the practicalities of everyday life.

14.98 Perhaps the strangest case is *Steeden v Carver [1999] STC (SCD) 283*. Miss Steeden's tax return was handed in to the Revenue at 10.30 on Monday 2 February. Her accountants had been told on the telephone by the Revenue that tax returns would be accepted if delivered 'at any time prior to Monday morning opening'. The Special Commissioner thought that the question to be decided was whether throughout Sunday 1 February the taxpayer had a reasonable excuse for not having delivered the return. The Revenue did not dispute the accountant's story. The Commissioner not surprisingly held that, 'reliance on Revenue advice as to the practical extension of a deadline, if unequivocally given, is as reasonable an excuse as can be found'. The strangeness lies in the fact that the case had to go to a hearing to establish what most people would consider to be a statement of the obvious.

Finality

14.99 For the purposes of the Taxes Management Act the amount of tax covered by an assessment cannot be deemed to be finally determined until that assessment can no longer be varied – whether by any Commissioners on appeal or by the order of any court [TMA 1970 s 118(4)]. The Revenue say that it follows that, in the case of a decision of the General Commissioners, a demand for a stated case under TMA 1970 s 56 (see **7.61**) will keep open the time limit until the final order of the courts or the prior settlement of the appeal (Investigation Handbook, para 4854).

Human rights

14.100 The UK is a signatory to the European Convention on Human Rights. The Human Rights Act 1998 incorporates that Convention, together with the First and Sixth Protocol to it, into UK law. There are three main convention rights that can apply to tax, Article 1 of the First Protocol and Articles 6 and 8 of the Convention. Article 1 of the First Protocol provides that 'every natural or legal person is entitled to the peaceful enjoyment of his possessions. No one shall be deprived of his possessions except in the public interest'. There is, however, a major proviso, namely that this provision is not to 'in any way impair the right of a State to enforce such laws as it deems necessary to … secure the payments of taxes or other contributions or penalties'.

14.101 The first UK tax case under Article 1 was *National and Provincial Building Society v United Kingdom ((1997) 69 TC 540)*. In that case it was common ground that the retroactive measure against building societies constituted an interference with the enjoyment of the societies' possessions. However, the European Court of Justice decided that there had been no violation of Article 1. According to the well established case law of the ECJ, such as in *Gasus Dosier-und Fördertechnik GmbH v Netherlands ((1995) 20 EHRR 403)*:

> 'an interference, including one resulting from a measure to secure the payment of taxes, must strike a "fair balance" between the demands of the general interest of the community and the requirements of the protection of the individual's fundamental rights'.

In determining whether this requirement is met a Contracting State enjoys a wide margin of appreciation and the Court will respect the legislature's assessment in such matters unless it is devoid of reasonable foundation. The Court commented that 'there is in fact an obvious and compelling public interest to ensure that private entities do not enjoy the benefit of a windfall in a changeover to a new tax payment regime', and felt that the actions taken by the UK could not be impugned.

14.102 The Administrative Court of the Queens Bench Division similarly dismissed a claim to apply Article 1 in *R (on the application of Professional Contractors Group Ltd v IRC [2001] EWHC Admin 236, [2001] STC 629*, which was a challenge against the IR35 legislation. The judge pointed out that in *X v France (Application 9908/82) 32 DR 266 (1983)* the Commission had said that:

> 'the legislation of most of the States … provides that the authorities should, when assessing income tax, take account in some cases of certain other factors distinct from income in the strict sense … Regulations of this kind should not, generally speaking, be considered incompatible with Article 1.'

In *Svenska Management Gruppen AB v Sweden (Application 11036/84) 45 DR 211 (1985)* it has said that:

> 'A financial liability arising out of the raising of taxes … may adversely affect the guarantee of ownership … However it is in the first place for the national authorities to decide what kind of taxes or contributions are to be collected. Furthermore the decisions in this area will commonly involve the appreciation of political, economic and social questions which the Convention leaves within the competence of the Contracting States. The power of appreciation of the Contracting States is therefore a wide one.'

14.103 The judge concluded that it did not offend against the concept of certainty for the common law of employment to apply to a service contractor and that, even where it involved additional expenses, it could not be said to interfere with their human rights so as to contravene Article 1.

14.104 *Lindsay v Customs and Excise Comrs [2002] EWCA Civ 267, [2002] STC 588* related to penalties. The judge felt that 'one must consider the individual case to ensure that the penalty imposed is fair. However strong the public interest, it cannot justify subjecting an individual to an interference with his fundamental rights that is unconscionable'. The judge felt that confiscating Mr Lindsay's car because he was bringing into the UK quantities of cigarettes and tobacco which he had purchased on behalf of friends was disproportionate, although whether his decision is based on Article 1 or on the ECJ concept of proportionality is not wholly clear.

14.105 Article 6 is the right to a fair trial. It provides that, 'In the determination of his civil rights and obligations or of any criminal charge against him everyone is entitled to a fair and public hearing within a reasonable time by an independent and impartial tribunal established by law'. It goes on to provide that everyone charged with a criminal offence must be presumed innocent until proved guilty according to law and sets out certain minimum rights that everyone charged with a criminal offence has: to be informed promptly of the nature of the charge against him, to have adequate time and facilities for the preparation of his defence, to defend himself in person or through legal assistance of his own choosing – to be given free when the interests of justice demand it – to examine witnesses against him and to obtain the attendance of, and examine, witnesses on his own behalf and to have the free assistance of an interpreter where necessary.

14.106 The most important case to date on Article 6 is *Customs and Excise Comrs v Han and Yau [2001] EWCA Civ 1040, [2001] STC 1188*. Customs sought a penalty for VAT evasion. The penalty where a taxpayer's conduct involved dishonesty is up to 100 per cent of the tax evaded. The VAT tribunal held as a preliminary point that the imposition of the civil penalty is a criminal charge for the purpose of Article 6 and that accordingly Mr Yau, who is a non-English speaker, was entitled to the benefit of the procedural safeguards. The Court of Appeal (in a consolidated appeal) upheld this ruling. It pointed out that the case law of the European Court of Human Rights (ECHR) makes clear that the concept of a 'criminal charge' has an autonomous convention meaning (*Engel v Netherlands (1976) 1 EHRR 647*). The ECHR effectively applied three criteria to determine whether a criminal charge has been imposed:

(*a*) the classification of the proceedings in domestic law;

(*b*) the nature of the offence; and

(*c*) the nature and degree of severity of the penalty that the person concerned risked incurring.

These factors together need to be weighed, giving substantially greater weight to (*b*) and (*c*) than to (*a*).

14.107 In an earlier case, *Georgiou v United Kingdom [2001] STC 80*, the ECHR had noted in connection with the same penalty provisions that as 'the penalty was intended as a punishment to deter re-offending, its purpose was both determent and punitive'. In the Georgiou case the penalty itself was substantial. The Court there considered the penalty to have been a criminal charge. The Court of Appeal in *Han and Yau* reviewed a number of ECHR cases. Applying these principles, and identifying the nature of the offence as fraud/dishonesty, it felt that the weight of Strasbourg authority is in favour of the taxpayer in the sense that, in the area of tax evasion at least, such authority does not require that the taxpayer should face imprisonment; it is sufficient that the penalty to which the taxpayer is subjected is substantial and its purpose is punitive and deterrent.

14.108 The same principle has been applied to direct tax penalties in *King v Walden (No 2) [2001] STC 822* which concerned penalties for income tax evasion. Jacob J in the High Court held that 'the system of imposition of penalties for fraudulent or negligent delivery of incorrect returns or statements is criminal' for the purpose of Article 6, as

(*a*) the system is intended to punish the defaulting taxpayer and to operate as a deterrent;

(*b*) the amount of fine is potentially substantial;

(*c*) the amount of fine is not related to any administrative matter;

(*d*) the amount of fine imposed depends upon the degree of culpability of the taxpayer, the less culpable the more mitigation; and

(*e*) it is accepted that generally it is not for the taxpayer to show that the determination of penalties was wrong; on appeal the burden of proof lies with the Crown in clear distinction to an appeal against an ordinary assessment.

14.109 However, this decision may need to be approached with caution. In the Han and Yau case Potter L J went out of his way to say:

> 'I have had drawn to my attention the decision of Jacob J in King v Walden in which, applying the criteria as considered in the Strasbourg authorities to which I have referred, and persuaded by the analysis and reasoning of the chairman in this case, he held that the system for imposition of penalties for fraudulent or negligent delivery of incorrect tax returns or statements is "criminal" for the purpose of Article 6(2). In doing so, he plainly went further than the decision in this case, the reasoning on which is largely premised upon penalties in respect of dishonesty. However, whereas the conclusions of Jacob J go further than those which I have expressed, they are not inconsistent with them.'

This suggests that Potter L J would probably take some convincing that penalties imposed for negligence could be classed as criminal.

14.110 It should also be mentioned that Nourse L J gave a dissenting judgement in *Han and Yau*. He felt that what ought to be regarded as criminal could vary from country to country.

> 'In this country we have, since 1689, developed a system of civil administration in which the executive, being subject to review by the courts, acts responsibly and fairly towards the individual citizen, the protection of whose rights is an integral part of the system. The assessment and collection of revenues due to the Crown is an important part of our civil administration. The VAT penalty system is fair, beneficial to the taxpayer and in the public interest. The rights of the taxpayer are already adequately protected. It would be folly, in the name of an abstraction, to introduce a further unnecessary protection, whose practical consequence would be to impair the efficiency of the system at no advantage to the taxpayers.'

14.111 The penalty after mitigation in *Han and Yau* was 90 per cent in one case and 50 per cent in another. That in *King v Walden* was 80 per cent. Jacob J referred to an exhaustive analysis of Strasbourg case law by Philip Baker, 'Taxation and the ECHR', 2000 BTR 211, which concludes:

> 'It now seems clearly established, therefore, that a tax-geared penalty can entail a criminal charge, and the issue of liability to penalties of 25% or higher has been regarded as involving the determination of a criminal charge.'

14.112 In *R (on the application of Morgan Grenfell & Co Ltd) v Special Comr [2001] EWCA Civ 329, [2001] STC 497* it was held that the Article 6 right to an oral hearing is usually thought to be associated with, and to flow from, a right to a public hearing, and seems completely inept to an appeal against a s 20 notice. In any event, the test under Article 6 is always whether the procedure taken as a whole was fair. For the Special Commissioner, in the context of the decision he had to make under s 20, to confine Morgan Grenfell to extensive written submissions was not so unfair as to call for intervention under Article 6.

14.113 Article 8 provides that 'Everyone has the right to respect for his private and family life, his home and his correspondence'. However, there is a caveat that a public authority can interfere with that right in accordance with the law where it 'is necessary in a democratic society in the interests of … the economic well-being of the country, for the prevention of … crime … or for the protection of the rights and freedoms of others'. Article 8 is clearly relevant in relation to the Revenue's information powers. It was held in *R v IRC, ex p Banque Internationale à Luxembourg SA [2000] STC 708* that in so far as the issue of a s 20 notice interferes with Article 8 rights, 'it is in my view clear that there was ample justification as required by Article 8(2). For the notices were issued according to law, in pursuit of a legitimate aim and necessary in a democratic society for protecting the taxation system and revenue.'

14.114 The decision of the ECHR in *Foxley v United Kingdom (2000) 8 BHRC 571* (a non-tax case) confirms that legal professional privilege is protected by Article 8, although the Court of Appeal in *R (on the application* *of Morgan Grenfell & Co Ltd) v Special Comrs* felt it unnecessary to rely on Article 8, which can be qualified in a proper case by the interests of the economic well-being of the country, because under domestic UK law legal professional privilege is unqualified by any considerations of public or private welfare. This was affirmed in the House of Lords where it was described as a fundamental human right long established in the common law. Such law is summarised in the non-tax case of *R v Derby Magistrates Court, ex p B ([1996] AC 487).*

Confidentiality and disclosure by the Revenue

14.115 The concept of confidentiality used to be fundamental to the UK tax system. A taxpayer could disclose information to the Revenue safe in the knowledge that it would not be disclosed to other agents of the government, such as the police or other third parties. That concept has been eroded significantly in recent years, but is still a cornerstone of the tax system.

14.116 Every employee of the Revenue has to make a declaration as being appointed that he

> 'will not disclose any information received by me in the execution of the duties which may from time to time be assigned to me by the Board of Inland Revenue except for the purpose of my duties or to the Board of Inland Revenue or in accordance with their instructions, or for the purposes of any prosecution for an offence relating to Inland recovery or in such other cases as may be required by law' [TMA 1970 s 6(4), (5) and Sch 1].

A person appointed to the Board and a General or Special Commissioner must make a similar solemn declaration of confidentiality [TMA 1970 s 6 and Sch 1].

14.117 This declaration is backed up by FA 1989 s 182, which makes it a criminal offence for any person to disclose any information which he holds or has held in the exercise of tax, tax credit or social security functions, in relation to any identifiable person [FA 1989 s 182(1)]. A breach of the provision renders the person liable on conviction or indictment to a fine up to the statutory maximum (£5,000) or imprisonment for up to two years or both. On summary conviction the penalty is again up to the statutory maximum but the magistrates can impose imprisonment of up to six months only in addition to that fine [FA 1989 s 182(8)].

14.118 Unfortunately, a taxpayer is likely to find it hard to invoke this protection, as any prosecution, other than by the Board of Inland Revenue, needs the consent of the Director of Public Prosecutions [FA 1989 s 182(9)], which seems unlikely to be given.

14.119 The section does of course permit disclosure either:

(*a*) with lawful authority;

(*b*) with the consent of the taxpayer (or person claiming tax credit); or

(*c*) if the information has already lawfully been made available to the public before the disclosure is made,

[FA 1989 s 182(5)].

14.120 For this purpose a disclosure is made with lawful authority only if it is made either:

(*a*) by a Crown Servant in accordance with his official duty;

(*b*) by any other person for the purposes of the function in the exercise of which he holds the information (and without contravening any restriction duty imposed by the person responsible);

(*c*) to the person responsible (in most cases the Board of Inland Revenue) or in accordance with an authorisation duly given by that person;

(*d*) in pursuance of any enactment or of any order of a court; or

(*e*) in connection with the institution of (or otherwise for the purposes of) any proceeding relating to any matter within the general responsibility of the Commissioners or the Board,

[FA 1989 s 182(6)]. It is unclear why (*e*) refers to both the Commissioners and the Board as the Board is defined as 'the Commissioners of Inland Revenue' [FA 1989 s 182(10)]. It may be the reference to the Commissioners is intended to refer to the General or Special Commissioners.

14.121 The author has been told by an Inspector that the section permits him to disclose information about a taxpayer's affairs to anyone he wants if he thinks that this will assist him with an enquiry under TMA 1970 s 19A and that he has had this specifically confirmed to him by the Revenue's Solicitors Office. This seems astonishing and in the author's view is wrong. In the case concerned, the Inspector did not carry out his threat to disclose information to a customer of the client. There is a clear difference between a power and a duty. Head (*a*) above does not seem at all apt to permit disclosure to third parties to seek to elicit further information from them.

14.122 Furthermore, when the legislation was introduced the Minister gave an assurance that:

> 'The powers in TMA 1970 ss 19A, 20 are not mutually exclusive. However, the Inland Revenue would not normally issue a notice under s 20 in order to obtain information that they had failed to obtain under s 19A. Very rarely, it might become clear, after the taxpayer had appealed against a s 19A notice, that s 20 was in fact the more appropriate section to use. A notice under s 20 cannot be issued by an Inspector unless the taxpayer has failed to take an opportunity to provide

the information voluntarily, and may be issued only with the consent of an independent Appeal Commissioner.' (Hansard, 19 April 1999, cols 425, 426.)

14.123 It is a defence for a person charged with an offence under the section to prove that at the time of the alleged offence:

(*a*) he believed that he had lawful authority to make the disclosure in question and had no reasonable cause to believe otherwise; or

(*b*) he believed that the information in question had been lawfully made available to the public before the disclosure was made and had no reasonable cause to believe otherwise,

[FA 1989 s 182].

14.124 Section 182 applies not only to Revenue staff. It extends to staff of the General and Special Commissioners (and of the tribunals under TA 1988 s 463 or 706 which are in practice administered by the Special Commissioners), the Controller and Advocate General, the National Audit Office and the parliamentary Ombudsman [FA 1989 s 182(2)–(4)]. Section 182 was introduced following the repeal of Official Secrets Act 1911 s 2, which previously provided the criminal sanctions for unauthorised disclosure.

14.125 Similar criminal penalties apply to an authorised disclosure by a person of information acquired by him in the exercise of his functions as a member of an advisory commission set up under the EC Arbitration Convention [FA 1989 s 182A]. That EC Convention (90/436/EEC) enables a taxpayer to require the competent authority (in the case of the UK, the Inland Revenue International Division) of one of its member states to seek to reach agreement with the authority of another member state to prevent it adjusting the profits of the taxpayer so as to create double taxation. If the two cannot reach agreement they are required to set up an advisory commission of experts to deliver an opinion on the elimination of double taxation.

Authorised disclosure

Foreign tax authorities

14.126 The Revenue are entitled to disclose information to a foreign tax authority in accordance with a double taxation agreement [TA 1988 s 815C]. In negotiating such agreement the Revenue are entitled to include provisions:

'with respect to the exchange of information foreseeably relevant to the administration or enforcement of the domestic laws of the UK and the laws of the territory to which the arrangements relate concerning taxes covered by the arrangements including in particular, provisions about the prevention of fiscal evasion with respect to those taxes.' [TA 1988 s 788(2) as amended by FA 2003 s 198.]

The precise rules governing what can be disclosed under a double tax agreement depends on the wording of the agreement.

14.127 Most of the UK's double tax agreements follow the OECD model. This provides that:

> 'Any information received by Contracting States should be treated as secret in the same manner as information obtained under the domestic laws of that State and should be disclosed only to persons or authorities (including courts and administrative bodies) involved in the assessment or collection or the enforcement or prosecution in respect of, or the determination of appeals in relation to, the taxes covered by the convention. Such persons or authorities shall use the information only for such purposes. They may disclose the information in public court proceedings or in judicial decisions.'

14.128 The OECD commentary points out that 'reciprocal assistance between tax administrations is feasible only if each administration is assured that the other administration will treat with proper confidence the information which it will receive in the course of their co-operation'. It emphasises that:

> 'the information received by a Contracting State may be used only for the purposes mentioned in para 1. If the information appears to be of value to the receiving State for other purposes than those referred to, that State may not use the information for such other purpose but it must resort to means specifically designed for those purposes (eg a case of a non-fiscal crime, to a treaty concerning judicial assistance).'

14.129 Accordingly, information received by a foreign tax authority under a double tax agreement could not be passed on by the tax authorities of that country to other officials responsible for the administration of, for example, exchange controls in that country.

14.130 Exchanges of information under double tax agreements of course work both ways. The Revenue can use this agreement to obtain information about a taxpayer's foreign assets or transactions from the tax authorities of the foreign country. The Revenue's instruction to their staff states:

> 'the information which a foreign Revenue may be able to provide is inevitably limited by their information powers and domestic procedures which differ widely throughout the world. The type of information sought should usually be restricted to that which could reasonably be expected to be obtainable and which relates to enquiries on which significant amounts of tax are potentially at stake. Regular sources of information available under UK domestic law should normally have been exhausted before a request is made. Inspectors should bear in mind

> that requests may involve a considerable amount of research by an overseas Revenue Official.' (Double Taxation Relief Manual, para 351.)

It seems likely that information in relation to a specific taxpayer is, similarly, normally routinely passed to the other country only where significant amounts of tax are at stake.

14.131 It should be realised that information can be exchanged under a double tax agreement in three ways; on request, automatically or voluntarily. There is automatic exchange of the routine items collected by tax authorities, usually from third parties, such as dividends, bank interest, royalties, pensions and commissions (Double Taxation Relief Manual, para 353). Information is likely to be volunteered to a foreign tax authority which comes to light in the course of a Revenue enquiry and is of such a nature that there is a reasonable suspicion that the tax laws of a foreign Revenue may have been abused or tax has been evaded or avoided (Double Taxation Relief Manual, para 352).

14.132 Within the EC there is a Mutual Assistance Directive in relation to direct and indirect taxation (77/799/EEC). This provides for exchange of information subject to the same sorts of safeguards as apply under double tax agreements. It specifically states that, 'all information made known to a Member State under this Directive shall be kept secret in that State in the same manner as information received under its domestic legislation' (Article 7).

14.133 It is specifically provided that the obligation as to secrecy imposed by the Tax Acts on Revenue staff is not to prevent disclosure of information under double tax agreements, the Arbitration Convention or the Mutual Assistance Directive [FA 1978 s 77; FA 1990 s 125(5); FA 2003 s 197; TA 1988 816(1), (2)]. However, such disclosure is not to be made unless the officer is satisfied that the foreign government is bound by, or has undertaken to observe, rules of confidentiality with respect to the information which are not less strict than those applying in the UK [TA 1988 s 816(2ZA); TCGA 1992 s 277(4); FA 2003 s 197(2)]. In practice that probably does not mean very much as Special Compliance Office, London, which deals with information exchanges, is likely to assume that the fact that the UK has entered into a double tax agreement with the country is itself evidence that such standards will be met. The Revenue cannot authorise information disclosed under the Mutual Assistance Directive to be used other than for the purposes of taxation or to facilitate legal proceedings for failure to observe the tax laws of the other country [FA 1978 s 77(3)].

14.134 The Treasury can make regulations for implementing (and dealing with matters arising from) any EC obligation created with a view to ensuring the effective taxation of savings income under the law of the UK and the laws of the other EC countries, and any arrangements made with a non-EC country with a view to ensuring the effective taxation of savings income under the law of the UK and the law of the other country [FA 2003 s 191(1)]. Such regulations can in particular require paying agents to obtain and verify information about the identity and residence of people to whom they make payments and to provide such information and details of the payments to the Revenue [FA 2003 s 191(2)]. The EC treaty envisaged has still to be finalised so no regulations have yet been made.

Domestic exchanges of information

With Customs and Excise

14.135 FA 1972 s 127 provides for exchanges of information between the Revenue and Customs and Excise. It provides that 'no obligation as to secrecy or other restrictions upon the disclosure of information imposed by statute or otherwise' is to prevent such exchanges. Such information can obviously not be disclosed by the recipient authority to anyone else other than for the purpose of any proceedings connected with a matter in relation to which the recipient authority performs duties [FA 1972 s 127(2)]. Guidelines agreed between the Revenue and Customs limit the extent to which information is exchanged at local level to investigation settlements and VAT control visits where significant irregularities have been found (Investigation Handbook, para 240). However, both Departments interpret FA 1972 s 127 as providing an open and unrestricted 'gateway' for the exchange of any information and the Revenue has authorised all its staff to pass information to Customs and receive information from them (Applicant Compliance Guide, para 19004). The two bodies are increasingly working together.

DTI and Office of National Statistics

14.136 The Revenue can supply to the DTI, the Department of Employment, or the Office of National Statistics, for the purpose of any statistical summary conducted (or to be conducted) by either, the names and addresses of employers required to operate PAYE and information concerning the number of employees in receipt of earnings paid by an employer [FA 1969 s 58(1)]. They can also disclose to the Office of National Statistics the name and address of the employer of a person who is one of a number of employees selected as a statistical sample for the purpose of a survey [FA 1969 s 58(2)]. The person in the DTI or ONS to which the information is supplied cannot disclose it to anyone else within his department, other than for the purpose of the statistical survey concerned, or to any other government department other than for a statistical survey being conducted by that department. They can, however, disclose it to the Northern Ireland Training Authority, a local planning authority, the Welsh Development Agency, Scottish Enterprise, Highland and Islands Enterprise, or a New Town Development Corporation for the purpose of functions of that body [FA 1969 s 58(4)]. They can also obviously disclose the information in the form of a summary so framed that particulars relating to an individual employer or employee cannot be ascertained from it [FA 1969 s 58(5)]. If any person makes an unauthorised disclosure he is liable on summary conviction to a fine up to £5,000 or on conviction on indictment to imprisonment for up to two years or a fine or both [FA 1969 s 58(6)].

14.137 Employment Relations Act 1999 s 39 authorises Revenue staff to supply to the DTI for any purpose relating to the National Minimum Wage Act 1998 any information obtained in the course of carrying out any Revenue function. It further authorises the DTI, with the authority of the Commissioners of Inland Revenue to pass on that information to an officer acting under s 13(1)(b) of that Act (ie, to the Revenue) or to an officer acting for the purposes of any of the agricultural wages legislation. FA 2000 s 148 authorises information obtained by the DTI under the minimum wage or agricultural wages legislation to be passed to the Revenue with the authority of the Secretary of State for Trade and Industry and to be applied for tax purposes. It also allows information obtained by the Revenue itself acting under the minimum wage legislation to be used for any tax purposes. The Revenue also have power to exchange information with the DTI in relation to community development finance institutions and community investment tax relief [FA 2002 Sch 16 para 43].

DSS

14.138 Both the Revenue and Customs can pass information to the DSS (or a person providing services to it) for use in the prevention, detection, investigation or prosecution of offences relating to social security or for use in checking the accuracy of information relating to benefits or National Insurance numbers or to any other matter relating to social security and (where appropriate) amending or supplementing such information [Social Security Administration Act 1992 s 122(1), (2)]. The DSS cannot onward supply the information to others unless it could have been applied direct by the Revenue to that other person – and even then they need the consent of the Revenue or Customs as appropriate [SSAA 1992 s 122(3)].

14.139 Information held by the Revenue specifically for the purposes of functions relating to contributions, statutory sick pay or maternity pay can of course be supplied to the DSS for use in relation to social security, child support or war pensions whether or not it is needed in connection with fraud [SSAA 1992 s 128E]. Similarly, Tax Credits Act 1999 Sch 5 para 2 permits the Revenue to pass information that they have obtained in connection with tax credits, to the DSS or the Benefits Agency for use for purposes relating to social security benefits, child support or war pensions.

14.140 The DSS can similarly pass to the Revenue and Customs any information which it holds which is to be used by the Revenue (or Customs) either:

(*a*) in the prevention, detection, investigation or prosecution of criminal offences which it is the Revenue's duty to prevent, etc;

(*b*) in the prevention, detection or investigation of conduct which attracts civil tax penalties;

(*c*) in connection with the assessment or determination of civil tax penalties;

(*d*) in checking the accuracy of information relating to (or provided for purposes connected with) any matter under the care and management of the Commissioners of Inland Revenue;

(*e*) (where appropriate) for amending or supplementing any such information;

(*f*) in connection with any legal or other proceedings relating to anything within (*a*) to (*e*),

[FA 1997 s 110(1)–(3)]. The Revenue must not pass on information received under (*a*) or (*b*) above unless such disclosure is authorised, either generally or specifically by the DSS [FA 1997 s 110(4)]. There is no similar restriction in relation to information supplied under the other heads.

14.141 The DSS can also pass to the Revenue any other information which it holds for the purposes of social security, child support or war pensions, but only if the Revenue require it for use for the purposes of functions relating to NI contributions, statutory sick pay or statutory maternity pay [SSAA 1992 s 121F]. The DSS can similarly pass to the Revenue information that it has obtained in relation to tax credits, but the Revenue can use that information only for the purposes of tax credits [Tax Credits Act 1999 Sch 5 para 3].

14.142 Data is automatically provided to the DSS/Benefits Agency (Applicant Compliance Guide, para 19005). Tax Credits Act 2002 Sch 5 para 4 similarly allows the Revenue to supply to the DSS or Benefit Agency any information which it holds for the purposes of its functions relating to tax credits, child benefit or guardian allowance, but only for use by the DSS for the purposes of social security, child support, war pensions or statistical studies.

14.143 Tax Credits Act 1999 Sch 5 para 4 similarly authorises the Revenue to pass information they have obtained in connection with tax credits to a local authority for use in the administration of housing benefits or council tax benefit. Sch 5 para 5 of that Act enables the Revenue to require a local authority to provide it with benefit administration information held by the authority for use by the Revenue in relation to tax credits (but not for any other purpose). The Revenue tell their staff that 'the transmission of information is limited to that on the WFTC/DPTC application form and WFTC/DPTC award details, and you must never reveal other tax information to local authorities'. Tax Credits Act 2002 Sch 5 para 7 similarly permits the Revenue to pass to local authorities for housing benefit and council tax benefit purposes information that it holds for the purposes of tax credits, child benefit or guardian allowances and para 8 allows information to be passed to the Revenue for such purposes.

Department for Education and Science

14.144 Tax Credits Act 2002 Sch 5 para 5 allows the Revenue to pass to the DfES for the purposes of such functions relating to employment or training as may be prescribed by Statutory Instrument information which it holds for the purposes of functions relating to tax credits, child benefit or guardian's allowance. Para 6 reciprocates by allowing the DfES to pass information to the Revenue for use in relation to tax credits, child benefit or guardian's allowances. Information relating to child benefit or guardian's allowance (but not tax credits) can also be passed to the DfES (or indeed any civil servant or other person) for the purposes of functions relating to the provisions of such services mentioned in Learning and Skills Act 2002 s 114(1) (to encourage, enable or assist participation by young persons in education or training) [TCA 2002 Sch 5 para 10].

Department of Health

14.145 Tax Credits Act 2002 Sch 5 para 9 permits the Revenue to supply to the Department of Health for the purposes of such functions relating to health as may be prescribed by statutory instrument information which it holds for the purposes of functions relating to tax credits, child benefit or guardian's allowance.

The Police

14.146 Until 2001 the Revenue could not even pass details of a criminal offence to the police other than where the police requested disclosure in cases involving murder or treason (Applicant Compliance Guide, para 19000). Even then staff were told 'Inland Revenue staff are not authorised to make disclosures to the police and requests for information should not be dealt with locally. All requests from the police for disclosure of information under protection orders should be referred to SCO' (Employer Compliance Handbook, para 6130).

14.147 However, Criminal Justice and Police Act 2001 s 19 provides that no obligation of secrecy imposed by statute or otherwise prevents disclosure of information held by the Inland Revenue or Customs made:

(*a*) for the purpose of facilitating the carrying out by any of the intelligence services of any of that service's functions;

(*b*) for the purposes of any criminal investigation whatever that is being, or that may be, carried out whether in the UK or elsewhere;

(*c*) for the purposes of any criminal proceedings whatever which have been or may be initiated, whether in the UK or elsewhere;

(*d*) for the purposes of the initiation or bringing to an end of any such investigation or proceedings; or (*e*) for the purpose of facilitating a determination of whether any such investigation or proceedings should be initiated or brought to an end,

[s 19(1), (2)].

14.148 The intelligence services for the purpose of (*a*) means the Security Service, the Secret Intelligence Service and GCHR [Regulation of Investigatory Powers Act 2000 ss 19(8) and 31]. A criminal investigation is defined as 'an investigation of any criminal conduct, including an investigation of alleged or suspected criminal conduct and an investigation of whether criminal conduct has taken place' [Anti-terrorism, Crime and Security Act 2001 s 20(1)]. Conduct is defined as including act, omissions and statements [s 20(2)]. Criminal conduct is any conduct which constitutes one or more criminal offences under the law of a part of the UK, or which corresponds to conduct which would do so if it took place in a particular part of the UK [s 20(3)]. Proceedings outside the UK are not to be regarded as criminal proceedings unless the charge relates to criminal conduct or to conduct which to a substantial extent consists of criminal conduct.

14.149 It should be noted that the provision is very widely drawn. Mere suspicion of a possible criminal offence is enough to absolve a Revenue officer from his obligation of secrecy. It does not even need to be a serious criminal offence. Note particularly the position in relation to offences committed overseas. Suspicion that a person has set up an overseas trust to evade a foreign tax would trigger a right to provide information to the foreign police. Suspicion that it was done to evade foreign exchange controls would not do so, as evading exchange control is not an offence in the UK.

14.150 There are three statutory safeguards. No disclosure can be made unless the person making it is satisfied that the making of the disclosure is proportionate to what is sought to be achieved by it [Anti-terrorism, Crime and Security Act 2001 s 19(3)]. Unfortunately, that is a very subjective test. It would be very hard to show that the officer was not so satisfied. The information can only be disclosed by the Commissioners of Inland Revenue or with their authority [s 19(4)]. In practice this means that disclosures will not be made by local tax offices but if an officer thinks that a disclosure is appropriate he will need to refer the matter to SCO (see s 108). Thirdly, the section does not override the Data Protection Act 1998, so information protected from disclosure by that Act cannot be disclosed [s 19(7)].

14.151 The Revenue and Customs have jointly issued a Code of Practice on the operation of those provisions (Press Release 11.2.2002). This states that staff of both departments must have regard to the Code as well as to their internal guidance and procedures when disclosing information under the Act. The Code provides that:

(*a*) In practice, disclosures are likely to be made only to the police, the NCIS and the National Crime Squad (para 2.5).

(*b*) The Revenue department will put in place Memorandums of Understanding with the recipient organisation before disclosure is made. These will establish procedures for the disclosure and receipt of confidential information (para 2.6). In particular, all potential recipients of information will have to demonstrate to the Revenue that they have a legitimate interest and that the information requested is needed for a specific stated purpose (para 3.11).

(*c*) Disclosure is not mandatory. No organisation can demand disclosure of information. The decision whether to release information is the responsibility of the Revenue (para 2.7).

(*d*) The Data Protection Act 1998 provides that personal information is not to be transferred outside the European Economic Area unless the country in question ensures an adequate level of protection for the rights and freedoms of people in relation to the processing of personal information about them (para 3.8).

(*e*) Only a limited number of Revenue staff will be authorised to make disclosures. Such people will receive detailed training and guidance so that they are fully aware of the security protocols, conditions and safeguards necessary to operate the provisions fairly and lawfully (para 3.12). The main ones will be the Inland Revenue Liaison Unit in London (which handles disclosure to the police under court production orders and disclosure under international agreements) and the Inland Revenue Office in Cardiff (which handles less substantial disclosures) (para 3.13).

(*f*) Disclosure of information will be on a case by case basis. There will be no disclosure of 'bulk' information (batches of data matching defined criteria produced in response to a general request) to the police and other law enforcement bodies (para 3.12).

(*g*) The Revenue's normal complaint handling procedures will apply (para 4.1). This is not much help as the disclosure will already have been made before the need to complain is recognised. Furthermore, there is not a lot of point in complaining to the officer in charge of one's tax office about a disclosure made by SCO!

Other governmental bodies

14.152 Information in relation to charities, in particular where the Revenue consider that a charity has been carrying on non-charitable activities or applying funds for non-charitable purposes can be exchanged with the Charity Commissioners [Charities Act 1993 s 10]. The names and addresses of employers and employees and the number of persons employed by individual concerns can be passed by the Revenue to the Business Statistics Office of the DTI or to the Department of Employment for the purpose of statistical surveys [FA 1969 s 58]. The Revenue can disclose information about pension schemes to the Occupational Pensions Board

[Social Security Act 1973 s 89(2)]. They can supply particulars of land and charges to a Land Registry [Land Registration Act 1925 s 129]. Information regarding option mortgages and qualification of housing associations for certain grants can be passed to the Department of the Environment [FA 1982 Sch 7 para 12; Housing Associations Act 1985 s 62]. Information required for the purpose of an investigation can obviously be passed to the Parliamentary Ombudsman [Parliamentary Commissioner Act 1967 s 8]. Information in connection with a National Audit Office report can obviously be made available to the NAO [National Audit Act 1983]. Information necessary for the discharge of functions under the Data Protection Act can be passed to the Registrar or Tribunal under that Act [Data Protection Act 1984 s 17]. Information in relation to National Insurance contributions, statutory sick pay or statutory maternity pay can be passed to the Health and Safety Executive, the Government Actuary's Department, The Office for National Statistics or the Occupational Pensions Regulatory Authority [SSAA 1992 s 122AA]. Information can be passed to the Financial Services Authority when this is needed for the purpose of their investigations [Financial Services and Markets Act 2000 s 35]. There are a number of statutory gateways under which information can be exchanged with the Department for Work and Pensions (Employer Compliance Handbook, para 6125). Some information is routinely exchanged electronically with that Department, mainly in relation to National Insurance. Information in relation to Redundancy Payments can be exchanged with the DTI (Schedule E Manual, para 5E 13841). Information in relation to Tonnage Tax can be exchanged with the DETR [FA 2000 Sch 22 para 34] and can also be provided to the police for the purpose of criminal investigation or proceedings [Anti-Terrorism Crime & Security Act 2001 Sch 4 and s 17]. The Revenue can disclose information to the Department of Agriculture and Rural Development in Northern Ireland (or an authorised officer of the Department) for the purpose of assisting it in carrying out its functions in relation to first year allowances for machinery or plant in Northern Ireland – and that Department can similarly provide information to the Revenue for the same purpose [CAA 2001 s 51].

The Inland Revenue

14.153 The Revenue do of course liaise internally, so information provided to them in relation to, say, inheritance tax will also be used for other tax purposes. It is specifically provided that information held by the Revenue for the purpose of functions relating to tax credits can be used for any other tax or NIC purposes by the Revenue and vice versa [Tax Credits Act 1999 Sch 5 para 2; Tax Credits Act 2002 Sch 5 para 2]. Similarly, information obtained by an officer for the purposes of the National Minimum Wage Act 1998 can be used by, or supplied to (with the authority of the Secretary of State if it is obtained under s 13(1)(a) of that Act) the Revenue for tax purposes [FA 2000 s 148(1), (2)]. So can information obtained by agricultural wages officers under that Act [FA 2000 s 148(3)].

Other people

14.154 The Revenue can of course provide information to third parties with the consent of the taxpayer. In the course of an enquiry they sometimes ask for bank mandates to be signed, ie, a letter authorising the bank to provide information to the Revenue. It is important to realise that armed with such a mandate the Revenue can obtain information, such as the bank manager's account notes, that is not available to the taxpayer himself. Where a student takes a statutory student loan he signs an agreement which authorises the Revenue to disclose to the Student Loan Company personal information, employment details and details of earnings and other income (Collection of Student Loans Manual, para 3104). Some provisions contain a specific right of disclosure. For example, the Revenue can disclose to a company that EIS relief has been given or claimed in respect of a particular number or proportion of its shares [TA 1988 s 310(9)].

14.155 The Revenue can of course seek information about any taxpayer from any third party who is willing to voluntarily provide it, but they cannot disclose anything about the affairs of the taxpayer concerned in order to do so. They tell their staff:

> 'Particular care should be exercised when making enquiries about an individual – remember if the person to whom you are talking knows you are an investigator, he or she may draw the conclusion telling them that the taxpayer is under investigation, and they will want to know why. Investigators are in a difficult position. You rely on the goodwill of those providing information. The best policy is to be frank and to make it clear from the outset that nothing can be given in return. Under no circumstances should you pretend to be anyone other than who you are when obtaining information. Accounts investigators should particularly beware of inadvertently providing information about other businesses. One of the grounds for investigation may be poor business result in comparison to other traders. Whilst it is legitimate to point this out, an investigator should never provide details about those other businesses. Within a local business community it will not be difficult for a trader to attribute even anonymised data to a particular competitor.' (Investigation Handbook, para 2427.)

Regulation of Investigatory Powers Act 2000

14.156 The Regulation of Investigatory Powers Act 2000 introduces a statutory framework for the techniques used by law enforcement, security and intelligence services. It deals with a number of issues such as interception of telephone and internet communications, surveillance and the scrutiny of the use of the powers of the intelligence services. Most of these are not of relevance to tax but ss 28 and 29, which deal with surveillance can be. This is because the Revenue is a 'relevant public authority' for the purposes of those sections [Sch 1]. The Act provides that surveillance is lawful for all purposes if an authorisation under the Act confers an entitlement to engage in such conduct and it is done in accordance with the authorisation [s 27(1)]. A person so authorised cannot be subject to any civil liability for any conduct which is incidental to conduct which is lawful under s 27(1) provided that such conduct is not itself such that a warrant should have been sought for it [s 27(2)].

14.157 Any person designated for the purpose of s 28 can authorise the carrying out of directed surveillance and any person designated for the purpose of s 29 can authorise a person to become a covert human intelligence source. All Revenue staff in Band C1 and higher are designated for the purpose of both sections. Where it is not reasonably practical for authorisation to be granted by such a person someone in Band C2 can grant authorisation (The Regulation of Investigatory Powers (Prescription of Offices, Ranks and Positions) Order 2000, SI 2000/2417). It is understood that Band C1 is a senior (but not fully trained) inspector grade.

14.158 Surveillance is directed if it is covert but not intrusive, is undertaken for the purposes of a specific investigation and is undertaken in such a manner as is likely to result in the obtaining of private information about a person [s 26(2)]. Surveillance is intrusive if it is carried out in relation to something taken place in residential premises or in a private vehicle and either involves the presence of an individual in the premises (or vehicle) or it is carried out by means of a surveillance device [s 26(3)].

14.159 A person is a covert human intelligence source if he establishes or maintains a personal or other relationship with a person for the covert purpose of using that relationship to obtain information or provide access to information to another person [s 26(8)]. A relationship is covert if it is carried out in such a manner that it is calculated to ensure that persons subject to the surveillance are unaware it is taking place [s 26(9)].

14.160 A Revenue officer can authorise surveillance under either section only if he believes it is necessary for the purpose of assessing or collecting tax and that the surveillance is proportionate to what is sought to be achieved by carrying it out [ss 28(2)), 29(2)]. The Revenue do not have power to authorise intrusive surveillance (although Customs do) [s 32].

Exercise of functions

14.161 Any function conferred by an enactment on the Commissioners of Inland Revenue (other than the making of statutory instruments) can be exercised by any officer of the Commissioners acting under their authority [IRRA 1890 s 4A].

Obstruction of officers

14.162 It is an offence to obstruct, molest or hinder an officer or other employee of the Revenue (or any person aiding such a person) acting in the exercise of his duties. The penalty is a fine of level 3 on the standard scale (£1,000) [IRRA 1890 s 11]. Fines imposed by the IRRA can be proceeded for and recovered in the same manner, and in the case of summary proceeding with the same power of appeal as any fine or penalty under any act relating to excise [IRRA 1890 s 36]. This will apply Customs and Excise Management Act 1979 ss 146–152 to such proceedings.

Impersonation of a Revenue Officer

14.163 It is an offence for a person to take or assume the name, designation or character of a Revenue officer for the purpose of:

(*a*) obtaining admission into any house or other place;

(*b*) doing (or procuring to be done) any act which that person would not be entitled to do on his own authority; or

(*c*) any other unlawful purpose.

The penalty on summary conviction is imprisonment for up to three months [IRRA 1890 s 12]. Although the Act refers to imprisonment with hard labour such a penalty was abolished in 1948.

Proceedings before Justices

14.164 Any officer or other person so authorised by the Commissioners of Inland Revenue or the Solicitor of Inland Revenue can prosecute, conduct, or defend any information complaint or other proceedings to be heard or determined by justices of the peace in the UK (or a sheriff in Scotland) if those proceedings relate to the Revenue or to any fine, penalty or other matter under the care and management of the Commissioners. If the authorised person is a solicitor he can also appear in the County Court in such matters [IRRA 1890 s 27].

Power to reward informers

14.165 The Commissioners of Inland Revenue have power to reward any person who informs them of any offence against any Act relating to the Revenue, or assists in the recovery of any fine or penalty. Such a reward cannot, however, exceed £50 without Treasury consent. The £50 figure has remained unchanged since 1890 [IRRA 1890 s 32].

Power to mitigate fines and stay proceedings

14.166 The Commissioners of Inland Revenue have power at their discretion to mitigate any fine or penalty incurred under the tax legislation.

They also have power to stay or compound any proceedings for recovery of any fine or penalty and to mitigate or entirely remit a fine or penalty even after judgement [IRRA 1890 s 35(1); TMA 1970 s 102]. The Treasury also have power to mitigate or remit a tax fine or penalty [IRRA 1890 s 35(2)].

Income tax decisions to apply to CGT

14.167 An assessment to income tax, a decision on a claim under the Income Tax Acts, or a decision on appeal against such an amendment or decision is conclusive so far as any liability to capital gains tax depends on the provisions of the Income Tax Acts [TCGA 1992 s 284].

The mutual assistance recovery directive

14.168 EC Council Directive 76/308/EEC (as amended by Directive 2001/44/EEC) makes provision for mutual assistance between EC tax authorities for the recovery of specified taxes duties and levies. It applies inter alia, to income tax, corporation tax, capital gains tax and petroleum revenue tax together with any claim to interest, civil penalties and costs in respect of a claim to such taxes. In the UK effect is given to the Directive by FA 2002 s 134. This applies to the recovery in the UK of amounts in respect of which a request for enforcement has been made in accordance with the directive by a tax authority in another EC country.

14.169 In response to such a request the Revenue can take such proceedings to enforce the foreign tax claim (by way of legal proceedings, distress, diligence or otherwise) as they can take to enforce a corresponding UK claim. Any enactment or rule of law relating to the corresponding UK claim applies equally to that foreign claim. This particularly applies to the laws on penalties and interest on overdue tax [FA 2002 Sch 39 paras 1, 2]. The Treasury have power to define by regulation what is a corresponding UK claim [FA 2002 Sch 39 para 3]. They do not appear to have yet done so.

14.170 Unless permitted by the Regulations, no proceedings can be taken against a person if he shows that proceedings relating to the foreign tax liability are pending, or about to be instituted, before a court, tribunal or other competent body in the foreign country. For this purpose proceedings are pending so long as an appeal can be brought against any decision in the proceedings, but the Revenue can take enforcement action in the UK if the foreign proceedings are not prosecuted or instituted with reasonable expedition [FA 2002 Sch 39 para 4].

14.171 No proceedings can be taken against a person in the UK if a final decision on the foreign claim has been made in his favour by a court, tribunal or other competent body in the other EC country.

14.172 It needs to be realised that all EC countries will have given legislative effect to the Directive. Accordingly, it will enable the Revenue to secure the enforcement of UK tax liabilities where a taxpayer has either moved to another EC country or has assets in such a country.

Index

A

L

M

N

O

P

R